John A. Naylor

THE ETHICS OF COMPETITION

THE ETHICS OF COMPETITION
AND OTHER ESSAYS

by

FRANK HYNEMAN KNIGHT, PH.D.

PROFESSOR OF ECONOMICS
UNIVERSITY OF CHICAGO

LONDON
George Allen & Unwin Ltd
MUSEUM STREET

FIRST PUBLISHED IN 1935
SECOND IMPRESSION 1951

PRINTED IN GREAT BRITAIN
BY BRADFORD & DICKENS, LONDON, W.C.1

PREFACE

THE purpose of this book is to make available to students of the social sciences some of Professor Knight's essays which have particular relevance to the problems faced by society to-day. While these articles are of general interest, most of them have appeared in technical journals, and are thus relatively inaccessible. The idea of publishing a collection suggested itself to a small group who had attended a dinner on the occasion of Professor Knight's forty-ninth birthday, November 7, 1934, but not until all arrangements had been made and the selection of the contents completed was Professor Knight informed of the project. The entire responsibility for the choice of articles thus falls on us; had the selection been made by the author, not only might the contents have been different, but some revisions might have been made.

Although we have attempted to choose articles which are representative of Professor Knight's work, the collection is not to be regarded as a synthesis of his thought. Perhaps, however, a unifying thread may be found in the problem of social control and its various implications. Only one article dealing with interest or capital theory has been included, because this is a subject about which Professor Knight has radically altered his views, furthermore, he is at present writing a book on this topic.

The compilation of the bibliography was a considerable task, since Professor Knight has kept no record of his publications. This was undertaken several years ago by Miss Alice Hanson and later was considerably expanded by Mr. Homer Jones; it has been brought up to date by Miss Gladys Hamilton.

We are greatly indebted to Professor Lionel Robbins of the London School of Economics and to Professor Jacob Viner of the University of Chicago for suggestions and assistance without which the project could not have been carried through. The advice of Professor Henry Simons has been particularly helpful in the selection of the articles; and we wish also to acknowledge the co-operation of the various other members of the Department of Economics at the University of Chicago.

For permission to republish the various selections included in this volume we are indebted to The Macmillan Company of New York, and Messrs. Macmillan & Co., to Messrs. F. S. Crofts and Company, The University of Chicago Press; and to the editors of the *Quarterly Journal of Economics*, the *Journal of Political Economy*, *The American Economic Review*, the *Zeitschrift für Nationalökonomie* (Julius Springer, Vienna), the *Journal of Economics* and *Business History*.

MILTON FRIEDMAN
HOMER JONES
GEORGE STIGLER
ALLEN WALLIS

THE UNIVERSITY OF CHICAGO
March 1, 1935

CONTENTS

BIBLIOGRAPHY

EVERY effort has been made to make this bibliography of Professor Knight's works complete up to March 1, 1935; and as far as possible, items in press on that date are included. Articles are arranged by the years of publication, and within each year they are listed approximately in the order of appearance; books, with the exception of the *Encyclopaedia of the Social Sciences*, are listed first in each year. The following abbreviations are used:

A.E.R.   *American Economic Review*
A.J.S.   *American Journal of Sociology*
J.P.E.   *Journal of Political Economy*
Q.J.E.   *Quarterly Journal of Economics*

1915 Review: "Thirteenth Census Report on Occupations," *A.E.R.*, v, pp. 184–8.

"Mechanical Devices in European Statistical Work" and "A Correction," *American Statistical Association Publication* 14, pp. 596–9, 700.

1916 "Neglected Factors in the Problem of Normal Interest," *Q.J.E.*, xxx, pp. 279–310.

1917 "The Concept of Normal Price in Value and Distribution," *Q.J.E.*, xxxii, pp. 66–100.

1919 Review: Henri Charriaut and Rauol Hacault *La liquidation financière de la guerre*, *J.P.E.*, xxvii, pp. 611–13.

Review: Bertrand Russell, *Proposed Roads to Freedom*, *A.J.S.*, xxv, pp. 227–8.

Review: Leonard S. Woolf, *Co-operation and the Future of Industry,* *J.P.E.*, xxvii, pp. 805–6.

Review: H. J. W. Hetherington and J. H. Muirhead, *Social Purpose*; and J. S. Mackenzie, *Outlines of Social Philosophy*, *J.P.E.*, xxvii, pp. 898–900.

1920 Review: Thorstein Veblen, *The Place of Science in Modern Civilization*, *J.P.E.*, xxviii, pp. 518–20.

1921 *Risk, Uncertainty and Profit* (New York: Houghton Mifflin Company). Discussion: "Traditional Economic Theory," *A.E.R.*, xi (Supplement), pp. 143–6.

1921 "Cost of Production and Price over Long and Short Periods," *J.P.E.*, xxix, pp. 304–35.

Review: Gustav Cassel, *Theoretische Sozialoekonomie*, *Q.J.E.*, xxxvi, pp. 145–53.

1922 Round Table, Chairman: "The Relation between Economics and Ethics," *A.E.R.*, xii (Supplement), pp. 192–3.

"Ethics and the Economic Interpretation," *Q.J.E.*, xxxvi, pp. 451–81.

"On the Other Hand," *The Signboard* (Issued monthly by Gamma Epsilon Pi), May, pp. 1, 3, and 4.

Review: C. R. Fay, *Cooperation at Home and Abroad*; Ramsay Muir, *Liberalism and Industry;* and Leo Pasvolsky, *The Economics of Communism*, *J.P.E.*, xxx, pp. 582–5.

1923 Discussion: "Economic Theory and Practice," *A.E.R.*, xiii (Supplement), pp. 105–7.

"Business Management: Science or Art?," *The Journal of Business*, State University of Iowa, March, pp. 5–9.

Review: O. F. Boucke, *A Critique of Economics*, *A.E.R.*, xiii, pp. 286–8.

"Some Books on Fundamentals" (Review of Hubert D. Henderson, *Supply and Demand*; A. C. Pigou, *The Economics of Welfare*; Lionel D. Edie, *Principles of the New Economics*; Alvin S. Johnson, *Introduction to Economics* (revised), *J.P.E.*, xxxi, pp. 342–59.

"The Ethics of Competition," *Q.J.E.*, xxxvii, pp. 579–624.

1924 "The Limitations of Scientific Method in Economics" in *The Trend of Economics*, Rexford Guy Tugwell, ed., pp. 229–67.

"Some Fallacies in the Interpretation of Social Cost," *Q.J.E.*, xxxviii, pp. 582–606.

Review: W. O. Hedrick, *The Economics of a Food Supply*, *Journal of Social Forces*, ii, p. 757.

Review: J. A. R. Marriot, *Economics and Ethics*, *Journal of Social Forces*, ii, pp. 757–8.

Review: D. Atkins, *The Economics of Freedom*, *A.E.R.*, xiv, pp. 718–9.

1925 Review: Fabian Franklin, *Plain Talks on Economics*, *Journal of Social Forces*, iii, pp. 353–4.

"On Decreasing Cost and Comparative Cost—a Rejoinder," *Q.J.E.*, xxxix, pp. 331–3.

Review: William McDougall, *Ethics and Some Modern World Problems*, *Political Science Quarterly*, xl, pp. 138–40.

1925 "Economic Psychology and the Value Problem," *Q.J.E.*, xxxix, pp. 372–409.

Review: T. N. Carver, *The Economy of Human Energy*, *Journal of Social Forces*, iii, pp. 777–8.

Review: F. S. Harris, *Scientific Research and Human Welfare*, *Journal of Social Forces*, iii, p. 778.

"A 'Scientific' Observation Regarding Socialism," *The Iowa Liberal* (May), pp. 5–6.

"Fact and Metaphysics in Economic Psychology," *A.E.R.*, xv, pp. 247–66.

Review: Clinton H. Scovell, *Interest as a Cost*, *J.P.E.*, xxxiii, pp. 468–70.

"A Note on Professor Clark's Illustration of Marginal Productivity," *J.P.E.*, xxxiii, pp. 550–62.

Review: Sir William J. Ashley, *The Christian Outlook*, *Political Science Quarterly*, xl, pp. 624–6.

Review: A. W. Small, *Origins of Sociology*, *A.E.R.*, xv, pp. 724–7.

1926 "Economics at Its Best" (review article on Pigou, *The Economics of Welfare*, 2nd ed.), *A.E.R.*, xvi, pp. 51–8.

Review: W. T. Foster and Waddill Catchings, *Profits*, *Political Science Quarterly*, xli, pp. 468–71.

Max Weber, *General Economic History*, translated by Frank H. Knight, London: George Allen & Unwin Ltd.; New York, Greenberg Company.

1927 Review: E. E. Hoyt, *Primitive Trade: Its Psychology and Economics*, *A.E.R.*, xvii, pp. 73–4.

Discussion: "Interest Theory and Price Movements," *A.E.R.*, xvii (Supplement), pp. 120–1.

Review: O. Fred Boucke, *Principles of Economics*, *J.P.E.*, xxxv, pp. 315–17.

Review: Frederick Soddy, *Wealth, Virtual Wealth and Debt. The Solution of the Economic Paradox*, *The Saturday Review of Literature* (April 16th), p. 732.

Review: David Atkins, *The Measurement of Economic Value*, *J.P.E.*, xxxv, pp. 552–7.

Review: U. G. Weatherly, *Social Progress*, *A.E.R.*, xvii, pp. 487–8.

Review: E. C. Hayes (ed.), *Recent Developments in the Social Sciences*, *A.E.R.*, xvii, pp. 686–7.

Review: J. Mayer, *The Seven Seals of Science*, *A.E.R.*, xvii, pp. 688–9.

1928 Review: Ogburn and Goldenweiser (eds.), *The Social Sciences and Their Interrelations*, *A.E.R.*, xviii, pp. 82–3.

Review: E. Dawson and others, *Teaching the Social Studies*, *A.E.R.*, xviii, p. 84.

"A Suggestion for Simplifying the Statement of the General Theory of Price," *J.P.E.*, xxxvi, pp. 353–70.

Review: G. H. Bousquet, *Essai sur l'évolution de la pensée économique*, *A.E.R.*, xviii, pp. 278–9.

Review: R. G. Hawtrey, *The Economic Problem*, *J.P.E.*, xxxvi, pp. 523–5.

"Homan's *Contemporary Economic Thought*," *Q.J.E.*, xliii, pp. 132–41.

"Historical and Theoretical Issues in the Problem of Modern Capitalism" (review article on Werner Sombart, *Der Moderne Kapitalismus*), *Journal of Economic and Business History*, i, pp. 119–36.

1929 "Freedom as Fact and Criterion," *The International Journal of Ethics*, xxxix, pp. 129–47.

Review: Christian Cornelissen, *Traité général de science économique*, Tome III, Vols. I and II: *Théorie du capital et du profit*, *A.E.R.*, xix, pp. 94–5.

Discussion: "Economic History," *A.E.R.*, xix (Supplement), pp. 156–8.

"Beauty and Economics," Manuscript of lecture given before Bureau of Personnel Administration, New York, March 28, 1929. (Mimeographed for private circulation.)

Review: Henri Sée, *Economic and Social Conditions in France during the Eighteenth Century*, *J.P.E.*, xxxvii, pp. 235–6.

"Absolutism, or—Absolutism!", *The New Humanist*, ii, 2 (May), pp. 1–3.

Review: P. Sargent Florence, *Economics and Human Behaviour— A Reply to Social Psychologists*, *J.P.E.*, xxxvii, pp. 363–4.

Review: Yves Guyot, *La science économique : ses lois inductives*, *Journal of the American Statistical Association*, xxiv, pp. 345–6.

1930 "Absentee Ownership," *Encyclopaedia of the Social Sciences*, i, pp. 376–8.

"Abstinence," *Encyclopaedia of the Social Sciences*, i, pp. 382–3.

Review: Horace Taylor, *Making Goods and Making Money*, *J.P.E.*, xxxviii, pp. 117–18.

"Fact and Interpretation in Economics," in U.S. Department of Agriculture (Graduate School), *Special Lectures on Economics* (February–March).

1930 Discussion: "The Theory of Economic Dynamics," *A.E.R.*, (Supplement), xx, pp. 35–7.

Review: Edward Jenks, *The Book of English Law*; and Munroe Smith, *The Development of European Law*, *J.P.E.*, xxxviii, pp. 237–8.

Review: Richard Ehrenberg, *Capital and Finance in the Age of the Renaissance*, *J.P.E.*, xxxviii, pp. 361–4.

Review: E. Lipson, *The Economic History of England*, Vol. I, "The Middle Ages," 5th ed., *A.E.R.*, xx, p. 278.

"Statik und Dynamik—zur Frage der Mechanischen Analogie in den Wirtschaftswissenschaften," *Zeitschrift für Nationaloekonomie*, ii, 1 (August), pp. 1–26. (Mimeographed in English as "Statics and Dynamics" for private circulation.)

1931 "Relation of Utility Theory to Economic Method in the Work of William Stanley Jevons and Others," in Stuart Rice, ed., *Methods in Social Science*, University of Chicago Press, pp. 59–69.

"Professor Fisher's Interest Theory: A Case in Point," *J.P.E.*, xxxix, pp. 176–212.

Review: Othmar Spann, *The History of Economics*, *J.P.E.*, xxxix, pp. 258–60.

"Davenport, Herbert Joseph," *Encyclopaedia of the Social Sciences*, v, pp. 8–9.

"Demand Curves—Theory," *Encyclopaedia of the Social Sciences*, v, pp. 69–72.

"Marginal Utility Economics," *Encyclopaedia of the Social Sciences*, v, pp. 357–63.

"Exchange," *Encyclopaedia of the Social Sciences*, v, pp. 666–9.

Review: Henry Dennison, *Organization Engineering*, *A.J.S.*, xxxvii, p. 316.

1932 "Das Wertproblem in der Wirtschaftstheorie," in *Die Wirtschafts-theorie der Gegenwart*, ii, Vienna, pp. 52–72.

"Social Economic Organization," "The Price System and the Economic Progress," "Demand and Supply and Price," "Distribution: The Pricing of Productive Services Individually," in *Syllabus and Selected Readings of the Second-Year Course in the Study of Contemporary Society*, University of Chicago, pp. 125–250. (These four items are an abstract of material mimeographed for private circulation at the University of Iowa during the years 1922–5.)

Review: Sherman H. M. Chang, *The Marxian Theory of the State*, *J.P.E.*, xl, pp. 130–1.

1932 Review: Sumner H. Slichter, *Modern Economic Society*, *A.J.S.*, xxxviii, pp. 130–2.

"The Newer Economics and the Control of Economic Activity" (Review article on Sumner H. Slichter, *Modern Economic Society*), *J.P.E.*, xl, pp. 433–76.

Review: Arthur O. Dahlberg, *Jobs, Machines, and Capitalism*, *J.P.E.*, xl, p. 573.

Review: Lawrence Dennis, *Is Capitalism Doomed?*, *A.E.R.*, xxii, pp. 512–13.

"Interest," *Encyclopaedia of the Social Sciences*, viii, pp. 131–43.

Review: Theodore Suranyi-Unger, *Economics in the Twentieth Century*, *J.P.E.*, xl, pp. 708–10.

Review: Alexander Gray, *The Development of Economic Doctrine*, *J.P.E.*, xl, pp. 711–13.

Review: Ludwig Mises and Arthur Spiethoff (eds.), *Probleme der Wertlehre*, Teil I, *A.J.S.*, xxxviii, pp. 471–2.

"Modern Economic Society—Further Considered" (a rejoinder), *J.P.E.*, xl, pp. 814–27.

1933 *Risk, Uncertainty and Profit* (with an additional introductory essay previously unpublished), London School of Economics and Political Science, Reprints of Scarce Tracts in Economic and Political Science, No. 16, London.

"Capitalistic Production, Time, and the Rate of Return," in *Economic Essays in Honour of Gustav Cassel*, pp. 327–42, London.

The Dilemma of Liberalism, Edwards Brothers, Inc., Ann Arbor, Michigan, 87 pages. (Planotyped for private circulation.)

"A Criticism of Professor Perry on 'The Arbitrary as Basis for Rational Morality,'" *The International Journal of Ethics*, xliii, pp. 148–51.

"Can We Vote Ourselves out of the Fix We Are In?," *The Christian Century*, l (February 1st), pp. 151–4.

Review: V. V. Obolensky-Ossinsky, S. L. Ronin, A. Gayster, I. A. Kroval, *Social Economic Planning in the Union of Soviet Socialist Republics*, *J.P.E.*, xli, pp. 131–2.

Review: Alvin Harvey Hansen, *Economic Stabilization in an Unbalanced World*, *J.P.E.*, xli, pp. 242–5.

Review: Harold F. Clark, *Economic Theory and Correct Occupational Distribution*, *J.P.E.*, xli, p. 260.

Review: George Soule, *A Planned Society*, *J.P.E.*, xli, pp. 421–3.

1933 Review: International Industrial Relations Institute, *World Social Economic Planning*, A.E.R., xxiii, pp. 357–9.

Review: Thomas C. Blaisdell, Jr., *The Federal Trade Commission*, A.J.S., xxxix p. 133–4.

Review: O. Fred Boucke, *Laissez Faire and After*, A.J.S., xxxix, pp. 148–9.

"A Reply" (to Joseph Mayer, "Pseudo-Scientific Method in Economics"), *Econometrica*, i, pp. 428–9.

Review: Samuel Howard Patterson, *Readings in the History of Economic Thought*, J.P.E., xli, pp. 557–8.

Review: George R. Geiger, *The Philosophy of Henry George*, J.P.E., xli, pp. 687–90; and *The International Journal of Ethics*, xliv, pp. 162–5.

1934 "Profit," *Encyclopaedia of the Social Sciences*, xii, pp. 480–6.

Review: Lionel Robbins, *The Nature and Significance of Economic Science*, *The International Journal of Ethics*, xliv, pp. 358–61.

"The Nature of Economic Science in Some Recent Discussion" (review article on Ralph William Souter, *Prolegomena to Relativity Economics*), A.E.R., xxiv, pp. 225–38.

"Social Science and the Political Trend," *University of Toronto Quarterly*, iii, pp. 407–27.

"The Development of Economic Institutions and Ideas" (Mimeographed for private circulation).

"Capital, Time, and the Interest Rate," *Economica*, xiv, pp. 257–86.

"The Common Sense of Political Economy (Wicksteed Reprinted)," J.P.E., xlii, pp. 660–73.

"The New Deal and Liberalism," in *Report of Midwest Conference on Industrial Relations*, School of Business, University of Chicago (October), pp. 35–44.

"Supply," *Encyclopaedia of the Social Sciences*, xiv, pp. 370–4.

"Taylor, F. M.," *Encyclopaedia of the Social Sciences*, xiv, pp. 541–2.

"Modern Thought: Is It Anti-Intellectual?," *University of Chicago Magazine*, xxvii, 1 (November), pp. 20–1, 23.

Review: William A. Scott, *The Development of Economics*, A.J.S., xl, pp. 413–14.

1935 "Intellectual Confusion on Morals and Economics," *The International Journal of Ethics*, xlv, pp. 200–20.

"Value and Price," *Encyclopaedia of the Social Sciences*, xv.

1935 Review: Bruno Moll, *Gerechtigkeit in der Wirtschaft*, *J.P.E.*, xliii, pp. 113–6.

Review: Jules Dupuit, "*De l'utilité et de sa mesure*," *J.P.E.*, xliii, pp. 119–20.

"The Ricardian Theory of Production and Distribution," Part I, *Canadian Journal of Economics and Political Science*, i, pp. 3–25; Part II, 1 (May).

"Professor Hayek and the Theory of Interest," *Economic Journal*, xlv (March).

Review: Ludwig Mises and Arthur Spiethoff (eds.), *Probleme der Wertlehre*, Teil II, *A.J.S.*, xxxix (May).

THE ETHICS OF COMPETITION

I

ETHICS AND THE ECONOMIC INTERPRETATION*

Bearing on problem of scope and method, 19.—Both economics and ethics deal with value, 19.—Economics as a pure science has given too little attention to separation of constants from variables, 20.— Sense in which wants can be considered as data, 20.—Economic interpretation as a theory of conduct, 22.—Are human motives predominantly economic?, 24.—Are they predominantly instinctive?, 25.—The adaptation theory, 26.—The pleasure theory, 27.— Economics as a study of the adaptation of means to ends, 30.— What becomes of ethics?, 31.—Three kinds of treatment of conduct, 36.

CERTAIN aspects of the doctrine of the "economic interpretation" form a natural and convenient avenue of approach to a consideration of the relations between economics and ethics and throw light on the scope and method of both these divisions of knowledge. It is this more general problem which is the object of attack in the present paper, which is not primarily an attempt to make a contribution to the technical discussion of the famous theory named in the title. This theory is useful for present purposes because it suggests the fundamental question as to whether there is really a place in the scheme of thought for an independent ethics or whether ethics should be displaced by a sort of higher economics.

Economics and ethics naturally come into rather intimate relations with each other since both recognizedly deal with the problem of value. Two of these lines of relation are especially interesting in their bearing upon the vexed problem of scope and method in economics. In the first place, the separation between theory and practice, or between science and art, offers special difficulties in this field, for reasons which it would carry us away from our central theme to elaborate

* Reprinted by permission from *The Quarterly Journal of Economics*, vol. xxxvi (1922), pp. 454–81.

here. The unfortunate but familiar result of this fact is that economists have spent much of their energy in disputations as to whether the science is properly concerned with facts and cause-and-effect relations, or with "welfare." In other provinces of science such controversies would seem absurd.

There is another and deeper source of confusion in the conception of the method of economics which also involves the relation between economics and ethics and which will lead directly into the problem of this paper. It relates to the ultimate data of economics, regarded as a pure science, dedicated to the search for truth and purified of all prejudices as to the goodness or badness of its principles and results. In this respect also economics has been far behind the natural sciences. Insufficient attention has been given to the separation between constants and variables; needless controversy and wasted effort have resulted from overlooking the fact that constants from one point of view may be variables from another, particularly that factors which are sensibly constant over short periods of time must be treated as variables when longer periods are under discussion.

Of the various sorts of data dealt with in economics no group is more fundamental or more universally and unquestioningly recognized as such than human wants. Yet one main purpose of the present discussion is to raise serious question as to the sense in which these wants can be treated as data, or whether even they are properly scientific data at all. We propose to suggest that these wants which are the common starting-point of economic reasoning are from a more critical point of view the most obstinately unknown of all the unknowns in the whole system of variables with which economic science deals. The answer to this question of whether and in what sense wants are data will be found to involve a clarification of the nature of economics as a science, of the nature of ethics, and of the relations between the two. If human wants are data in the ultimate sense for scientific purposes, it will appear that there is no place for ethical theory in the sense in which ethicists have conceived that subject, but that its place must be taken by economics. It will be interesting to observe that in view of a logically correct distinction between ethics and economics, the great majority of economists not only, but in addition no small proportion of thinkers calling themselves ethicists, have not really believed in ethics in any other sense than that of a more or less "glorified" economics.

To state the fundamental issue briefly at the outset, are the motives with which economics has to do—which is to say human motives in general—"wants," "desires" of a character which can adequately be treated as *facts* in the scientific sense, or are they "values," or "oughts," of an essentially different character not amenable to scientific description or logical manipulation? For if it is the intrinsic nature of a thing to grow and change, it cannot serve as a scientific datum. A science must have a "static" subject-matter; it must talk about things which will "stay put"; otherwise its statements will not remain true after they are made and there will be no point to making them. Economics has always treated desires or motives as facts, of a character susceptible to statement in propositions, and sufficiently stable during the period of the activity which they prompt to be treated as causes of that activity in a scientific sense. It has thus viewed life as a process of satisfying desires. If this is true then life is a matter of economics; only if it is untrue, or a very inadequate view of the truth, only if the "creation of value" is distinctly more than the satisfaction of desire, is there room for ethics in a sense logically separable from economics.

In a more or less obscure and indirect way, the treatment of wants as data from which and with which to reason has already been challenged more than once. More or less conscious misgivings on this point underlie the early protests made by economists of the "historical variety against the classical deductive economics, and the same is true in a more self-conscious way of the criticism brought by the modern "historismus," the "institutional economics" of Veblen, Hamilton, and J. M. Clark. Thus especially Clark,* whose position most resembles that herein taken, observes that the wants which impel economic activity and which it is directed toward satisfying are the products of the economic process itself: "In a single business establishment one department furnishes the desires which the other departments are to satisfy." Hitherto the chief emphasis has been placed on the factual instability of wants and their liability to be changed as well as satisfied by business activity. This is usually coupled with a deprecating

---

* "Economics and Modern Psychology," *Journal of Political Economy*, January and February, 1918. The quotation is from page 8.

attitude, a tendency to regard the growth of wants as unfortunate and the manufacture of new ones as an evil; what have not advertising and salesmanship to answer for at the hands of Veblen, for example! From the standpoint of hedonism, which is to say of the economic philosophy of life, this conclusion is undoubtedly correct. If the Good is Satisfaction, there are no qualitative differences, no "higher" and "lower" as between wants, and that is better which is smaller and most easily appeased.

It is not on any sentimental or idealistic ground, but as a plain question of the facts as to how the ordinary man conceives his own wants and interprets them in conduct that we shall argue against this view of the matter. Wants, it is suggested, not only *are* unstable, changeable in response to all sorts of influences, but it is their essential nature to change and grow; it is an inherent inner necessity in them. The chief thing which the common-sense individual actually wants is not satisfactions for the wants which he has, but more, and *better* wants. The things which he strives to get in the most immediate sense are far more what he thinks he ought to want than what his untutored preferences prompt. This feeling for what one *should* want, in contrast with actual desire, is stronger in the unthinking than in those sophisticated by education. It is the latter who argues himself into the "tolerant" (economic) attitude of *de gustibus non disputandum*; the man in the street is more likely to view the individual whose tastes are "wrong" as a scurvy fellow who ought to be despised if not beaten up or shot.

A sounder culture leads away from this view, to be sure, but it leads to a form of tolerance very different from the notion that one taste or judgment is as good as another, that the fact of preference is ultimately all there is to the question of wants. The consideration of wants by the person who is comparing them for the guidance of his conduct and hence, of course, for the scientific student thus inevitably gravitates into a *criticism of standards*, which seems to be a very different thing from the comparison of given magnitudes. The individual who is acting deliberately is not merely and perhaps not mainly trying to satisfy given desires; there is always really present and operative, though in the background of consciousness, the idea of and *desire for a new want* to be striven for when the present objective is out of the way.

Wants and the activity which they motivate constantly look forward to new and "higher," more evolved and enlightened wants and these function as ends and motives of action beyond the objective to which desire is momentarily directed. The "object" in the narrow sense of the present want is provisional; it is as much a means to a new want as end to the old one, and all intelligently conscious activity is directed forward, onward, upward, indefinitely. Life is not fundamentally a striving for ends, for satisfactions, but rather for bases for further striving; desire is more fundamental to conduct than is achievement, or perhaps better, the true achievement is the refinement and elevation of the plane of desire, the cultivation of taste. And let us reiterate that all this is true *to the person acting*, not simply to the outsider, philosophizing after the event.

In order to substantiate and support the doctrine thus sketched we turn to consider briefly the opposite view, which is that of the "economic interpretation." Historically this doctrine is associated with the so-called "scientific" socialism,* but we are here interested in it not in connection with any propaganda or policy, but simply as a theory of conduct, as one answer to the question of the relation between economics and ethics. Our first task is to find out what the doctrine really means.

The somewhat various statements of the theory reduce in general to the proposition that the course of history is "determined" by "economic" or "materialistic" considerations. All of these terms raise questions of interpretation, but the issue may be stated briefly. In the first place, the course of history is a matter of human behaviour, and we shall as already indicated consider the problem in its broader aspect as a general theory of motivation. As to the word "determined," it is taken for granted that conduct is determined by motives; the statement is really a truism. The issue then relates to the fundamental character of motives; are they properly to be described as materialistic, or economic, in their nature? Between these two terms it is better to use "economic"; a "materialistic" motive would seem to be a contradiction

---

* It would be hard to imagine a more ill-mated team than fatalism as the credal basis for revolutionary propaganda, and a mechanistic philosophy of ruthless force and class war as the background for a moral transformation of the world!

in terms; a "motive" is meaningless unless thought of as a phenomenon of consciousness. The opposite view would merely throw us back upon a denial that conduct is determined by motives at all. Without attempting a philosophical discussion of this question we shall take the common-sense position.*

Are human motives, then, ultimately or predominantly economic? If the expression, "economic motive" is to have any definite and intelligible meaning, it must be possible to distinguish between economic motives and other motives. The expression is, of course, widely used in learned and scientific discussion as well as in everyday speech, with the feeling that such a differentiation exists, but examination fails to show any definite basis for it or to disclose the possibility of any demarcation which is not arbitrary and unscientific. In a rough way, the contrast between economic and other wants corresponds to that between lower and higher or necessary and superfluous. The economic motives are supposed to be more "fundamental"; they arise out of necessities, or at least needs, or at the very least out of the more universal, stable, and materially grounded desires of men. The socialistic popularizers of the theory under discussion have leaned toward the narrower and more definite and logical conception of downright necessities.†

The view of the man in the street, as shown by students beginning the study of economics, and also common in text-book definitions of the science, is that the economic side of life is summed up in "making a living." But what is a living? If by a living we mean life as it is actually lived, everything is included, recreation, culture, and even religion; there is no basis for a distinction between the economic and anything else, and the term has no meaning. At the other extreme would be the idea of what is really necessary, the physiological requisites for the maintenance of life. Even this turns out on examination to be hopelessly

* In the writer's opinion a pure-science attitude in psychology leads inevitably to behaviourism, to a discussion of stimulation and response with consciousness out of it —i.e., away from "psychology." But it is false to the facts. Scientists must recognize that we cannot free any science, not even physics, to say nothing of psychology, entirely from subjective elements and formulate it in purely objective terms.

† Quotations could be multiplied, from socialists and others, to illustrate and prove the statement. Marx, indeed, is typically vague and metaphysical. Perhaps as clear a statement as any is that of Engels: "The determining consideration is always the production and reproduction of actual life." (From an article in the *Sozialistische Akademiker*, quoted in Ghent, *Mass and Class*, chap. i.)

ambiguous. Does "life" mean the life of the individual only, or that of the group or race? If the latter, does it include the increase of numbers, or only their maintenance at the existing level, or some other level? Does what is "necessary" refer to conditions under which life *will* be preserved or numbers maintained or increased, or only those under which it *could* be done? and under what assumptions as to the tastes and standards, and the scientific and technological equipment of the people? Even if we think of a population rigidly controlled as to their reproductive function (which is scarcely conceivable), the birth rate necessary to maintain numbers at a constant level would depend upon the death rate and hence would vary *widely* with the scale of living itself. We doubt whether the conception of necessity can even theoretically be defined in sufficiently objective terms to make it available for scientific purposes.

Between these two extremes of what people actually get and what they rigorously require in order to live, the only alternative is some conventional notion of what is "socially necessary," or of a "decent minimum." It is obvious that such a conception of a "living" is still more indefinite than the others, and the way seems to be closed to any objectively grounded differentiation between the making of a living and any other kind or portion of human activity.*

Another common-sense notion of the meaning of economic activity is that it includes everything which involves the making and spending of money or the creation and use of things having a money value. It will presently be argued that this is substantially correct for practical purposes as far as it goes, though it directly or indirectly covers virtually the whole life activity of a modern man and has to be limited to certain aspects of that activity. It is interesting to ask how much of our ordinary economic activity (economic in the sense indicated) is concerned with things which can reasonably be argued to be "useful"— not to say necessary—if by useful we mean that it contributes to health and efficiency, or even to happiness. If we begin with food, the most material and necessary of our requirements, it is obvious that but a fraction of a modest expenditure for board in an American town

---

* The contrast between work and play may come to mind in this connection, but a little scrutiny will show that it affords no help from the difficulty. In a subsequent paper something will be said concerning the economic and ethical bearing of play.

would come under this head.* And proceeding in order to our other "material" needs, clothing, shelter, furniture, etc., it is apparent that the farther we go the smaller the fraction becomes. And it is not a large fraction of a fairly comfortable income which goes for all these items, if the purely ornamental, recreative, and social aspects are excluded.

Moreover, when we scrutinize the actual motives of actual conduct it is clear that the consciously felt wants of men are not directed toward nourishment, protection from the elements, etc., the physiological meaning of the things for which money is spent. They desire food, clothing, shelter, etc., *of the conventional kinds and amounts*. It is an ethnological commonplace that men of one social group will starve and freeze before they will adopt the ordinary diet and garb of other groups. Only under the direst necessity do we think in terms of ultimate physical needs as ends; the compulsion to face life on this level is equivalent to abject misery. A large proportion of civilized mankind would certainly commit suicide rather than accept life on such terms, the prospect for improvement being excluded. This interpretation of motives, which is the nearest approach to a definite meaning that can be given to the economic interpretation, is almost totally false. It is simply contrary to fact that men act in order to live. The opposite is much nearer the truth, that they live in order to act; they care to preserve their lives in the biological sense in order to achieve the *kind* of life they consider worth while. Some writer (not an economist or psychologist!) has observed that the love of life, so far from being the most powerful of human motives is perhaps the weakest; in any case it is difficult to name any other motive or sentiment for which men do not habitually throw away their lives.†

When we turn from the preservation of individual life to that of the race as a motive a similar situation is met with. Men will give up their lives for the group, but not for its *mere life*; it is for a better or at least a worthy life that such sacrifices are made. The life of the individual is logically prior to that of the group, as our physiological needs are

* A considerably larger proportion may, of course, be "necessary" in the sense that under the actual conditions a person could not obtain and live upon the requisite quantities of protein and calories in the cheaper forms in which they might be had.

† One of the most serious defects of economics as an interpretation of reality is the assumption that men produce in order to consume. Except for those very low in the economic scale the opposite is as near the truth, and the motives of a large part of even "lower-class" consumption are social in their nature.

logically prior to the higher ones, but again that is not the actual order of preference. Probably few civilized men would refuse to die for their fellows if it were clear that the sacrifice were necessary and that it would be effective.

But when materialistic interpreters speak of the perpetuity of the group as a motive they are likely to have in mind not this result in the abstract, but rather sex-feeling, the means by which continuity and increase are secured in the animal world. Here again they are squarely wrong; social existence and well-being in the abstract are more potent than sex attraction in any crude interpretation. With sex experience as with food, it is not the thing as such which dominates the civilized individual. His sex requirement is as different from that of animals as a banquet with all fashionable accompaniments is from the meal of a hungry carnivore which has made a kill, or a buzzard whose olfactory sense has guided him to a *mellow piece of carrion*. It is again a question of fact, and the fact patently is that when the biological form of the motive conflicts with the cultural, aesthetic, or moral part of it—as more or less it about always does—it is the former which gives way. Sex debauchery is, of course, common enough, but this also rather obviously involves about as much cultural sophistication as does romantic or conjugal love, though of a different kind.*

On every count this biological interpretation of human conduct falls down; no hunger and sex theory of human motives will stand examination. It will not be denied that human interests have evolved out of animal desires, and are ultimately continuous with them; and an understanding of animal behaviour can throw light on human problems, but only if interpreted with the utmost caution. Man has risen clear above, or if this seems to beg any philosophical questions he has at least gotten clear away from the plane where life is the end of activity; he has in fact essentially reversed this relation. It is not life that he strives for, but the good life, or at the ultimate minimum a decent life, which is a conventional, cultural concept, and for this he will throw away life itself; he will have that or nothing. He has similar

* It is of interest that the conduct which men denounce by calling it "bestial" (in the field of sex and elsewhere) is typically of a sort in which the "beasts" never indulge. Animals are not promiscuous on principle, but merely indifferent to the individual; they are rarely subject to the peculiar notion from which man is as rarely free, that one individual of the opposite sex is for sexual purposes different from others.

physical requirements with the animals, but has become so "particular" as to their mode of gratification that the form dominates the substance. A life in which bare existence is the end is *intolerable* to him. When his artificial, cultural values are in ultimate conflict with physical needs he rather typically chooses the latter, sacrificing quantity of life to quality, and it is hard to see how he could be prevented from doing so. We can scarcely imagine a slave society placed under physical compulsion so effective that men would permanently live in it. If they were given the least sight or knowledge of their masters and their masters' way of life, no provision however bountiful for all physical wants would prevent some irrational individual from setting up a cry for "liberty or death" and leading his willing fellows to the achievement of one or the other. It is a familiar historical fact that it is not the violently oppressed populations which rebel, but those whose milder bondage leaves them fairly prosperous.* The assumption of the materialistic, or economic, or biological interpretation of conduct is that when men must choose between some "real need" and a sentimental consideration they will take the former. The truth is that when the issue is drawn they typically do the reverse. For any practical social purpose, beauty, play, conventionality, and the gratification of all sorts of "vanities" are more "necessary" than food and shelter. †

* We have omitted mention of the class struggle historically associated with the economic interpretation. It may be remarked in passing that the effective motive of insurrection, and especially of its upper-class leadership, is essentially idealistic. Revolutions would rarely if ever succeed without the belief that the cause is *right* in the minds of *both parties* to the struggle. The pet notion of Labriola, that people make up sentimental reasons for their acts when their real motives are materialistic will also gain more in truth than it will lose by being inverted. Back of the much exploited economic motive in international antagonisms also, conventional and sentimental considerations are clearly to be seen. What men fight over in war is the conflict between cultures, devotion to which is proverbially unconnected with any objective superiority.

† This thesis cannot be elaborated and emphasized as it deserves to be. Some reference ought to be made to the most notorious advocate of the opposite view among social philosophers, Herbert Spencer. His work is a development of the principle that all human values are to be gauged by the standard of tending to the "increase of life," which principle he views as axiomatic from the angles of right as well as necessity. Our contention is that actually the increase of life is rather a by-product of activity, in a sense a necessary evil.

It is interesting to note that "quantity of life" cannot be given an objective meaning as a measurable quantity, to say nothing of its ethical character. Life is a highly heterogeneous complex whose elements resist reduction to any common denominator in physical terms. How compare the quantity of life represented by a hog with that in a human being? They are different *kinds* of things. To common sense, a handful of fleas

Some attention must now be given to another method of interpreting conduct, closely related to the biological and like it aimed at supplying an objective measure of well-being. This is the theory that man has inherited certain *instincts* which must achieve a substantial measure of successful expression in action or the individual will develop maladjustment, baulked disposition, and unhappiness. We cannot go at length into the failure of this theory either to explain actual behaviour or to yield ideal requirements, and fortunately it is unnecessary to do so as the doctrine is now properly passing out of favour.* The significance to be claimed for the theory is that of supplementing the biological interpretation. Certain acts not now useful in the biological sense are assumed to have been so in the past under different conditions, and the organism has become so adjusted to them that its normal functioning depends upon their continued performance.

If instincts are to be scientifically useful, it must surely be possible to get some idea of their number and identity. But there has always been substantially unanimous disagreement on this point. Logically the choice seems to lie between a meaningless single instinct to do things-in-general and the equally meaningless hypothesis of a separate instinct for every possible act. Between these two views is a free field for arbitrary classification. Such fairly concrete lists as have been given consist chiefly of enumerations of the possible alternatives of action in possible types of conduct situations, and largely reduce to pairs of opposites. For a single illustration, an animal in danger may fight or run. Hence our theorists come forward with an "instinct" for each of these types of reaction. This of course tells us nothing of what we want to know which is, *which one* of the possible reactions will take

would seem to contain more "life" than a town meeting or the Royal Society, but Mr. Spencer would hardly contend that it represents more "value." The only purely physical measurement of life that is readily conceivable would be a determination of the quantity of energy in ergs involved in metabolic change in a unit of time.

A confusion essentially the same as that of Spencer seems to underlie the contrast between industrial and pecuniary values developed by Veblen and Davenport. There is no mechanical measure of values which will bear examination, and we cannot compare values or kinds of value without having something to say about value-standards for reducing to common terms magnitudes infinitely various in kind.

* Cf. Ellsworth Faris, "Are Instincts Data or Hypotheses," *American Journal of Sociology*, September, 1921.

Also C. E. Ayres, "Instinct and Capacity," *Journal of Philosophy*, October 13 and 27, 1921.

place. It is not enlightening to be told that conduct consists in choosing between possible alternatives.

A mere classification of feelings or cravings has some interest, however void of scientific utility it may be, but the psychologist can hardly claim to have "discovered" the emotions. In this connection it is interesting to consider the extent to which motives do fall into pairs of opposites. There are numerous such couples or polarizations which cut deeper into human nature than do the proposed instincts. Our reasons for wanting things come down in astonishingly large measure to the desire to be like other people, and the desire to be different; we wish to do things because we can, or because we cannot; we crave companionship, of the right kind, but the requirement of privacy, even solitude, is equally imperative; we like the familiar, also the novel, security but likewise adventure, and so on. Acquisitiveness, the instinct which should be most saleable to the economist, is perhaps but the opposite of our alleged gregariousness, one being essentially the desire to exclude others from certain interests and the other the desire to share them. All these, like selfishness and unselfishness, have some meaning, but are hardly suitable bases for a scientific classification. It is significant that McDougall, the father of the modern instinct theory, regarded the feeling element as the only stable part of the instinct, both stimulus and reaction being subject to indefinite shift and change. The unsuitability of such a view as a foundation for the superstructure built upon it in the way of scientific laws of *behaviour* hardly calls for comment.*

* The logical defect of the instinct theory is a misconception of the aims and methods of scientific procedure, which fallacy also pervades the attempt to make psychology scientific. The significance of instincts would lie in the application of the analytic method to the study of consciousness (here, on its conative or volitional side). Analysis in natural science means different things in different cases, the general basis of its employment being that a thing can be explained by showing what it is made of. In some cases we can predict the whole from the parts by simple addition, in others by vector addition, as of forces in mechanics. In other cases we can only predict empirically as in chemistry. The properties of the compound (except mass) bear no simple or general relation to those of the elements, but we do know by experiment that the same compound can always be obtained from the same elements by putting them together in the same way (and conversely). The case of colours is interesting. One spectral colour is physically as primary as another, yet a few are primary *in the sense that* we can get the others by mixing them. *None of these assumptions hold* in the study of consciousness, and analysis must be given a very special meaning in this field if it is to have any meaning at all. In our opinion Professor Bode has put an eternal quietus on much of what passes for

From the instinct theory we turn naturally to the ancient doctrine of psychology and ethics to which it is a handmaiden, that the end of activity is a "harmonious adjustment" of the organism, a smooth and unobstructed functioning of the digestive, neuro-muscular, and glandular systems (and perhaps the reproductive also, and any special structures concerned with tending the young or other social activities) and for consciousness the feeling of satisfaction or comfort that goes with this condition.* Freudianism and abnormal psychology have seemed to confirm this view, and Thorndyke† also though rather guardedly speaks of behaviour as controlled by "satisfiers" and "annoyers." Perhaps a sufficient comment on the hedonistic theory would be to run through again the main categories of economic wants, food, clothing, shelter, amusement, etc., and simply ask the candid question as to what fraction of the ordinary man's expenditure for any of them makes him "feel better" or is expected to do so. The higher one is in the economic scale, the more successful in doing what all are trying to do, the larger is the proportion of his consumption which tends to make him less, and not more, "comfortable."

The authors of great imaginative literature—always indefinitely better psychologists than the psychologists so-called—have never fallen into any such palpable delusion as the belief that men either strive for happiness or expect to be made happy by their striving. The same has been true of philosophers and religious thinkers of all time, and even economists have recognized the futility of attempting to satisfy wants. It is obvious that wants multiply in at least as great a ratio as the heads of the famous hydra. Greeks as well as Hindus, and Epicureans as well as Stoics and Cynics perceived at the dawn of modern culture that it is indefinitely more "satisfactory" and "economical" to repress desire than to attempt to satisfy it. Nor do men who know what they do want—and who have not sapped their vitality by

science in psychology. See his paper on "The Doctrine of Focus and Fringe," *Philosophical Review*, 1914.

* The socialists have assumed hedonism rather than argued it. Spencer regarded it as also axiomatic that life-sustaining activities are necessarily pleasure-giving (*Data of Ethics*, Sec. 34) and vice versa. Modern pragmatism seems to run in terms of the same two-fold assumption that The Good is identical with both the biologically beneficial and the actually desired. It seems to us that critical thought confirms common sense in repudiating both parts of this dogma.

† *The Original Nature of Man.* New York, 1913.

unnatural living or too much of a certain kind of thinking—want their wants satisfied. This argument of economists and other pragmatists that men work and think to get themselves out of trouble is at least half an inversion of the facts. The things we work for are "annoyers" as often as "satisfiers"; we spend as much ingenuity in getting into trouble as in getting out, and in any case enough to keep in effectively. It is our nature to "travel afar to seek disquietude," and " 'tis distance lends enchantment to the view." It cannot be maintained that civilization itself makes men "happier" than they are in savagery. The purpose of education is certainly not to make anyone happy; its aim is rather to raise problems than solve them; the association of sadness and wisdom is proverbial, and the most famous of wise men observed that "in much wisdom is much grief, and he that increaseth knowledge increaseth sorrow." Thus the pursuit of the "higher things" and the crasser indulgences are alike failures if the test is happiness.

But the test is not happiness. And by this we do not mean that it ought not to be, but the simple fact that that is not what men want. It is a stock and conclusive objection to utopias that men simply will not live in a world where everything runs smoothly and life is free from care. We all recall William James's relief at getting away from Chatauqua. A man who has nothing to worry about immediately busies himself in creating something, gets into some absorbing game, falls in love, prepares to conquer some enemy, or hunt lions or the North Pole or what not. We recall also the case of Faust, that the Devil himself could not invent escapades and adventures fast enough to give his soul one moment's peace. So he died, seeking and striving, and the Angel pronounced him thereby "saved": "Wer immer strebend sich bemüht, den können wir erlösen." The pleasure philosophy is a false theory of life; there abide pain, grief, and boredom: these three; and the greatest of these is boredom. The Hindus thought this question of happiness through to the end long ago, and reached the inevitable conclusion—Nirvana—just life enough to enjoy being dead.*

* There is an incident in the Life of Pyrrhus, as told by Plutarch, which shows the nature of man and his motives as much better than all the scientific psychology ever written that it merits repeating substantially as that author tells it.

"When Pyrrhus had thus retired into Epirus, and left Macedonia, he had a fair occasion given him by fortune to enjoy himself in quiet, and to govern his own kingdom in

The idea of a distinction between economic wants and other wants must be abandoned. There is no definable objective, whether subsistence, gratification of fundamental impulses or pleasure, which will serve to separate any of our activities from the body of conduct as a whole. Nor, we aim especially to emphasize, is there any *definable* objective which properly characterizes any of it. It simply is not finally directed to the satisfaction of any desires or the achievement of any ends external or internal * which can be formulated in propositions and made the subject of logical discourse. All ends and motives are economic in that they require the use of objective resources in their realization; all are ideal, conventional, or sentimental in that the attempt to define objective ends breaks down. Behind them all is "the

peace. But he was persuaded, that neither to annoy others, nor to be annoyed by them, was a life insufferably languishing and tedious. . . . His anxiety for fresh employment was relieved as follows. (Then follows a statement of his preparations for making war against Rome.)

"There was then at the court of Pyrrhus, a Thessalonian named Cineas, a man of sound sense, and . . . who had devoted himself to Pyrrhus in all the embassies he was employed in . . . and he continued to heap honours and employments upon him. Cineas, now seeing Pyrrhus intent upon his preparations for Italy, took an opportunity. when he saw him at leisure, to draw him into the following conversation: 'The Romans have the reputation of being excellent soldiers, and have the command of many warlike nations: if it please heaven that we conquer them, what use, Sir, shall we make of our victory?' 'Cineas,' replied the king, 'your question answers itself. When the Romans are once subdued, there is no town, whether Greek or barbarian, in all the country, that will dare oppose us; but we shall immediately be masters of all Italy, whose greatness, power, and importance no man knows better than you.' Cineas, after a short pause, continued. 'But, after we have conquered Italy, what shall we do next, Sir?' Pyrrhus, not yet perceiving his drift, replied, 'There is Sicily very near, and stretches out her arms to receive us, a fruitful and populous island, and easy to be taken. . . .' 'What you say, my prince,' said Cineas, 'is very probable; but is the taking of Sicily to conclude our expeditions?' 'Far from it,' answered Pyrrhus, 'for if heaven grant us success in this, that success shall only be the prelude to greater things. Who can forbear Libya and Carthage, then within reach? . . . And when we have made such conquests, who can pretend to say that any of our enemies, who are now so insolent, will think of resisting us?' 'To be sure,' said Cineas, 'they will not; . . . But when we have conquered all, what are we to do then?' "Why, then, my friend,' said Pyrrhus, laughing, 'we will take our ease, and drink, and be merry.' Cineas, having brought him thus far replied, 'And what hinders us from drinking and taking our ease now, when we have already those things in our hands, at which we propose to arrive through seas of blood, through infinite toils and dangers, through innumerable calamities, which we must both cause and suffer?'

"This discourse of Cineas gave Pyrrhus pain, but produced no reformation. . . ."

* The term happiness is as heterogeneous as any other; its only meaning is that the end of action is *some* state of consciousness. Besides being as vague as possible this statement, in the view of practically all thinkers on ethics who were not hoodwinked by economic logic and the price system itself, is false.

restless spirit of man," who is an aspiring rather than a desiring being; and such a scientifically undescriptive and unsatisfactory characterization is the best we can give.*

For the purpose of defining economics the correct procedure would appear to be to start from the ordinary meaning of the verb to economize, that is, to use resources wisely in the achievement of *given* ends. In so far as the ends are viewed as given, as data, then all activity is economic. The question of the effectiveness of the adaptation of means is the only question to be asked regarding conduct, and economics is the one and all-inclusive science of conduct.† From this point of view the problem of life becomes simply the economic problem, how to employ the existing and available supplies of all sorts of resources, human and material, natural and artificial, in producing the maximum *amount* of *want-satisfaction*, including the provision of new resources for increased value production in so far as the present population finds itself actually desiring future progress. The assumption that wants or ends are data reduces life to economics,‡ and raises

* This reasoning refutes alike such classifications of wants as Professor Everett has given in his very charming book on Moral Values (chap. VII, esp. sec. II) and the distinction between industrial and pecuniary values already mentioned. All of Everett's kinds of value are economic; in fact nearly any specific value belongs to most of his classes.

In regard to "real ends," we should note the futile quest of a Summum Bonum by ethical thinkers.

† For purposes of academic division of labour this will have to be restricted by excluding the technological aspect of adaptation and restricting economics to the general theory of organization. Most of the attention will practically be given to the theory of the *existing* organization, through private property and competitive free exchange, which makes economics virtually the science of prices. Our definition of the economic aspect of behaviour includes not only technology as ordinarily understood but the techniques of all the arts.

‡ That is, on the practical or conduct side. A word may be in place as to the relation between economics as a science thus broadly conceived and related sciences. Conduct is not co-extensive with human behaviour; much of the latter is admittedly capricious, irrational, practically automatic, in its nature. Different actions have in various degrees the character of conduct, which we define with Spencer as "the adaptation of acts to ends," or briefly, deliberative or rational activity. Much that is at the moment virtually reflex and unconscious is, however, the result of habit or of self-legislation in the past, and hence ultimately rational. But there is a place for the study of automatic responses, or behaviourism, and also for psychology, which should not be confused with the former. We have by no means meant to repudiate the attempt of biology to explain the end or motives which the science of conduct uses as data. This is altogether commendable, as is also the effort to explain biology in physico-chemical terms. These researches should be pushed as far as possible; we object only to the uncritical assumption that they have explained something when they have not, and to dogmatic assertion (either way) as to how far it is intrinsically possible to carry such explanations.

again the question with which we started out, Is life all economics or does this view require supplementing by an ethical view of value?

The conception of economics outlined above is in harmony with the traditions of economic literature. The "economic man," the familiar subject of theoretical discussion, has been much mistreated by both friends and foes, but such a conception, explicit or implicit, underlies all economic speculation. The economic man is the individual who obeys economic laws, which is merely to say that he obeys *some* laws of conduct, it being the task of the science to find out what the laws are. He is the *rational* man, the man who knows what he wants and orders his conduct intelligently with a view to getting it. In no other sense can there be laws of conduct or a science of conduct; the only possible "science" of conduct is that which treats of the behaviour of the economic man, i.e., economics in the very broad sense in which we have used the term. A scientific principle necessarily takes the form that under given conditions certain things can be counted upon to happen; in the field of conduct the given conditions are the desires or ends and the rationale or technique for achieving them.

The objections raised to the notion of the economic man, are however also sound in their own way. They reduce to the proposition that *there is no such man*, and this is literally true. Human beings do not in their conscious behaviour act according to laws, and in the concrete sense a science of conduct is an impossibility. They neither know what they want—to say nothing of what is "good" for them—nor act very intelligently to secure the things which they have decided to try to get.*
The limitation on intelligence—knowledge of technique—is not fatal to the conception of a scientific treatment of behaviour, since people are "more or less" intelligent, and "tend" to act intelligently, and all science involves a large measure of abstraction. Far more essentially is the limitation due to the fact that the "given conditions," the causes at work, are not really given, that wants are not ultimately data and the individual more or less completely recognizes that they are not.

The definition of economics must, therefore, be revised to state that it treats of conduct *in so far* as conduct is amenable to scientific treatment, in so far as it is controlled by definable conditions and can

* From this point of view again the animals are superior to man, in that they are more intelligent, sensible; a hog knows what is good for him and does it!

be reduced to law. But this, measured by the standard of natural science, is not very far. *There are no data* for a science of conduct in a sense analogous to natural science. The data of conduct are provisional, shifting, and special to individual, unique situations in so high a degree that generalization is relatively fruitless. *For the time being*, an individual acts (more or less) *as if* his conduct were directed to the realization of some end more or less ascertainable, but at best provisional and vague. The person himself is usually aware that it is not really final, not really an "end"; it is only the end of the particular act, and not the ultimate end of that. A man engaged in a game of chess acts *as if* the supreme value in life were to capture his opponent's pieces; but this is obviously not a true or final end; the circumstances which have led the individual to accept it as end for the moment come largely under the head of accident and cannot be reduced to law—and the typical conduct situation in civilized life is analogous to the game in all the essential respects.

A science of conduct is, therefore, possible only if its subject-matter is made abstract to the point of telling us little or nothing about actual behaviour. Economics deals with the form of conduct rather than its substance or content. We can say that a man will in general prefer a larger quantity of wealth to a smaller (the principal trait of the economic man) because in the statement the term "wealth" has no definite concrete meaning; it is merely an abstract term covering everything which men do actually (provisionally) want. The only other important economic law of conduct, the law of diminishing utility, is almost as abstract; its objective content is covered by the statement that men strive to distribute income in some way most satisfactory to the person at the time among an indefinite number of wants and means of satisfaction rather than to concentrate upon one or a few. Such laws are unimportant because they deal with form only and say virtually nothing about content, but it is imperative to understand what they do and what they do not mean.

If one wishes to study the concrete content of motives and conduct he must turn from economic theory to biology, social psychology, and especially culture history. Culture history is not, therefore, a method of economics, as the historic quarrel would lead one to think, but a different field of inquiry. It gives a *genetic*, and not a *scientific* account of its subject-matter. History has, indeed, tried to become a science and the effort has brought forth numerous "philosophies of history," but it is open to grave doubt whether "laws" of history exist and whether the entire project is not based on a misconception.*

If a science of economics is limited to the abstract form of conduct and the treatment of conduct in the concrete takes the form of history rather than science, what is to be said of ethics? In addition to the explanation of conduct in terms of motives and the explanation of the motives, common sense does raise another kind of question, that of the *evaluation* of motives. But we are met at the outset with the logically insuperable difficulty that the criticism of an end implies some *standard*, which can logically only be another end, which to enter into logical discourse must be viewed as a datum, like the first. Hence, scientifically we can never get beyond the question of whether one end conflicts with another and if so which is to be sacrificed. But this mere comparison of ends as given magnitudes belongs to the economic calculation involved in creating the maximum amount of value or want-satisfaction out of a given fund of resources; hence there seems to be no place for anything but economics in the field of value, and scientifically there is none. If we are to establish a place for ethics really distinct from economics and independent of it, it must be done by finding ends or standards which are something more than scientific data.†

For those to whom ethics is only a more or less "glorified" economics, virtue is correspondingly reduced to an enlarged prudence. But the essential element in the moral common sense of mankind seems to be the conviction that there is a difference between virtue and prudence, between what one "really wants" to do and what one "ought" to do; even if some religious or other "sanction" makes it

* It is impossible to discuss at length the relations between historic (genetic) and scientific explanation. The distinction is perhaps sufficiently well established to justify using the terms without a lengthy philosophic analysis. Our point of view is not that either of these is "higher" than the other; we merely insist that they are different and that each can fulfil its special purpose best by recognizing the difference.

† It was remarked early in the present discussion that one leading school of ethicists (the hedonistic) merely enlarge the principles of economics and do not believe in any other ethics. Economists have usually held to this view—the principle is the same whether their good is called pleasure or want-satisfaction, so long as it is held to be quantitative—and now the same position is being taken up by the realistic school of philosophers who regard value as a real quality in things. Cf. R. B. Perry, *The Moral Economy*.

ultimately prudent to do right, at least it remains true that it is prudent because right and not right because prudent or because there is no difference between the two. A considerable part of the literature of ethics consists of debate over the validity of this distinction and of moral common sense, which is to say over whether there is any such thing as ethics or not, and the question creates perhaps the most fundamental division between schools of thought. There was no difficulty for the Greeks, who had no word for duty or conscience in their language, and there is none for the modern "pagan" who considers these things as out-worn puritan superstitions. It must appear dogmatic to seem to take sides on the question without working out an entire philosophic system in justification of the position, but we wish to point out that *if* there is to be a real ethics it cannot be a science, and to cite a few reasons for believing in the possibility of a real ethics.

The first of these considerations is the argument developed in this paper that the view of ends as scientific data breaks down under examination. The second is that the rational, economic, criticism of values gives results repugnant to all common sense. In this view the ideal man would be the economic man, the man who knows what he wants and "goes after it" with singleness of purpose. The fact is, of course, the reverse. The economic man is the selfish, ruthless object of moral condemnation. Moreover, we do not bestow praise and affection on the basis of conduct alone or mainly, but quite irrationally on the motives themselves, the feelings to which we impute the conduct.

We cannot dwell on the moral habitability of the world under different hypotheses or argue the question whether such implications constitute "evidence" for the hypothesis in question. The disillusioned advocate of hard-headedness and clear thinking would usually admit that the "moral illusion" has stood the pragmatic test and concede its utility while contending that it is scientifically a hoax. But it is pertinent to observe that the brick-and-mortar world cannot be constructed for thought out of purely objective data. There is always a feeling element in any belief. Force and energy are notoriously feelings of ours which we read into things, yet we cannot think of anything as real without force as a real. Apparently we are incapable of picturing anything as existing without putting a spark of our own consciousness into it. Behind every fact is a theory and behind that an interest. There is no purely objective reason for believing anything any more than there is for doing anything, and if our feelings tell us nothing about reality then we know and can know nothing about it. From this it is an easy step to see that the intolerable repugnance of the idea that not only duty and right, but all effort, aspiration and sacrifice are delusions is after all as good a reason for believing that they are not as we have for believing that the solid earth exists in any other sense than seeming to us to do so.

But the main argument for the validity and necessity of a real, non-scientific, transcendental ethics comes out of the limitations of scientific explanation. We have seen that the "scientific" treatment of conduct is restricted to its abstract form, that its concrete content can only be explained "historically." But in dealing with human problems we are constantly thrown back upon categories still more remote from the scientific, upon relations which cannot be formulated in logical propositions at all, and we must admit that a large part of our "knowledge" is of this character. That figurative language does convey a meaning, however, is indisputable, and it is commonly a meaning which could not be expressed literally. When Burns says that his Love is "like a red, red rose," etc., when Kipling tells us of Fuzzy-Wuzzy that " 'E's a daisy, 'e's a ducky, 'e's a lamb," their words meaning something, though it is not what they say! William James has commented on the effectiveness of these comparisons whose physical basis is undiscoverable, illustrating by the statements that a certain author's style is like the atmosphere of a room in which pastilles have been burning. Let anyone take even a science text-book and try to translate all the figurative expressions into literal, purely logical form, and he will realize how impossible it is to describe the world in terms which mean definitely what they say.

Of this general description must be the criticism of values, as it is the character of aesthetic and literary criticism. Our values, our standards, are only more obviously of the same character which our desires reveal on examination—not describable because not stable, growing and changing by necessity of their inner nature. This is, of course, intellectually unsatisfactory. The scientific mind can rest only in one of two extreme positions, that there are absolute values, or that very individual desire is an absolute and one as "good" as another. But neither of these is true; we must learn to think in terms of "value-standards" which have validity of a more subtle kind. It is the higher goal of conduct to test and try these values, to define and improve them, rather than to accept and "satisfy" them. There are no rules for judging values, and it is the worst of errors to attempt to make rules—beyond the rule to "use good judgment"; but it is also most false to assert that one opinion is as good as another, that *de gustibus non disputandum est*. Professor Tufts has put the question in a neatly epigrammatic way which emphasizes its unsatisfactoriness from a rational, scientific standpoint: "The only test for goodness is that good persons on reflection approve and choose it—just as the test for good persons is that they choose and do the good."*

If the suggestions above thrown out are sound, there is room in the field of conduct for three different kinds of treatment: first, a scientific view, or economics and technology; second, a genetic view, or culture history, and third, for a Criticism of Values. The discussion of the latter will, like literary and artistic criticism, run in terms of suggestion rather than logical statement, in figurative rather than literal language, and its principles will be available through sympathetic interpretation rather than intellectual cognition.†

* See essay on "The Moral Life," in the volume entitled *Creative Intelligence*, by Dewey and others. Professor R. B. Perry in a review as beautifully illustrates the inevitable scientific-economic reaction to this viewpoint. See *International Journal of Ethics*, vol. 28, p. 119, where Professor Perry, referring to the statement quoted above, says: ". . . it cannot appear to its author as it appears to me. I can only record my blank amazement."

† There is obviously a need for a better terminology, if history and criticism are to have their methods properly named and if they are to be adequately distinguished from the "sciences." Such adjectives as genetic and normative, used with the word science are objectionable, but perhaps the best we can do. They do not sufficiently emphasize the contrasts.

It should be noted that some writers have attempted to make ethics scientific on the basis of somewhat different logical procedure from that sketched above. They regard the end of conduct as the production of some "stage of consciousness" (pleasure or happiness) but assume that the common-sense being does not know the effects of acts and hence that special study of past experience (on the basis of the *post facto* satisfactoriness of results) is necessary to secure rules for guidance. This reasoning does not separate ethics from economics, however, as it is again a mere question of technique for securing recognized ends.

II

THE ETHICS OF COMPETITION*

The central position of the value problem in economic policy.—The necessity of formulating ideals, of an "absolute ethics," 44.—Outline of article, 45—I. Contrast between theory and practice of laissez-faire individualism, (a) in its value scale and organization of resources to produce values; (b) in its distribution of produce, 47.—II. Business as a game, 62.—The problem of a standard for judging games, 63.—Elements of a game: ability, effort, and luck, 63.—Criticism of the business game, 64.—III. Competition as a motive, 65.—It is efficient as an incentive in getting things done, 65.—The question of what things; ethical versus economic view of life, 66.—Contrast of emulation with pagan ideal of perfection, 66.—With Christian ideal of spirituality, 71.

IN the previous paper the writer undertook to argue against the view of ethics most commonly accepted among economists. The argument was not directed against hedonism as such, but against "scientific" ethics of any kind, against any view which sets out from the assumption that human wants are objective and measurable magnitudes and that the satisfaction of such wants is the essence and criterion of value, and which proceeds on the basis of this assumption to reduce ethics to a sort of glorified economics. It was pointed out that any such view consistently reduces the "higher" wants to a secondary position as compared with "lower," and interprets human life in biological terms. But the fact is that human beings do not regularly prefer their lower and more "necessary" needs to those not easily justified in terms of subsistence or survival value, but perhaps rather the contrary; in any case what we call progress has consisted largely in increasing the proportion of want-gratification of an aesthetic or spiritual as compared to that of a biologically utilitarian character, rather than in increasing the "quantity of life." The facts, as emphasized, are altogether against accepting any balance-sheet view of life; they point rather toward an evaluation of a far subtler sort than the addition and

* Reprinted by permission from *The Quarterly Journal of Economics*, vol. xxxvii (1923), pp. 579–624.

subtraction of homogeneous items, toward an ethics along the line of aesthetic criticism, whose canons are of another sort than scientific laws and are not quite intellectually satisfying. We cannot accept want-satisfaction as a final criterion of value because we do not in fact regard our wants as final; instead of resting in the view that there is no disputing about tastes, we dispute about them more than anything else; our most difficult problem in valuation is the evaluation of our wants themselves and our most troublesome want is the desire for wants of the "right" kind.

The purpose of the present paper is to develop and supplement the argument already given, first by re-emphasizing the necessity of a defensible criterion of values as a basis for passing judgment on questions of policy; and secondly by inquiring into the standards of value implicit in the *laissez-faire* or individualistic social philosophy and raising certain questions in regard to them. On the first head, fortunately, we can be brief. It is a thesis which calls for no elaborate demonstration that social policy must be based upon social ideals. An organized system must operate in accordance with a *social* standard. This standard will of course be related in some way to the values of the individuals making up the society, but it cannot be merely identical with them; it presupposes some process of organizing the various individual interests, weighing them against each other and adjudicating conflicts among them.

It is impossible to form any concept of "social efficiency" in the absence of some general measure of value. Even in physics and engineering, "efficiency" is strictly a value category; there is no such thing as mechanical efficiency. It follows from the fundamental laws of the indestructibility of matter and of energy that whatever goes into any apparatus or process comes out *in some form*. In purely mechanical terms, all efficiencies would be equal to one hundred per cent. The efficiency of any machine means the ratio between the *useful* output and the total output. In simple cases the distinction between useful and useless may be so sharp and clear as to give rise to no discussion—as in the case of the mechanical energy and the heat generated by an electric motor. But when more than one form of useful output (or costly input) is involved, the necessity arises for having a measure of usefulness, of value, before efficiency can be discussed. The efficiency relations of a steam engine may be much changed when the exhaust steam is applied to heating. In so complicated a problem as that of social efficiency, where the elements of outlay and of return are both infinitely numerous and diverse, it is no wonder that the process of valuation has become the heart and core of the study. It must ultimately be recognized that only within rather narrow limits can human conduct be interpreted as the creation of values of such definiteness and stability that they can serve as scientific data, that life is fundamentally an exploration in the field of values itself and not a mere matter of producing given values. When this is clearly seen, it will be apparent why so much discussion of social efficiency has been so futile.

Perception of these obvious fundamental principles at once cuts the gound from under one of the lines of criticism of the economic order which has attracted wide attention. It is an idea sponsored especially by Dr. Thorstein Veblen and copied by others, that there is some distinction between "pecuniary" and "industrial" employments* and that society ought to take the control of industry out of the hands of "financiers" and put it into the hands of "technicians."†

This notion rests on the same obvious fallacy, the idea that society has a choice between producing more goods and producing more value, and that it is the part of wisdom to prefer the former. It is difficult to take either part of the proposition seriously. The quantity of goods, if there is more than one kind, must so obviously be measured in value units. The proposal of leaving it to technicians in the respective fields to say how much social productive power shall be expended in each is merely grotesque; military experts would use it all for the army and navy, the medical men could usefully employ it all, and more, for health, and so on. There is no more important function of a first course in economics than to make the student see that the whole problem of social management is a *value* problem; that mechanical or technical efficiency is a meaningless combination of words.

Indeed there can be no question, as the course of the argument will show, that the valid criticisms of the existing economic order relate chiefly to its value standards, and relatively much less to its efficiency in the creation of such values as it recognizes. We shall furthermore

* Publ. Amer. Econ. Assoc., 3d ser., vol. ii, 1901.
† *The Vested Interest and the State of the Industrial Arts*, pp. 63, 89, 99.

insist that not merely a measure of value but ideals of value are pre-requisite to any intelligent criticism of social processes or results. This is not, like the proposition regarding efficiency, a self-evident truth. It is quite arguable that the determination or criticism of policy involves only a comparison of alternative possibilities and a choice of that which is considered preferable. It is arguable, and the contention is in fact often put forward, that values are purely relative, that it means nothing to say that anything is good or bad except in comparison with a worse or better alternative. It is a practical question: does the judging faculty actually work by reasoning out alternatives and deciding which is preferable, or does it not rather formulate ideals and compare actuality and potentiality with these, and with each other indirectly, by so comparing them with an ideal? No doubt both methods are used, and are useful; but we contend that in regard to the larger and higher questions, the ultimate problems of moral and social life, the formula-tion of ideals is a necessary step. There is a place, and a vital place, for an "absolute" science of ethics. Its dicta will not be really absolute, for they never cut loose entirely from the real world and its possibilities of growth and transformation, and they will always grow and change. But at least they are not "merely" relative; they must be beyond the immediately attainable, and will often lie in the field of the actually impossible, patterns to be approached rather than objectives to be achieved.

We contend not merely that such ideals are real to individuals, but that they are a part of our culture and are sufficiently uniform and objective to form a useful standard of comparison for a given country at a given time. Normal common sense does judge in terms of ideals, of absolute ethics in the sense indicated, and not merely in terms of the best that can be done; else it would be linguistically equivalent to call a situation hopeless and to call it ideal, which is clearly not in accordance with usage. In what follows we shall appeal to what we submit to be the common-sense ideals of absolute ethics in modern Christendom. No pretence will be made of drawing up a code of such principles; they are frequently not of a character to fall readily into propositions. There will be no attempt to "settle" moral questions or set up standards, but only to bring out the standards actually involved in making some familiar moral judgments in regard to the economic system, and to examine them critically. The argument will therefore be negative in tone, and the need for brevity may occasionally give it something of the flavour of an "attack"; but let it be stated here that we are not advocating or proposing change. The question of *policy* is a question of alternatives, a purely relative matter; we are concerned here with the question of *ideals*, which we assume may be carried further, into the realm of considerations at least "relatively" absolute. Even if the competitive system is better than any available substitute, a clear view of its shortcomings in comparison with conceivable ideals must be of the highest value in making it better than it is.

An examination of the competitive economic order from the standpoint of its ethical standards will fall naturally into three parts. In the first place, the contention already put forward, that wants are not ultimate data or to be identified with values, does not mean that they are not real and important. We can never get entirely away even from physical needs, requirements for life, for health and for comfort, small as such motives really bulk in civilized behaviour. Moreover, at any given time and place the existing stage of culture sets minimum requirements which are imperative in character. It is true within limits that the purpose of economic activity is to satisfy wants, and the fact raises a group of questions for consideration in an appraisal of any system of economic organization. We must inquire first into its value standards, in the economic or quasi-mechanical sense, its manner of dealing with wants as they exist, its mechanism for comparing and equating and perhaps selecting among the various wants of the various persons and classes of persons which make up the society. It is hardly necessary to remark that the questions *which* wants and *whose* wants are to be satisfied are in fact closely bound up together. The system's answer to this two-fold question constitutes its social economic value scale; and very different social value scales may be formed from the same set of individual wants by different methods of selection, equation, and combination. The more distinctly ethical aspect of this issue is of course the old problem of social justice, relating to the system's treatment of the wants of persons and classes; but that is by no means separable from the question of ranking different wants of the same person. A second inquiry under the same head, of a more mechanical sort but still distinctly a problem of values, deals with the *efficiency* of the system in using its available resources in creating the values which it recognizes, that is, in producing the largest quantity of "goods" as measured by the standard which it sets up.

Another question, ethically more fundamental than these but inseparable from them, and one which must be considered in the first section of the inquiry, follows directly from recognizing the provisional character of wants and the obvious fact that the wants which an economic system operates to gratify are largely produced by the workings of the system itself. In organizing its value scale, the economic order does far more than select and compare wants for exchangeable goods and services: its activity extends to the formation and radical transformation, if not to the outright creation, of the wants themselves; they as well as the means of their gratification are largely products of the system. An examination of the ethics of the economic system must consider the question of the kind of wants which it tends to generate or nourish as well as its treatment of wants as they exist at any given time.

The second of the three main standpoints to be considered corresponds to an aspect of economic life which is rapidly securing more adequate recognition among economists, the fact that the motive of business is to such a large extent that of emulation as such. Industry and trade is a competitive game, in which men engage in part from the same motives as in other games or sports. This is not a matter of want-satisfaction in any direct or economic sense; the "rewards" of successful participation in the game are not wanted for any satisfying power dependent on any quality which they possess as things, but simply as insignia of success in the game, like the ribbons, medals, and the like which are conferred in other sorts of contests. Our second main task will therefore be to raise the question, w*hat kind of game* is business? Is there anything to be said about games from an ethical point of view, any basis for judging them or ranking them as games, and if so, is business a relatively good, bad, or indifferent game?

The third division of the paper will deal briefly with the more fundamental aspects of the problem of values from the standpoint of absolute ethics. Economic activity is a large part of life, and perhaps tends to grow in relative magnitude. The issue as to the influence of the economic system on character can be treated only superficially, but should at least be raised. Emphasis will be placed on the particular phase of competitive emulation as a motive and of success in a contest as an ethical value. The competitive economic order must be partly responsible for making emulation and rivalry the outstanding quality in the character of the Western peoples who have adopted and developed it. The modern idea of enjoyment as well as of achievement has come to consist chiefly in keeping up with or getting ahead of other people in a rivalry for things about whose significance, beyond furnishing objectives for the competition itself, little question is asked. It is surely one function of ethical discussion to keep the world reminded that this is not the only possible conception of value and to point out its contrast with the religious ideals to which the Western world has continued to render lip-service—a contrast resulting in fundamental dualism in our thought and culture.

Throughout the discussion it will be necessary to keep in mind the close inter-connection among these several aspects of the economic system. Economic activity is *at the same time* a means of want-satisfaction, an agency for want- and character-formation, a field of creative self-expression, and a competitive sport. While men are "playing the game" of business, they are also moulding their own and other personalities, and creating a civilization whose worthiness to endure cannot be a matter of indifference.

I

Discussion of the merits of free competition, or *laissez-faire*, takes on an especial interest in view of the contrast between the enticing plausibility of the case for the "obvious and simple system of natural liberty," and the notoriously disappointing character of the results which it has tended to bring about in practice.* In the later

* It should be stated that for simplicity we shall speak of "the" competitive system, though the discussion relates to a "purely" competitive system, as understood by the economic theorist. It is superfluous to remark that such a system has never been closely approximated in reality, or perhaps advocated by any writer taken seriously by any large group—certainly it was not advocated by Adam Smith. The idea of a purely individualistic order is a logical device, necessary to separate for study the tendencies of individualism from those of socialism. It would go a long way toward clarifying discussion if it were generally recognized on both sides that there are no one-hundred-per-cent individualists and no one-hundred-per-cent socialists; that the issue is one of degree and proportion.

eighteenth and early nineteenth centuries, under the influence of the "classical economists," of the Manchester liberals, of the political pressure of the rising bourgeoisie and the general force of circumstances, rapid progress was made toward the establishment of individual liberty in economic affairs. But long before complete individualism was closely approached its consequences were recognized to be intolerable, and there set in that counter-movement toward social interference and control which has been going on at an accelerating pace ever since. The argument for individualism, as developed by its advocates from Adam Smith down, may be summarized in a sentence as follows: a freely competitive organization of society tends to place every productive resource in that position in the productive system where it can make the greatest possible addition to the total social dividend as measured in price terms, and tends to reward every participant in production by giving it the increase in the social dividend which its co-operation makes possible. In the writer's opinion such a proposition is entirely sound; but it is not a statement of a sound ethical social ideal, the specification for a utopia. Discussion of the issue between individual freedom and socialization, however, has largely centred around the truth of the proposition as a statement of the tendencies of competition, rather than around its ethical significance if true. Those who do not like the actual tendencies of the system as they appear to work out when it is tried—and that is virtually everybody—attack the scientific analysis. We propose to argue in the first place that the conditions of life do not admit of an approximation to individualism of the sort necessarily assumed by the theory, and secondly that there are in the conditions of actual life no ethical implications of the kind commonly taken for granted as involved in individualism in so far as it is possible of realization.

The careful statement of the meaning of individualism falls within the province of the economic theorist rather than that of the ethical critic. It is an accident of the way in which economic science has developed, and especially of the peculiar relation between science and practice in this field, that so little serious effort has been made to state with rigour and exactitude the assumptions involved in the notion of perfect competition, the premises of pure economics. Literary writers on economics have been interested in administrative problems, for which the results of any exact treatment of principles are too abstract to be of direct application, and have not generally been trained to use or appreciate rigorous methods. The mathematical economists have commonly been mathematicians first and economists afterward, disposed to oversimplify the data and underestimate the divergence between their premises and the facts of life. In consequence they have not been successful in getting their presentation into such a form that it could be understood, and its relation to real problems recognized, by practical economists. The critical reader of general economic literature must be struck by the absence of any attempt accurately to define that competition which is the principal subject under discussion. A clear formulation of the postulates of theoretical individualism will bring out the contrast with practical *laissez-faire*, and will go far to discredit the latter as a policy. In the present paper the attempt to state the presuppositions of a competitive system cannot be carried beyond a bare outline; it will be developed with reference to our special purpose of showing that in the conditions of real life no possible social order based upon a *laissez-faire* policy can justify the familiar ethical conclusions of apologetic economics.

1. In the first place, an individualistic competitive system must be made up of freely contracting individuals. As a matter of fact, a rather small fraction of the population of any modern nation enter into contracts on their own responsibility. Our "individualism" is really "familism"; all minors, the aged, and numerous persons in other classes, including for practical purposes the majority of adult women, have their status-determining bargains made for them by other persons. The family is still the unit in production and consumption. It is hardly necessary to point out that all arguments for free contract are nullified or actually reversed whenever one person contracts on behalf of another.

2. Moreover, the freest individual, the unencumbered male in the prime of life, is in no real sense an ultimate unit or social datum. He is in large measure a product of the economic system, which is a fundamental part of the cultural environment that has formed his desires and needs, given him whatever marketable productive capacities he has, and which largely controls his opportunities. Social organization through free contract implies that the contracting units know

what they want and are guided by their desires, that is, that they are "perfectly rational," which would be equivalent to saying that they are accurate mechanisms of desire-satisfaction. In fact, human activity is largely impulsive, a relatively unthinking and undetermined response to stimulus and suggestion. Moreover, there is truth in the allegation that unregulated competition places a premium on deceit and corruption. In any case, where the family is the social unit, the inheritance of wealth, culture, educational advantages, and economic opportunities tend toward the progressive increase of inequality, with bad results for personality at both ends of the scale. It is plainly contrary to fact to treat the individual as a *datum*, and it must be conceded that the lines along which a competitive economic order tends to form character are often far from being ethically ideal.

3. It is universally recognized that effective competition calls for "fluidity," the perfect divisibility and mobility of all goods and services entering into exchange. The limited extent to which this assumption fits the facts of life sets limits to the "tendency" of actual competition, which in many cases nullify the principle. Here, as in the case of other assumptions, it is illegitimate to draw practical conclusions from a "tendency," however real, without taking account of contradictory tendencies also, and getting the facts as to their relative strength. One of the dangers of reasoning from simplified premises is the likelihood that the abstract factors may be overlooked in drawing conclusions and formulating policies based thereon.

4. One of the most important prerequisites to perfect competition is complete knowledge on the part of every competing individual of the exchange opportunities open to him. A "perfect market" would involve perfect, instantaneous, and costless intercommunication among all the traders. This condition is really approximated quite closely in the case of a few commodities dealt in on the organized exchanges; but the market for most consumption goods is very crude in its workings. As regards the productive services, abstract pecuniary capital does indeed flow through a highly developed market; but the market for labour, land, and real capital, and their uses, leaves wide margins for "bargaining power" and accidental aberrations. Both the organization of production and the distribution of the product diverge correspondingly from the theoretically ideal results.

5. Competition further requires that every actual or potential buyer of every saleable good or service shall know accurately its properties and powers to satisfy his wants. In the case of productive goods this means knowledge of their technical significance. In an industrial civilization as complex as that of the modern world it is clear that the divergences from this "tendency" must often be more important than the tendency. Indirect knowledge is available to offset direct ignorance in many subtle ways, and yet no individual can know enough to act very closely according to the ideal of perfect intelligence. Moreover, perfect competition does not stop at requiring knowledge of things as they are; the competitor must foresee them as they will be, often a very considerable distance in the future, and the limitations of fore-knowledge are of course more sweeping than those of knowledge.

6. The results of intelligent action are the purposes to which it is directed, and will be ethically ideal only if these ends are true values. Under individualism this means that the wants of individuals must be ideal, as well as their knowledge perfect. We have commented enough on the fact that the social order largely forms as well as gratifies the wants of its members, and the natural consequence that it must be judged ethically rather by the wants which it generates, the type of character which it forms in its people, than by its efficiency in satisfying wants as they exist at any given time.*

* On the character of wants, see an article by A. F. McGoun in *The Quarterly Journal of Economics* for February, 1923. Professor McGoun appears to intend his argument in part as a criticism of my former paper already referred to; but as he begins by drawing curves to represent want-variations, whereas my main contention was that wants are not the sort of variable that can be adequately represented by curves, it would take too much space to bring the argument to a clear issue. I should not question that the observations made in his paper have great value.

Very wise and penetrating remarks on the character of various wants will be found at many points in Wicksteed's *Common Sense of Political Economy*. Patrick Geddes's essay on John Ruskin in the Round Table Series is a brilliant argument for the reduction of all economic values to aesthetic standards. The essay on Phases of the Economic Interest, by H. W. Stuart, in the volume on *Creative Intelligence*, ably emphasizes the explorative, experimental character of much of our activity, in contrast with the static conception of wants demanded by economic logic. Many of the "higher" wants are keenly satirized in Veblen's *Theory of the Leisure Class*. A sober discussion of the problems involved, of much greater scientific significance, is found in the later chapters of G. P. Watkins's volume on *Welfare as an Economic Quantity*.

The activity of business in the way of manufacturing wants has received much attention in the literature of late, again under the leadership of Veblen. It is a serious fallacy to condemn this sort of activity without discrimination. Whether it is good or bad to create wants depends altogether on the character of the wants created. One cannot con-

7. Another sweeping limitation to the actual workings of free competition arises from the fact that men do not have free access to such imperfect markets as exist. No error is more egregious than that of confounding freedom with free competition, as is not infrequently done. As elementary theory itself shows, the numbers of any economic group can always make more by combining than they can by competing. Under freedom all that would stand in the way of a universal drift toward monopoly is the fortunate limitations of human nature, which prevent the necessary organization from being feasible or make its costs larger than the monopoly gains which it might secure. But universal monopoly is self-contradictory, and against any such tendency social action is the only recourse. The workings of competition educate men progressively for monopoly, which is being achieved not merely by the "capitalist" producers of more and more commodities, but by labour in many fields, and in many branches of agriculture, while the producers of even the fundamental crops are already aspiring to the goal.*

8. The individualistic competitive organization of want-satisfying activity presupposes that wants and the means of satisfying them are individual, that is, that wants attach to things and services which gratify the wants of the person consuming them without affecting other persons. As a matter of fact, what is desired is more largely a matter of human relations than goods and services as such; we want things because other people have them, or cannot have them, as the case may be. Then, too, the appurtenances of civilized life can be furnished to an individual only by providing them for the community, and we want to live in a civilized community as well as to live in a

demn advertising and salesmanship out of hand, unless one is prepared to repudiate most of education, and of civilization in general; for most of the desires which distinguish man from the brutes are artificially created. Ethically, the creation of the right wants is more important than want-satisfaction. With regard to the facts in the case, we may observe that business is interested in the fact of change in wants more than in the character of the change, and presumably effects chiefly those changes which can be brought about most easily and cheaply. Our general moral teaching would indicate that it is easier to corrupt human nature than to improve it, and observation of the taste-forming tendencies of modern marketing methods tends perhaps to confirm the view and to substantiate a negative verdict on individualistic activity of this sort.

* The resemblance of this argument to that of Marx is evident. There seems to be ground for treating Marx's conclusions seriously even though his supporting logic, based on the alleged universal superiority of large-scale methods of production, must be repudiated.

civilized way ourselves. With rare exceptions exchanges or contrasts between individuals affect for good and for ill persons not represented in the bargain itself, and for these the bargain is not "free." Social action is necessary to promote the exchanges which diffuse benefits on others for which the parties cannot collect payment in the market, and to suppress those which diffuse evils for which the contracting parties do not have to pay. A typical illustration is the improvement or use of property in ways which add value to or subtract value from neighbouring property. In a developed social order hardly any "free exchange" between individuals is devoid of either good or bad results for outsiders.

9. An exchange system cannot work at all according to "theory" without a scientific unit for measuring values. Society has to take over or carefully control activities which have to do with the circulating medium. With the use of credit highly developed, the control of banking and currency involves a large measure of control over all business, but really free banking would soon reduce all exchange relations to chaos.

10. An economic organization must employ its available productive power in part to provide for current needs of society and in part to provide for future growth. If this second function is to be performed intelligently through individual initiative under competitive organization, each member of the system must make a correct comparison and choice between his own present wants and future social requirements. The weakness of competitive individualism in this field is well recognized, since manifestly progress is essentially a social fact. In an individualistic system provision for progress depends upon the interest of present individuals in future individuals—engendered to an uncertain extent and with uncertain consequences on the form of progress by the family system—or upon their interest in progress itself or some form of it as an ideal value, or upon some accidental connection which makes progress a by-product of activities directed toward other ends. None of these, nor all together, produce results invulnerable to criticism; but the problems of social action in the same field are likewise so difficult and the ideal of progress itself so vague that it is impossible in short compass to say anything of value about the relation of different forms of social organization to the solution of the problem. It is a fact that social interference has gone further in this field than in that of

controlling current production and consumption, as witness especially the social provision for education and scientific research.

11. All human planning and execution involve uncertainty, and a rational social order can be realized through individual action only if all persons have a rational attitude toward risk and chance. But the general human attitude is proverbially irrational, and much social limitation of individual freedom is called for. Not only is it necessary to prohibit gambling, but provision has to be made for placing control of resources and the direction of wealth-production in the hands of persons reasonably fit and competent to take responsibility; and the freedom of these individuals to take chances has to be further restricted by general regulations. Thus no society has in fact ever treated productive resources as private property in any strict sense. It seems likely, however, that a socialistic society would err rather on the side of over-conservatism than on that of recklessness.

12. The last heading in this list of reasons why individualism and competition cannot bring about an ideal utilization of social resources will be the ethics of distribution. In a competitive system distribution is effected by a marketing process, the evaluation of productive services, and is of course subject to all the limitations of marketing in general, as enumerated in the last half-dozen pages. But that is not the main point. It is a common assumption—for which the exponents of the "productive theory" are partly responsible—that productive contribution is an ethical measure of desert. This has improperly tended to bring the theory itself, as a causal explanation of what happens in distribution, into disrepute; because those who are misled into accepting the standard, but cannot approve of the result realized, react by attacking the theory. An examination of the question will readily show that productive contribution can have little or no ethical significance from the standpoint of absolute ethics. (The question of practicability, it must be kept in mind, is eliminated by the boundaries set for this discussion; we are dealing with ideals and not inquiring whether or in what respects the possibilities of the real world may be harmonious with our moral cravings.) The examination of productivity as a standard of desert must again be handled in outline.*

* The "specific product" of any agency is what it enables society to produce more than could be produced without it, with no reference to what it could produce by

(*a*) In the first place, as already noted, there is only a "general tendency" to impute to each productive agency its true product. The factor of ignorance is especially important here, since correct imputation would require perfect technological knowledge and foresight. Human beings do not live on averages, and it is only to a very limited extent that a system of free exchange can make it possible for one to live this year on what he may (or may not) earn next year. To a still more limited extent, if at all, can the particular individual whom the tendency passes over live, through free exchange, on the compensating extra share of a more favoured person.

(*b*) The tendency to place each productive agency in the position where it will make the greatest contribution is far less effective even than the force which adjusts remuneration to actual contribution. A social system which sets artists to shining shoes and pays them what they are worth in that occupation is no less open to condemnation than one that sets them to work at their art and pays them what they would be worth as boot-blacks.

(*c*) The product or contribution is always measured in terms of price, which does not correspond closely with ethical value or human significance. The money value of a product is a matter of the "demand," which in turn reflects the tastes and purchasing power of the buying public and the availability of substitute commodities. All these factors are largely created and controlled by the workings of the economic system itself, as already pointed out. Hence their results can have in themselves no ethical significance as standards for judging the system. On the contrary, the system must be judged by the conformity to ethical standards of these facts of demand rather than by the con-

---

itself. We assume that this is a correct use of the word "product," since it is generally true in cause-and-effect relations that "the cause" is only the deciding factor in the antecedent situation, and that which factor is regarded as deciding is largely a matter of point of view.

We recognize also that specific productivity is the only possible basis for organizing productive resources intelligently, since maximum specific contribution all round is the condition of maximum total product.

It should be kept in mind also that the absolute ethics of distribution are not affected by the fact of organization and the interconnection of the products of different agencies. In a society characterized by individual self-sufficiency, but recognizing the same ethical principles, the obligation of the more efficient or more industrious or more lucky individual who secured a superior share to divide up with others would be as great and as small as it is in a developed system of free enterprise.

formity to demand of the actual production and distribution of goods. And the final results diverge notoriously from the ethical standards actually held. No one contends that a bottle of old wine is ethically worth as much as a barrel of flour, or a fantastic evening wrap for some potentate's mistress as much as a substantial dwelling-house, though such relative prices are not unusual. Ethically, the whole process of valuation is literally a "vicious" circle, since price flows from demand and demand from prices.

(*d*) The income does not go to "factors," but to their owners, and can in no case have more ethical justification than has the fact of ownership. The ownership of personal or material productive capacity is based upon a complex mixture of inheritance, luck, and effort, probably in that order of relative importance. What is the ideal distribution from the standpoint of absolute ethics may be disputed, but of the three considerations named certainly none but the effort can have ethical validity.* From the standpoint of absolute ethics most persons will probably agree that inherited capacity represents an obligation to the world rather than a claim upon it. The significance of luck will be discussed below in connection with the conception of business as a game. We must contend that there is a fallacy in the common position which distinguishes between the ethical significance of the income from labour and that from other factors. Labour in the economic sense may represent either a sacrifice or a source of enjoyment, and the capacity to labour productively derives from the same three sources as property ownership, namely, inheritance, luck, and effort of acquisition, and with no obvious general difference from the case of property in their relative importance.

(*e*) The value of any service or product varies from zero to an indefinite magnitude, according to the demand. It is hard to see that

---

* We find a fairly general agreement among serious writers that the principle of *need*, which would practically amount to equal sharing as a general rule, is the ideal basis of distribution. Among authors of general treatises at least the following have so committed themselves: Taylor, *Principles of Economics*, 8th ed., p. 511; Taussig (with a "perhaps"), *Principles of Political Economy*, 3d ed., vol. ii, p. 475. In an ideal world we may assume that all men would put forth equal effort, so that distribution according to effort would become identical with the ideal. In the present writer's view, effort— i.e., *conscientious* effort—is a better principle; it is more in accord with common-sense ideas of desert, which hardly go to the point of treating all men as equally deserving, and is less obviously impossible of practical application.

even when the demand is ethical, possession of the capacity to furnish services which are in demand, rather than other capacities, constitutes an ethical claim to a superior share of the social dividend, except to the extent that the capacity is itself the product of conscientious effort.

(*f*) The value of a productive service varies from zero to indefinite magnitude, according to its scarcity. The most vital ministrations become valueless if offered in superabundance, and the most trivial performance becomes exceedingly valuable if sufficiently unique and rare, as when a human monstrosity satisfies an economic demand by letting people look at him. It is hard to see how it is more meritorious merely to be different from other people than it is to be like them— except again, possibly, if the capacity has been cultivated by an effort which others refused to put forth.

(*g*) Finally, it may be pointed out that modern society does accept and honour the claim of the entirely helpless to a tolerable human existence, and that there is no difference in principle between this recognition in the extreme case and admitting that differences in degree of competence from no valid basis for discriminatory treatment in distribution. But, after all, does anyone really contend that "competence," as measured by the price system, corresponds to ethical merit? Is it not obvious that "incompetence" follows just as surely if not quite so commonly from being too good for the world as from being blameworthy in character?

Thus the competitive system, viewed simply as a want-satisfying mechanism, falls far short of our highest ideals. To the theoretical tendencies of perfect competition must be opposed just as fundamental limitations and counter-tendencies, of which careful scrutiny discloses a rather lengthy list. Its standards of value for the guidance of the use of resources in production are the prices of goods, which diverge widely from accepted ethical values; and if the existing order were more purely competitive, if social control were reduced in scope, it seems clear that the divergence would be enormously wider still. Moreover, untrammelled individualism would probably tend to lower standards progressively rather than to raise them. "Giving the public what it wants" usually means corrupting popular taste. The system is also inefficient in utilizing resources to produce the values which it sets up, as brought out with startling force by the report on Waste in Industry, by a Committee of the Confederated Engineering Societies. It distributes the produce of industry on the basis of power, which is ethical only in so far as right and might are one. It is a confessed failure in the field of promoting many forms of social progress, and its functions in this regard are being progressively taken over by other social agencies. Left to itself, such a system "collapses" at frequent intervals through dilution of its value unit and through other causes which produce violent oscillation instead of the equilibrium of theory.

It is expressly excluded from the field of the present paper to pass any practical judgment upon the competitive system in comparison with any possible alternative. But in view of the negative tone of the discussion, it seems fair to remark that many of these problems are exceedingly difficult and that many of the evils and causes of trouble are inherent in all large-scale organization as such, irrespective of its form. It must be said also that radical critics of competition as a general basis of the economic order generally underestimate egregiously the danger of doing vastly worse. Finally, let us repeat that practically there is no question of the exclusive use of entire abolition of any of the fundamental methods of social organization, individualistic or socialistic. Economic and other activities will always be organized in all the possible ways, and the problem is to find the right proportions between individualism and socialism and the various varieties of each, and to use each in its proper place.

II

In turning from the want-satisfying aspect of economic activity to consider other of its value problems we enter upon a much harder task. There is little in the way of an established tradition for guidance, and the material is far less amenable to detailed subdivision or to treatment with scientific definiteness. All that can be attempted here is to raise questions and suggest lines of investigation.

It is an essential point in our criticism of established dogma that it has accepted in too narrow and final a sense the view of the economic system as merely a mechanism for satisfying those wants which are dependent upon exchangeable goods and services. Economists have given a belated and even yet not general and adequate recognition to the want-creating side of the system, and to wants as economic products at the same time that they serve as ends and guides of production. Still less attention has been paid to aspects of the organization problem which do not fall naturally under the subject of the satisfaction of wants at all, in the ordinary sense of wants for goods and services. But when we consider that productive activity takes up the larger part of the waking lives of the great mass of mankind, it is surely not to be assumed without investigation or inquiry that production is a means only, a necessary evil, a sacrifice made for the sake of some good entirely outside the production process. We are impelled to look for ends in the economic process itself, other than the mere consumption of the produce, and to give thoughtful consideration to the possibilities of participation in economic activity as a sphere of self-expression and creative achievement.

As soon as the question is raised, it becomes apparent that there are other values involved in production besides the consumption of the goods produced. Since the light of psychological criticism has been turned upon economic theory there has been a growing recognition of the inadequacy of the old treatment of production as mere sacrifice or pain undergone exclusively for the sake of consuming the product. The satisfaction derived from consumption itself is seen to be derived largely from the social situation rather than from the intrinsic qualities of the goods, while the mere fact that wealth is so largely accumulated, or devoted to all sorts of purposes manifestly not in view when its production was undertaken, is sufficient to prove that consumption is not the only motive of production. On the contrary, the persons most actively and successfully engaged in creating wealth not untypically limit their consumption to the point of living rather abstemious personal lives, which they must do to keep fit to meet the physical and mental demands which their business interests make upon them. At the bottom of the social economic scale, the satisfaction of physical needs is undoubtedly the dominant motive in the mind of the unskilled labourer. Higher up, consumption becomes less and less a matter of physiology and more a matter of aesthetics or the social amenities. Still higher, this in turn becomes mixed with a larger and larger proportion of the joy of activity not dependent on any definite use to be made of its results. Traditionally, economics has been vague on the character of economic motives, implying at one time wealth-possession and at another wealth-consumption as fundamental, and never working out clearly the relations between these essentially contradictory impulses or between them and other possible motives.

Turning to look for motives attached to production as an activity rather than to the product, the most obvious is its appeal as a competitive game. The desire for wealth takes on more or less of the character of the desire to capture an opponent's pieces or cards in a game. An ethical criticism of the industrial order must therefore consider it from this point of view. In so far as it is a game, what kind of game is it? There is no doubt that a large amount of radical opposition to the system arises in this connection. The propertyless and ill-paid masses protest not merely against the privations of a low scale of living, but against the terms of what they feel to be an unfair contest in which being defeated by the stacking of the cards against them is perhaps as important to their feelings as the physical significance of the stakes which they lose. In a higher social class, resentment is aroused in the hearts of persons who do not like the game at all, and rebel against being compelled to play it and against being estimated socially and personally on the basis of their success or failure at it.

Increasing attention to this "human side" in economic relations is familiar to all in the demands of labour leaders, who talk much more than formerly of "control" and much less of wages and hours. The same shift in emphasis is manifest in the entire literature of economic discontent. When the sentiment grows strong enough, the personnel problem begins to interfere seriously with business operations, and the ruling classes are forced to pay heed to it. It is probably within the truth to say that inequality in the enjoyment of the produce is now less important as a source of opposition to the competitive system than is the far greater inequality in the distribution of economic power, opportunity, and prestige. The feeling of antagonism is no doubt accentuated by the contrast between the political rhetoric about liberty and equality, on which our citizens are so largely fed, and the facts of autocracy and servitude which labouring people (rightly or wrongly) feel to characterize their actual lives.

Economists and publicists are coming to realize how largely the efficiency of business and industry is the result of this appeal to intrinsic interest in action; how feeble, in spite of the old economics, is the motivation of mere appetite or cupidity; and how much the driving power of our economic life depends on making and keeping the game interesting. A rapidly growing literature on "incentive" is a witness to this awakening. As long as we had the frontier and there was not only "room at the top" but an open road upward, the problem was not serious. But in a more settled state of society, the tendency is to make the game very interesting indeed to a small number of "captains of industry" and "Napoleons of finance," but to secure this result by making monotonous drudgery of the lives of the masses who do the work. There are limits beyond which this process cannot be carried without arousing a spirit of rebellion which spoils the game for the leaders themselves, not to mention the effect on the output of products upon which people have become dependent.

The problem of an ethical standard or ideal in terms of which to judge the economic order is of a different and far more difficult sort when we leave the field of more or less comparable burdens and quantities of goods, to consider power and prestige as ends. In a competitive game it is absurd to speak of equality as an ideal, a fact which much radical discussion overlooks. Some of the criticisms brought against existing society amount to condemning a foot-race as unfair because someone has come out ahead. We must bear in mind, too, that the system is a want-satisfying agency at the same time that it is a competitive game, and that the two functions are inseparable, while the two sets of ideals are different. For efficiency in the production of goods a large concentration of authority is necessary. But this concentration violates the principle of equality of opportunity in the game; and when power of control carries with it the right to consume product accordingly, as it actually does, the result is flagrant inequality in this respect also. There appears to be a deep-seated conflict between liberty and equality on the one hand and efficiency on the other. There is little comfort for democratic, equalitarian idealism in the study of evolutionary biology, in which the highly centralized or "cephalized" forms have always come out ahead. Yet apparently human society is different in some degree at least, for there appears to be a tendency for autocracies, aristocracies, and systems approaching a caste organization to be beaten out in history by the apparently less efficient "democracy," though democracies have not in practice approached closely to the equalitarian ideal.

In a system which is at the same time a want-satisfying mechanism and a competitive game we seem to find three ethical ideals in conflict. The first is the principle already mentioned, of distribution according to effort. The second is the principle of "tools to those who can use them." This is a necessary condition of efficiency, but involves giving the best player the best hand, the fastest runner the benefit of the handicap, and thus flagrantly violates the third ideal, which is to maintain the conditions of fairness in the game.

An attempt to formulate accurately the conditions of a fair and interesting game leads into difficult problems. The difference between play and work is subtle, and remains obscure after all the attempts of psychologists to deal with it. It is an old and ever-fascinating dream that all work might be converted into play under the right conditions. We know that almost any kind of work may become infused with the play spirit, as is more or less typically true of the creative arts, the higher professions to some extent, and notably business itself, as already observed. Yet definitions of play carry us little beyond the statement that it is enjoyable activity. It is usually defined as activity which constitutes its own end, is performed for its own sake.* But this view will hardly stand examination. We cannot think of any human activity, however "playful," which is entirely spontaneous and self-contained. Perhaps the random movements of a baby's hands and feet fit the description; but the games and recreative activities of an adult or a child look more or less beyond the mere bodily movements; they have an objective, if nothing more than to build a block house to be immediately torn down, and on it they are dependent for their peculiar interest. Perhaps we can say that in play the objective usually follows so closely upon the activity that the two are naturally thought of as a unit, or that the result occupies the attention so fully as to exclude the effort from consciousness altogether, while in work they are contrasted and the activity is presented to the mind as a means, over against the end. At least, the feeling tone of play can often be imparted

* For an excellent brief discussion of the use of the term "play" see C. E. Rainwater, *The Play Movement*, Introduction. Dewey's definition, a typical one, covers "those activities which are not consciously performed for the sake of any reward beyond themselves." See also the lecture on Work, in Ruskin's *Crown of Wild Olive*.

to work more or less voluntarily by fixing attention upon the objective, thus crowding the effort out of consciousness. The power to induce this shift of attention in other persons seems to be an important factor in leadership.

We are here concerned rather with the special psychology of competitive games than with the general problem of play, which includes non-competitive social ceremonial as well as solitary random play and formal games played solitaire. A few general statements may be made with some confidence in regard to the difference between a good competitive game and a poor one. In the first place, there are three elements which affect the question of who is to win and thus contribute to the interest: these are ability to play, effort, and luck. It is also significant that the ability of play brought to the game on any particular occasion is, like all human capacity, a compound of innate endowment and "education" acquired from the previous expenditure of effort in play or practice, or perhaps in some closely related activity of either a recreative or a serious character. A good game must test the capacity of the players, and to do this it must compel them to exert effort. At the same time, it must involve more than a purely objective measure of capacity (assuming maximum effort). The result must be unpredictable: if there is no element of luck in it there is no game. There is no game in lifting weights, after one once knows how much can be lifted, even though the result measures capacity. Where "records" are made, the interest centres in the unpredictable fluctuations in the powers of men (or horses, etc.) from one trial to another.

A good game calls for some reasonable, though far from definite, proportion among the three elements, capacity, effort, and luck— except that apparently most human beings are susceptible to fascination by pure chance, in spite of the obvious fact that a competitive game of pure chance involves a logical contradiction. Certainly there is general agreement that games of skill are "superior" to games of chance. Effort is called forth by interest, and intelligent interest is dependent on the fact that effort makes some difference in the result. But effort is futile or superfluous if there is too great a difference in the abilities of the players, and the game is spoiled. Even the hunter who considers himself a sportsman always gives his quarry a chance. Finally, it will no doubt be admitted that some games are "higher class" than others, depending presumably on the human qualities necessary to play them successfully and to enjoy them. The actual ranking of games would, it is true, raise the same problems of value standards which beset the path to objectivity in all fields of artistic criticism; and here also we should have to appeal to a general consensus and perhaps admit within limits the equal validity of opposing judgments.

No doubt different judges would disagree in their ranking of business as a competitive game, but the principles sketched above suggest some shortcomings. Its outcome is a very inaccurate test of real ability, for the terms on which different individuals enter the contest are too unequal. The luck element moreover is so large—far larger than fairly successful participants in the game will ever admit— that capacity and effort may count for nothing. And this luck element works cumulatively, as in gambling games generally. The effects of luck in the first hand or round, instead of tending to be evened up in accord with the law of large numbers in the further progress of the game, confer on the player who makes an initial success a differential advantage in succeeding hands or rounds, and so on indefinitely. Any particular individual may be eliminated by the results of his first venture, or placed in a position where it is extraordinarily difficult to get back into the game.*

Again, differences in the capacity to play the business game are inordinately great from one person to another. But as the game is organized, the weak contestants are thrown into competition with the strong in one grand mêlée; there is no classification of the participants or distribution of handicaps such as is always recognized to be necessary to sportsmanship where unevenly matched contestants are to meet. In fact the situation is worse still; there are handicaps, but, as we

---

* In the matter of luck it is even more difficult than in the case of want-satisfaction to measure the relative strength of different tendencies. Opinions will differ as to the ideal amount of luck in a game as well as in regard to the amount which there actually is in business. The cumulative working of the luck element will probably be more generally acknowledged to be a real evil. It is worth observing that the excessively crucial character of single decisions is a common phenomenon in all phases of life, a leading source of its tragedy and pathos. Rarely are we given enough "trials" in planning any feature of our careers to test the judgment which we actually possess. And when one thinks of the possibilities of developing better judgment, one is face to face with the essential tragedy of the brevity of life itself.

have seen, they are distributed to the advantage of the strong rather than the weak. We must believe that business ability is to some extent hereditary, and social institutions add to inherited personal superiority the advantages of superior training, preferred conditions of entrance into the game, and even an advance distribution of the prize money.

The distribution of prizes diverges from the highest ideal of sportsmanship in another way. In a competition where the powers of the contestants are known to be unequal but the inequalities are not well enough determined to permit the classification of the players or an equalization of chances by means of handicaps, it is possible to sustain interest by offering a larger number of prizes less unequal in value. This method brings about an automatic classification of the contestants by the progress of the game itself. But in the business game the tendency is to multiply inequalities of performance in the inequality of distribution of the stakes. Let us suppose that we are organizing a footrace among a thousand men taken at random from the general population. At one extreme they might be all lined up on a mark and made to race for a single first prize; at the other, the prize money might be distributed equally, irrespective of the results of the race. From the standpoint of sport, the one proceeding would be as absurd as the other. If the critics of competition tend to make a fetish of equality, the system itself does undoubtedly go very far to the opposite extreme.

Admitting that business success tends in the large to go with business ability, we must face the question of the abstract merit of such capacity as a human trait, and hence of business as a game. It can hardly be denied that there is a preponderance of cultivated opinion against it. Successful business men have not become proverbial for the qualities that the best minds and most sensitive spirits of the race agree in calling noble. Business as it is and has been does not commonly display a very high order of sportsmanship, not to mention the question which will be raised presently as to whether sportsmanship itself is the highest human ideal. As to the human qualities developed by business activity and requisite to enjoyment of and successful participation in it, there is no objective measure and no opinion will be accepted as free from "prejudice" by those who disagree with it. We shall dismiss the subject by quoting a statement by Ruskin, which can hardly be waived aside as valueless or unrepresentative. "In a community regulated by laws of demand and supply, but protected from open violence," he says, "the persons who become rich are, generally speaking, industrious, resolute, proud, covetous, prompt, methodical, sensible, unimaginative, insensitive, and ignorant. The persons who remain poor are the entirely foolish, the entirely wise, the idle, the reckless, the humble, the thoughtful, the dull, the imaginative, the sensitive, the well-informed, the improvident, the irregularly and impulsively wicked, the clumsy knave, the open thief, the entirely merciful, just, and godly person."*

However favourable an opinion one may hold of the business game, he must be very illiberal not to concede that others have a right to a different view and that large numbers of admirable people do not like the game at all. It is then justifiable at least to regard as unfortunate the dominance of the business game over life, the virtual identification of social living with it, to the extent that has come to pass in the modern world. In a social order where all values are reduced to the money measure in the degree that this is true of modern industrial nations, a considerable fraction of the most noble and sensitive characters will lead unhappy and even futile lives. Everyone is compelled to play the economic game and be judged by his success in playing it, whatever his field of activity or type of interest, and has to squeeze in as a side line any other competition, or non-competitive activity, which may have for him a greater intrinsic appeal.

III

We must treat still more inadequately our third main question, which from the point of view of pure ethics is the most important of all—the question of the ethics of competition as such. Is emulation as a motive ethically good or base? Is success in any sort of *contest*, as such, a noble objective? Are there no values which are real in a higher sense than the fact that people have agreed to strive after them and to measure success in life by the result of their striving? It seems evident that most of the ends which are actually striven after in the daily lives of

* Taken from *The Cry of Justice: An Anthology of Social Protest*, by Upton Sinclair, p. 752.

modern peoples are primarily of this character; they are like the cards and checker-men, worthless (at best) in themselves, but the objects of the game; and to raise questions about the game is to make one's self disagreeable. To "play the game" is the current version of accepting the universe, and protest is blasphemy; the Good Man has given place to the "good sport." In America particularly, where competitive business, and its concomitant, the sporting view of life, have reached their fullest development, there have come to be two sorts of virtue. The greater virtue is to win; and meticulous questions about the methods are not in the best form, provided the methods bring victory. The lesser virtue is to go out and die gracefully after having lost.

We do not mean to beg the question whether the spirit of rivalry is ethically good, but only to state it in a form which raises it sharply. It cannot be denied that appeal to the competitive motive may be a source of interest in activity. The issue raised is in part the old as doubtless scientifically unanswerable one of pleasure *versus* discipline as the fundamental moral value. The hedonist would say that, as a matter of course, whatever adds to the pleasure adds to the value, and would ask only whether more is added than is taken away.

But here we appear to run into the obverse of Mill's paradox of hedonism, which is perhaps the paradox of life. It is in fact much easier to argue that the introduction of the contest motive into economic life has made it more efficient than that it has made it more pleasurable! Candid observations of industrial operatives at work, and of their frenzied, pathetic quest for recreation when off duty, alike fail to give the impression of particularly happy existence. As already observed, economic production has been made a fascinating sport *for the leaders*, but this has been accomplished by reducing it to mechanical drudgery for the rank and file. In the large is the competitive urge a lure, or is it rather a goad? Is it positive or negative, especially when we recall that for the masses the competition is in the field of consumption, with production regarded purely as a means? From the standpoint of pleasure, does the normal human being prefer a continuous, unquestioning, and almost deadly competition, or the less strenuous atmosphere of activity undertaken for ends that seem intrinsically worth while, with a larger admixture of the spectator attitude of appreciation? Current comment on the rush of life and the movement toward guilds and medievalism indicate a widespread feeling of opposition to the competitive tendency.*

If on the other hand one adopts the view that the end of life is to get things done, the case for competition becomes much stronger; but even here misgivings arise. It is hard to avoid asking, *what things*. If it is thought to be important which things are done, competition may be entirely indifferent and unselective, equally effective as a drive toward worthy and unworthy ends. If so, the selection of ends must be left to accident or to some other principle. There seems to be a tendency, however, for competition to be selective, and not in a very exalted sense. It is hard to believe that emulation is as effective in the "higher" fields of endeavour as it is in relation to material concerns or mere trivialities.

It is possible to hold that it does not matter what is done, that all activity develops personality equally, or that action and change as such are what make life worth living. From the point of view of mere interested activity, if we are to bring into question neither the character of the result nor that of the interest (beyond the fact that it is an "intelligent" interest, the result a foreseen result), the organization of life on a competitive basis would seem to be abundantly justified. Perhaps the organization tends to foster a philosophic attitude which will justify theory; and if so, we have a sufficient "economic interpretation" of the vogue of pragmatism. Interpreting life in terms of power as such, including "intelligence" as a form of power, there can be little question that competitive business has been an effective agency in bringing the forces of nature under human control and is largely responsible for the material progress of the modern era.

It is in terms of power, then, if at all, that competitive economics and the competitive view of life for which it must be largely accountable are to be justified. Whether we are to regard them as justified at all depends on whether we are willing to accept an ethics of power as the basis of our world view. And as Fichte said, "Was für eine Philo-

---

* Bertrand Russell, in his *Principles of Social Reconstruction*, makes the distinction between competitive and non-competitive values virtually equivalent to good and bad, the devotion to the former the primal sin of the modern world. H. G. Wells, in an early book, *In the Days of the Comet*, drew an idyllic picture of a world with competition eliminated. On the other hand, modern socialism has perhaps more commonly accepted competitive emulation as a motive, claiming only that under socialism it would be moralized and turned toward social welfare instead of private gain.

sophie man wählt hangt davon ag was für ein Mensch man ist." But like most aphorisms this may be turned around without ceasing to be equally true: the sort of person one is depends on the sort of philosophy one chooses. It is the eternal law of reciprocal cause and effect; as just suggested, the system tends to mould men's minds in the channels which will justify the system itself, and in this sense there is a partial truth in the "economic interpretation," which we have gone to such lengths to attack and repudiate.* But the matter does not, cannot, rest there. The whole question is, are we to accept an "ethics of power" à la Nietzsche, or does such an acceptance involve a contradiction in terms and really mean the rejection of any true "ethics" altogether? Most of us have been taught in various connections not only that there is some sort of contrast between ethics and power, between right and might, but that the contrast is fundamental to the nature of morality. In these days it is eminently respectable to hold that all ideas of this sort belong to those childish things which one must put away on becoming a man. It is a part of the modern scientific world view, and a legitimate part. To many of its "tough-minded" advocates, one who calls it in question must class himself as not merely "tender-minded," but "feeble-minded" as well.

And "logically" they are inevitably right! A strictly scientific discussion of general world problems leads inexorably to fatalism, to a mere question of power, to the relegation to a land of dreams of any ethics which involves questions of another sort than that as to which of two forces is the greater in magnitude. The question at issue must be clearly recognized to be precisely this: whether the logic of science itself is universally valid; whether there is or is not a realm of reality which is not comprehended in factual categories and describable in terms of definite meaning combined in propositions subject to empirical verification. Or, more accurately, it is the question whether knowledge of any such reality is possible, or whether it can be intelligently discussed. The tough-minded scientist, if candid, will admit that there *may be* such a reality, but will insist that we cannot talk about it "intelligently." Which of course is true, in the nature of the case, if to talk intelligently means to talk scientifically, which are

* See the paper above referred to: "Ethics and the Economic Interpretation," in the *Quarterly Journal of Economics* for May, 1922.

to him equivalent terms. To the modern mind any attempt to argue such a question is fraught with the greatest difficulty, since the modern mind itself is moulded into conformity with the scientific view of what is meant by intelligent discourse. Two facts, however, must apparently be accepted. The first is that one may also find "respectable" company in the belief that the scientific world view not only finds no place for many of the most fundamental data of human experience, but that, tested by the canons of its own logic, it is ultimately riddled with contradictions; numerous minds of demonstrated competence in the field of science itself hold this view. The second fact is that people do manage to "understand each other" more or less, in conversation about things which are not matters of scientific fact, but of interpretation, as in discussions of art and of character or personality.

Assuming that all ethical standards other than that of quantity of accomplishment, the ideal generated by the institution itself, are not to be dismissed *a priori* as manifestations of incompetence to discuss the question, we may close the discussion by referring briefly to the relation of some historic types of ethical theory to the problem of the evaluation of competition. From the standpoint of hedonism, the question would be simply whether competition has added to the pleasure of living. This question has been raised above, and we shall recur to it presently. In our view the nineteenth-century hedonists were not ethical hedonists anyway. They held, or assumed, the position of psychological hedonism, which involves the question-begging procedure of using pleasure as a synonym for motive in general, and to attack or criticize it at this day would be to slay the slain. They were really utilitarians in the sense in which the term was used by Paulsen, referring to the judgment of human actions by their consequences and not in accordance with formal rules. On the crucial question, how to judge the consequences, they were commonly silent or vague. But examination will show that nineteenth-century utilitarianism was in essence merely the ethics of power, the "glorified economics" to which we have referred before. Its outcome was to reduce virtue to prudence, its ideal the achievement of the greatest *quantity of desired results*. It was scientific, intellectual, in the naturalistic, pragmatic conception of knowledge as instrumental to power, that is, as power itself. As to the purposes for which power *ought* to be used, the true problem of ethics, they had nothing to say in any definite or systematic way; the fact of desire was tacitly accepted as the essence of value. Spencer bravely reduced the whole system to an ethical absurdity by explicitly carrying desire back to an ultimate justification in the desire to live, postulating that any species "must" desire what is good for it in a biological sense; and for all the group, survival power was in fact the final measure of rightness.

It seems to the writer almost superfluous to deny the appropriateness of the term "ethics" to any such conception. The conditions of survival are merely the laws of biology. It may well be the part of prudence to act in accordance with them, assuming that one *wants* to survive, but it can hardly be associated with the notions of right or duty, and if these have no meaning beyond prudence the whole realm of ethics is illusory.* Ethics deals with the problem of choosing between different kinds of life, and assumes that there is real choice between different kinds, or else there is no such thing as ethics. The ethical character of competition is not decided by the fact that it stimulates a greater amount of activity; this merely raises the question of the ethical quality of what is done or of the motive itself.

With this so-called ethics of scientific naturalism may be contrasted, as general types of ethical thought, true ethical hedonism or eudemonism, the Greek and the Christian views. From the standpoint of the first, the happiness philosophy, little need be added to what has already been said. Competition may form an added source of pleasure in activity, especially to the winner or, in the progress of the game, to those who stand some chance to win. But it is more likely to become a goad, especially when participation in the contest is compulsory. There is a fairly established consensus that happiness depends more on spiritual resourcefulness, and a joyous appreciation of the costless things of life, especially affection for one's fellow creatures, than it does on material satisfaction. A strong argument for co-operation, if it would work, would be its tendency to teach people to like each other in a more positive sense than can ever be bred by participation in a contest—certainly in a contest in which the means of life, or of a decent life, are felt to be at stake. The dominance of salesmanship in

* These writers could find no place for and would have to reject an ethical obligation to live.

the business world, as well as the spirit of economic rivalry, must also tend to work against the appreciation of the "free goods."

It should be observed also that while the principle of "whom the Lord loveth he chasteneth" is hard to apply as a maxim of practical morality, it is generally admitted that human nature is likely to show up morally finer under adversity than in security and ease; also that few people can be trusted with much power without using it to the physical damage of others and their own moral discredit.

Surely no justification of competition as a motive is to be found in the Aristotelian conception of the good as that which is intrinsically worthy of man as man, or the Platonic idea of archetypal goodness. The outstanding characteristic of Greek ethical thought was the conception of the good as objective, and of the moral judgment as a cognition. A thing should be done because it is the thing to do, not because it is or is not being done by others. Virtue is knowledge, and the good is intellectually conceived, but the meaning of these statements contrasts as widely as possible with the modern reduction of virtue to prudence and of choice to a calculation of advantage. The intellectual equality in Greek ethics is the capacity of discrimination between true and false values, which is a wholly different thing from the ability to foresee changes and adapt means to ends. The one runs in terms of appreciation as the other runs in terms of power. The ideal in the one case is perfection, in the other that of bigness. To be sure, the Greeks were far from indifferent to recognition and glory, and the contest spirit played a large role in the life of the people, as shown in the national games. But the ideal seems always to have been the achievement of perfection, and the education of the people to recognize superior merit, not merely to win. Certainly it was not the mere winning of power.

Christianity has been interpreted in so many conflicting ways that one must hesitate to bring it into a scientific discussion; yet even this wide range of uncertainty will not admit competitive values into Christian thought. If there is anything on which divergent interpretations would have to agree, it would be the admission that the Christian conception of goodness is the antithesis of competitive. We are by no means forced to believe that the central figure of the Gospels was an ascetic; he never condemned pleasure as such, and seems to have had his own pleasure in life. But his participation in any sort of competitive sport is not to be imagined. Among his most characteristic utterances were the fervent exhortations that the last should be first and that he who would be chief should be the servant of all. The Christian ethical ideal contrasts as sharply with the Greek as either does with modern ideas derived from natural science and political economy. We have said that any *ethical* judgment of activity must be based not upon its efficiency, the quantity of results accomplished, but on either the character of those results or the character of the motive which led to the action. The Greek view fixes attention upon the character of the result, and gives an essentially aesthetic conception of ethical value; Christianity centres attention upon the motive, and its ideal of life may be summed up in the word "spirituality," as the Greek ideal is summed up in "beauty" or "perfection." As the Greek identified virtue with knowledge, assuming it to be inconceivable that one should recognize true values and not act in accordance with them, Christianity (more explicitly as formulated by Paul—Romans 7: 15; Galatians 5: 19–23) makes virtue consist in conscientiousness, in doing what one believes to be right, rather than in the correct perception of objective goodness. It must be admitted that if it is hard to describe or define beauty, it is enormously more difficult to discuss spirituality in terms that seem at all intelligible to a scientific and utilitarian age. Both ideals agree in differing from economic (scientific, pragmatic) ethics in that they are *qualitative* in their ideals, whereas the last is merely quantitative. It seems fairly clear to the writer that it is from Christianity (and from Kant, who merely systematized Christian, or Pauline, principles) that modern common sense derives its conceptions of what is ethical as stated when that point is explicitly under discussion.

The striking fact in modern life is the virtually complete separation between the spiritual ethics which constitutes its accepted theory of conduct and the unethical, uncriticized notion of efficiency which forms its substitute for a practical working ideal, its effective values being accepted unconsciously from tradition or the manipulations of commercial sales managers, with a very slight admixture of aesthetic principles. For "spirituality" is preserved in practice a smaller and smaller fraction of the seventh day, by a smaller and smaller fraction of the population; and even that is more and more transformed by organizations into a mere contest in membership and display, with a larger or smaller admixture of the element of aesthetic diversion and a smaller or larger admixture of pure commercialism. The spirit of life in the "Christian" nations and the spirit of Christianity offer an interesting study in the contrast between theory and practice. And all the while there are multiplying evidences of a genuine spiritual hunger in the modern peoples. They have got away from the spiritual attitude toward life, and do not know how to get back. Science is too strong for old beliefs, and competitive commercialism too strong for old ideals of simplicity, humility, and reverence.

Thus we appear to search in vain for any really ethical basis of approval for competition as a basis for an ideal type of human relations, or as a motive to action. It fails to harmonize either with the Pagan ideal of society as a community of friends or the Christian ideal of spiritual fellowship. Its only justification is that it is effective in getting things done; but any candid answer to the question, "what things," compels the admission that they leave much to be desired. Whether for good or bad, its aesthetic ideals are not such as command the approval of the most competent judges, and as for spirituality, commercialism is in a fair way to make that term incomprehensible to living men. The motive itself has been generally condemned by the best spirits of the race. In academic life, for example, though every (American) institution feels itself compelled to use credits, marks, and honours, they are virtually never defended as intrinsically worthy, incentives to effort.

Whether it is possible to bring about improvement by substituting some other basis of social organization for competitive individualism is a question beyond the scope of this paper. Its purpose has been merely to bring out fundamental weaknesses of competition from the standpoint of purely ideal standards, and so to establish bases for comparison with any other possible system. Summarizing the argument, it was first emphasized by way of introduction that any judgment passed upon a social order is a value judgment and presupposes a common measure and standard of values, which must be made as clear and explicit as possible if the judgment is to be intelligent. Efficiency is a value category and social efficiency an ethical one. Now the standards which underlie a competitive system, according to orthodox economic theory, are the actual desires of the individual members of society. Competition is supposed to effect a comparison of these, and to organize the resources of society in such a way as to satisfy them to the greatest possible extent in order of magnitude— that is, it is supposed to "tend" to do so. The first main task of the paper was therefore to enumerate the more fundamental and obvious limitations on this tendency, or counter-tendencies which are in many cases quite as important as the tendency itself. Economic theory must isolate the ideal tendencies with which it can deal most readily; but no practical conclusions as to the real beneficence of the system can be drawn until the actual relative importance of the tendencies recognized by the general theory—which in endeavouring to explain always seems to justify—are measured in comparison with divergent tendencies and these taken into account.

In the second division of the paper it was pointed out that the competitive economic life has value implications on the production side, the most notable of which is its appeal as a competitive game. An examination from this point of view reveals notable shortcomings of business considered purely as a game. There is also a certain ethical repugnance attached to having the livelihood of the masses of the people made a pawn in such a sport, however fascinating the sport may be to its leaders.

Finally, we have called in question from the standpoint of ideal ethics the predominance of the institution of sport, or action motivated by rivalry, and in particular have contrasted it with the Pagan ethics of beauty or perfection and the Christian ideal of spirituality.

ECONOMIC PSYCHOLOGY AND THE
VALUE PROBLEM*

The basic difficulty in economic theory is the philosophical problem of the meaning of explanation in connection with human behaviour. I. Motive or desire in human conduct is the analogue of force in mechanics, 77.—II. Is force real or merely symbolic, leaving movement (behaviour in the case of human beings) the only fact open to description or study? 81.—This question is merely formal in physics, for we know forces by their effects alone, and hence unambiguously if at all; but in the realm of conduct, we know motives in ourselves directly and in others by communication, in addition to inferring them from observed behaviour, and the two sources of information disagree considerably. III–IV. The intellectually embarrassing but unescapable fact of purposiveness, in thought as well as conduct, 86.—V. The place of motives and their treatment in economics, which has to be critical as well as descriptive and logical—a branch of aesthetics and ethics as well as of science, 97.—VI. The objective of economic activity and the point of view of social criticism of the economic order, 102.

AT the present moment economic interest and discussion are in one of their periodic swings away from the more philosophical aspects of the subject, in the direction of the empirical and the concrete. Expressions of weariness and impatience with methodology and speculation and all generalities are the familiar note. We are urged to be "scientific" in the manner of the laboratory sciences, to devote ourselves to the observation of "facts," and to eschew generalization and all assertions outside the realm of empirical verification. Such movements come and go. The balance between observation and analysis will always be a shifting one. The philosophical interest never dies out, and will always come into its own—and be overdone in its turn. Not for any long period, certainly, can any science which deals with human conduct and social policy remain

* Reprinted by permission from *The Quarterly Journal of Economics*, vol. xxxix (1925), pp. 372–409.

aloof from the broad and difficult but unescapable problems connected with the nature of value and its relation to reality and the methods by which both are tested and known. The great names in the history of economic thought are to a remarkable extent prominent also in the history of moral science and of logic, and it is no more probable than from the standpoint of economics it is desirable, that this condition of affairs will be greatly changed in the future.

Indeed, economics stands, in a somewhat peculiar sense, at the meeting point of the three great branches of thought or fields of intellectual endeavour. The science which deals with the satisfaction of wants is, in the first place, a science of ways and means, and hence concerns itself with the entire body of natural science in its pragmatic aspect as a technique for controlling nature and bending natural forces and materials to the will of man. And in this natural science, as a technique of prediction and control, are included the facts and laws of human behaviour as well as those pertaining to the behaviour of external things. But the study of want-satisfaction must consider also the wants themselves, and if it is to have anything to say about policy, it must consider them critically; hence it comes into the closest relation with those disciplines which undertake the criticism of values, that is, with aesthetics and morals. Between and around these two fields of facts and values is the central problem of philosophical inquiry, the problem of knowledge, which in fact can least of all be neglected by the student of any phase of conduct. For surely it is a commonplace which it would be unpardonable to ignore, that human beings act, not on the basis of fact and reality as such, but on the basis of *opinions* and *beliefs about facts*, and what is called *knowledge*, but which at best falls notoriously short of the implications of that term. From a logical point of view therefore, one who aspires to explain or understand human behaviour must be, not finally but first of all, an epistemologist. These general problems of scope and method all come to a focus in the central question of the relation between motive and conduct, which is one of the meanings of that most ambiguous and meaningless of words, the term "psychology."

I

The economist meets the problem of conduct and motive at every point and stage of his work, but perhaps first and most unavoidably in the study of consumption. *Why* do men purchase goods, and particular amounts of different goods? More specifically, what answer that will be in any degree enlightening can be given to the question why the amount of any good purchased bears a fairly definite relation to its price, decreasing as the price increases, if other conditions are unchanged? Relatively narrower and less important aspects of this problem will here be passed over, in order to come at the central issue without delay or distraction of interest.*

This central issue is nothing less than the question whether conscious desires or conscious states of any sort can be regarded as "causing" or "explaining" conduct. The scientific study of behaviour is notoriously unable to find a place for conscious states as causes, and the weight of psychological opinion is increasingly against treating them as such. Psychologists began a long generation ago, with the advent of the James-Lange theory, to hold that feeling results from action rather than action from feeling; that we desire because we act rather than act because we feel desire. Accepting this view, we should have to say that the consumer feels a desire for a good because

* One of the side issues is the question whether desire is to be treated as relative or absolute. It seems clear to the present writer that desire, which, as will appear, is the analogue in psychology of force in mechanics, is, like any other force, relative in nature. One force is not merely *measured* by another force, but its existence as a magnitude is conditioned by that of some equal force in opposition. Value, similarly, is an aspect of choice, and valuation is intrinsically a comparison of values. But no practical confusion is likely to result from taking the theoretically erroneous position that desire is an absolute, and discussion therefore appears to the practically minded as a mere logomachy.

Another issue more intimately related to the central problem is that of the correct method of aggregating units of desire or satisfaction into totals. Passing over the further question of the relation between quantity of desire and quantity of satisfaction, it is a fundamental principle that the attractive force of a unit of commodity decreases with the increase in the number of units. The question is whether the value of a supply is to be regarded as the sum of the values of the units considered successively or as the product of the value which one unit actually has in the given supply into the number of the units. In technical language, is "consumers surplus" real? The analogy of mechanics does not throw light on the question, because a mechanical force produces the same effect in a combination that it does when acting alone. Thus the answer to the question depends on one's fundamental conception of economics, whether and in what sense values are to be viewed as analogous to mechanical forces.

he purchases it. Still more recently the tendency is simply to leave desire and satisfaction and all feelings out of the scientific discussion of behaviour and treat every action as a response of the organism to a situation or stimulus.

From a strictly scientific point of view this position seems unescapable. Science, we are perpetually reminded, deals with *observed facts*, and their relations of coexistence and sequence. It must rigorously exclude "metaphysical entities" of every sort. And a feeling, manifestly, is not an "observed fact"; it is an inference from the behaviour itself, or at most it is "reported," which is to say that it is inferred from a report, which report itself is but an observed behaviour fact. Conscious states are certainly never observed through the senses, they are not directly observed in any sense in any other person; and it is far from clear just what it means, or how true it is to say that one observes even his own conscious states as such. The question is acutely controversial. If we do explain actions by feelings, we must go on to explain feelings by the situations in which they arise in connection with the character of the "organism," its "character" being just its behaviour habits as ascertained by previous observation. An explanation which stops at facts of consciousness is idle and useless. The purpose of knowledge is to predict, and the use of prediction is control. But we can predict only on the basis of some readily observable and identifiable mark or condition. It is useless to know that a human being who feels in a certain way will act in a certain way, unless we have some perceptible indicator of the feeling, which indicator can be only a behaviour fact. Equally useless is it from the standpoint of control unless we know how to produce and manipulate feelings, and this can be done only by means of established behaviour sequences.

Thus, unless it is assumed that feelings have some real existence apart from the observable physical facts pertaining to the organism, they are superfluous in explaining behaviour, and if they do have such a real existence, they actually make prediction and control impossible to the extent that they function as causes. If the desire which (as we say) prompts an act is rigorously dependent upon (correlated with) the situation in which it arises, then it is simpler and more satisfactory to predict the act from the situation directly, especially as the desire itself can never be observed and has to be inferred from previous behaviour. If the desire is *not* perfectly correlated with the situation, then to that extent the act which it "causes" cannot be predicted from previously known data at all. Knowledge of coexistences and sequences among facts which cannot be observed is futile, even if we assume that it can be real. There would be absolutely no point to measuring the specific gravity of lead or the tensile strength of iron if we had no way of knowing when we had lead or iron to deal with except to measure the density or strength as the case might be. We do not dissect a dog to find out what is inside of that particular dog, and the significance of knowledge as to what is inside of dogs as a class depends on the possibility of identifying the members of that class in some simpler way than by dissecting them. Just so, it is futile, even if possible, to know that a certain desire causes a certain act, unless we have some way of knowing when that desire is operative other than to wait and see if the associated conduct takes place. The utility of science depends on its ability to distinguish between edible mushrooms and poisonous toadstools *without* eating them and awaiting the result. The cogency of this reasoning seems to leave no possible way of escape. At most, it may from this point of view conceivably be a matter of purely scientific, abstract interest that certain feelings go with certain conduct; it is surely evident that we cannot logically regard the conscious state as causing or explaining the conduct in any significant sense.

And yet we do, habitually, and for all practical purposes universally, look at the matter in just this "unscientific" way. Professor Watson and his confrères may expostulate with us all they like about the error of our ways—we go right on thinking of conduct as in the main the effect of desire, and it seems impossible to talk sense about it from any other point of view. Where reason and common sense are found in such flagrant contradiction, the verdict of common sense cannot be brushed aside without examination from a point of view above the position of the conflicting claimants; philosophy must be called in to arbitrate the controversy If the two are simply left to fight it out, the result is a foregone conclusion; all the dynamic power is on the side of common sense and it will go on doing what it finds irresistibly convenient—"in erring reason's spite." The further course of the argument will sketch the philosophic aspects of the question, and will show that in this instance the position of common sense is better grounded in terms of the ultimate and inclusive facts of experience than is that of scientific logic. In the process it will also become increasingly clear that the sharp distinction between observation and inference or fact and "metaphysical entity," stressed so much by the scientific dogmatist, is based on a naïve dualism which is wholly untenable. The truth is not only that the fundamental concepts of science are as different as possible from the "facts" of the plain man's experience, but also that even these latter are far indeed from the character of immediate sense-data. On the other hand, much that the devotee of natural science methods dismisses contemptuously as "mere emotion" may turn out to have as strong a claim to a counterpart in ultimate reality as can be put forth by any human experience whatever. It will throw light on the problem to consider briefly the analogous case of physical science in its effort to explain the "behaviour" of material objects.

II

Mechanics is generally thought of and defined as the science which studies the action of "forces." Yet the physicist constantly recognizes that he really knows nothing about force, and that if such an entity exists, it is not open to human observation. The uneducated man is likely to say that we know forces by their effects; but to the worker, who has been taught to think critically about what he is doing, it is clear that we really know only the effects themselves. We assume, or infer, the forces, for no objective reason, but because it pleases a certain queer bias in our minds to do so. It seems to "simplify" our thinking. All that physics or any science can really do is to describe what is observed to happen; and the careful and candid scientist is especially conscientious in eschewing any knowledge of what "makes" things happen, or whether anything does. The "laws" of science are mere statements of dependable coexistences and sequences among events. The goal of scientific "explanation" is simply to formulate these laws in terms as general as possible.

And yet in practice, it is admittedly impossible to get along without the notion of force! Mechanics has always used the notion freely,

while explicitly recognizing that it stands for no real existence known
to us, but is simply a convenient way of saying that things happen
according to law; that is, that the same thing always happens under
the same conditions. It is easy, as it is common, to disparage "metaphysical" entities like the Kantian Ding-an-sich and Spencer's
Unknowable. But the simple, indispensable notion of force is of
exactly the same character; and the candid thinker has to recognize
on every plane of experience that our thinking cannot be carried on
without such conceptions. They have to be accepted as realities as
much as any of our thought-content.

For an illustration, consider the most familiar case of force, namely,
gravitation. We say the apple falls to the ground because the earth
"attracts" it, and that the planets are controlled in their orbits by a
similar attraction. Yet it is clear that all we can observe, or know, is
that the bodies do move along courses and at velocities which can be
described by unvarying formulae. What then is the use of the idea of
gravitation? and what was the great discovery of Sir Isaac Newton?
The discovery was simply this: that the *same* formula is applicable to
all these cases. Newton's inspired idea was that the moon is all the time
falling toward the earth, and that the law or formula of its fall might
be the same as that which Galileo had found for the fall of objects
toward the ground at the earth's surface. The path of the moon under
the influence of inertia alone would not bend around the earth, but
would bear away in a straight line at a tangent to the actual orbit.
Thus the moon is at every moment "falling" away from its natural
course along a line roughly at right angles to it and toward the centre
of the earth. Calculation at first showed that the formula for the rate
of its fall was *not* the same as that found by Galileo (with allowance
for the thinning out of the intensity of the attraction with the distance);
but when more accurate astronomical measurements were made, the
guess was confirmed and the great discovery established. Newton
further found that the same formula would explain the elliptical shape
of the orbits in the solar system and the other mathematical relations
which had been noticed by the great German astronomer Kepler and
named Kepler's Laws. Newton's law of gravitation "explained" all
these phenomena by reducing them to a common principle and showing
the essential similarity between the mysterious movements of the

heavenly bodies and the familiar movement of things falling to the ground. As to *why*—in any other sense—*any* of the movements happen as they do, or happen at all, it has absolutely nothing to say.

From a scientific point of view the problem of economic behaviour is parallel to that of the celestial motions. The "desire" which we say "makes" men buy goods is analogous to the "attractive force" which makes objects fall to the surface of the earth and planets fall toward the sun. What we really observe in the economic situation is the fact that a good is purchased, just as what we observe in the other case is the fact of movement. The notion of desire serves to simplify the statement, in accordance with our mental prejudices, in the one case, as the notion of attractive force does in the other.

In economic and other human behaviour, however, the situation is complicated by the fact that we *feel* desire in ourselves and associate the feeling in a definite way with our actions, while other human beings can and do talk to us about their desires in relation to their conduct. Thus we appear to have an additional reason for believing that feelings have something to do with response to situations. Candid reflection unquestionably shows that, in fact, the idea of force in connection with the motion of objects in space is a feeling of effort which we read into them on the basis of our own experience. But for our feeling of our own weight, we should not have the idea of gravitation as a force in any other sense than a law of motion; we should never form the idea of space and motion at all if we lacked the power of voluntary movement in ourselves. Just so, too, logically speaking, we merely "infer" consciousness in other human beings from the "movements" of speech, facial expression, and the like, by which, as we say, they "communicate" with us. There is no clear logical reason why we do not regard the behaviour of objects generally as communicative—at least until our attention is called to the problem and we have thought hard about it for a time—any more than there is a clear logical reason why we do so interpret certain behaviour facts in human beings. Careful examination of the matter will show that this fact of *communication between consciousnesses* is the fundamental fact of knowledge and the nearest we can ever get to an "ultimate" in human experience. For the present it is needful only to record two obvious facts, more or less contradictory between themselves. The first is that, logic notwithstanding, we do recognize some behaviour as communication from other minds and do not so interpret other behaviour. The second is that no human being really disbelieves in the reality of force as an element in the external existent world, any more than he doubts the fact of consciousness in his fellow human beings. The contradiction between logic and common sense is aggravated rather than resolved by appealing to the analogy between mechanics and human behaviour.

This brings us to the threshold of the fundamental difficulty in economic psychology. In mechanics there can be no discrepancy between forces and their effects, because we have no source of information regarding the forces except the effects themselves. We "infer" the force from the effect, and in the nature of the case the force is always exactly what is required to "explain" the effect observed. But in human behaviour we have two sources of information in regard to desire (which is the analogue of force), and the two sources *disagree* more or less. Each of us is immediately aware of innumerable desires which do not, to our knowledge, find expression in any outwardly observable behaviour, and has immediate knowledge to the effect that the acts most directly prompted by desire do not exactly express the desires as felt and often diverge grotesquely from them. No experience is much more common than surprise or disappointment at the things we find ourselves doing. Likewise our communication with other human beings acquaints us with the same situation in regard to them. The knowledge of human desires we get through social intercourse reveals them as divergent in a very considerable degree from the desires which are necessary to explain in the scientific sense the behaviour which we observe.

Here is the heart of the paradox. We have two sources of information in regard to the causes of human behaviour, but they do not tell the same story, and yet we cannot disbelieve in the validity of either of them. We "know" that there is a causal relation between desire and conduct, and we "know" also that the causes do not accurately or closely correspond with the effects. This is the eternal dilemma of hedonism.* In saying that conduct is always controlled by the

---

* The term hedonism is here used to designate the explanation of conduct by *desire*, not pleasure. This is the correct formulation of a scientific ethics, or rather, again, of

strongest desire, we may mean either of two things, either desire as the analogue of force in physics, or desire *as felt*. In the former interpretation the statement is a mere truism; in the latter it is merely false. The hedonist must take his choice between these two "horns."*

For the purposes of an economics which will be scientific in the sense of laboratory science, the course to be pursued is well marked out. It will be, like mechanics, behaviouristic in theory but not so in terminology or in fact. It will employ freely the concept of desire as an explanation of behaviour, as mechanics employs the concept of force as an explanation—because it is irresistibly convenient to do so. And it will carefully make it plain, as does its sister science in the corresponding case, that the concept is "really" but a short-hand manner of expressing the fact that there is uniformity of sequence or "law" in human responses to situations. And everyone whose common sense is not suppressed by logical sophistication will know that in the one case as in the other it is "really" no such thing! that desire and force are parts of the real universe with at least as good an epistemological pedigree as any observed behaviour datum. This aspect of the matter will be more fully considered later on. For the moment the significant point is that scientific economics must keep sharply separate and distinct the two conceptions of desire, namely, the desire which explains observed behaviour and is the analogue of force in mechanics, and desire as known by the individual human being in himself directly, and in other individuals through language and social intercourse.

Thus scientific economics is restricted in its data to behaviour

a scientific theory of conduct, for a scientific ethics is a contradiction in terms. The idea that quantity of satisfaction corresponds to quantity of desire is one which seems quite too unreasonable for any thinking person to entertain. When the hedonist speaks of quantity of pleasure, he means quantity of *anticipation* of pleasure, that is, he means quantity of desire. (In the writer's opinion even anticipation of pleasure is not really identical with desire, as a fact of experience.)

* Historically the doctrine described is known as psychological hedonism and is distinguished from ethical hedonism. The latter is the doctrine that pleasure *ought* to be the goal of every action. This position involves all the difficulties of outright idealism with numerous others peculiar to itself; but discussion in detail is outside the field of the present paper.

The question-begging character of hedonistic reasoning also appears in its implication that all human beings are of necessity absolutely selfish. We all like what we like and dislike what we dislike, undoubtedly. But the contention that there is no difference between selfishness and unselfishness is practically a conclusive *reductio ad absurdum* of the doctrine which leads to such a position as a conclusion.

facts. It cannot deal with feeling facts, except as a mode of expressing behaviour facts, for two reasons. In the first place, the facts of desire and satisfaction cannot be accurately observed and measured, and scientific economics must dogmatically and rigorously identify them quantitatively with their objective expressions in measurable goods or services taken up or given off, just as the physicist identifies forces quantitatively with their expressions in movement.* The second reason for the exclusion of feeling facts, as known through sources independent of their expression in action, is that this second kind of knowledge, in so far as it gives verifiable information, contradicts to a considerable extent that furnished by the first source. Therefore economics, in dealing with these data also, would be trying to ride two horses at the same time over courses too divergent for comfort. It is better to leave distinct sets of data to different sciences; and the facts of consciousness and their relation to the facts of behaviour form the province of the already well-established disciplines of psychology and ethics.†

III

So much for the methodology of economics as a science, in the straight and narrow sense of the term, as the generalized statement

* Economics, like physics, may have to add the concept of "potential" movement, a notion still more obviously a convenient instrumental fiction.

† When economic psychology is given the above interpretation, and the instrumental, non-ontological character of desires and motives as used in economics is sufficiently emphasized, there can be no objection to stating the principles of utility and disutility in the conventional form. Otherwise, they are true only in rough approximation to the facts of experience.

The classical economists also sensed the difficulty in the scientific treatment of human behaviour, and the famous "economic man" represents their method of meeting the problem. Some such device is imperatively required. This one is to be criticized only for its vagueness as to the place of consciousness in the interpretation of behaviour. The hedonistic man, the selfish man, and the "rational" man are closely related conceptions, all designed for the same function. All reduce, if consistently applied, to the thesis developed above, that the scientific man is one who does what he wants to do and whose wants are consistently related to the situation in which the man is placed. Followed out, this really means, as we have shown, simply the mechanistic view of man as an automaton, one whose conduct is in accordance with law in the scientific sense—that is, completely describable in terms of uniform relations to his situation. He may be conscious, but only in an "epi-phenomenal" sense, and consciousness is to be left out of the scientific description of behaviour. The French philosophers of the Enlightenment carried the idea to its necessary logical limit, as the English hedonists did not. It has been a historical trait of the English mind to place truth ahead of consistency!

of verifiable coexistences and sequences in its special field. But it is not the whole end of life to be scientific—a fact sometimes overlooked. Science itself is instrumental, relative to prediction and control, and controlling events is more than understanding them in the scientific sense. Economics especially is by no means as separable from its corresponding art as are the natural sciences—and separation of these latter is not as complete as it sometimes appears. We should like to insist on the imperative and equal importance of two things: that the economist must be more than a scientist, and that he must know when he is a scientist and when he is something else. Practically speaking, he is always more or less of a reformer as well, and one of his special difficulties is that of combining these two roles without confusing them to the detriment of both. In connection with the problem of control, the function of the scientist is to answer the question "how?" —how things can be done. But before anything is done some one has first of all to answer the question "what?"—what is to be done, what is desirable. This question makes it necessary to consider the relation between motive and conduct from an entirely different point of view. To the reformer's prior question, the technique of science has, in the nature of the case, no answer at all to make; and we must contend also that the reformer's task of carrying out "control" includes enormously more than following scientific directions.

Too much emphasis cannot be given to the first point. The *first* step toward control is to answer a question as to *what* shall be done. *This question can be answered only in terms of motives, in just the sense in which science cannot consider them.* Science, as has been shown, can recognize motives only as causes, as the uniform antecedents of acts. In this sense there can be no question about them, except to find out what they are, which is to say, to get back of them to some observable behaviour fact as an identification mark and eliminate them from the discussion. One may feel curiosity as to which of two motives or desires *is* the stronger, but that is just another way of saying that one is curious as to what will action *will* be performed; that the stronger desire dominates is a truism; and anything of the nature of "choice" between motives, that is, anything of the nature of decision or *real control*, is excluded from the moment the scientific point of view is adopted. The whole field of interests, as interests, lies outside the realm of science, in a realm which it must treat as non-existent. It can only view ends as forces, which is to say as fictitious links between antecedent and consequent in behaviour, manufactured to humour a mental caprice.

Now a human being cannot live in the realm of science alone; he cannot really treat or regard himself as an organism automatically expressing its nature in responses to situations. *To live, on the human plane, is to choose.* Possibly we can conceive of life reduced to the plane of scientific curiosity, but there would still be curiosity itself as an interest calling for explanation. One must still choose to be curious; and the attempt to explain this choice in terms of a given motive as cause raises the necessity of explaining that motive by a mechanical cause or by a choice. Thus one either eliminates control or embarks on an infinite regressus of explaining choices by motives and motives by choices without end—an absurdity. Curiosity is one motive which obviously cannot be reduced to uniformity of sequence. It is of its essence that the stimulus situation is *not* uniform in physical turns, nor the physical result of the action foreseeable. Intellectual problem-solving activities can be discussed only in terms of quality of conscious experience.* Even the attempt to explain mechanically all *other* interests except the scientific interest in explaining them reduces life to a basis of pure contemplation not to be approximated outside a Lamaist monastery, and one which is clearly the antithesis of the ideal of control actually preached in scientific literature. There is no escape from the "prior question" which, everywhere in life, is the question of the end; and the asking of this question involves recognizing the existence of ends as something entirely different from scientific causes of acts. The economist as a scientist may adhere to behaviourism; as a reformer and as a man, he must have a psychology and an ethics, else, as a brilliant English economist recently put it, he may possibly support life, but cannot be expected to enjoy it.

Closely connected with the recognition of ends which are facts but

---

* In fact, these statements also apply to all the so-called instincts in man. The uniformity in both stimulus and response is in the internal conscious tone, not in the physical situation or the physical act. It would be in the interest of clear thinking to restrict the term "instinct" to innately determined uniformities of response to stimulus in the objective, physical sense. This would practically exclude the term from discussion of human behaviour.

not causes is the second point, that the application of scientific technique is by no means all of the process of control; in the field of human activity there are also causes which are not "facts," in the scientific sense. The natural scientist, even if he does turn artist and engineer, confronts the disturbing, non-scientific factor of purpose in a relatively simple form; purposes *toward* his material are implied in the fact that he studies it; but at least his problem is not complicated by purposes *in* it. But this is just what the social scientist does meet at every turn. Every one of the human beings whom he seeks to understand and potentially to control, harbours his own purposes of understanding and control in regard to all the rest, including the scientist himself. Social control is a phrase used very freely these days; it is one of those terms much easier to use than to define. The notion of self-control in the individual is difficult enough. Who is the controller and who the controlled? who the potter and who the pot? Social self-control involves the same difficulties *plus* innumerable others. It is self-control *plus* mutual control, and both involved to the *n*th degree. The social scientist cannot, without being grotesque, place himself over against society in the relation of a gardener to his vegetables. Even in experimenting with the higher animals, it might well be necessary to go outside the realm of behaviour technique, to take some account of the creatures' feelings in order to achieve any large success in getting them to do one's will. Surely the man who would undertake to treat human society merely as material for scientific manipulation, to control it by finding the laws of its response to stimuli and devising stimuli to provoke the responses he might desire, would have to be classed as a monster or an imbecile. He might have abundant intelligence, of the scientific sort, but would be lacking in "sense." There is nothing forcibly to prevent an individual from arguing that conflicts of purpose within human beings are liquidated on the principle of composition and resolution of forces; but he cannot really apply the theory to himself, and the attempt to apply it without substantial modifications to others or to society will lead to undesirable consequences.

Let it be understood that we are not discussing metaphysics, but practical methodology. The scientific dogmatist is free to maintain that "really" it is altogether a matter of technique, of mechanical cause and effect. This cannot be disproved, and may be "true" in the metaphysical sense. All we are asserting is that, practically speaking, people have to be treated both as if they had feelings and as if the feelings and attitudes of the person who is attempting to influence them also made a difference. It may be "true" that the attitude of the controller operates only by influencing his own behaviour and that only this has any influence over others. But it is certain that the "others" do not think so, and just as certain that the technique of control cannot in fact be reduced to behaviour formulae with feelings left out, though some persons can of course act a part more effectively than others, as individuals also differ in gullibility. In practice, the "spirit" of an action counts, as well as the action itself, and is often vastly more important. The relation of mutuality must be recognized. The man who expects to influence others must work more through their feelings and his own than through explicit physical stimulus and response. The interpretation of human conduct in terms of "behaviour patterns," inherited or acquired, in relation to "situations," may be metaphysically correct, but it will not work.*

The matter may be summed up by saying that human control is in practice a phenomenon of art and morals to a greater extent than it is one of mechanical technique. Art and morals themselves *may* be *theoretically* reducible to technique, and do unquestionably consist in part of the application of established causal principles in the production of effects foreseen and willed. But anyone who asserts that they

* Speech in particular cannot without absurdity be treated as mere physical behaviour, and the behaviouristic term "language habit" does grave injustice to the richness and variety of life. The notion of habit is of possible applicability to the utterance of words used in a purely literal sense—if any language outside of mathematical symbols ever is strictly literal, an assertion open to doubt. It will not fit at all the other type of language, which is more important and more common in cultural intercourse, the figurative, suggestive use. Language as an artistic medium must not be confused either with the mere tool of factual communication or with mechanical incitement to action. Actual speech almost always contains a considerable admixture of the first element. No two people talk identically the same language. The great majority of sentences spoken or written express and convey to the hearer or reader ideas to some extent original and unique. How we ever learn to communicate thought and feeling seems profoundly mysterious. Induction by association appears wholly inadequate to explain the result, certainly in a creative literary genius and his readers. The writer is impelled to believe to some extent in an intuitive "faculty" of communication and interpretation. Yet our communication is admittedly very imperfect. Two critics get very different impressions from a book or poem; and in social science and philosophy, discussions of fact have a way of transforming themselves into arguments about what somebody really said. Yet communication of new ideas and emotions is a fact, and one which resists mechanistic explanation.

involve nothing more than that, or that mechanical process is their essential nature, simply places himself outside the discussion of the things of art and morals. Art, after all, is "expression"—of ideas and emotions; and the potency in human relations of sympathy, anger, personal force, and feeling attitudes generally, is not to be gainsaid. At this point the economist and sociologist would do well to take lessons from the experience of the older sciences of human control, the law and medicine. The inadequacy of mere rules and the necessity for a humanized administration of law have surely been demonstrated to the satisfaction of the most critical, as has also the impossibility of limiting attention to the behaviour facts without regard to the "intent" of the law and the "intention" of the accused of crime or of the parties to a contract. Even in medicine, which is supposed to be a matter of purely physical cause and effect, we observe a remarkable shift in emphasis from chemical to moral factors. In the personal relations side of business administration, the vogue of "scientific management" was short-lived, and has long since given place to emphasis on the "human element."

IV

The foregoing is all on the plane of practical expediency and is chiefly negative in import. It has aimed to show what the economist can *not* do, namely, that he cannot restrict himself to the canons and methods of objective science, if he wishes to have a part in improving social life.* The interpretation and control of human events call for *more* than that. The discussion would be incomplete without some attempt at a suggestion as to what the "more" is to be; what can be said of aesthetics and ethics, beyond the fact that they are "not" natural sciences altogether? and what is the relation of economics to all three? The practical discussion in the previous sections of the paper leads to reflections which seem to the writer to throw some

* It would, of course, be possible to quibble over the meanings of both the terms "objective" and "science." They are used here in the sense in which natural scientists use them, to refer to verifiable observation through the senses. The writer agrees with the behaviourists in holding that verbal reports of introspection used in the "science" of psychology are not observation in the same sense. The further course of the discussion will, it is hoped, make the matter clearer.

light on the deeper phases of the value problem. The general drift of these can be indicated in a few paragraphs.

The corner-stone of the scientific attitude is scepticism; it must insist on nothing so much as the repudiation of all "emotion" as a source of knowledge; to science, faith, and will-to-believe are synonyms for sin. Thus in human relations the scientific attitude is well summed up in the aphorism quoted by Schopenhauer that whoever forgives and forgets throws away dearly bought experience. Morality, as the term is used, is therefore as antithetical to science as faith itself. The effect of this sceptical attitude is sharply to accentuate the naïve dualism of the plain man, the distinction between the real and the imaginary, the objective and the subjective, or, as Walter Lippmann most naïvely puts it, between the world outside and the pictures in our minds. No criticism can be made of this position, in its place— that is, *adopted for the purposes of science.* Certainly nothing is more needed in the thinking of the public to-day than the cultivation of regard for facts—in questions of fact; the objective attitude—in situations where the objective attitude is the thing that is required!

Science *is* to be criticized, however, for making the sceptical attitude a universal and only virtue, and this not so much because this *ought not* to be done as because it *cannot* be. It is merely ignoring fact not to recognize that the sceptical attitude itself is an emotion, and likewise the intellectual satisfaction that comes from scientific comprehension and explanation. The sceptical attitude is assumed for a purpose and is justified because it serves a purpose: it is a means and not an end, and the ends which it serves must be at least as real as the data of sceptical science. Scepticism or detachment and disinterestedness as an absolute principle leads to the position ascribed to the members of the ancient school of Pyrrho, that they would not admit that they denied, and doubted whether they doubted. A will-to-believe is, after all, the only alternative to a dogmatic negation of thought and of life.

In science and in philosophy there is great danger that the cultivation of the sceptical attitude may be over-done. It is in a way of becoming a new dogmatism, as false and pernicious as the medieval dogmatism of faith, which made belief as such a virtue, meritorious in proportion as the doctrine believed was absurd and incredible. In economics and sociology, certainly, the great desideratum of the present day is less an increased development of the scientific spirit than it is a spirit of critical discrimination between questions of fact and questions of value and purpose, between scientific problems in the proper sense and problems of taste and judgment, with the use of an appropriate and significantly different method of attack on the two sets of problems, when they have been separated. Scientific dogmatism naturally denies the existence of everything which will not pass its tests as a fact. Hence it is reduced to the dilemma of denying conscious purpose altogether or attempting to treat purpose on the level of fact, and it is impossible to do either, as we have already demonstrated. In consequence, we have as the prime desideratum in social science, as just suggested, a penetrating and rigorous study of ends, the recognition of the kind of things they are and the development and application of an effective methodology for studying them. What is required is nothing less than the basing of social science upon a sound philosophy of knowledge and reality.

Now it is a philosophical commonplace that the sharp dualism of fact and wish disintegrates at the first flash of critical scrutiny. This relation is closely connected with the relation between observation and inference; and between these two things science is equally insistent upon drawing a sharp distinction. What is "really" perceived, and what is "only" inferred or seen because it is wished? The least examination shows that no clear separation can be made. In discussing the problem of economic demand it was pointed out that science regards our knowledge of the desires of any person except ourselves as an inference from behaviour of some sort—speech, gesture, facial expression, and the like. Consciousness is not an observed fact, but, like force in mechanics, a "convenient" assumption (convenience being obviously a purposive, emotional category), and cannot be admitted as a scientific datum. But reflection makes it clear not only as already suggested, that we "infer" force, and the consciousness of other persons, from our own consciousness, but that we cannot perceive the objects themselves as real without making this inference to a certain extent, without reading our own experience into them. This has been familiar matter since the days of Hume, who also— hard-headed Scotsman and thoroughgoing sceptic that he was—

agreed with the theologian Berkeley that the primary as well as the secondary qualities of objects all resolve themselves into mental states of the experiencing subject. Hume added only that the subject himself also disappears in the same mental states. Other "subjects" of course share the same fate.

No logical answer has ever been given to the reasoning of Hume, and it seems clear that his conclusion must be accepted as logically final. Approaching the matter sceptically and reasoning logically, there is no such thing as the perception of reality, and all that exists is the flow of conscious experience of which "I" am immediately aware. This is solipsism, but with "I" understood to be not a self in any real sense, but just a stream of consciousness. Now of course modern psychology recognizes, and the candid student must see, that the stream of consciousness is in fact even less real than the objects. States of consciousness, sensations, and their like are artificial constructions, the result of the scientific psychological analysis of experience, bearing little relation to the facts of life as directly known. In fact, philosophy, at last accounts, was still seeking for the "immediate data of experience," and in the writer's opinion it will still be seeking for them as long as the problems of thought have any challenge for the human mind.

Such being the result of the subjective, or psychological approach, it is next to be noted how similar have been the results of the objective, scientific study of reality, based on the naïve realism of the plain man, but otherwise submitted to the tests of the sceptical mind. The attempt of science to find what is real in human behaviour reduces it first to mechanical movements and physiological processes, in themselves sufficiently different from the "immediate" experience or observation of life. The rest is inference and emotion. But physiology just as inexorably dissolves into chemistry, and chemistry into physics, and all that physics leaves of reality is electric charges moving in fields of force—things far more unreal than the characters in the most fanciful work of fiction. Moreover, the experts in science and scientific method (*vide* Mach, Pearson, Russell) are frankly sceptical of the reality of any of it, and talk in terms of concepts useful for the purposes of analysis, and of the simplification of our thought processes.

The answer at the end of every line of inquiry is instrumentalism.

Reality is not what is logical, but what it suits our *purposes* to treat as real. This was the upshot of the thought of Kant, the next great name in the history of philosophy after Hume; for, as Professor Fite has shown,* it was the great German thinker who made the transition from scepticism to pragmatism.† The logical study of "data," under which they always evaporate, has given place to the critical study of thought from a functional, that is purposive, point of view. Reality is the sum of the factors which condition purposive activity, including purposive thought, which must not be conceived of as always standing in an incidental relation to behaviour.‡ The freeing of thought from emotion and metaphysical entities would mean its annihilation. It is impossible to perceive or imagine the real world without recognizing the equally real character both of purposes and of intellectual concepts. Thought is impossible without these non-factual data.

The real "Copernican Revolution" in thought was just this shift in viewpoint, the recognition of purpose as more fundamental than fact, and of observation as relative to use, or in any case relative to interest of some sort, and in some sense and some degree creative. For the essential character of purpose is its vital, dynamic quality; it is evolutionary; its nature is to grow cumulatively. When thought gives up the quest of reality in any other sense than experience organized in relation to some purpose—which may be that of attaining more knowledge as well as any other use—the two great departments of thought come to be history and criticism. The problem of ontology is merged, on the one hand, in the problem of genetics and on the other, in the problems of ideals and ways and means. As shown above, to make the objects of scientific observation the only reality is merely to say dogmatically that scientific curiosity, thus narrowly defined arbitrarily, shall be the only legitimate interest in life. When the fact is faced that we have other interests, just as real, it is clear at once that scientific reality is subordinate to a wide field of purpose.

* *Philosophical Review*, 1914, p. 410.

† This is true in spite of all the pedantry of Kant himself and of the absolutistic interpretations of his doctrine by his German followers down to Schopenhauer. Schopenhauer's voluntarian was eclipsed, and, for western taste, spoiled, by his pessimism.

‡ This is the great weakness of the popular American brand of pragmatism. There is no reason for looking to any field of action or achievement to justify action or achievement in any other field; each one may and certainly does define its own values and provide its own ends, though in a relation amounting to unity with all the others.

Moreover, by scientific logic itself, purposes are real in so far as men agree in recognizing them as such, for that is what the scientific test of reality reduces to.

In the study of any phase of the problem the outstanding fact is the social nature alike of thought and achievement and of purpose itself. All are aspects of *social* evolution. The essence of association is communication. There can be no question that we build up our knowledge of an external world through the interchange of experience with our fellow beings. The individual learns from others to perceive and observe, to interpret the "buzzing booming confusion" which experience in the raw must be (though no one who can talk about experience has any immediate unsophisticated knowledge of what it is) into a world of objects, movements, relations, and forces. Thus observation itself, understood in anything approaching its scientific meaning, is a power socially developed and trained in the individual, and produced in the course of history by the accumulation of communicated and compared experiences. Only in this way do we learn even to see with anything like accuracy. And always we see largely what we expect to see, what fits into our organized knowledge of the world. And the structure of our thinking is notoriously that of our language, our medium of communication.

So far from our knowledge of the consciousness of other persons being an "inference" from a "perception" of their behaviour, it turns out that the very capacity to perceive is developed through and dependent upon intercommunication between minds as conscious centres. Knowledge of that which we say we infer is logically prior to knowledge of that which we say we observe, since it is a condition of observation itself. And always, the test for distinguishing "real" observation from imaginary is the possibility of verification, which means comparison with the communicated observations of other persons. Observation in the scientific sense is therefore restricted to the limits of possible communication; and nothing very far from the common experience of the race, accumulated and organized into concepts and symbolized by speech forms, could be observed even if it existed.* There is no such thing as either immediate or positive

* The common identification of "observed fact" with "sense data" is manifestly a confusion. The perception of an object rests upon ages of mental sophistication. More-

knowledge, it is all a matter of the relative cogency of reasons, or usefulness of believing one thing as compared with another. Scientific truth is a critical rather than a logical category.

V

Further development of the argument in its philosophical bearings lies outside the purpose of this paper. These are worked out along what the writer considers the correct lines in the writings of Bergson and James.* The implications for economics may be pointed out under two headings, though the issues are closely related. The first is the interpretation of wants as springs of action and agencies of control, or economics in its more scientific aspect. The second is the somewhat larger question of the fundamentals of social policy and economic organization.

Under the first head the essential point is that economics is a branch of aesthetics and ethics to a larger extent than of mechanics. This of course implies that aesthetics and ethics themselves are not to be reduced to economics, and by way of economics to behaviour mechanics. The wants with which the economist is concerned in explaining the consumption and production of wealth are sharply distinguished both from desires as causes and from desires as effective stimuli to action. They have to be thought of and treated as much more than forces, conscious or unconscious, which dissolve into mere phenomenal uniformity of coexistence and sequence. On the one hand, desires have a primary, assertive, creative, and experimental character; they are choices. On the other, they have a cognitive quality. The person choosing and acting has a feeling of laying hold on an external verity, closely akin to the peculiar "tang" of actual perception of objects as contrasted with dreaming or imagining—the quality which Hume called vividness. The motive of conduct is more or less a

over, as we have previously remarked, no observation in the true sense is quite compulsory and unavoidable; no objectification will stand up under hard sceptical scrutiny; every perception of reality is more or less a voluntary act. Thought is saturated with purpose and concepts, emotion and metaphysical entities.

* Dewey's position seems ambiguous to me; in so far as it is naturalistic and intellectualistic, I am out of sympathy with it, as I am also with any "idealism" of an absolutistic or monistic tendency.

judgment of real worth as well as a conscious impulse to act; and this conscious impulse again is more than the bare fact that action follows stimulation in some determinate way. Scientific logic easily shows the feeling of objectivity in connection with value to be illusion and "mere emotion"; but the same process even more easily and surely makes illusion of our ordinary perceptions of external reality. So, the reflection is on scientific logic; for we cannot be absolute sceptics and live. Hence we come perforce around the circle. Observation cannot be freed from emotion; and values have to be conceded a degree of objectivity, and value of some sort a reality even prior to that of the data of sense-observation, which, for its part, always contains an emotional element.

It follows, as has been already suggested, that the method of social prediction and control is as closely akin to the method of art and of aesthetic criticism as to the method of laboratory science. Economics has, of course, problems of both sorts, but the former are the more extensive and fundamental. The motives underlying economic behaviour have no discoverable general and uniform relation to organic needs, even if these could be defined in purely objective terms, which cannot in fact be done. The identification of motive and need, or the reduction of actual human wants to biological terms, rests on assertion contrary to evident fact. Wants are culture products, to be judged by culture canons and understood and controlled through culture categories. Even our food and clothing, in all their concrete content, and by far the larger part of their money cost, represent social and aesthetic and not biological values. To a large extent, of course, the phenomena of culture are reducible to law in their own sphere, whether the behaviour in question is conscious or unconscious. So also artistic production is in part the application of objective technique in the production of effects conceived and defined in advance. The part in either case that is based on deliberate creative choice can never be distinguished and measured. But it is the crucial part. One main objective in life is to get routine and repetitive activities down to the level of unconscious habit, or to relegate them to machines or slaves of some sort, and set one's own time and energies free for activities which involve originality, initiative, exploration, creation. It is always possible to assert that there is a mechanical law covering every detail of conduct if we could discover it,* but the assertion is mere dogma, and practical procedure calls for the opposite assumption.

Moreover, motives resist reduction to any common measure or principle in any terms simpler in their own kind than value itself. That motives in their vast variety are in some sense a manifestation of a "will to live," that all values may be evaluated in terms of "quantity of life," has the appearance of an approach to scientific treatment, and is a common assertion of the scientific dogmatist. The notion is familiar in the classical literature of both orthodox and socialistic economic theory, and it is interesting to find thinkers so far apart as Herbert Spencer, John Ruskin, and Dr. Thorstein Veblen speaking essentially the same language at this point. Passing over again the evident fact that a "will" to live is more than the *fact* of living, or else is a mischievous use of words, we find it hard to tell what these writers mean by quantity of life, and perhaps harder to tell what they think they mean by its value. If number of individuals is the measure of life, as Professor Carver has courageously maintained, it would appear that insects or bacteria represent the "highest," the most successful, forms. The only other objective measure that suggests itself is the quantity of energy involved in the metabolic process and this standard would hardly yield a ranking in value which would meet with general acceptance. The word "adaptation" is freely used as if it represented something more objective and scientific than moral goodness as a conception of success in life; but the notion will not stand examination. It is, in fact, a good example of the substitution of sound for sense; it either looks back to the maintenance and increase of life and encounters the difficulties already suggested, or else looks forward to some aesthetic or moral standard.

Marx, and Veblen following him, seem to have in mind some metaphysical "principle" of life, a concept belonging to the intuitive

* That is, it is possible to assert, and impossible to disprove either of these two propositions: (1) That conscious motives are mechanical forces merely, and axiomatically account exactly for conduct, or (2) the more rigorously positivistic view that motives, like all forces, are fictitious, and the sequence of physical changes the only reality. In practice, our contention is that it must be assumed *both* that force is more than phenomenal uniformity of sequence, *and* that human motives are more than mechanical forces. If the practical necessities of thinking and acting are regarded as indicating the nature of reality—and they are the only indicators we finally have—this amounts to a demonstration of some sort of philosophic idealism.

thought realms above such requirements as definition or measurement —and in the writer's opinion not devoid of significance if its "un-scientific" character is recognized instead of asserting the contrary. Ruskin, even more clearly, really meant simply value, conceived in aesthetic and moral terms. His famous dictum, "There is no wealth, but life," therefore means merely that there is no value but value. This, too, in the connection and for the purpose of Ruskin's preaching, is anything but nonsense. It is exactly what our overscientifically minded students of social problems still need to be told, with all possible emphasis.

Life, *as life*, is no more a value than it is a quantity in the scientific sense. There is hardly a need for arguing about the value of mere physiological process, and hardly more need to point out that con-sciousness, as such, is not a value either. Everything depends on what kind of consciousness it is, its quality. No doubt life has to be poor and hard if it is not to be regarded as "better than none"; but to a negligible extent does the question of living or not living come up in practice. Thought and effort under all ordinary conditions take life for granted and are directed toward securing one kind of life rather than some other kind. And in the ultimate test, anaesthesia and euthanasia are chosen in preference to a conscious existence which is too far from the expectations and standards of the individual. More-over, in the ordinary day's work, men constantly risk life, or know-ingly shorten it, and in the last resort throw away a life by no means intolerable, for the chance of a "better" life, for themselves or for others. That human beings are by nature idealists and sentimentalists seems to be as incorrigibly and obstreperously a "fact," for practical purposes, as any verifiable scientific observation.

Space does not admit nor does the purpose of this paper require elaboration of philosophical implications beyond the main contention that the fruitful study of economic and social problems demands recognition of *values* as data of a different character from factual observations in a uniform behaviour sequence. Science itself is purpos-ive, instrumental; and when it is intelligent and candid, it makes no pretences in regard to throwing light on the nature of ultimate reality. It treats of the data of experience from the standpoint of classification and analysis, because that is the most fruitful method for prediction and control in a large part of the field. It is not to be assumed without demonstration that the method is completely and universally applicable, even in a narrowly practical sense; and there is an inherent contradiction involved in applying it to purposive behaviour as such. Science itself loses its meaning when the effort is made to lift the categorical distinction between purpose and the means of its fulfilment. Furthermore, is there anything more absurd intrinsically than the idea that thought and feeling minister to, and are justified by, their promotion of the physico-chemical process of metabolism? Measured by the ultimate test employed by science itself, the test of intelligent communicability, the higher values seem to have a claim to real existence as high as that of the data of observation, which are by no means immediately known, but are constructed by elaborate purposive inference and organization of "immediate sense-data," whose own existence is in fact hypothetical. Candid introspection shows that ends, purposes, cannot be described in the static type of categories used by science. Only in part do they fall into classes, or remain identical with themselves from moment to moment. Yet we can discuss them in their uniqueness and describe them in their growth and change. Our minds do have an apparatus of thought and communication different from that of scientific logic, and language is an instrument of this higher process as well as of the lower and more exact.

Economists have erred egregiously in assuming that behaviour can be dealt with in objective, scientific terms alone, or that purpose, being recognized as in some sense real, can be handled with the same type of intellectual apparatus. The purposes of men are inherently dynamic and changing; want-satisfying activity is not in the main directed toward gratifying existing desires sharply defined as data in the conduct problem; it is largely explorative in character; a repetitive experience is looked upon more or less as a necessary evil and its motive as a goad rather than an end. The problem of human life is less that of getting preconceived results than of finding out the results of actions and acquiring "better" wants. We do things to prove that we can, and to find out whether we like to; the problem is largely to understand the problem itself, and as with smaller problems, understanding it largely carries the actual solution with it as a matter of course. The consumer and producer of wealth commonly does not realize it, but it is true that much of his activity is in response to the poetic injunction, "Know thyself." Curiosity is very largely synonymous with the supposedly broader term, "interest." Knowledge of self cannot be separated from knowledge of the world, nor either knowledge from that which is known. As we know more, both the self and the world are enlarged, and this growth is life.

VI

The point of view developed above has direct significance also for the central practical problem of economic theory, which is that of evaluating competitive individualism as a system of social organization, in comparison with a system based upon conscious, intelligent cooperation and on moral motives in place of the mechanical interaction of self-seeking activities. The commonly recognized function of economic organization is to utilize the limited resources at the command of the social group in bringing about the largest possible satisfaction of the wants of its members. But the form of organization also goes far to determine what is to be wanted, and to mould the attitudes of persons toward their work and toward each other. The main defence of the competitive system against an increasing volume of criticism has rested upon its efficiency, and the candid student must probably concede its superiority on that score. True, that efficiency itself is disappointingly low. As measured by the most objective standards attainable, the results can hardly be more than a third of those theoretically possible with existing material resources and technical knowledge, and are probably well below that figure. But in recent years thoughtful opinion has been tending to place less emphasis on efficiency in achieving objectives taken for granted, and to give increasing recognition and weight to this other question of the type of objectives generated and the general philosophy of life inculcated in people.

The World War and its aftermath have greatly accentuated this shift in emphasis and change in standards of judgment. Critical attention has been focused, not merely on the glaring discrepancy between the actual principles of social action and the ethical-religious pretensions of Western civilization, but also on the practical consequences which follow from the Machiavellian-Mandevillian standards which make intelligent selfishness equivalent to virtue, and power and cunning the main components of our human ideal. The values which animate our economic activity are being made explicit and subjected to critical scrutiny as has not been done before since the industrial era began. People in high places are coming to feel that much of our toil and trouble serves no end but to feed the increasing fires of competitive display and greed of power, and are asking whether life has to be a relentless struggle for distinction and domination, or whether a bit more of friendliness might not be worth some sacrifice, if necessary, of the touted physical ease and comfort which few get and fewer have time to enjoy. There is more willingness to envisage a world presenting less "progress" toward goals which seem dubious, and a lower rate of consumption of "goods and services" whose connection with goodness and serviceability is not always clear.

This does *not* mean, as some have too hastily inferred, that the economic system is to be criticized because it manufactures our wants, or because it charges as much for making them as for gratifying them, or even more. *That would be true in any social system, and desirable.* The development of wants is really much more important than their satisfaction; there is no poverty so deplorable as poverty of interests. There is no issue as between "natural" wants and "artificial"; all human wants are more artificial than natural, and the expression natural wants, if it has any meaning, can refer only to those of beasts. By the same token, human wants are more "sentimental" than "real." The issue is between artificial sentimental wants which are good and artificial sentimental wants which are bad. This is especially true as we come to realize that standards of living and of work are largely but reflected desires for one type or another of human relationship, that we want things, mainly to be like others or to be different from them, to emulate or dominate, be agreeable or arouse envy, and so on. It may be ever so demonstrable that competition is really but a method of cooperation, and even a very "good" method as far as effectiveness and low organization cost go; and it may yet be far more important that competition teaches men to *think* of each other as competitors and not as co-workers, and to *see* their relation to their work as that of the slave to his treadmill. The incentives to work may have value significance as well as the results. It is even beginning to be asked whether it is really inevitable, and in that sense right, that in a vast social cooperation the "superior" individuals (meaning the more powerful) must be paid for their superiority, and for the interesting creative and directive work which must admittedly fall to the superior, by being given as a matter of course vastly more than an equal share of the inadequate product of the joint enterprise. Even the mechanical efficacy of "material" rewards in calling out the most and best that men have to give is being questioned, as it is more clearly perceived that the actual incentive is not really material in the main, but social and sentimental and far removed from the love of comfort and ease.

These considerations are mentioned to indicate the basis on which the competitive system is to be judged, not to pass judgment upon it. "There is much to be said on both sides." At most, argument can only point out the direction of progress, not draw the specifications for revolutionary transformation. And aside from the fact that there are limits, regrettably narrow, to the possible sacrifice of efficiency, and assuming that a social order not based fundamentally on self-interest can be made to function, it must be observed in addition that the moral issues are not all one-sided. Commercialism has certainly been a powerful agency in the development of tolerance. The strength and self-reliance which it emphasizes must always have a prominent place in the ideal character. Moreover, it is uncertain how far the unfortunate attitudes of people toward each other and toward their work are really due to any particular system of organization, and how far they are incidental to large-scale cooperation as such, irrespective of the type of mechanism which controls the distribution of burdens and benefits. The aim of the later sections of the present paper has been merely to develop a point of view from which intelligent judgment of the question is possible. That point of view may be summed up in the paraphrase already proposed of Ruskin's famous dictum: "There is no Value but Value." The necessity for a thoroughgoing acceptance of this point of view has been established by an examination of the perplexities of economic methodology.

THE LIMITATIONS OF SCIENTIFIC METHOD IN ECONOMICS*

I. The Meaning of Science

SINCE economics deals with human beings, the problem of its scientific treatment involves fundamental problems of the relations between man and his world. From a rational or scientific point of view, all practically real problems are problems in economics. The problem of life is to utilize resources "economically," to make them go as far as possible in the production of desired results. The general theory of economics is therefore simply the rationale of life.—In so far as it has any rationale! The first question in regard to scientific economics is this question of how far life is rational, how far its problems reduce to the form of using given means to achieve given ends. Now this, we shall contend, is not very far; the scientific view of life is a limited and partial view; life is at bottom an exploration in the field of values, an attempt to discover values, rather than on the basis of knowledge of them to produce and enjoy them to the greatest possible extent. We strive to "know ourselves," to find out our real wants, more than to get what we want. This fact sets a first and most sweeping limitation to the conception of economics as a science.

Even this statement of the scientific view of life as the conscious utilization of resources for given ends involves stretching the term scientific as compared with its most exact signification. It involves conceding the reality and potency of conscious thinking and planning, which in the narrowest meaning of science are illusory. From a *rigorously* scientific viewpoint, life is a mere matter of mechanics; what human beings think of as practical problems of conduct are subjective illusions; thinking and planning and all subjectivity are illusions; human actions are a detail in a cosmic panorama of the transformation of motion. But since it is impossible to discuss value

* Reprinted from *The Trend of Economics*, edited by Rexford G. Tugwell, by permission of F. S. Crofts and Company, Publishers.

in purely objective terms, we must simply assume the reality of the conscious data and leave it to philosophy to reconcile the contradiction, or to decide that it cannot be reconciled. We have to accept the common-sense notion of value or worth as our starting-point.

Two sorts of experience are recognized as having worth, or as capable of having it, an active and a passive; one is creation or control, and the other appreciation. These are not strictly separate experiences, but rather "aspects" of experience, yet they are practically separable to a large degree. The worth of active creation or control is a kind of appreciation; usually, the worth of the experience of activity depends more or less upon a feeling of worth toward or appreciation of some "result" brought about. But though the two things are usually more or less associated and overlapping, we are all familiar with extreme cases in which on the one hand the feeling of worth is nearly or quite purely passive and on the other the worth of an activity is nearly or quite independent of the character of the result. The literature of value, like that of science, shows a bias for monism, so there is a tendency to reduce all value to "contemplation" or to the "joy of being a cause," according to the temperamental predilections of the particular writer, but a candid observer must accept both, and all sorts of mixtures of the two.

Each of these fundamental categories also exhibits two sub-types. In the case of appreciation we distinguish an effective or emotional or aesthetic, and a cognitive or intellectual pleasure. The mixtures and interrelations of these are again complex, but again we do separate, more or less, a worth which is pure appreciation from a worth which is a matter of "understanding." We do care to understand things which we feel to be repulsive, and we do care for things which we feel no impulse to try to understand. Sometimes the one sort of worth contributes to the other, and sometimes they appear to conflict. The aesthetic experience of the cultivated person is in part a matter of understanding how a painting, say, or a piece of music or a poem produces its effect, but also the aesthetic experience may be endangered by too much analysis. In general, it appears that beauty must involve a certain amount of illusion; the "machinery" must not be too manifest, or the interest in it too strong, or the effect is lost.

In the field of activity, also, there is a separation, less easy to make clearly, between that which is *spontaneous*, going to its end directly and immediately, and that which involves a conscious, calculated marshalling of means. The distinction holds for both the activity whose worth is inherent and that whose worth lies rather in the result which it produces. In creation and control as in appreciation, there is more or less conflict between understanding and enjoying. We strive to understand the how and why of our actions, to analyse the technique; and yet when this process is carried too far, and it becomes altogether a matter of routine manipulation of means to produce an effect preconceived and foreseen, there is a loss of interest in the action. It might be interesting, if space allowed, to go into the problem of classifying our value experiences on the basis of the various combinations of these types, but our purpose is merely to sketch certain aspects of the meaning of science in connection with the field of values.

The immediate purpose of science is to enable us to *understand*, which again covers the understanding both of beauty and of the technique of action. But our modern, sophisticated way of thinking tends more and more to subordinate the desire for understanding as such to a desire for control. It can hardly be doubted that the spirit of science itself makes for this interpretation. A scientific age tends to relegate understanding for its own sake to the realm of sentiment and romance, an order of value regarded rather contemptuously in comparison with considerations of practice and power. The value of science is found in the *results* which it makes it possible to achieve, and science itself takes its place as a tool, tending toward the level of necessary evils. The love of science is brought by the scientific spirit into the position of a sentiment to be viewed apologetically. In the scientific, evolutionary, view of the world, too, the scientific interest is "explained" as a Spencerian transfer of attention from the real end to the means, which becomes erected into a pseudo-end.

Some rather obvious restrictions in outlook which arise from giving too predominant a place to science may be mentioned at this point. A scientific atmosphere obscures if it does not eclipse a considerable part of the field of values. It centres attention on the results of activity, weakening or destroying the value of the process. In addition, it emphasizes the quantitative aspect of the result which can be treated scientifically as against the qualitative or aesthetic aspect which cannot. For these reasons activity comes to be concentrated along lines where results can be predicted and brought about "efficiently," that is, in the largest possible quantity with relation to a given stock of resources or productive power. This means concentration in lines of essentially repetitious work as contrasted with the spontaneous and creative. For science, manifestly, cannot direct creation in any true sense; it can only copy, or at best rearrange old elements in new combinations. True creation, which is the field of art, involves the invention of new ends as well as new means for reaching them. Science is always striving to "understand" art and produce its effects by the calculated application of rules; but to the extent that it succeeds in its endeavour the result is no longer art in the true sense. The evil is multiplied by the fact that because science can never explain why this is so, it tends to deny the fact. Real creation involves a very different technique; or, it is better to say, it is not a matter of technique at all, but a kind of psychic sympathy or entering of the mind of the artist into his medium and a handling of it from the inside, whereas science works externally. Yet the contradiction already referred to is conspicuous here. The artist needs a great deal of scientific knowledge and technique; but when his work becomes reduced to these terms it ceases to be art and becomes merely copy-work.

We should note, however, that the satisfaction of the understanding or the successful production of a calculated effect *when it first happens* in any particular problem is very closely akin to the experience of creative activity. The expansive feeling of elation or mastery which comes with *discovery*, or sometimes even with learning from another person, is much like that of true invention.

The scientific interpretation of science is that "knowledge is power"; it is not a value in itself, but subordinate to activity, whose value, in turn, is in its results; it is "instrumental." We must accept this conclusion as true by definition; that is what is meant by scientific knowledge, which is our point here. Whether this pragmatic epistemology carries with it a pragmatic metaphysics, an interpretation of reality in terms of end and means, depends perhaps on whether one identifies scientific knowledge with knowledge in general. It is one of the philosophic assumptions of this essay that this *cannot* be done, that neither man nor his world can be understood in terms of categories derived from the exigencies of adapting means to given ends.

But to proceed with the definition of science: From the standpoint of knowledge, the problem of control is a problem of *prediction*. Conduct, which is the adaptation of means to ends, is necessarily forward-looking. To behave intelligently means to act in the light of valid knowledge as to what would happen in the given situation in the absence of interference from myself, and of the changes in this course of events which will result from any contemplated action of mine. In case I cannot bring about any change in the natural progress of events, or at least not any desirable change, I must still be able to foresee the progress itself, in order to react intelligently toward it. From the standpoint of a strict view of conscious behaviour, we are not interested in the world as it is, except as a basis of predicting what it will be in the immediate or remote future to which conscious plans of action relate.

Science, then, is merely the *technique of prediction*. It is the mental mechanism or process by means of which we act intelligently. From the scientific standpoint (or this quasi-scientific view which accepts motives as real causes) to "live" intelligently and to "act" intelligently are interchangeable expressions. And to act "intelligently" (shifting the emphasis) means to act in such a way as to bring about the result foreseen and intended; it goes without saying that any result brought about by deliberate action is a desired result. It is important to keep in mind that not all control is scientific in the sense of involving conscious, deliberate adaptation of means to the production of desired ends. Control begins in the control of our own bodies, since it is only upon them that mind or purpose can act directly. It is questionable how far this control of our muscular systems is ever "scientific" at any stage, and it is certain that it tends strongly to become unconscious and automatic, reverting to our second type of control experience noted above. Such fundamental activities as speech, for example, are probably learned in the first place by a process of trial-and-error or by accident involving little conscious adaptation. A good part of it is no doubt "instinctive," such as the modulation of the voice to convey emotion. Any skilled technique when well learned, drops largely below the threshold. A trained pianist or typist thinks as little about the keys he strikes as does any normal person about the position of his vocal organs in articulation, and the skilled mechanic uses his tools in much the same automatic way; they have in effect become a part of his body. Perhaps the military strategist too may come to manipulate his army with little more thought than the skilled driver of a motor car gives to his pedals and controls.

It is clear, however, that for all this tendency of any instrumental adjustment to become unconscious, there is no such tendency in life as a whole. Instead of progressing toward the condition of unconscious automata, we are called upon constantly for more thinking; the mental strain involved in conscious as compared with unconscious activity increases continuously, and the mysterious liability to error which is characteristic of conscious responses in contrast with mechanical adjustments grows greater instead of decreasing.

II. The Technique of Prediction, or the Logic of Science

All science may be regarded as an elaboration and refinement of the principle that we judge the future by the past. A scientific treatment of the problem of prediction and control must assume that this is just as true whether the process is one of conscious or unconscious knowledge, deliberate or automatic response. Even if man, like the lower animals, inherits adaptive reaction patterns, the basis of the adaptation is the same. A scientific world view has no possible place for the intuitive, or any other foresight of *new* truth, in advance of perception. Its fundamental assumption is that *truth is always the same* and is known through perception and memory. But that truth is always the same is equivalent to saying that the world is always the same. Change is unreal, or in so far as there is real change, the world is knowable only historically, the future is unpredictable.

The paradox, that if the world is always the same there is no problem of prediction, while if it is not always the same prediction is impossible, is resolved by means of two fundamental notions, law, and rearrangement, or analysis-synthesis. The essential idea in law is change of an interchanging character, that a thing does not change in "essence" if it changes predictably, since it remains true to its nature which is to change in the same unchanging way. Any predictable change, and any that science can discuss, is therefore analogous to movement along a path which can be represented by an equation, and of which any part can be calculated from the formula for any other part, however small.

The conceptual hiatus between a static and a changing world is further bridged in another way by the idea of rearrangement of the same elements in different combinations. Ultimately, both of these ideas merge in laws of rearrangement in the literal sense of spatial movement. Science refuses to credit the idea of internal, independent changes in simple elementary things, even in accordance with law, and insists on reducing all change to changes in the relations of unchanging elements or units. So the ordinary objects of experience are split up hypothetically into elements in terms of whose rearrangements are explained those changes in sensible things which are not brought into correspondence with external changes. A complete scientific explanation of the world would leave nothing but actual, literal motion. Of course the idea of such an explanation cannot be taken very seriously. The human mind baulks at the outset at the notion of movement without something that moves, and the logical process of reducing change to motion attentuates the moving particles into a form imperceptible to sense and unreal to imagination. Moreover, practically speaking, mechanics itself has never been able to get along without the notion of force, which is quite clearly a mode of consciousness and not an existence perceived in the outside world. For practical purposes, again, we must stop far short of the ideal of rigorous scientific conceptions, and survey the process by which our minds organize that sort of provisional knowledge on which conduct is based (outside of scientific laboratories, and in large part within them also).

To begin with, consciousness organizes the "big, buzzing, booming confusion," which is experience in its raw state, into a world of objects, existing and moving and changing in space and time. Our behaviour is concerned with the properties of *things*, including their modes of behaviour, which are truly properties as much as are the sense qualities. Properties and modes of behaviour of things form the content of knowledge and the subject-matter of thought as the basis of action.*
The axiom at the basis of practical thinking, the principle of identity

* The "new" logic of modern mathematics and neo-realist philosophy, dealing with empty relations and pure order, if it has any relation to conduct at all, has so little that it can be left out of account in such a survey as the present.

or static principle already referred to, is simply that things remain "essentially" the same, that they have an inner nature which does not change. They may change as far as sensible properties are concerned, but only according to unchanging "law" and in definite relation to other things. We may state this axiom simply in the proposition that the same thing will behave in the same way under the same circumstances. The idea of a "thing," or identity itself, is just the recognition of permanence or sameness in the organization of qualities, as is clearly shown by what happens in reasoning.

If behaviour meant only dealing with "the same things in the same circumstances," in a literal sense, there would be no occasion for thinking as we use the term. Intelligence would be a matter of *mere* memory. But the variety of things with which we have to deal is indefinitely too great for our minds to become acquainted with them; they do not remain the same in the perceptual sense, and the "circumstances" (which means their relations to other things) are similarly complicated and variable. These two facts, the mentally unmanageable complexity of manifoldness of the things which make up our world, and their habit of apparent change, necessitate the activity of thinking. In this sketch we shall not go into the logic of atomism by which sensible change is supposed to be reduced to rearrangement in space, and which belongs more to philosophy than to the logic of practice. Our study will concern itself only with the manner of formulation of those factual laws of change by means of which it is possible to predict the future and to behave intelligently.

The first step in the simplification of experience, and the simplest form of inference, is the act of classification in the sense of assimilating identically similar things. The principle of prediction involved is that not merely the same thing but *like* things behave in the same way under the same conditions, or that what is true of one member of a class of similars is true of all. The principle is of very limited application, as there are few classes of objects alike in all respects. It holds nearly enough to be useful in the case of such natural classes as different leaves from the same plant or plants of the same variety, specimens of the same mineral, etc., and more accurately of such artificial things as machines of the same model, samples of the same purified chemical compound or other "standardized" objects.

In practice this principle merges into a second one which involves inference of a more developed type. Classes are formed of objects similar *in certain respects*, though they may be different in other respects. The principle of prediction here is that things alike in some particular will be or behave alike in some other respect. The formal logic of the syllogism (restricting it for the moment to universal propositions only) represents this process of reasoning by classification. The syllogism itself states the results rather than the process of inference, as is readily shown. If we consider the famous syllogism,

> All men are mortal
> Socrates is a man
> Therefore Socrates is mortal,

it is evident that if Socrates is a man, we could not know that all men are mortal without already knowing that Socrates is so. Or, taking a different view, if mortality is an essential attribute of manhood, we could not know that Socrates is a man without knowing first that he is mortal. Hence we could in no case know both premises without previously knowing the conclusion, and it cannot be said that we really infer the conclusion from the premises.

To bring out the real nature of the process of prediction of the future from the present or inference of what is not known by direct observation from what is so known, the propositions must be stated differently. What is known is that *other* men have been mortal, or, more accurately, that other "things" having certain observable attributes marking them as members of the class "Man" have turned out to have the attribute mortality, and that (minor premise) the object Socrates has these other attributes. It is inferred that he will be found to have the attribute mortality previously found associated with the class marks.

All inference is essentially of this character. An object perceived to have certain qualities is inferred to have others not open to observation but previously found associated with those which are observed. Most of our ordinary recognition of objects is really on this basis, we perceive relatively little, and infer most of what we think we perceive. Reasoning power is the capacity to single out *essential* characteristics, marks from which relatively much can be inferred, and associate with them the qualities really connected. The wide applicability of the principle, the possibility of inference and prediction, depends on the *fact* that the objects of experience do fall into significant classes having a great number of attributes in common. If the qualities of objects were assorted at random in the world we simply could not infer, and intelligence would be impossible. The dogma of the "uniformity of nature" therefore covers the stability or permanence of things *and the reality of classes.*

The theory of inference requires extension in several ways beyond the simple cases covered by syllogisms made up of universal propositions. The case where either premise is a particular proposition was treated by the old logicians, but not in a way to make it very fruitful for practical guidance. If we say that *some* men die of consumption and that X is a man, the conclusion that X *may* die of consumption is of little utility. Modern logic is able to go much farther, through the use of the theory of probability or statistics; but it seems best to note two other modern devices which do not sacrifice universality in the conclusion, before commenting upon this theory. The first relates to quantitative similarity as a basis of classification and inference. Many attributes (always including activities) are variable in degree rather than simply present or absent. In fact science is largely concerned with the question how much of one is associated with how much of another. It is fundamental to our knowledge of nature that the qualities found associated in a small number of cases make it possible to construct the whole functional relation between two magnitudes.

The second device carries the same idea still further. If we find a certain quantitative relation between A and B and between B and C, or between, say, A and different proportions of B and C, it is often possible to construct from measurements of a few cases a functional relation among the three variables by which innumerable cases can be interpreted.

In these statements we purposely avoid using the term "cause" or "force." It is far better to say simply factors or variables, for anything which the words cause and force add to the mere idea of uniformity of association is unreal and misleading. What is meant by saying that nothing happens without a cause is merely that every change is associated with other changes, and that all are mathematical functions of time. The terms antecedent and consequent are also to be used with caution. The inferred quality or response may be subsequent in time to that from which it is inferred, or it may not; it may be only a potentiality, like the fact that a blow or contact with a hot iron will injure flesh *if* it happens, the practical significance of which knowledge is to prevent its happening. A cause in the ordinary sense need not be antecedent to its effect, as for instance when we cause an increase in the tension of a spring by stretching it. Probably the *commonest meaning of cause* is that it is the phenomenon which we can control directly, and by controlling which we are able indirectly to control another phenomenon upon which we cannot act directly. The idea of cause may have other meanings, but it would complicate this discussion unduly to go into more detail. The notion of force has long been recognized as a reading of our muscular sensation of effort into physical changes. We know only the effects, never the force (except in the case of our own muscles); force is, as Poincaré has said, a convenient conceptual device for simplifying certain equations.

The subject of the composition and resolution of variables, or synthesis and analysis, calls for one further observation. Sometimes the qualities of the compound can be predicted from those of the elements by addition, and sometimes by more complicated methods, and sometimes not at all. We can add forces in mechanics, and predict the resultant *a priori*; we can form chemical compounds, but cannot predict the result, or discover any general relation between the properties of the compound and those of its elements (except the mass), but we can be sure that the same elements combined in the same way will always give the same compound. This fact is useful because and only because the elements are definite substances identifiable by other and simpler means than testing for the particular phenomenon we wish to predict—the formation of the compound. There is much loose talk about the "analysis" of mental phenomena, which as we shall see later on is largely a pernicious use of words; in general these cannot be taken apart or combined experimentally, and neither "elements" nor "compounds" have any general marks of identification.

We return now to the question of the particular proposition and the theory of statistics. Though it may not be possible to draw any conclusion by which conduct may be guided from the premise that some men die of consumption, a premise stating that of any large number chosen without bias, a constant proportion will meet this fate may be very useful. For oftentimes our plans relate or can be made to relate to a large group of cases instead of a single case. Thus in business, if it is possible to tell how many buildings will burn, the individual owner of any one building may protect himself by clubbing together with other owners in an insurance organization of some sort. If a dealer knows what proportion of his accounts will prove un-collectable he can make allowance for this item as a cost of doing business and be as safe as if he could control the contingent event itself. Even where cases cannot be classified objectively, it is sometimes possible to estimate probabilities, and the mere fact of taking chances one after another, even where there is no similarity in the ventures, produces if it is done "intelligently" a tendency to cancel out gains and losses.

A final consideration practically quite as important as any of the foregoing is that very little indeed of any person's actual knowledge of the world is derived in any way from his own observation and re-flection, that an overwhelmingly preponderant portion comes through other persons by a process of *communication*. Thus the basic fact which makes possible any effective mastery of the world by anyone is the fact that the world of objects is the same for all minds. Knowledge is not practically usable unless it is "dependable," and the chief canon of dependability is that it can be demonstrated to and verified by and through other persons. Science is nearly restricted to the field within which such demonstration and verification are practicable, that is, to data which are in fact the same for all normal observers, *and which can in fact be communicated* so accurately as to compel all to recognize the identity. It is hardly thinkable that without effective intercommunica-tion we could ever form the idea of a real world or that conscious, intelligent thought would be possible.

The combination of all these methods of prediction gives rise to an elaborate and complicated technique, which is all useful and indis-pensable in scientific research. Yet as a matter of fact, none of it is ordinarily employed with any definiteness or accuracy in reaching the practical decisions of everyday life, even those relating to the material world. (In the prediction of human behaviour and social changes, this is much more strikingly the case, as will be seen in our next section.) For a simple illustration, consider the forecasting of the weather. The scientific meteorologist indeed follows something of the formal methodology outlined above, measuring variables, determining functional relations, calculating probabilities, *et cetera*. But the farmer or old salt who uses no such process of analysis and measurement may often predict the weather with as much reliability. His processes are largely unconscious, whether truly intuitive or only unconsciously rational. (The scientific dogmatist will insist that there can be no real intuition, but we are not so sure, especially in the field of human interpretation and communication.) In any case, the practical decisions of everyday life, even those regarding material nature, are only to a small extent scientific, whatever one may care to assume as to the ultimate theoretical possibility of a scientific determination of the issues. People make little pretence of enumerating exhaustively the variables upon which a conclusive demonstration would depend, and less pretence of measuring them, and have only the vaguest idea of the functional relation between observed factors and those to be inferred. What actually takes place in any practical situation such as predicting the course of prices, locating oil wells, or forecasting crop yields, and still more so in the more fundamental things such as deciding whether to go to college, selecting an occupation for life, and the like, is that the person makes an *estimate*, by a process only in a small degree conscious, and not describable in any considerable detail. Most decisions are enormously complicated by the fact that we do not know what we want, or why, as has been emphasized by the psycho-analysts.

We are now ready for the next step in the argument—the specific problem of applying scientific methods to the prediction of human phenomena. These two introductory sections have aimed to clarify the meaning of science as a technique of prediction, and the conditions requisite to scientific prediction in any field of data. These conditions may be regarded as a part of the definition of science. Knowledge usable for prediction in the guidance of conduct must consist of propositions which state unchanging truth and hence can be made only with regard to data which are ultimately static. Merely historic facts are of no direct practical use, and it would conduce to clear thinking to separate sharply scientific from historical truth in the terminology.

In general, a scientific proposition must hold good for a class of objects or situations; it states a dependable association or a numerical probability of an association between an attribute not open to direct observation and one which is so, and usually expresses a quantitative relation between the two. In general, truth cannot be considered scientific unless it is demonstrable, which means that it must be alike for all observers and accurately communicable. The scientific view of experience postulates a world which is independent of observation, and hence is of course really the same for all observers. But it is to be noted that there can be no scientific evidence for this view beyond the actual tendency of observers to agree. There is in fact the widest divergence in the amount of agreement among different observations according to the character of the data. There is never any close agreement quantitatively, but science has in many fields evolved a technique of *measurement* which compels agreement. In the field of human attributes and behaviour, all these prerequisites, the stability of the data, their assimilability into classes, even their objectivity and especially the possibility of their objective measurement—will be found subject to sweeping limitations which set corresponding limits to the scientific treatment of the phenomena.

III. THE SCIENTIFIC TREATMENT OF HUMAN DATA

A very large portion of the conduct of any human being is related in some way to other human beings, and if it is to be intelligent, it must be based upon correct prediction of their behaviour; and, needless to say, we desire and need the power of controlling the behaviour of persons quite as commonly as in the case of other phases of the "environment." It goes without saying that we do predict more or less correctly in this field, and act more or less intelligently in relation to other persons. We know what to expect of them under various circumstances, we count upon them in innumerable ways without being disappointed in the outcome in anything approaching the proportion of cases called for by the law of probability if our predictions were unfounded. And we do influence the conduct of others by deliberate action. But does this unquestioned fact of prediction and control by common-sense methods prove the possibility of scientific treatment? The question is whether it is possible to *improve upon the performance of common sense*, as science has done in the realm of physics and biology, by the conscious formulation and use of rules based upon a wider comparison and more careful analysis of cases.

At the outset we are confronted with a problem as to what *is* the method of common sense in predicting human behaviour, and what the correct relation to it of the method of science. It is fairly clear that common sense does not reach its conclusions in this field by comparing and analysing cases as objective phenomena, treating human beings as "things," and observing their uniformities. It *connects actions with feelings* and pictures behaviour in the closest association with, if not by means of, an idea of the *conscious attitude* of the other person. The behaviour attributes of human beings constitute character or person-ality, which is thought of in a quite different way from such physical qualities as the fluidity of water or the explosiveness of dynamite. Should science proceed in the same way, and associate feelings with situations and actions with feelings, or should it establish its relations between situations and actions directly?

The latter seems the simpler course, and the youngest of the sciences, calling itself Behaviourism, has arisen to advocate this method of procedure. The behaviourist points out that primitive man attributes consciousness to inanimate objects just as we attribute it to ourselves and our fellow beings, and contends that we should grow out of the childish practice in the one case as we have in the other. There is no way of demonstrating whether any reaction is conscious or not, or what sort of consciousness if any accompanies it, not to mention the problem of finding where in the evolutionary scale consciousness appears. It is a plausible inference that the proper procedure is to ignore consciousness and infer the responses of human beings to situations from previous observation and analysis of their responses to situations. The behaviourist (in the exuberance of his enthusiasm) is likely to go farther and deny outright that consciousness actually has anything to do with behaviour or that there is any such thing. But in this he is turning philosopher and carrying the discussion outside the field of science. The practical question is whether the notion of consciousness is *useful* in prediction. It might indeed be just as useful if consciousness did not "really exist" as if it did, and it is the usefulness, not the existence, which practically concerns us. Scientific discussion does not always keep science separate from metaphysics as it should do.

It is impossible to argue at length in this paper the issues involved in behaviourism; we can only state briefly our own position, which is that consciousness *is* useful, and its recognition necessary and inevitable, in the interpretation of human behaviour. The reason is simply that we cannot help ourselves. (And it may be admissible to step over into the domain of the metaphysical problem long enough to note that the same reasoning justifies accepting the ontological reality of consciousness, that it is the only sort of reason we ever have for believing in the existence of anything.) As a matter of fact we never succeed entirely in eliminating consciousness from our ideas of material things. We have noted that mechanics has not been able to do without the notion of force, though whatever force is, more than motion, is a fact of consciousness. It is impossible to construct in thought a world of real objects in purely objective terms; if objects are to have the qualities of consistent behaviour they are inevitably thought of as possessing rudiments of mind. We interpret the behaviour of the most material thing by to some degree putting ourselves in its place. Still more true is this when we come to consider the behaviour of living things. Purely mechanical biology remains an aspiration of the scientific intellect. Some sort of teleology is inevitable in speaking of the phenomena of life. The *will* to live and to increase is more than the *fact* of living and increasing, and we cannot account satisfactorily to ourselves for the facts of the lowest animal and plant life without recognizing an *element of striving* as well as processes and results.

In the field of human behaviour we have indefinitely stronger reasons for accepting consciousness as real and potent, in the fact of *communication*. The conclusive reason for believing that an action is conscious is that the subject can *tell us so*, and tell us about the motives. Logically, the behaviourist is right; we do not perceive consciousness, in any other person at least; we cannot prove or verify it; we only infer it from behaviour. But in spite of logic we all recognize that as a matter of fact we know consciousness more surely and positively than we know the behaviour from which theoretically we infer it. We cannot scientifically explain, except most superficially, how we communicate feelings or read expression in the looks and acts and words of others. Yet if anything in human life is clear it is that our whole intellectual life is built upon the fact of communication. Without it we could never develop the idea of objectivity, the foundation of scientific reasoning, and as noted in the preceding section, the test of reality is the possibility of verification, which depends on communication with the consciousness of others.

If the objective cannot exist without intercommunication, it is a truism that the subjective cannot be discussed without it. There is a mystery about our being able to talk and understand each other in regard to purely subjective experiences, but there is no question of the fact. It would appear, especially in view of the fact that we have no knowledge of purely objective reality, that we must concede some sort of consciousness to anything that can be made a subject of intelligent discourse. In connection with the problem of conduct it is surely clear that if consciousness is denied and a behaviouristic position assumed, an end is put at once to the possibility of discussing values or motives. We might discuss activity—though it is not easy to see how the discussion could have any "meaning"—and even the "cause" of activity (in the phenomenalistic use of that word), but there would be no such thing as a "reason" for activity; the idea of reasons would become meaningless and the subject-matter of all discussion of values unreal.

How do these considerations affect the possibility of scientific prediction of conduct? Within limits, it is possible to discover laws of behaviour, as such, in the objective sense. The term "man" denotes a very real and distinct class of "object"; seldom is there disagreement as to whether any particular specimen belongs to the class. And yet, outside of physiological processes and reflexes (and even these are not at all uniform) it is astonishingly hard to find traits or characteristic definite reactions which one can confidently infer from membership in the class, which are common to substantially all members of it. Even laughing, crying, and talking are not definite reactions to definite stimuli. In this field the "laws" which we may hope to reach are at best statistical in character, and even these are subject to narrow limitations, for reasons which will be pointed out presently.

The behaviour of human beings depends upon their *previous history*, and the history of no two individuals is the same or closely similar, *in essential respects*. The difficulty is that the reactions assuming them, to be determinate, are affected *in a large degree* by *imperceptible* differences in the situation. This is illustrated by the stories of "clever" animals. Dogs and horses have frequently seemed to their trainers to be reacting to spoken commands, but careful experiment has shown that this was not true at all, that they were really dependent upon some "cue" involuntarily and unconsciously given by the trainer himself and so subtle in character that careful study has sometimes failed to disclose just what it was. The wide divergence in the results obtained by different persons attempting to influence people *by the same technique* is a familiar fact, as also that the effects of laws and administrative measures seldom correspond to the expectations of their framers. Even in the case of the elemental and "gross" motives this is true. Who can say whether a specified punishment will reduce a particular crime? whether dropping bombs on any enemy population will weaken or strengthen their military morale? whether raising wages will cause men to work harder or to loaf, or what the effect of a change in the price of diamonds will be upon the sales? It depends!

These considerations form a convenient transition from the behaviouristic method to the "psychological," which attempts to give a scientific treatment of consciousness. "It depends," in such cases, upon how people feel and think others feel, on their own mood and temper, and the attitude which they see back of the "stimulus." Suppose, then, we accept conscious states and attitudes as data for the prediction of behaviour: how is the prospect for scientific treatment, superior to the judgment of common sense, affected? We doubt whether it is much improved, if at all; we question the possibility of any prediction which leaves consciousness out of account and builds upon stable relations between stimulus and reaction, but we also doubt whether the formal methods of science can be carried far in the field of conscious data. The argument of the behaviourist seems much more conclusive in its negative aspect than it is as a basis for construction. There is no doubt whatever that a competent judge of human nature could study the situation in any such case as those named above and render an opinion which would be valuable as to the probable outcome. But can he, or anyone else, state the data on which his conclusions would rest, and the character of the "functional relation" between the knowns and unknowns? The question appears to be self-answering.

We have no objective identification marks for moods and tempers, as shown by the fact that description of them runs practically in terms of the conduct to be anticipated. We say a person or a crowd is in the mood for certain acts, or in the frame of mind where such and such things are likely to happen. We make the prediction of behaviour directly, unconscious of the objective character of the "data," and use it to characterize the latter. Such expressions as an "ugly" or "jovial" mood have really no deeper or different meaning, they suggest conduct rather than identifiable marks from which conduct is to be predicted. We predict by simply "knowing," without any conscious process of inference, what to expect.

This does not mean that the art of prediction and control of the behaviour of people cannot within limits be taught and learned. But it is taught and learned by a very different method than that of giving and following rules. Painting and story-writing can be taught and learned, but not in the main by *telling how* to paint and write, and it is to the study of the fine arts that one must turn for an understanding of the methods of communication generally, in the field where facts of consciousness are involved. Intuitive and intellectual or unconscious and conscious processes are involved and interrelated in ways which go beyond the scope of this paper or the writer's competence to begin to discuss. It appears that formal statements do not carry us far beyond such truisms as that men in a mood for some activity are "likely" to do it under "appropriate" conditions.

The whole question is one of empirical fact: are there objectively recognizable features in the situation which are uniformly associated with the different possible eventualities? The insertion of feelings as factors between the stimulus and the reaction only makes it more clear that the sequence simply is not uniform as far as our senses can discriminate; we can count upon people neither to feel in a certain describable way under conditions identical within the limits of perception and verification, nor to act in the same way under the promptings of the "same" feelings; we cannot count upon the same person to repeat himself, much less other persons to copy him. Perhaps *if* the person and the stimulus were really the *same*, the same conduct would follow; but it is the most characteristic attribute of persons to change in unpredictable ways, and the "stimulus" being in practice usually some "reaction" of another person or persons, is equally fluctuating and uncertain. It is futile, practically speaking, to argue. the question whether the same stimulus "really" produces in the same or a similar subject the same reaction; the fact confronts us that whether we speak in behaviouristic or psychological terms, the same stimulus, *within the power of perception or any available test to determine*, acting on the same subject, similarly defined in terms of the available means of knowing identity and similarity, *does not* produce the same conduct, within the practical requirements of classification.

It would be hard to over-emphasize the importance of the fact that the practical usefulness of scientific principles depends upon our ability to infer with certainty (or a known degree of probability) and in general quantitatively, a large number of *facts which cannot be observed directly* from *facts which can be easily recognized and measured*, or from historical data easy to obtain. It would be useless to know the solubility of sodium chloride if we had no way easier than measuring its solubility of telling when we had sodium chloride to deal with. In dealing with human behaviour, there is a lack of recognizable marks for the sort of non-observable characters we are interested in inferring, if indeed there is any fundamental human nature which determines behaviour. There is an abundance of identification data, easily ascertained, but no discoverable connection between these and what we wish to know. It is easy to find out many things about a human being's ancestry, race, education, and the like, and some traits and capacities can be identified and measured with a degree of accuracy, but nothing seems to follow with any certainty from such facts. We could not tell from a man's antecedents or life history or from his stature or his "I. Q." such simple things as whether he would take sugar in his coffee, or would drink coffee at all, whether he would have the qualities of leadership or could be trusted with money. Literature and conversation are replete with generalizations about the behaviour of "women," "Jews," "The English," even about citizens of one county or town in contrast with another, about "Yale men," "Methodists," men of a certain family name, and so on *ad lib.*; but everyone who has given any study to the question knows that when such statements are definite enough to test they are trivial or false. There are indeed many negative generalizations which are dependable, as that a man cannot be a competent physician without a scientific education, or that cripples do not make good messenger boys, but the contrary positive assertion is rarely valid.

To repeat, it is possible for a good judge of human nature to form opinions with a high degree of validity as to what individuals or groups are likely to do under conditions present to observation. Moreover, it is possible to convey information and describe situations intelligibly to a considerable extent, and to make general statements regarding the art of judging human nature which have some degree of helpfulness. But none of this is done by the methods of science. It is all in the field of art, and not of science, of suggestion and interpretation, and not accurate, definite, objective statement, a sphere in which common sense works and logic falls down, and where, in consequence, the way to improve our technique is not to attempt to analyse things into their elements, reduce them to measure and determine functional relations, but to educate and train our intuitive powers.

All the foregoing argument is further strengthened and emphasized by the development of the psycho-analytic method in psychology, involving the introduction of subconscious mind. We cannot elaborate here the significance of this movement, but it is evident that while its postulates may be useful as the basis of a technique of control in certain special cases, they introduce enormous new difficulties and uncertainties in the way of reducing behaviour at large to general laws. In so far as the new theories are sound they show that men's real motives are often quite other than they think them to be, and extremely difficult to come at. The human propensity for "rationalizing" of which some of Dewey's followers have made so much, and the distinction between "good reasons" and "real reasons" so genially portrayed by James Harvey Robinson are kindred developments which emphasize the difficulty of predicting human behaviour from motives. As to psycho-analysis, it seems clear that the last part of this term is used in a sense so different from its ordinary scientific meaning as to be descriptively misleading. The procedure would be much more accurately called psycho-interpretation.

Besides behaviourism and psychology, there is a more or less definite and distinct line of attack on the problem of scientific prediction in human affairs, which goes under the general designation of sociology, in which we include the philosophy of history and social psychology. Under this head we must first allot a few words to the theory of human instincts. The controversy on this subject is a rather disheartening piece of logomachy, and for our purpose the matter may be very briefly disposed of. No one has ever denied that there is an innate element in human behaviour; what people do and like to do is not altogether a matter of training and historic accident. On the other hand, it appears that no one has contended that (beyond a few simple reflex movements) human beings inherit any preformed action patterns by virtue of which, independently of teaching, they will do any definite thing under any definite circumstances. Many activities, such as eating, sexual mating, talking, fighting, fleeing from danger, and the like are very readily and naturally learned. Yet it is most essential to observe that these are not specific activities, that the concrete content of all of them, what is eaten and how, the forms of courtship and family life, the language spoken and so on—are after all acquired, and within astonishingly wide limits one type of content is acquired as readily as another. In Professor McDougall's original version of the instinct theory it did not in fact profess to be a theory of conduct at all, as he expressly insisted that both stimulus and the reaction in the case of any particular instinct are indefinitely modifiable, that only the central part, the feeling, is a stable datum. Moreover, the instincts are valueless for prediction for another obvious reason. They include all possible types of reaction to fundamental situations, and do not pretend to tell us anything as to which type of reaction will follow in any given case. An animal in danger may fight, or run away, or perhaps feign death; whatever he does, the theory gives us an "instinct" to do just that. It is not practically helpful to be told that some one of the possibilities of a situation will eventuate, though it may have a power, somewhat difficult to account for, of satisfying after the event—a certain type of craving for a reason why.

For the content of reactions, the prediction of actual behaviour, we are thrown back upon what is more properly perhaps the province of sociology, the study of social inheritance, of *mores* or institutions.

The history of the attempt to define culture and found a science of culture by discovering laws of its development and change is one of the most fascinating of all subjects of inquiry. We cannot in the present connection even refer to the individual proposals that have been made, or summarize the arguments that have been advanced pro and con in regard to the possibility of a science, or a philosophy, of history. It is enough for our purpose to point out that among those who ought to be most competent to judge, the historians themselves, few indeed believe at the present day in the fruitfulness of such endeavour, or express serious respect for the attempts of sociologists and philosophers to formulate laws of culture evolution. The function of the historian is to find out and show "wie es eigentlich gewesen," or as Professor A. C. McLaughlin has expressed it, to learn what happen*ed* and to steer clear of generalizations as to what happen*s*. The same historian is frankly sceptical about the project of making history "useful." On this point the profoundest of the philosophers of history himself remarked, with a touch of bitterness perhaps, that the only thing to be learned from history is that men will not learn from history. Sir Leslie Stephen puts the case still more strongly in his familiar warning that when an author asserts that "history proves," a point, the reader should simply read instead, "I propose to assume without evidence."

The present writer would hasten to say that he does not understand these authors to mean that the study of history is really not useful, and that he himself considers history the one subject about which no one can ever know as much as he needs to know. But the usefulness of history is not in giving us rules which can be made the basis of inference and prediction; it is not in this respect a science, but rather an art. The study of history works in a quite different way, through training the judgment, giving insight into human life. The useful knowledge of history is chiefly unconscious knowledge and its application will also be unconscious. As we have remarked of the interpretation and prediction of human situations in general, the basis of the inference is not consciously known. Often, indeed, the premises can be discovered and put into words *afterward*, but that again is more history, but not science.

The primal question in regard to a science of history is simply the question in regard to any science, which we have repeatedly stated: is the material dealt with stable (in its elements at least) classifiable and verifiable? that is, *are* there (in it) "laws" to be discovered? The truth about history and culture could hardly be better stated than it has been (paradoxical to observe) by the father of the new Historismus in American economics, Dr. Thorstein Veblen: . . . "there are no cultural laws of the kind aimed at [by the early German Historical School] beyond the unprecise generalities that are sufficiently familiar beforehand to all passably intelligent adults."* Yet Dr. Veblen goes on to build up a science of history of his own (in the field of economics at least), based upon *causal laws* most sharply distinguished from "uniformities of sequence in phenomena," upon causes which "*determine* the course of events," which "*make* the uniformity or variation." This, according to him, is "modern science," and compared with it the "natural laws" . . . "of the nature of empiricism" are "quite fatuous." It would be a waste of white paper for the present writer to give any extended criticism of this position. If I know anything at all about modern science, its first principle is the complete repudiation of all causes that "determine" or "make"; the first article in its creed is the declaration that human knowledge is limited to empirical generalization concerning the uniformities of phenomena. Moreover, the only alternative to this empirical view is a belief in entelechies of some sort, and of all such notions Dr. Veblen is as scornful as he is of the "aphoristic wisdom" of empiricism.

Of course science does make a working distinction between causal laws and empirical laws, but it is all a matter of degree of generality. That "quinine is good for ague" is an empirical law in comparison with the statement that quinine is a specific poison for the animal parasite which "causes" the malaria by interfering in definite ways with the normal physiology of the blood. But one is entitled to ask "why" poisons are poison and why the destruction of red corpuscles by the *plasmodium malariae* produces the familiar symptoms, and these questions could only be answered by descriptive propositions of a

* *The Place of Science in Modern Civilization*, p. 262. This statement is again much more extreme than I should make myself. It is a question of *how far* beyond common sense a scientific study of history can go. I should contend, not only for the power of history to educate common sense, as already indicated, which is a very different thing from yielding scientific laws, but also that there is possibility of systematizing common-sense judgments and improving their accuracy, within limits. The study of history can undoubtedly find some "laws" if the term is not taken too rigidly.

still more general character. Except for a higher degree of generality we could never reach a "cause" in any other sense than that in which the presence of swamps "caused" malaria in the days before the parasites and their mosquito carriers were known.

There is another theory of human nature put forth under the caption of sociology by Dr. Wm. I. Thomas and the "Chicago School." It is a theory of interaction between human nature and socially inherited institutional "values." It proposes to explain human conduct in terms of these values and the "attitudes" of the reacting individuals. It is an interesting theory and offers in the writer's opinion much greater possibilities for throwing light on behaviour than does the science of behaviourism. It may be of great practical value as an aid in educating common sense, and should be infinitely more efficacious than the childish doctrine of instincts in making events seem more intelligible afterwards. But when it comes to the prospect of finding "laws" which can be used practically for *predicting* conduct—that is a different question, and one in regard to which we must entertain grave doubts until its possibility is demonstrated. For this ambition to be realized the same list of assumptions given for other sciences must hold good; these attitudes and values must be stable, reducible to a manageable number of classes and, most improbable of all, the sociologist must be able to discover objective marks of identification by which they can be recognized before they express themselves in conduct. We suspect that it may prove possible by this means to "explain" conduct in the *post facto* sense to a large extent; that is, it may be possible to show that much of it is really according to law, to show *afterwards* that what resulted in any case was what should have been expected from the "forces" at work. But if these "forces" cannot be identified and measured, simply, in some other way than by waiting for the effect which it is desired to predict, it is obvious that there is no hope of prediction.

One after another, all avenues of escape are apparently closed, and we are forced back upon the conclusion already several times stated, that human phenomena are not amenable to treatment in accordance with the strict canons of science. They will not yield generalizations which can be used as the basis of prediction and the guidance of policy, because there are no generalizations about them which are true; that is, no generalizations about our observations of them. Whether, say, to an infinite intelligence, they would be analysable into uniformities, whether any characterization could be permanently true, or whether truth itself changes, is another question, belonging to metaphysics. But as far as our observations go, they simply are not uniform; human beings do not maintain their identity as to behaviour traits and do not fall into a manageable number of behaviour classes with objective and measurable identification marks; and this s practically true whether we do or do not attempt to use conscious states or attitudes as data in the classification. Each part of this proposition may be given a few final words of elaboration.

The fundamental fact in the way of a science of human nature is a familiar characteristic shared by all the higher animals, that the reaction of an individual to an "object" depends not only or mainly on the individual and the object, but on the *previous history* of the individual. Of course one can object that what the individual *is* at the moment determines the reaction, that his past history operates only by changing him. This cannot be proved or disproved as a theory, but is practically untrue, as there is no possible way of observing the changes, if any, made in the individual by his experience. The phenomenon is variously designated as associative memory, or mnemism;* or on the lowest plane, the conditioned response; or on the highest plane by saying that the individual reacts not to the object as such but to what it *means* to him. Or in Bergson's more picturesque phrase, the animal carries its past with it into the future in a cumulative process of growth. Long before he is adult, a being with man's sensitiveness to passing experience and his capacity for conscious and unconscious memory has become such an unique aggregation of attitudes toward meanings that there is no use in talking about accurate classification; he has to be treated as an individual. In addition he is highly unstable, and most especially is largely unknowable, since as already observed, the associations which condition his responses are quite inaccessible to observation. No life history could conceivably be detailed and accurate enough to make them available as scientific data. And, to repeat, the

* See Bertrand Russell, *The Analysis of Mind*, chapter iv, and the work of Semon there referred to. The Freudian psychology has served greatly to emphasize the role of the past in the present behaviour of human beings.

"stimulus," in most of the conduct which we need practically to predict, consists of "reactions" of other persons, and is therefore equally unclassifiable and in large part unknowable.

We may grant that in their responses to certain "elemental" stimuli and urges people are appreciably similar. They all experience the motives of hunger and sex, fear and anger, and so on. And even though the concrete mode of expression of these motives is almost entirely derived from training and social suggestion, cultural background is also relatively stable in reference to these elemental things. Given familiarity with one's nationality, social class, education, etc., it may in fact be possible to predict a good deal about the probable course of his life. If he grows up in the United States he will no doubt eat the flesh of swine, cattle, sheep, and abstain from that of cats, dogs, horses; he will be monogamous (in theory), will give some sort of acceptance to some conception of Christianity (at least as opposed to other religions); if in the Southern part of the country, he will think himself imbued with an antipathy to negroes as a race (though this is largely a misapprehension) and so on.

There is no doubt, moreover, that scientific study can give a much more accurate idea than that of common sense as to the actual probability of many contingencies and vicissitudes of life. There is some possibility, in these elemental reactions, of finding "laws" which have some value—laws of a "statistical" character. We can learn something about the effects of various causes on birth-rates, marriage, divorce, etc. In the sphere of eonomic activity especially, no one will gainsay the value of statistics and the statistical study of cause and effect. At best, however, the difficulties of defining units and getting reliable information at the sources, and all the obstacles familiar to workers with official statistics, set serious limitations on the method. It so often costs more to get the facts than is involved in the policy in question, or the process takes so long that the question has to be settled or settles itself before the results of investigation can be made available. A current news item remarks upon a discrepancy of something like forty per cent in the figures put out by two governmental departments on the amount of cotton in the United States, *last* December, not in the future.

In addition to all the staggering practical difficulties of statistical study of social phenomena, the method is subject to two sorts of general limitation. In the first place, it is restricted, as noted, to the "elemental" factors in life. But the progress of mankind is away from the elemental, away from the natural, in regard to which we may be supposed more or less stable and similar, to the artificial, where we are capricious and divergent. Let any one candidly estimate the fraction of his own activity or of his expenditure of income which is devoted to elemental needs, to the maintenance of health and efficiency. Even though his budget be relatively very modest, the fraction will be quite small. A German scholar lecturing in this country recently remarked that it is astonishing how easy it is to live on an income worth about a hundred American dollars a year, when everyone else is doing likewise.

The other limitation is that it is only with reference to individuals in distinctly individual relations that differences cancel out or reduce to percentages. Wherever they in any sense constitute a real group, wherever the reactions have any way of influencing each other, a very different situation is met with. Even suicide has been known to become epidemic. When there is any effective means of inter-communication among the individuals subjected to the action of a cause, they cease to act as individuals and the effect becomes a matter not of statistics but of group psychology. We say that a group is "organic," meaning simply that the action of individuals in groups is not necessarily related in any simple or discoverable way to their actions as individuals. Prediction of the behaviour of groups offers all the insuperable difficulties of prediction of individual behaviour; they simply are not stable, or reducible to manageable classes or to be characterized in any objective terms other than those which describe their conduct itself. Groups, and societies, like individuals, carry their past with them into the future and grow in historical uniqueness. They also react to meanings rather than situations, and are quite as sensitive and erratic as the individual.

We seem to be forced to the conclusion, not that prediction and control are impossible in the field of human phenomena, but that the formal methods of science are of very limited application. Common sense does predict and control, and can be trained to predict and control better; but that does not prove that science can predict and control better than common sense. And it seems very doubtful whether in the majority of social problems the application of logical methods and canons will give as good results as the informal, intuitive process of judgment which, when refined and developed, becomes art. Art is not science, and only within narrow limits can it be reduced to science (in which case of course it ceases to be art). It seems to us that science is a special technique developed for and applicable to the control of physical nature, but that the ideal so constantly preached and reiterated, of carrying its procedure over into the field of the social phenomena rests on a serious misapprehension.

Nor is it, we may suggest, a misapprehension only as to the character of the material to be worked with. It would carry us outside the field of this paper and into a discussion of a very different character to argue the moral question involved in the very notion of social control. In practice this can only mean either something on the order of self-control, which is obviously a very different thing from the manipulation of cause and effect, or else the control of one part of society by another part. No doubt each individual and class in society is anxious enough to get hold of a technique of controlling the rest of society; but is that an aim about which the social philosopher should concern himself so seriously? Within limits it is; for in any organized system a part of the individuals must be in control of the rest. In this sense social control is an adjunct to law. But law itself, most of us admit, should be minimized; the ideal is *freedom*, no control. Also, in any actual society there are children and innumerable adults of all degrees of incompetence to control themselves intelligently, in regard to whom an effective technique of control is a real desideratum. But approaching the problem from this concrete standpoint manifestly puts it in a very different light than simply transferring the ideal and methods of the scientific control of nature over to the field of controlling men.

But the only point we have wished to develop in this paper relates to the pure theory of methodology. In this field we have striven to implant doubts as to the extent to which, in view of the actual character of human data, we may improve upon the results of common sense by the use of the formal methods by which such progress has admittedly been made in the way of mastering physical nature. We may help to clinch the point by suggesting that the mental process of predicting and controlling human behaviour may be analogous to the process of recall in memory. The power of recall is an unquestionable fact, and it is probably true that it can be developed by training, to some extent. But no scientific analysis has told us *how* to recall, described a technique or formulated rules for recalling more effectively. We set the mind to work at the task of digging up a missing name or fact; we know that mental process accompanied by effort is going on, though the attention may be elsewhere and the mind, consciously, otherwise occupied. We cannot tell what the process is in any terms which will facilitate it; we only know that after a certain period of effort and the confused feeling that the mind is at work on the problem, the datum sought for comes into consciousness—or that it does not, as the case may be.

It may well be the same with the problem of predicting and controlling the behaviour of our fellows. The process seems to resist analysis or formal description. It is a problem of interpretation, of formulating a result and inventing a technique for bringing it about, not of verified observation, of methodical inference and control by the application of formulas. One must simply *learn* to interpret and to lead his fellows. It is like aesthetic interpretation and creation; one lives with the problems, discusses, attempts to formulate judgments intelligible to others and to embody his ideas in creative work, and to understand the judgments of others and appreciate their work. And finally he finds himself understanding and being understood, and his results turning our more or less in harmony with his intentions.

The kind of thing which human nature is is shown by the forms of language used in describing it. Discussion of human nature, like discussion of art works, runs to a relatively slight extent in terms of objective, sensible qualities, but predominantly in language which suggests rather than asserts; its meanings are conveyed by figurative rather than literal forms of expression. It is difficult to appreciate the relative importance of figurative language as compared with literal. By far the greater part of written and spoken discourse is more or less figurative, and it not only conveys a meaning, but usually a meaning which it would be impossible to express directly, scientifically. People are far more concerned with meanings than with sense qualities, and meaning, being a subjective phenomenon, must be suggested rather than stated. The behaviourist-materialist may insist that expressions like "a stalwart soul," and "my love's like a red, red rose" are "really" based on physical similarity of some attenuated sort. But he cannot point out in terms of sense qualities wherein the resemblance consists, and his assertion is therefore mere dogma, as far from the "facts" of experience as the ravings of any mystic. One is just as free to believe that there is more to it than physical resemblance in any sense, that there is a realm of meanings no less real than the verifiable world of physics. It is doubtful whether any language except possibly the arbitrary symbols of mathematics and symbolic logic, is entirely literal, just as it seems that reality cannot be thought of in purely objective terms. The meanings which are conveyed, but not expressed, by figurative language, cannot be taken apart and put together, and it is a misuse of the term "analysis" to apply it to our thought concerning them, just as all the rest of the technique of natural science is misapplied in their sphere.

IV. Economics as a Science

In spite of all the foregoing, there is a science of economics, a true, and even exact, science, which reaches laws as universal as those of mathematics and mechanics. The greatest need for the development of economics as a growing body of thought and practice is an adequate appreciation of the meaning, and the limitations, of this body of accurate premises and rigorously established conclusions. It comes about in the same general way as all science, except perhaps in a higher degree, i.e., through abstraction. There are no laws regarding the *content* of economic behaviour, but there are laws universally valid as to its *form*. There is an abstract rationale of all conduct which is rational at all, and a rationale of all social relations arising through the organization of rational activity. We cannot tell what particular goods any person will desire, but we can be sure that within limits he will prefer more of any good to less, and that there will be limits beyond which the opposite will be true. We do not know what specific things will be wealth at any given place and time, but we know quite well what must be the attitude of any sane individual toward wealth wherever a social situation exists which gives the concept meaning. In the same way we know that in any productive operations on this earth there are some general relations between quantity of resources used and quantity of product turned out.

These principles are only less abstract than those of mathematics. It is never true in reality that two and two make four; for we cannot add unlike things and there are no two real things in the universe which are exactly alike. It is only to completely abstract units, entirely without content, that the most familiar laws of number and quantity apply. Yet no one questions the practical utility of such laws. They are infinitely more useful than they could be if they ever did fit exactly any single concrete base, since all that they lose in literal accuracy they gain in generality of application. By not being strictly true in any case they are significantly true in all.

It is not necessary to regard the general, *a priori* laws of mathematics or economics or such mechanical principles as inertia as being "intuitively" known in any inscrutable way. They may all be more advantageously treated as mere facts of observation, characteristics of the world we live in, but characteristics so obvious that it is impossible to escape recognizing them and so fundamental that to think them away would necessitate creating in the imagination a different type of universe. The "necessary" character of axioms is undoubtedly due, not to their being created or given to experience by mind, but rather on the contrary to the fact that the mind has not the creative power to imagine a world fundamentally different from that in which we actually live.

This conception readily fits the character of the general laws of economic theory, such as diminishing utility and diminishing returns. The former is a general statement of the *fact* that men with a given quantity of exchange power do not (unless they are feeble-minded) expend it all upon the first commodity they run across, or the one which happens to be uppermost in mind at the moment, but distribute it in some more or less determinate way over the available goods. There *is* a valid distinction between the intelligent and stupid or insane expenditure of money.

In the same way there is, and every normal adult *knows* that there is, a general law of the relation between quantity of resources expended and quantity of goods produced. It is a fact of the world we live in that "goods" are usually produced, not by single agencies working alone but by a combination of resources, in much the same way that "satisfaction" is produced by consuming a variety of goods; and the character of the dependence is much the same in the two cases. In a universe governed by a general law of increasing returns the output of goods would be increased by decreasing the amount of resources devoted to their production. Such a universe would be bedlam.

It is a common objection to deductive economic theory that from obvious principles only obvious conclusions can be established and nothing really significant can come out of it. This assertion is belied by the facts of economic science itself, not to mention mathematics, where a structure of boundless and ever-growing scope and intricacy is built up on the basis of a few simple axioms. Yet it all "works"; its conclusions are descriptive of reality and are indispensable in predicting and controlling the phenomena of the physical world. In economics also, the significance of the conclusions of general theory is patent. They are not "obvious," since the ablest students are not in agreement in regard to many of them, nor useless for practical purposes, since the broad outlines of social policy depend upon them and are quite commonly misguided through the failure of legislators and administrators to understand and follow them.

Nor are the general laws of economics "institutional." They work in an institutional setting, and upon institutional material; institutions supply much of their content and furnish the machinery by which they work themselves out, more or less quickly and completely, in different actual situations. Institutions may determine the alternatives of choice and fix the limits of freedom of choice, but the general laws of choice among competing motives or goods are not institutional— unless rational thinking and an objective world are institutions, an interpretation which would make the term meaningless. Economic activity consists in the use of certain resources by certain processes, to produce "wealth." The content of the concept wealth is largely institutional, and the resources available and processes known and used at any place and time for producing wealth are in a sense historical products; but there are general laws of production and consumption which hold good whatever specific things are thought of as wealth and whatever productive factors and processes in use.

For illustration we may consider the assertion commonly made even by economists who do not recognize the function of general laws, that the way to understand price fixation is to study the machinery and process of marketing. The mode of organization of the market may indeed have a good deal to do with price, and that in at least two ways. It brings the buyers and sellers of the goods more or less perfectly into communication with each other, furnishing the channels through which the real price-fixing forces, the facts of demand and supply, work out more or less freely and effectively to a determinate result. In addition, what we call marketing machinery and organization includes a large element of direction of energy into manipulation of demand, creating real or fictitious qualities in the goods marketed, through true or false information, or through mere psychological compulsion in the form of suggestion and exhortation. In so far as these things are present and operative, they are, of course present and operative; but they do not affect the fact that in the large the conditions of supply and demand determine the prices of goods. Other considerations produce aberrations from the result of perfect intercommunication among buyers and sellers who know the goods and their wants, but they are to be understood only as producing *aberrations from* the fundamental tendency and hence in subordination to it. They are of the nature of friction, divergence of materials from conditions taken as standard, and the like, in the workings of the laws of mechanics in actual machines.

There is a close analogy between theoretical economics and theoretical physics. Both treat of the relations between cause and effect, between force and change, without reference to the question of what forces may actually be at work in any particular case or what effects it may be desirable to produce. In both fields, the *application* of the principles does depend precisely upon these questions of the particular ends in view and means at hand, and upon all the conditions present. But the application of principles is impossible without principles to apply. It is no argument against the practical value of pure theory that taken alone it does not yield definite rules for guidance. It is a recognized fact that laboratory physics could not have made anything approximating its actual progress in modern times without the aid of a relatively separate development of mathematical theory by men who have not been experimenters.

The laws of economics are never themselves institutional, though they may relate to institutional situations. Some, as we have observed are as universal as rational behaviour, the presence of alternatives of choice between quantitatively variable ends, or between different means of arriving at ends. Others are as universal as "organized activity," independent of the form or method of organization. A large part of the extant body of economic theory would be as valid in a socialistic society as it is in one organized through exchange between individuals. Other laws relate to behaviour in exchange relations, and of course have no practical significance where such relations are not established. Still others cover behaviour in situations created by even more special institutional arrangements, as for example the differences in business conduct created by the custom of selling goods subject to cash discount or by the existence of a branch banking system as contrasted with independent banks. An intelligent conception of the meaning of science requires a clear grasp of the meaning of classification and subclassification, of laws of all degrees of generality. Each law is universal in the field to which it applies, though it may not give a complete description of the cases which it fits. Quite commonly a law has the form "*in so far as* the situation is of such a character, such things will happen." Any law is significant if it gives a sufficient part of the explanation of a sufficiently common type of occurrence.

Scientific laws fall into a sort of hierarchical order from still another point of view than that of the classes of phenomena to which they apply. A law states that under given conditions given changes will occur. But the "given conditions" may be only relatively given, and may themselves be changing in relation to other causes which condition them, and so on. After explaining an event in terms of causes immediately at work, it may be necessary to explain those causes, bringing in other causes to be explained in turn. To a large extent these stages in the process of explanation fall in different sciences, one taking as data the results of another; but sometimes several stages may fall within the province of one science. The latter is true in economics, and the problem of what are to be treated as data becomes especially troublesome. We shall return to this point shortly.

If the term economics were to be interpreted in the literal sense, as covering all behaviour which involves the adaptation of means to ends and the "economizing" of means in order to maximize ends, then economics would be an almost all-inclusive science. It would take in about all of what we call rational behaviour, since thinking is just the technique for guiding the performance of this function. But the study of this vast field falls into certain natural divisions, and after all the generations of discussion there is still need for clear delimitation of these and recognition of the methods appropriate to each. The process of want-satisfaction, or rational behaviour, involves certain elementary factors: (1) the wants to be satisfied, (2) the goods, uses or services of goods, and human services, which satisfy them, (3) intermediate goods in a complicated sequence back to (4) ultimate resources, on which the production of goods depends, (5) a series of technological processes of conversion, and (6) a human organization for carrying out these processes. This human organization again is two-fold, including (6-a) the internal organization of productive units or enterprises, which belongs rather to the field of technology than to that of the other phase which is (6-b) the social organization of production and distribution in the large. Theoretical economics as the term is generally used is concerned almost exclusively with the very last factor, the general social organization, in which the nation and to a large extent the world is the unit.

As a basis of division of labour in the investigation and study of a field which is still vastly too broad for a single science, it is tacitly agreed to separate further certain *methods* of organization as fields for different groups of workers. The most important division is that between *political organization*, on the one hand, covering the various methods such as monarchy, democracy, etc., based on territorial sovereignty, and on the other hand what has come to be called *the* economic organization, worked out through exchange in markets and prices of goods and services. Thus economic theory has in practice come to be restricted to the analysis of social interaction and co-ordination through the price mechanism, that is, of organization through the competitive sale for money by individuals (really by families) of productive services (of person and "property") to business enterprises, and the competitive purchase from business enterprises with the money obtained of goods for consumption. It is the business enterprise, variously constituted, which carries on the actual production. Thus of the three main elements in economic life, wants, resources, and organization, economic theory deals directly with one aspect of the organization, and only incidentally with the other elements. Wants are in the province of psychology, sociology, and ethics; resources fall in various other sciences, and the technological aspect of organization to a vast number, and the internal organization of business to a special branch of economics.

The great fact which makes economic theory so vague and so difficult is the confusion already referred to as to the relations between cause and effect or the interpretation of "given" conditions, or in scientific terms, the separation of the constants and independent variables, from the dependent variables. This problem underlies the crude distinction often drawn between "static" and "dynamic" economics, and between short-time and long-time views of the price problem. It is also central to the issue between the conceptions of economics as deductive theory and as "institutional" economics. All these contrasted notions are purely relative, matters of degree; at one extreme we might have a discussion limited to the abstract theory of markets, at which point indeed some of the mathematical treatments virtually stop; at the other extreme we should have the philosophy of history (in the economic field, however defined) and that is what institutional economics practically comes to. It should go without saying that all are useful and necessary.

To begin with, needless confusion has been caused by the unfortunate use of the terms "static" and "dynamic." These are highly objectionable because they have in mechanics a definite meaning unrelated to the main issue in economics. The problem of conditions of equilibrium among given forces—"statics" in the proper sense—is often important in economics, but is after all subsidiary, as indeed it is in physical mechanics. The larger question is that of whether the forces acting under given conditions tend to produce an equilibrium, and if so how, and if not what is their tendency; that is, it is a problem in dynamics. This type of problem has been too largely passed over hitherto, leaving a fatal gap in the science. The crying need of economic theory to-day is for a study of the "laws of motion," the *kinetics* of economic changes. Physics could hardly have made a start until two sorts of resistance to change were sharply distinguished, that is, inertia and friction. The centring of economic theory about the possibility and condition of equilibrium has caused the study of the laws governing economic changes in time to be neglected. The least serious attempt to formulate and use the concepts of mass, momentum, energy, etc., or their analogues, in relation to economic change, and to measure economic force and acceleration, would have shed a flood of light on the contrast between mechanics and economics and the methodologies of study in the two fields.

We can hardly over-emphasize the contrast between economic dynamics in this proper sense—the study of the laws of change under given conditions—and the major problem above indicate, as to what conditions are to be treated as given. At the very outset we are confronted with a question in regard to which confusion reigns supreme, the question whether and in what sense human wants are to be considered in economics as data (or independent variables). We are not called upon to argue this question here, but merely to point out that it is by no means simply answered. Wants are usually treated as *the* fundamental data, the ultimate driving force in economic activity, and in a short-run view of problems this is scientifically legitimate.* But in the long-run it is just as clear that wants are dependent variables, that they are largely caused and formed by economic activity. The case is somewhat like that of a river and its channel; for the time being the channel locates the river, but in the long-run it is the other way.

Similar statements hold for the other half-dozen elements in the economic problem. The means of want-satisfaction and the resources used to produce them, and the technology and business organization according to which the process is carried out—all are *data*, causes, independent variables, in some regards and with reference to some time periods, and all are effects, dependent variables, in other regards and with reference to other time periods. The only ultimately in-

---

* The argument of earlier sections of the essay should have made it clear that only within restricted limits are wants to be regarded as data for science in any case. Civilized people act perhaps as much by way of experimentation in wants and satisfactions as they do in response to wants for definite things. But explorative behaviour cannot be rationally directed in the sense in which action directed toward a foreseen result is rational, and it is apparently without the pale of strictly scientific treatment.

dependent variables are those features of nature and human nature which are in fact outside the power of economic forces to change, and it would be hard to say what these are. Even the laws of technology and physiology operate in economic relations as people believe them to be rather than as they are, and our beliefs concerning them are by no means fixed or independent of economic events.

Such a mass of interrelated data seems to call for a combination of three methods of treatment which must logically be sharply differentiated. The first is economic theory in the recognized sense, a study, largely deductive in character, of the more general aspects of economic cause and effect, those tendencies of a price system which are independent of the specific wants, technology, and resources. The second division, or applied economics, should attempt a statistical and inductive study of the actual data at the particular place and time, and of the manner in which general laws are modified by special and accidental circumstances of all sorts. That is, on the one hand it should get the facts as to the wants, resources, and technology in the situation to which the study is intended to apply, and the precise form of such functional relations as the general theory cannot describe more accurately than to say for example that they are "decreasing"; and in the second place it should ascertain and take account of facts and principles too special in character for the general theory, or which are not matters of general agreement. The argument of the third section of this paper should prove that this branch of the science is subject to very narrow limitations; the data lack the stability, classifiability, and measurability requisite to scientific treatment, and actual economic practice must as we have argued be at least as much an art based on wide general knowledge and sound judgment as a science with accurate premises and rigorous conclusions.

The third division of economics is the philosophy of history in the economic field, or what some of its votaries have chosen to call "historical" and others "institutional" economics, studying "the cumulative changes of institutions." In so far as it aspires to practical utility it will endeavour to predict long-period changes in the factors which applied economics accepts as data and attempts to observe and use as bases of inference. As far as can be seen now, this third division, even more than the second, is a field for the exercise of informed judgment rather than for reasoning according to the canons of science. The movements of history are to be "sensed" rather than plotted and projected into the future.

Within the compass of the first division of economics, that of economic theory, there is a practically limitless number of problems and points of view which may afford bases for separating independent variables from dependent. But we can distinguish some four or five levels in the stability of data, corresponding to stages in the causal sequence, causes at one stage becoming effects of more general ·and stable causes at the next. First. The price situation *at a moment* is the resultant (as far as it can be explained in terms of general forces) of a tendency to equilibrium between offers to buy and offers to sell, all of which are based upon speculative opinions. Neither the actual supplies of goods nor the ultimate demand operate *directly*; they act only indirectly in so far as the facts control the opinions of the traders, which opinions fix the prices. In highly organized markets there is a fairly effective focusing of the real speculative opinions of the persons who have any active interest in the market. In the great bulk of consumption goods there is no well-organized market, and the price at any time and place is subject to influence within rather wide limits on each side of the true competitive level by a wide variety of accidental and special factors, especially by "monopoly" in divers forms and degrees.

Second. For most commodities there is a more or less definite production period or interval within which the supply available in the world market at least will not be much affected by price changes. As regards agricultural crops the period is sharply fixed. As regards manufactured goods it is less definite, but there is usually relative stability of supply for some period, though it may be much more quickly responsive to price changes in one direction than the other. In any case the phenomenon of a period within which supply is fairly unchangeable is general enough to justify recognition of a theory of price with reference to it. For this problem the physical quantity of supply available, or for which commitments have been made, is the supply datum, and the demand curves of the ultimate consumers are the constants on that side of the price adjustment.

Third. For longer periods of, say, a decade, the situation is more complex. The supply of any particular good is obviously a dependent variable, responsive to price forces rather than causal of them, through the shifting of productive power from one industry to another. But for such periods the total productive power of society may be treated as roughly constant (or subject to considerable change only from causes outside the regular workings of the price system). Also the population and its consumptive habits, the distribution of wealth, knowledge of technical methods, and the like may be viewed as *reasonably* independent variables. These, then, are the "causes" which control and in terms of which we explain the "dependent variables" with reference to this period, the prices of goods and of productive services and the apportionment of productive power among different industries and of product among different persons. Within such a period the extent to which productive power can actually be moved about, and at what cost, depend upon causes special to each individual situation and about which no generalization can be made.

The largest reservation called for in assuming the fixity of the data controlling production and consumption over a period of years relates to the permanence of wants. As the standard of living rises, the economic interests of people are transferred more and more out of the sphere of fundamental needs into that of aesthetic and social gratification and pure experimentation. Thus wants become more unstable and as a result the interest of producers is centred more in the field of arousing wants or changing them to fit particular products and less in the field of studying wants and producing goods to fit them. Yet although the bulk of the national expenditure now has little relation to strict physiological needs if social and aesthetic standards were to be disregarded, it is still true that most of it fits into a fairly stable set of cultural values. Only over longer periods, of generations, do the fundamental social standards and ideals change greatly. The study of such long-time changes would seem to be the most conspicuous task of institutional economics, though similar reasoning applies in a not much smaller degree to changes in the other fundamental factors of the economic situation. No one would belittle the importance of studying these historic movements in the general structure of social standards and relations which presents the fourth level stage in economic causality. But neither, we think, can anyone contend that such a study should displace the other branches of economics which either are fairly independent of institutions or take them as they are at a given time and place and use them in explaining the immediate facts of economic life.

The prospect of actually predicting the historical changes of institutions does not, as we have repeatedly observed, look very promising to us. The possibilities seem to be restricted to two main lines of approach. Institutions might be treated as entities on their own account and internal, inherent laws of growth and change found in them, which could be projected into the future. This sort of independent change, of an animistic character, is not in favour with the modern scientific mind, for the reason presumably that experience generally shows changes to be "explicable" in terms of relations to larger, more fundamental changes, in a sequence leading back to geologic and astronomical causes. This is the other alternative, to explain human culture and its movements in terms of general laws of nature and of biology, as already suggested. The work of Buckle represents perhaps the most thoroughgoing attempt yet made in this direction, and his leadership has not produced much of a school of followers. The theories of natural selection and the materialistic interpretation of history have had hard sledding and have not got far, even in explaining the past, nor anywhere in sight of the goal of power to predict. The fact seems to be that man is at heart a sentimentalist, as far, in general, as he can be and live, or at little farther. Only the animals are really "sensible," knowing what is good for them and doing it. The formula which will predict changes in the motives and conduct of men, either by discovering an internal law or by relating them in some determinate way to the predictable facts of nature, is not, we believe, likely to be discovered soon. The statements that "history repeats itself" and its equivalent, that "human nature is always the same" are true, in a sense. But it is a sense that cannot be defined, and such a sense that definite inferences drawn from the principle are more likely to be false than true. Trained judgment and human insight seem to be more effective in predicting the future than any discoverable law, and that is not going very far.

So our argument is chiefly a recital of the limitations set by the nature of the data upon the scientific treatment of human problems in general and those of an economic character in particular. In the realm of physical nature the exact methods of science have carried understanding and control enormously farther than common sense could go. But this was because the data are relatively stable, reducible to classes of manageable number, and especially classes with recognizable and measurable indices. None of these essential features seem to hold good of human data. Moreover, in any deep view of the case, the problem of understanding and controlling human behaviour is radically different in character from that of explaining the material world and using it. Physical objects are not at the same time trying to understand and use the investigator! The practical problem of getting along with our fellow human beings must be attacked in the main by a method very different from the technique of natural science, a different kind of development and refinement of common sense, which carries us rather into the fields of aesthetics. In a limited field in economic data, due largely to the fact that exchange has reduced the factors to definite measurable quantities, we can have an exact science of the general form of relations. It can tell us little in the concrete, and its chief function is negative—to offset as far as possible the stupid theorizing of the man in the street. The real sociology and economics must be branches of literature as much as of science. In fact they need to be both, and commonly succeed in being neither. It is no wonder that these sciences are still in the stage of violent disagreement among their followers as to what they are and what they are about. The first step toward getting out of this slough, we suggest, is to recognize that man's relations with his fellow man are on a totally different footing from his relations with the objects of physical nature and to give up, except within recognized and rather narrow limits, the naïve project of carrying over a technique which has been successful in the one set of problems and using it to solve another set of a categorically different kind.

V

MARGINAL UTILITY ECONOMICS*

The founders of modern utility theory are generally recognized to be W. Stanley Jevons, author of *The Theory of Political Economy* (1871), Karl Menger, author of *Grundsätze der Volkswirtschaftslehre* (1871), and Léon Walras, the first instalment of whose *Eléments d'économie politique pure* appeared in 1874. These three men, working independently and belonging to different branches of European culture, came practically at the same time to the same position. Yet the central doctrine of marginal utility, now one of the most familiar in economic theory, was not a new discovery made by them or by any other writer usually associated with the marginal utility or Austrian school. After the work of the founders received general recognition, numerous statements of similar doctrine, varying in clearness and elaboration, were found scattered through the earlier literature. Some were by men who had been recognized in their day on other grounds, others by men who had died unheard of. If the most pathetic case is that of Gossen, the strangest is that of the famous economist Senior. This thinker, characterized by brilliant insights and inability to build upon them, not only stated the utility principle but especially emphasized its main consequence, namely, that cost affects price only indirectly through supply; yet he worked out his value theory as a whole on the Ricardian principle of subjective cost, without incorporating this premise. The utility theory had apparently to wait for the "fullness of time" and to be stillborn many times before it could live.

At the present time marginal utility analysis, in one or another of its numerous variants, is firmly established in the economic thought of all important countries. The country where utility theory first rose to dominance is Austria, hence the identification of "Austrian school" with marginal utility doctrine. The great triumvirate of Vienna, Menger, Böhm-Bawerk, and Wieser, were the first to sketch in the

* Reprinted from *The Encyclopaedia of the Social Sciences*, edited by E. R. A. Seligman. By permission of The Macmillan Company, Publishers.

main outlines of the new theory; they enlisted an imposing array of followers including Sax, Philippovich, and Zuckerkandl, and trained a number of younger economists of whom Schumpeter and Hans Mayer are probably the best known. In Germany utility theory encountered opposition from the historical school, which was rapidly attaining prominence after the middle of the nineteenth century. Menger found himself therefore fighting the battle not merely of marginal utility but of the "exact" deductive method in social science; and allied with him was Dietzel, an economist who was nearer to the classical theory than to the Austrian school. The opposition in Germany was overcome only very slowly; not until after the war did marginal utility receive its full share of academic recognition in that country. In France the ground for utility theory was prepared by the writings of Condillac and J. B. Say. Although the mathematical performances of Walras met with disfavour, the theory was not forced to fight for survival; yet except for Walras French economics made no significant contribution to the theoretical exploitation of the utility principle. Italian economists, led by Pantaleoni and Pareto, took up particularly the mathematical variant of the new theory. Among other continental writers of the marginal utility orientation must be specifically mentioned Wicksell in Sweden, Pierson in Holland, Birck in Denmark, and Bilimovič in Russia.

In the English-speaking countries the acceptance of marginal utility was a reaction from the theories of the classical school, which had dominated economic thought since the publication of Adam Smith's *Wealth of Nations* (1776). In England the new theory was popularized by William Smart, the translator of Wieser and Böhm-Bawerk, and P. H. Wicksteed, a follower of Jevons. Despite an obvious reverence for the classical tradition and no less pronounced coolness toward Jevons, Marshall was even more responsible for the acclimatization of a modified form of marginal analysis in England. In the United States, where classical doctrines were not as strongly entrenched, Carey's influence was on the wane when utility theory found a thoughtful and original exponent in J. B. Clark. The other American writers with marginal utility leanings are Patten, Fetter and Irving Fisher, all of whom made original contributions on the specific problems.

It has always been recognized—it could not fail to be, as soon as the phenomena came under scrutiny at all—that a thing must be desirable in order to have power to command value in exchange. But the Smith-Ricardo school considered desirability only a condition of exchange value; they rejected it as a determinant of value on the empirical ground that there seems to be the widest discrepancy in fact between the usefulness of commodities and their prices. Smith cited the example of water and diamonds, previously used by Locke and Law; Ricardo, that of gold and iron. Dismissing utility as a cause of price, they fell back upon cost, which likewise had necessarily been recognized as a factor from the beginning of speculation on the subject. Smith believed that in a primitive state commodities might be expected to exchange on the basis of labour costs, and that in a developed exchange economy the cost which determines price consists of the money payments made by producers for the labour, capital, and land necessary to produce a commodity. Ricardo's highly abstract mind disliked the pluralism of Smith's treatment and his failure to integrate arguments proceeding from different standpoints. He conceived the idea that the theory of value could be made simple and unitary on the basis of labour cost alone. Several difficulties stood in the way, of which the most important were the roles of land and capital in production. The surplus theory of land rent, which had been stated by Smith, Hume, and Anderson and was getting recognition through West and Malthus and according to which rent is the effect and not a cause of price, seemed to Ricardo to remove the difficulty in the matter of land and was therefore used by him as the corner stone of a new system. If Ricardo was dissatisfied with the assumption of uniform capital outlays in various branches of production, the device by which he got rid of capital as a major cause of price differences, Senior's concept of abstinence, reduced capital cost to homogeneity with labour cost in terms of subjective sacrifice. After him the formulation of value theory on the basis of sacrifice cost remained unshakable down to the "revolution" inaugurated by the marginal utility theorists. Yet the recognition of "non-competing" strata of labourers by Mill and Cairnes made it impossible longer to take the labour cost theory literally. At the same time the classical theory of distribution, also built around the surplus theory of rent, was placing an increasing strain on every mind free from prepossession and was virtually abandoned in J. S. Mill's overhauling of the classical system. When Mill also recanted on the wages fund theory, the wreck was so complete that a new start became inevitable.

In formal statement the new doctrine of Jevons and Menger seemed revolutionary indeed. It explained price in terms of utility, summarily rejected by the writers of the old school, and squarely inverted the accepted relation between cost and price by holding cost to be derived from price and not its cause. The key to the change of view was the recognition of the homely fact that commodities are esteemed not in accordance with their significance in general, but with that of any small unit of the available supply. All the units of any commodity being alike, that unit which is employed for the most important use can be replaced by the unit in the least important employment, and an equal value must attach to both. Hence the effective use value of any good decreases rapidly as the supply increases, and the paradoxes seen by the earlier writers vanish. The use value of a unit of either water or iron is very small, because it is so abundant that it is available for trivial uses; but it would increase almost indefinitely if the supply were reduced, while gold and diamonds would be little esteemed if abundant.

This conception of the use value of the single unit of a commodity, determined by the importance of the "last" unit, or the unit in the least important use, is now generally called "marginal utility," Smart's rendering of the German *Grenznutzen* of Wieser (in his translation of Wieser's *Der natürliche Werth* in 1893). The term was not used by any of the founders of the theory. In his paper delivered before section F of the British Association in 1862 (reprinted in 4th ed. of the *Theory*, pp. 303–14) Jevons called it "coefficient of utility" and in the book of 1871 "final degree of utility." Menger's term was simply "importance," that of Walras, "rarity." Jevons and Walras defined the notion with quantitative precision, using the mathematical theory of infinitesimals; Menger spoke only of units or portions as understood in everyday usage.

In attempting to explain price in terms of marginal utility the Austrian theorists encountered considerable difficulty when they found that the utilities of articles of the same price must be very different to rich and poor buyers. The difficulty was really imaginary and was due to reasoning in terms of absolute rather than relative utilities. Jevons saw and emphasized the truth that the doctrine of utility determining price involves only comparisons by each individual buyer for himself of the different uses for his purchasing power large or small; no comparison as between one individual and another, whether of utilities or disutilities, is called for.

From explaining price on the basis of use value as in turn dependent on scarcity, it seemed a natural step to reason that where goods come into existence through production, as most of them do, the means of production, or cost goods, will be valued to the same extent as the products to which they give rise and on the same principles. Any one unit of a productive resource will be valued in accordance with the least important unit of product for which it is available, i.e., according to the satisfaction actually dependent on its use. It is due primarily to Menger that the foundation was laid for a new approach to the valuation of "indirect goods," "goods of higher order," or productive resources. Jevons had a deeper insight at some points but did not break away from the influence of the older British approach completely enough to develop his theory of supply systematically, and the later Austrian writers became confused over side issues. The values of production goods constitute at the same time the money costs of production and the incomes through which product is distributed. The fruits of the new viewpoint were ultimately greater in the field of distribution than in that of the explanation of price.

As regards price theory, critical reflection soon revealed that the revolution was by no means so great as it appeared to be from the change in form of statement. On the one hand, men found a great deal of utility theory implicit in the treatment of the classical economists; and, on the other, there was much cost theory in Jevons and Menger. Smith argued that if in a primitive community it costs twice as many days' labour to kill a beaver as to kill a deer, then one beaver will exchange for two deer. With reference to this statement two observations must be made. The first is that if the labour is not of the same kind, freely transferable from one occupation to the other, the reasoning loses all force and meaning. The second is that the reasoning is valid not only for labour but also for any other cost good, such as an acre of ground, which is freely transferable from one employment to another. If the society for any reason has its choice between definitely limited amounts of two commodities, the above reasoning will still hold without any cost being involved. The real argument, not stated by Smith but necessarily implied, is that value depends on amount produced, producers being supposed to employ the resources in the production of the more valuable product. Far from being opposed to the utility principle, the cost theory presupposes its operation at every moment of the adjustment. It is clear also that Ricardo and his successors were fully aware of the role of demand. On the other hand, both Menger and Jevons saw, the latter the more clearly, that if price depends on utility as determined by scarcity, then scarcity in turn is generally the result of the high cost of production. Jevons gave the utmost typographical prominence to the words (*Theory*, 2nd ed., p. 179):

Cost of production determines supply;
Supply determines final degree of utility;
Final degree of utility determines value.

The essential achievement of marginal utility in price theory was that of forcing a new realistic approach to the problem as a whole, centring attention upon the behaviour of actual human beings in competitive relations, each attempting to make the best of his situation in the buying-and-selling economic system. In this marginal utility theory was really following the example set by Adam Smith. Ricardian economics ran in terms of a sort of metaphysical necessity; the actual workings of competitive processes in bringing about the results contended for were assumed rather than clearly expressed, and for this reason much error as well as misplaced emphasis crept into the statements.

The greatest improvement introduced by the marginal utility viewpoint came in the field of distribution theory as a by-product of the changed view of cost. The classical Ricardo-Senior-Mill theory of distribution was utterly unrealistic. It did not consider the problem as one of the valuation of services furnished to production, under competition or monopoly, but as a matter of the successive slicing off of the social income by the three main economic classes found in the society of post-feudal Europe. Smith and Malthus, basing themselves upon an entrepreneur cost theory of price, afforded clear intimations of a realistic approach, but the building of a pain-cost theory of value around the pillar of the residual theory of rent threw all into the discard. It was the truly revolutionary contribution of the utility approach to force consideration of costs and distributive payments as integral parts of one general valuation problem, which has been gradually recognized as that of explaining economic organization under the influence of price facts and motives of individual self-interest.

In the formulation of explicit laws of price the utility theorists were no nearer the truth than the classical economists. The case of the deer and the beaver itself proves that the classicists were wrong in so far as they held that pain-cost has anything essential to do with price fixing. But prices are no more determined by psychological utilities than psychological disutilities. The essential principle is that producers choose the larger return from any productive activity irrespective of its being painful, pleasant, or indifferent and that amount produced in relation to demand fixes prices. When any two commodities can be produced with the aid of the same resources of whatever sort, freely transferable from the one use to the other, the prices of those commodities must in equilibrium be such that the alternative products of the same or equal units of resources exchange for each other. Price is determined by cost rather than utility but by cost in a physical, technical sense, not that of pain or sacrifice.

Comparisons of sacrifice, however, may be and commonly are involved in greater or less degree, and the operation of the utility principle is the basis of the whole process of adjustment. This is the alternative cost theory which is definitely the product of the utility approach. But alternative cost requires much explanation and qualification to fit it accurately to the facts of economic life. The reasoning assumes that all productive resources are freely and continuously transferable from one use to another, so that, as more of one good and less of its alternative are produced, the amount of the latter given up in increasing the output of the former by one unit remains unchanged. But this condition of constant cost rarely describes the situation exactly. In general, some of the resources are freely transferable, others not; and frequently some factors are available only in very large blocks, so that the most efficient organization requires very large-scale production. The first condition will give rise to increasing cost, and the latter to decreasing cost in the earlier stages of expansion of an industry. Given an indefinitely long time for readjustment, including changes in form of capital, retraining of labour, and whatever else may be involved, the law of constant cost is not far from the truth. Under such circumstances utility determines quantities produced but cannot affect the final equilibrium price. On the other hand, the factors of production are hardly transferable instantly in any degree; for a very short period the condition approximates that of fixed supply. In so far as this is the case, price is determined by the relative utilities of the supplies as they stand, cost exerting no influence at all. Problems actually encountered fall between these two limits; the longer the period over which one looks ahead, the greater the extent to which prices at the end of it will correspond to physical cost conditions and the less the role of utility. For ordinary producers' calculations the role of cost is certainly far the greater, but the actual quoted price at any moment, the price at which consumers buy from dealers, reflects rather the demand conditions, supply being "given." The influence of relative utility as compared with that of relative cost depends on the comparative elasticities of the two curves. In the short run, supply is highly inelastic and demand conditions predominate; in the long run, supply generally has practically infinite elasticity and predominates over demand, the latter being always of intermediate elasticity.

Where increasing cost is due to the more intensive exploitation of the non-transferable factors with increasing proportions of factors drawn in from without, utility and cost work together in determining price, the relative influence of each depending on the elasticities of the two curves. Where increasing cost is due to the fact that production depends on cost goods of special qualities, the supply of which is actually an increasing function of price, the price may be said to depend on the effects of both utility and cost, the latter in the sense of disutility. In general, however, the supply of labour is little dependent on disutility considerations; nor is the supply of capital for short periods, since it is an accumulating good. Moreover, labour and capital are employed so generally over the field of production that changes in the supply of either have to be very extensive to exert much influence on the relative supply of different commodities and hence on their prices.

The Austrians admitted the effect of cost on price through control of amount produced held that cost is finally measured by the value of cost goods, which is derived from the value of products, and hence that utility finally controls price. The premise may be accepted as true, but the conclusion is fallacious. In so far as the costs of two commodities consist of different quantities of the same cost goods, these costs are relative physical magnitudes and are not measured by utility; this condition is much more typical for costs generally than that of distinct factors producing distinct products.

Similarly in the field of distribution the utility theorists gave the correct approach but in formulating the general principle fell into confusion. It is true that the distributive shares are simply the values of the productive services and that these are derived from product values. But in the effort to make utility the sole explanation these writers tended to argue as though different cost goods have different products or groups of products. In so far as that is true, the values of the cost goods may be said to reflect the relative utilities of the products. But the general situation is rather that ultimately all the productive resources cooperate in making each product. Hence the relative "utilities" of units of different resources depend on the relative physical quantities which they respectively contribute to each product. This sets the problem of imputation (*Zurechnung*), the division of a joint effect among cooperating causes.

Imputation was discussed by the Austrians at great length, but they reached no agreement among themselves and did not arrive at a clear and sound analysis. Here the first attempt was the best. Menger gave a fairly clear, if brief, sketch of the process of competitive imputation based on the essential fact that, while the factors almost always have to cooperate in production, any single one being practically ineffective alone, the proportions in which they are employed are variable, this makes it possible to divide the product of their joint activity among them by finding the effect of substituting a small quantity of one factor for a small quantity of another. Most of the school failed to see that the proportions are in fact variable almost without physical limit and that the producer's problem is precisely that of deciding upon the correct proportions of factors along with the problem of fixing the output for the enterprise. The main difficulty was that economists as a class had remained ignorant of the fundamental logic of quantitative variation applicable to problems of joint causation, which had been worked out in connection with physical mechanics a century or more before. The way out was pointed especially by Marshall in England and J. B. Clark in America. The purchase of productive services by entrepreneurs follows exactly the same principles as the purchase of final products by consumers. The complementary relationship may be present or absent in either case. Buyers substitute small quantities of one productive service (or commodity) for small quantities of any other until they arrive at such proportions—varying from buyer to buyer—that they obtain from the last unit of each productive service (or commodity) equal additions to the final product (or to "total satisfaction"); competition sets all the prices in such a way as to clear the market.

The problem of interest presents a special difficulty in distribution theory, because the payment takes the form of an abstract arithmetical rate and not of a specific sum for the use of a concrete productive instrument. Ricardian economics had discussed the share of capital in the social income but had done nothing significant toward explaining the return as a rate, and the problem became a favourite one with the utility school. While Jevons made a brilliant attack on it, which was never adequately appreciated, Menger's work was very weak at this point. Böhm-Bawerk made it his main life work (*Kapital und Kapitalzins*, 2 vols., 1884–9) and under his influence and stimulation notable work has been produced in America (Fetter, Fisher, and others). As Böhm-Bawerk interpreted the problem of developing a theory of interest in harmony with marginal utility principles, it involved refuting productivity and use theories as well as Senior's abstinence doctrine (which Senior unaccountably never employed to explain the rate of interest but only the role of capital in connection with the prices of goods) and explaining the phenomenon in terms of a difference in subjective appreciation of present and future goods. Some critical students think this is what Böhm-Bawerk actually achieved. Undoubtedly a more general view is that, after almost a thousand pages of prolix argumentation, he gave in a few pages a none too clear but reasonably correct statement of the productivity theory, somewhat vitiated by the admixture of the wages fund view of the relation between capital and wages. The utility approach does not necessarily call for a psychological explanation of interest, in such terms, for instance, as the discount of future satisfactions; the simple theory that interest is a ratio between the net value product of capital goods and their money cost, as held by Wieser, would seem to be quite adequate.

It is generally claimed that the marginal utility doctrine and movement is responsible for two contributions of great scientific value. First, it focused attention on demand, which had been passed over and taken for granted by the Ricardians. In this connection the importance of its contribution cannot be overestimated. Demand has ever since been recognized as the driving power behind economic activity and economic organization, although generally physical cost relations exercise a much greater control over the superficial fact of exchange ratios. In the second place, it is claimed that utility theory carries the analysis of demand beyond the surface facts of quantity and price, that it "explains" demand. On this issue there is wide disagreement and the keenest controversy. On the one hand, some form of marginal utility theory is almost universally presented in textbooks, and it seems impossible to discuss economic behaviour in a utilitarian civilization without using utility concepts. On the other hand, the theory is not merely rejected by able critics as unreal and preposterous; it is in fact a favourite point of attack for the enemies of abstract theoretical economics as such.

The issue involves all the philosophical problems connected with the concepts and methodology not merely of economics but of all the sciences dealing with man. The utility theory should be seen as the culmination, historically and logically, of the rationalistic and individualistic intellectual movement of which the competitive economic system itself is one aspect and modern science and technology are others. To its admirers it comes near to being the fulfilment of the eighteenth-century craving for a principle which would do for human conduct and society what Newton's mechanics had done for the solar system. It introduces simplicity and order, even to the extent of making it possible to state the problems in the form of mathematical functions dealt with by the methods of infinitesimal calculus. Moreover, in harmony with eighteenth-century cravings, it claims to furnish a guide for social policy; it can be harnessed to the very practical purpose of proving that if only the state will limit itself to the negative function of defence against violence and predation and leave men free to pursue their own interests, individual self-seeking directed by market competition will bring about a simultaneous maximum of want-satisfaction for all concerned, which in this world view is the desideratum back of all thought and activity. The utility theorists were contemporary with Herbert Spencer and were philosophically his comrades in arms.

The reaction against utility theory is in part the natural reaction against the view of the world and of man which it embodies, in favour either of a more spiritual or less mechanistic view or one less apologetic and more radical; but in part also it is a reaction in precisely the opposite direction, toward more "scientific" conceptions. Under the first banner march those critics to whom the "economic man" is a caricature or a calumny or both. Some insist on treatment in terms of organic social purpose, historical forces, or culture patterns. Others insist on a degree of freedom and spontaneity or of realism in detail that would exclude any treatment except the recording of events as they happen and their imaginative interpretation. Of some of these protesters it must be said briefly that they do not understand either the logic or the purpose of the utility analysis. As a matter of course, the utility description of behaviour as an affair of comparing and choosing is valid only in so far as men compare and choose; no one in his senses has thought of it as the exclusive form of all activity in all historic time. More specifically, the "patterning" of interests does not invalidate the principles of utility analysis at all, so long as substitution is possible through varying proportions; and that is clearly the fact over a considerable field, whatever its precise extent may be.

In the more rigorous versions of the theory, however, there is an element of paradox and unrealism. The notion of increments of satisfaction undoubtedly implies that the value of life as a whole is some definite increasing function of the quantities of the various means of satisfactions available, which hardly agrees with common sense. It also implies the well-known consumers' surplus a quantity of free satisfaction representing the difference between what is paid for goods at the uniform market price per unit and what an omniscient monopolist could theoretically make the consumer pay by selling to him successive small portions at the maximum price for each separately. It would be hard to locate this free satisfaction in the consciousness of a typical consumer. It is necessary at least to distinguish sharply between valuing goods as increments to a supply of goods and valuing them as increments to a total satisfaction. In fact, the entire theory is much more convincing in the loose, common-sense formulation of Menger than it is in the more refined mathematical version of Jevons and Walras.

Critics of utility theory from the opposite direction contend that it is subjective and unscientific and advocate a treatment of economic phenomena by statistical methods using only physical magnitudes, quantities, and prices. They deny that utility explains demand or adds anything to the demand curve or schedule taken as a fact. Logically, they can put up a strong case. The analogy of utility theory with Newtonian principles does not stand up well under examination. In mechanics, if the forces are not directly accessible, at least the conditions under which they act and the effects are measurable and do repeat themselves accurately from one case to another. In economic behaviour the opposite is the case. Under no real circumstances can the behaving subject himself, not to mention any outside observer, ever know even afterward whether or not he actually performed in such a way as to realize maximum possible total satisfaction; and it is even less possible to repeat the choice experimentally with controlled variations. Indeed, on the basis of knowledge gathered from one's own experience and intercourse with others it seems that men do not balance alternatives correctly. All that can be claimed is that there is an effort to do so, with more or less approximation to this result; but the introduction of error into the reaction puts the whole relation on a categorically different basis from cause and effect in nature. On the other hand, the advocates of a purely statistical science do not seem to realize that economics, if it is to have any relation to human problems of means and ends, must be concerned with goods and services not in themselves, but as representing values or sacrifices. These cannot be treated as physical things but must be defined in the same vague and shifting terms as the human impulses, successes, and failures which the scientific mind finds such unsatisfactory material.

STATICS AND DYNAMICS*

SOME QUERIES REGARDING THE MECHANICAL ANALOGY IN ECONOMICS

THE frequency and familiarity with which the terms static and dynamic are used in economic literature contrast somewhat strangely with the paucity of discussion of their meaning, and the comparative abundance of argumentation regarding the necessity for such a distinction throws into even stronger light the lack of effort at clear definition. Marshall's usage is typical; he constantly uses the terms static and dynamic, and kindred expressions like *caeteris paribus* and "unchanging general conditions of economic life," and repeatedly insists on the importance of clearness in regard to them; but he nowhere offers a complete list of the static data, or "other things," or attempts a clear statement of the principles at issue. There are exceptions to this procedure of course; notably the work of J. B. Clark, Schumpeter, and the mathematical school of Walras and his successors. It is not the intention in this paper to go through the literature, or selected specimens of it, and give a detailed criticism. Neither is there any serious pretence of supplying in a positive, constructive way all that seems to be wanting. The aim is merely to raise certain questions, without attempting to give the final answers.

The terms statics and dynamics are of course borrowed from theoretical mechanics. Most of the writers who have used them were no doubt aware that the analogy of economic theory to mechanics is subject to limitations, like all analogies. Schumpeter, indeed, explicitly remarks (*Wirtschaftliche Entwicklung*, p. 75) that there is no connection with mechanics, which we suggest is as far from the truth as an assumption of complete parallelism. There is a real and important relation, or the words would not have been taken over, and the

---

* Translated from "Statik und Dynamik—zur Frage der Mechanischen Analogie in den Wirtschaftswissenschaften," *Zeitschrift für Nationalökonomie*, vol. ii (1930), pp. 1–26, and reprinted by permission.

constant use of the concepts of friction and inertia is additional proof
that the analogy of mechanics exerts a large influence on the thinking
of economists. It is from this standpoint that we approach the subject;
the mechanical analogy seems to deserve a searching examination and
an effort to clarify some of the questions involved in its use.

The root idea in economic statics is clearly the notion of *equilibrium*,
and hence of *forces* in equilibrium. At the outset we are confronted
with the fact that critically-minded physicists have always felt the
notion of force objectionable. From Newton down they have regarded it as metaphysical and unreal, and have struggled to eliminate
it from their conceptual systems. It seems to be unquestionable that
for reflective common-sense (if these more or less contradictory terms
may be used together) there is a repugnance for action-at-a-distance,
and a strong urge to find explanations in the strictly mechanical terms
of impact. Manifestly this question cannot be followed up here.
We merely note that the "mechanical" theories of gravitation and
other forces have never taken root in physics, and that the role played
by potential energy seems to make the elimination of metaphysical
forces out of the question. The significance for thought of the new
approach to the whole problem through relativity theory is not clear,
even if the new theories receive such verification as is possible, and
the analogy which is significant for economics is certainly that of the
older Newtonian mechanics; indeed engineers will undoubtedly
continue to use the old concepts, whatever may happen in a certain
narrow realm of theoretical physics. Our point here is that in using
the mechanical analogy the notion of force is involved and that it is a
most troublesome one in its original context.

As compared with mechanics, the notion of force will be much
more or much less troublesome in economics according as any particular thinker leans toward one or another type of psychology,
which is to say one or another world-view. The student with a
materialistic and hence a behaviouristic bias who cares about consistency had perhaps better give up at once such notions as force and
tendency and equilibrium, and restrict the matter of his discourse to
statistical trends, correlations, etc., in the field of physically measurable
magnitudes. That is, he will practically cease to talk of human beings
and their wants, sacrifices, and satisfactions, and deal exclusively with

commodities and prices. This indeed is what a good number are doing at the moment—with whatever it may be of clearness as to the logical basis of the urge back of the movement. If terms like equilibrium and tendency are used in such a system it must be in the sense of statistical modes and mathematical limits, which is not the meaning they have in general usage. For the non-materialist, whether idealist, dualist, pluralist, or what-not, so long as he considers it possible and important to speak intelligibly about mental life, the idea of force in human behaviour is clearer and more real than in nature. For the human analogue of force is motive, and men do assume (when not trying to prove a contrary theory) that they have some knowledge of motives, from personal experience and intercommunication with their fellows, and this contrasts with the inaccessibility of any such knowledge regarding forces in inanimate nature.

In mechanics, change or process means motion, and analogically we speak of social processes as movements. The simplest case of mechanical equilibrium is that of the mutual cancellation of two or more forces (velocities?) giving complete rest. The economic analogue is the equilibrium of a market in which no economic process (ex-change) is induced. As soon as we consider the process by which such an equilibrium is established, we enter the field of dynamics, and the basic problems involved in the use of the analogy of mechanics are forced upon the attention.

In an experimental set-up to illustrate mechanical equilibrium, the forces unavoidably act through things having mass—weights or springs—and hence act upon these masses as well as upon each other. If friction could be eliminated from such a system it would never actually come from any other position to a stationary equilibrium, but would perpetually oscillate or move around some circuit which could be represented by an equation. With friction present, in addition to inertia, as it always is in an actual case, important distinctions have to be made, as there are different kinds of friction. With friction of the sort presented by solid bodies in contact, the system, released from any point other than that of theoretical equilibrium, may remain at rest, or if it moves it will come to rest. But the point of rest and nature of the movement toward that point will vary widely with the character of the friction (relation between standing and moving friction) and its magnitude relative to the inertia of the system and the degree of disequilibrium of the starting-point. Details are irrelevant here, but damped oscillation is one significant possibility. The actual point of rest might be the theoretical equilibrium point, but that result is highly improbable.

Another type of friction is that represented by the resistance of a fluid to motion of a solid through it, which depends on its density and viscosity. If our experiment is performed with the whole apparatus suspended in water or mercury or molasses, the point of rest will be that of theoretical equilibrium, with or without oscillations, even though its motion may be indefinitely slowed down. A case more or less intermediate between solid and liquid is presented by sand or shot.

These cases suggest questions which it seems the economist might profitably examine. It is crude at best to attribute any continuing divergence of conditions from those of theoretical equilibrium to "friction" as economists generally do, since the theory of a frictionless system calls not for equilibrium but for perpetual oscillation. This, however, assumes the presence of inertia, and raises the question of the relation between friction and inertia, or their possible analogues, in economics. It seems that the analogy in the mind of economists in discussing the tendency toward equilibrium is that of movement against a viscous friction, with inertia absent or negligible. The presence of a significant amount of inertia would mean a tendency toward oscillation, and a careful study in the light of this analogy of the tendency toward cyclical swings so common in economic phenomena, might be both theoretically illuminating and practically significant. If the economic behaviour of an individual has the nature of response to any condition which in turn responds to the behaviour but only (for whatever reason) after a certain interval or lag, the first response will naturally go too far and set up oscillations. In the second place, the difference between viscosity friction and that between solid surfaces might well prove suggestive also.

Philosophically, the possibilities of inquiry along the line of a serious working out and carrying over of the mechanical analogy, and determination of its applicability and limitations, seem to the writer most alluring. Large results would of course depend on genius in the investigator, or slow development through discussion. We should remember that it required roughly two and a half centuries (Galileo to Meyer, Joule, and Rankine) for physicists to work out a clear definition of their fundamental concept energy. In the background of course is the ultimate problem of psychology, especially the role of conscious deliberation and effort in comparison with automatic response. Traditional economic thought has occupied a sort of middle ground in this regard; it accepts deliberation regarding means as real, but treats ends as given in the situation and argues that deliberation regarding ends (which common sense accepts without question) is "really" deliberation regarding means. An objectively scientific view, of course, takes the further step and argues that all deliberation is "really unreal" at least as to making any difference in the process or result; in this view, conscious states are, at most, "events" in a certain time-space configuration, along with physical changes, but without any more dynamic quality. The question seems to boil down to the nature of *error*, and its correlate, effort. The scientific urge is against this notion, craving automatic exceptionless uniformity, i.e., an ultimately unchanging as well as passive nature of things.*

In the basic "economic law," of uniform price in a market, the assumption is perfect knowledge of conditions on the part of all economic subjects. It is surely conceivable that study might show to what degree the "resistance"—ignorance, prejudice, etc.—which prevents the facts from conforming to such obvious tendencies is really analogous to inertia or friction of the different types. The universal and unavoidable use of the terms friction and inertia in describing human responses shows that they have scientific and not merely analogical significance. The concepts, however, need to be sharply differentiated, as the law in the two cases is different; a force acting against (viscous) friction produces motion at a speed proportional to the force; acting against inertia it produces motion accelerating at a rate proportional to the force.

Whatever we conceive to be the "force" back of human behaviour, whether conscious interests, or "real advantage" (conceived bio-

* The working postulates of orthodox economics are those of British utilitarianism, given classical expression by Hume; it is assumed that men may be mistaken as to means but not as to ends. The question may be raised whether the notion of physical force does not like that of motive involve contingency, a kind of error, which would explain its repugnance to the scientific intellect.

logically, hedonistically, aesthetically, or ethically), or merely the physical situation of the organism, the project of a proper mechanics of the process forces upon us a number of interesting questions. Mechanics runs in terms of three ultimate dimensions, time, space, and mass (which is supposed to have a more empirical standing than force), and to these must be added in application to reality the different types of friction as already noted. Only the time dimension seems to carry over directly and be available for use in such a field as economics. Yet it appears that we cannot reduce the economic process to quantitative terms unless we can give workable meaning to space and to mass, and to space not merely in the aspect of measurable distance, but in that of direction as well. We do constantly speak of direction in economic changes and even of degrees of opposition or parallelism; when the notion is made precise it is that of "angle" between changes. Perhaps it will some time be possible to use the notion of a "field" of social force and process in a definite sense which might be represented by coordinates. Perhaps the notions of momentum and energy and their respective laws of conservation, so vital to physical thinking, have real analogues in the competition of the market. In mechanics action and reaction are equal; a force produces equal momentum (though not equal energy) in opposite directions. In mechanics, friction converts a measurable quantity of mechanical energy into an "equal" quantity of heat though momentum is conserved. If such relations cannot be interpreted, it would seem advisable to find some way of avoiding the mechanical analogy and developing a less misleading terminology.

It will be observed that most of the discussion so far has really dealt with dynamics; not the abstract conditions of equilibrium (an equalization of forces acting in all "directions") but the nature of changes (movement) toward equilibrium have been considered. This procedure should serve to emphasize a fundamental contrast between the use of terms in economics and in mechanics. The discussion should have made it clear that no science of economic dynamics exists, as it could not exist prior to a definition of elementary magnitudes and units such as just suggested, and this is so far from accomplishment that the suggestion of its possibility probably strikes the reader as strained or fanciful. At best it may be said that the statistical economics now being prosecuted with so much zeal in various quarters might yield data for some of these definitions, though the inquiries are not consciously oriented toward any such general scientific aim. In actual usage economic dynamics, or dynamic economics, has become merely a critical and negative term to refer to the limitations of "static" analysis, or more exactly to any particular author's objections to any other author's use of the equilibrium concepts. Its least vague usage is that of a sort of catch-all for stressing changes in given conditions in contrast with adjustments to given conditions. In practice it suggests an insistence that there are no given conditions, which view if consistently maintained would mean that there are no predictable reactions and that science is impossible. This issue cannot be discussed here; the only answer in any case would be to point to the "history and prospects" of economics. Our concern is with definitions of concepts, and our present point is that there is no economic dynamics in the meaning the term should have if it is to be used at all. Economic literature includes no treatment of the relations between measured force, resistance, and movement. What it calls dynamics should be called evolutionary or historical economics. Mechanics, conversely, has no place for evolutionary categories; it assumes constancy in its ultimates, believing (until recently) that mass and energy are "really" neither created nor destroyed. In any case the general properties of materials are unchanged in mechanical transformations.

Our next task is to call attention to a certain relativity in the notions static and dynamic and attempt to define with some care the important stages or terms in a series of economic processes in which relatively more stable conditions, i.e., conditions undergoing slower processes of change, serve for theoretical analysis as a framework or setting of given conditions with reference to shorter-period adjustments. These shorter-period adjustments, then, have the character of "tending" to establish equilibrium with reference to their respective given conditions at any given time, though with a certain lag due to the fact that the latter are also in fact continuously changing. Due primarily to the influence of uncertainty or ignorance of the future, which is associated with changes in the conditions in which economic subjects act, many other disturbances and maladjustments ensue, in addition to the time lag. With regard to the final stage in the series, we shall have to inquire more particularly as to whether the longest-run processes which the economist has to consider have the equilibrating character, and hence whether the problem of economic evolution or progress can be given the form of a problem in dynamics. In the interest of clearness as to the nature of the relations and adjustments involved, we first call to mind some of the uses of the notion of equilibrium in connection with natural phenomena.

At first sight the idea of static conditions may seem to be merely that of *caeteris paribus*, but a little reflection will show that frequently much more is involved. It is true that the study of the causal relation, or correlation, between any two magnitudes which are involved in an interrelated system requires that the other be held constant. In the more precise language of mathematics, causality is a functional relation involving a large number of variables and the relation connecting any two, when separable at all, is a partial. derivative which is a function of all the others and at best can only be stated independently by giving each of the others some fixed value. In a general case the relation of dependence may be mutual for all the variables in a function. But in real examples the relation is not typically mutual and elements which are to be treated as variable and those which are to be treated as fixed cannot be chosen arbitrarily. Equilibrium in nature is generally a phenomenon of adaptation in a real sense; one group of factors adapt to another group (as well as to each other); as between the groups, the adjustment is predominantly or wholly in one direction; rather typically, particularly in economics, the framework factors themselves are in motion independently, as already suggested, dragging the adapting group behind them instead of moving to meet the latter.*

* All the possible types are met with in economics. The relation between price and cost illustrates an adjustment which is mutual as to direction of movement but with such a difference in speed and range that it is generally justifiable to say that cost of production "determines" price and not inversely. Changes in the cost of any one commodity reflect the relative movement of all competing industries using the same resources in production, and hence are likely to be small in comparison to the change in price in the process by which the two are brought to equality. It seems inevitable and correct to speak of the relatively fixed magnitude as cause, as we say the level of the water in the ocean controls that in the bay, or that the earth attracts the falling apple, or that we tie the boat to the bank, even though the relation is mutual.

The most common example borrowed from nature to illustrate static equilibrium in economics is that of water tending toward its level. Here there is no room for question as to the separation between the process and its setting, between the factors changing and the factors in relation to which they change. The "given conditions" are (1) the quantity and fluid properties of the water and (2) the shape and size of the drainage basin or system of interconnected containers in which it is free to move under the influence of (3) the force of gravity. What is variable is the position of the water or the various portions which make up its fluid mass. (The illustration is also in point in connection with the questions raised in the first part of this paper, the analogical meaning of gravity and inertia and the various sorts of friction and of the actual character of the process which might take place under slightly different conditions.)

What interests us here is merely the character of an equilibrating change. There is a fixed or presumptively fixed sort of conditioning factors and a process which moves toward a state of rest by establishing equilibrium with relation to the given conditions. The prevalence of this general type of situation in the world is striking. The wind, for another example, results from a disequilibrium in the atmosphere, a difference in pressure corresponding to the difference in water level, and its blowing operates to equate the pressure and bring the process to a stop. Electric current is a similar flow from high to low "potential." All the movements and processes of ordinary observation seem to represent a flow of energy "down hill" and toward a level at which it would be at rest. Most of them are finally derived from the redistribution of the solar heat energy, which itself gives every indication of having the same character. Its flow perpetually maintains the disequilibria which causes the flow of water and air, and hence the phenomena of life. The fundamental cosmic mystery is the origin and destination of a universe which science pictures as an irreversible reaction. (If the analogy of a frictionless system holds, the solar energy must complete a circuit sometime, in some way, but that is not our problem here.)

In economics we are chiefly concerned with equilibrium not as a state of rest but as a *process* in equilibrium, with a slower process forming the "given condition" within which a more rapid one takes place and tends toward a moving equilibrium. Thus the flow of solar energy and the form, position, and movement of the earth condition the complete circular process of evaporation of water from the ocean and its return flow thither through the streams. This circular process is in equilibrium when the amount of water reaching the sea is the same as the amount leaving it by evaporation, and, when at every point in the complex circuit, the quantities arriving and leaving are equal, the flow neither expanding nor contracting. It is obvious that after any change in the solar radiation or any of the numerous other given conditions, all of which do in fact undergo changes, a considerable interval must elapse before equilibrium will be established. It follows that the system never really is in equilibrium ("moving equilibrium") at any point; but its tendency toward such a state is the main feature to be made clear in a scientific description of it. (The role of friction and inertia in producing a lag in the adjustment of processes toward a moving equilibrium with their given conditions is considerably different from the case of tendency toward stationary equilibrium, but the differences need not be elaborated here.)

In economics, as previously remarked, this general type of relation is exemplified in a series of stages. The notion of a series of "cases" in price theory, extending from short-run to ultimate long-run is especially familiar in the great work of Marshall, who recognizes four main "cases" in his price theory.* Some modifications of his results appear necessary in the light of a systematic survey of the material from the special viewpoint of the principle here under discussion; detailed contrast between our cases and Marshall's is not called for, but a few significant divergences will be noted in passing. There seems to be a hiatus in his series at the very beginning, at the short-run end. His scheme does not take sufficient account of the fact that in the actual fixation of the prices of commodities which have a highly organized market and a definite price at a moment, the market is made and the price at any moment fixed, not by owners of supply and prospective consumers (as is assumed also in the mathematical systems), but by a class of professional traders who come in between these primary groups. This fact makes it needful to introduce an additional

* *Principles of Economics*, book v, chap. v, especially sec. 8.

stage in price theory, with its own given conditions and position of equilibrium.

In the wheat pit of a grain exchange, for example, the given price-determining conditions at any moment are the opinions, dispositions, and financial power of the various traders. Actual demand by consumers, and actual supply alike, are outside of the market and operate only indirectly, through the opinions of traders as to what these facts are and are likely to be in the future as far ahead as they attempt to predict. The variables in the situation are the price and the distribution among the traders of claims against each other to deliver or accept the commodity. The total volume of such claims, or the amount in the hands of any individual, bears no determinate relation to an actual quantity of wheat or to any physical or human reality. The condition of equilibrium is simply that the price and distribution of claims be such as to make the total effective buying disposition equal to the total effective selling disposition, measured in bushels, relative to traders' attitudes as they are at the moment.

Over a longer period, roughly bounded by harvest-time in the main wheat belt in the case of this commodity, the opinions of traders are no longer data in the price situation, but themselves perpetually tend to "equilibrate" in relation to the facts of physical supply and consumers' demand, and to carry price with them. These facts therefore become the data for a different equilibrium or "normal," the price for the season as a whole. These data are properly separable, as those of the former case were not, into conditions of "supply" and of "demand." Producers or actual owners of wheat and its consumers are distinct if somewhat overlapping groups, and possession of wheat and need for it are distinct facts, which is not true of buyers and sellers in the speculative market or of the motives which determine their role one way or the other. Demand now includes the purchasing dispositions and purchasing power of all users of wheat, including present owners, measured for the season or unexpired part of it, while supply is the amount of wheat in the market as a whole, practically the wheat-consuming world. (Allowance for carry-over and for overlapping of seasons in different regions may for brevity be ignored.) For other things than agricultural crops, the "season" is indefinite, but there is a period within which relative unresponsiveness of supply to price changes is an important given condition in price fixation. The variables for this second case, of limited period with fixed supply, are the price and the distribution of the supply over the season and among the purchasers. The condition of equilibrium is that the price be such as to distribute the supply over the season and among consumers in accordance with the principle of equalization of marginal utility ratios with price ratios over the entire field.

Over a still longer period—in general a period of a few years—supply cannot be treated as a datum, but is one of the chief variables in the situation, and the same is only less true of the incomes of purchasers. This brings us to the thorny question of what is more or less properly called *the* static economy, the problem of defining the conditions under which economic life will have continuity but not growth, production and consumption running along in a uniform volume, and without change in general character. As remarked at the outset, the essential feature of such an economy, to make it most useful as a tool of analysis, have received surprisingly little intensive consideration. The task presents serious difficulties; in fact it is impossible to give a rigorously accurate definition for either unchanging volume or unchanging character of economic life without departing so far from reality as to make the significance of the treatment dubious.*
Yet the notion may be both real enough and definite enough to be useful, even though a certain element of arbitrariness in definition must be accepted. We can only give our own formulation with a brevity which must seem dogmatic, but may serve for illustration.

The main given conditions of statically continuous economic life fall naturally, first, into the categories of (1) wants and (2) means of satisfaction, the latter meaning the ultimate resources of produc-

* Rigour would demand a community of immortal individuals who never learn nor forget and never change their minds or tastes, absolutely standardized commodities and implements and processes of production, and resources which can neither be increased nor used up nor misapplied. In the mathematical treatments, one would expect such rigour. In fact these authors assume rather a sort of statistical uniformity which sacrifices realism without achieving the definiteness needed in deductive theory. Moreover, their systems of equations strive rather ineffectually to get beyond a general *a priori* instability for any position of the system other than that of perfect equilibrium. They are not seriously to be compared with the equations of mechanics which show the magnitude and direction at any point of stresses associated with disequilibrium, and of their resultant.

tion.* Under productive resources, again, it is inevitable to separate (2-A) actual "things," human beings and other physical agencies, from (2-B) the general level of "culture" in its aspect of economic productive power. This latter in turn includes technology (2-B-a) in the narrow, external sense of physical and chemical processes and the like, and also (2-B-b) in the human sense of the technique of business organization. This sub-classification involves much overlapping, especially since technical development logically inheres in human beings, their traits and capacities; but such an enumeration seems necessary for clearness.

In addition to these main groups of data, certain further conditions have to be constant. Not merely the total supply of productive resources but also (3) the distribution of their ownership, including both external goods and personal capacities, must be unchanging. (4) Monetary conditions must be specified in some form (which is hard to do very realistically, since a constant price-level cannot be defined and under frictionless conditions any system "tends" toward indefinite inflation). (5) Finally, it must be remembered that in several

* This "Austrian" view that the quantities of the productive services are fixed under any given conditions cannot be defended at length here. It is not rigorously true to fact but is as nearly exact as any other general assumption in economic theory. The amount of any productive service forthcoming is theoretically affected by a psychological factor and relative irksomeness, odium, etc., must be taken into account when any productive resource is transferred for one use to another. But in the writer's opinion the classical economists seriously confused the "cost" to a nation or individual of its income as a whole, which is properly pain or sacrifice, with the "cost" of any particular unit of commodity which determines its price. The "pain" of labour and abstinence as a general fact has virtually nothing to do with price determining cost. In theory relative pain is an element in price, since it is an element in cost, but in fact labour is notoriously paid rather in inverse than direct ratio to pain, showing that the role of pain is insignificant. The supply of labour in any use is, like that of other factors, a matter of the relative attraction of competing uses, and to a quite negligible degree a matter of the general supply price of the factor.

A more serious objection to the view taken herein relates to the unrealistic character of any classification of the productive factors. Manifestly the classes are not only indefinitely numerous, if one thinks of effectively homogeneous types whose units are really interchangeable, but shift their boundaries with the lapse of time. In the ultimate long run any human being or thing with productive qualities practically without limit has to be replaced or renewed and can be replaced with something else (a thing of other qualities) embodying the same "quantity" of abstract "investment" on the one hand and "productve capacity" on the other. In a broad sense they are practically all capital. An examination which cannot be given in detail here would show that these facts do not essentially affect the argument. The productive factors are merely allowed whatever freedom of transformation they actually possess along with movement from one field of use to another. Any classification implied relates to the situation after equilibrium is reached.

regards an exchange system is incapable of standing alone; many economic functions have to be carried on or controlled by society as a unit, that is, by the government. Hence public policy in its various phases (which need not be enumerated—the whole political, legal, and moral system is involved) must be included among the constants of the economic system. In particular, the state must be assumed to exclude or set fixed limits to the creation of monopolies or the use of monopoly power.*

So much for the given conditions of the static economy. The variables in the process of establishing equilibrium are three: (1) The prices of final goods and services; (2) the prices of productive services (including a quasi-rent on intermediate goods somewhat in excess of maintenance and replacement charges passed on to other resources); (3) the allocation of productive resources among industries and among enterprises within each industry. (The "distribution" of final products among those who supply productive services is taken care of by the prices of the services and ownership).

The conditions of equilibrium are all included under two parallel statements of marginal equalization—aside from the fact that all income is expended in consumption, which is included in the definition of the static economy. These statements are: (1) prices of final goods and services are set at such levels that consumers in behaving

* Constancy in many respects would be secured for the static economy concept by assuming habitation on the part of the people. But this is hardly consistent with economic behaviour.

One of the most interesting controversial points regarding the static economy can only be mentioned here. That is Schumpeter's view that all capital-goods would be completely analysed into land and labour and would as capital-goods receive no income (interest or quasi-rent). It seems to the writer that under any realistic conditions as to wants and conditions of supply, goods requiring a longer time to produce must have greater value for the same expenditure of ultimate resource-services other than time. The supply of "time" in production is limited by the supply of consumable goods in general, and it must command a price unless all goods are free and the conditions of economic life consequently non-existent. Cf. Böhm-Bawerk's criticism of Schumpeter, *Zeitsch. f. Volkswirtsch., Soz. u. Verw.*, XXII; also article by E. von Beckerath, *Schmollers Jahrb*, Vol. 53. We agree with Schumpeter (and others—Pantaleoni and Wieser) that apart from the influence of interest itself there is no general preference of present to future satisfactions and no occasion for assuming such in the static economy. To make the conception realistic we must imagine a natural stationary equilibrium of the capital supply, such as the stationary state contemplated by J. S. Mill, the interest rate being sufficient to prevent the consumption of capital already saved without bringing about further saving.

economically (i.e., expending their incomes in such a way as to secure equal increments of utility from equal expenditures) exactly exhaust the supplies of all goods produced; (2) the prices of productive services are set at such levels that producers (entrepreneurs) in behaving economically (expending their respective productive outlays, i.e., costs, in such as to secure equal product increments of equal market value for equal outlays) exactly exhaust the supplies of all productive services (the supplies forthcoming at the prices offered, if one does not assume the supplies fixed).

Inspection will show that these two statements involve several other conditions. It is mere repetition to observe that production costs in money are equal to prices of goods, and productive resources receive (through "imputation") product increments equal (in price) to the productive increments they contribute at the margin. The phenomenon of "rent" in the ordinary meaning is taken care of, since it makes no difference in principle in the workings of the competitive process whether any type of productive service is used in making many products or in making only one—though it makes a difference no less than inversion in the causal relation between the payment for the service, as a cost item, and the price of the product (if a productive resource is used in industries generally, its remuneration is a cause with reference to the price of any one product; if it is used in only one product, its remuneration is an effect of the price of that product). Competition between entrepreneurs in the same industry (making a given product) fixes the price paid for the service at the value of its productive contribution just as effectively and in the same way as if the competition is spread over any number of industries. The only case not explicitly provided for is that in which the entire supply of a productive agency is a monopoly in the hands of a single entrepreneur, where in fact the distributive share would be a residuum merely. Other monopolies of particular markets, of products, and of productive processes, as such, corners, etc., we exclude here for brevity.*

* The static economy pictured here is one in which all economic processes are absolutely continuous without expansion or contraction. It may be observed in passing that the conception is not affected by cyclical periodicities in conditions, such as the succession of day and night or the seasons, alternation of productive activity and consumption, etc., provided that ultimate repetitiveness is realized and

We now arrive at the fourth and final step* in the series of longer-run processes, each providing a setting or framework of conditions theoretically treated as given, to which shorter-run processes tend to adjust themselves so as to establish equilibrium. The first was price-fixation by traders in a speculative market; the second price fixation by producers and consumers in a market where supply and demand are given for a limited period; the third was the case of continuous production and consumption of unchanging volume and general pattern; after this comes the problem of growth and change. (We may say simply "growth," assuming, according to custom, that both qualitative and quantitative changes represent improvement.) The particular question which concerns us in this connection has to do first with the "equilibrating" character of these longest-run, secular or historical, changes which constitute growth and second with the applicability of mechanical notions and terms to the treatment of these changes. We must see clearly what the changes are and what is their setting or given conditions—which now take us outside the sphere of economic phenomena—and inquire whether the correct

all changes are fully foreknown and taken into account in the economic behaviour of all persons affected. In many connections the uncertainty which is associated with change is more important for economic theory than the change itself. This suggests that regular continuous growth might also be admitted in the static economy as such growth would not involve unpredictability (cf. Schumpeter). We raise no question as to the legitimacy or importance of studying a society in which growth is present but uncertainty absent and where consequently the ideal of marginal equalization of returns in relation to outlays of every sort is continuously realized. This admission does not affect the significance of the different separation made above, between a (perfectly adjusted) society with growth absent and with growth present. As to the term static economy, it seems relatively more suitable to the concept pictured here—to the elimination of growth rather than the elimination of uncertainty. In strict conformity with the mechanical analogy, the term statics should relate, as suggested at the outset, to equilibrium in a commodity market.

* It will be noticed that we come out with the same number of main "cases" as did Marshall (see above, p. 170) although we inserted at the beginning the stage of the speculative market. Marshall's distinction between short-run and long-run normal price is omitted because it seems to us misleading to draw a general demarcation between fixed capital (human and non-human) and that which moves freely from one industry to another. Moreover, there is a more fundamental difference of view. Marshall refuses to treat the shorter-period adjustments clearly as *transfers* of fluid resources from and to other uses. That is, he refuses, in this and other connections, to separate sharply productive changes under static conditions, i.e., changes compensated by inverse changes in other industries, from changes which affect the social aggregate. This refusal, in our opinion, leads him into a number of errors, especially the error of treating land as categorically different from other capital goods. (cf. below, p. 180).

scientific treatment of economic progress should view it as in its turn a movement toward a position of stability in relation to the (extra-economic) conditions which form its environmental setting.

That the processes of economic growth do take place inside a world of conditioning circumstances is a fact which does not call for argument. To make a detailed list, however, separating economic changes from surroundings which do not change or change independently of economic events, seems to be an impossible task. It is one of the problems of economic science itself to discover and mark out its own boundaries. The demarcation would not be excessively difficult on the side of the physical universe and its laws, or that of man himself in the physiological sense, but on the side of psychology and social institutions it is much more forbidding.* In any event, the general idea is clear, and that is all that is needed here.

As to the variables involved in the processes, it is enough to say that those which call for discussion are, as in the earlier stages of the argument, those which were the data for the preceding stage. This list—the given conditions of a static economy also presented difficulties, as the reader will recall. With reference to the main factors, the fact of progressive change in the actual world is evident enough: the available supplies of (nearly all) the productive factors are increasing, technology and business organization are improving, and consumers' wants are expanding, and, we assume, being raised to "higher" levels. Our question is, are these changes properly to be regarded as resulting from "forces" which they progressively "equiliberate" and destroy, as the flow of water or air destroys the difference of level or pressure, thus advancing toward a condition in which the changes would cease. In this case we may be sure that economic growth is not being and will not be maintained by progressive change in the setting itself, creating disequilibrium as fast as growth

* In this connection we have again to face the important factor of one's conception of man's nature and place in the Cosmos. The "scientific" view assumes that changes in man can be completely accounted for in terms of external and prior natural conditions. A theory which recognizes ends and allows man real initiative in changing himself or his environment is in contradiction with a scientific conception of human nature and transfers the discussion to a different realm of discourse. In the writer's opinion the contradiction is insurmountable in the present stage of intellectual development. Philosophy and experience have not taught us concepts which enable us to think comfortably in the terms of what experience and common sense force us to recognize as real and valid.

removes it. If progress is a movement toward equilibrium, it must in the nature of the case be a stationary one.

The British classical economists, notably J. S. Mill, assumed economic progress to be an equilibrating process, and thought that the equilibrium was near at hand. Among a large group of economists to-day we meet with the opposite assumption in a more or less clear form, namely that progress is self-exciting and cumulative. It has even been argued by the historian Henry Adams that the law of economic advance is a geometric progression. The modern successors of the "classicals" have gotten away from the express assumption of the imminence of a stationary state, but we still find the discussion of long-run changes running in terms of a tendency toward equilibrium; the nature of the equilibrium and of the given conditions to which it relates are not clearly stated, and when examined seem to imply the assumption which has been formally dropped. The remainder of this paper will be devoted to a brief survey of the main long-run adjustments or elements of progress from this standpoint.

For this purpose it seems best to adopt a somewhat different classification of the progress variables (formerly the constants of the static economy). All the elements are bound up in man himself, as consumer, labourer, owner, or entrepreneur, and in discussing growth it is not convenient to separate sharply the different capacities in which the same individuals function.

We may begin with the element of population, i.e., with man "in the abstract," the bare fact of numbers. This of course is one of the favourite topics of the older economics and one which has always been treated in a way to exemplify the equilibrating principle. Recent discussion has been more cautious and has reacted far enough from the assumption that a given psychological standard of living controlling the birth rate is a fixed condition which, along with a total production of necessaries increasing much less rapidly than numbers, determines a definite equilibrium population and wage level.

The case appears to be an instructive one in a methodological sense. There can be no doubt that the natural principle of biological increase under given conditions (as affecting individuals) is a constant ratio (which might be a rate of decrease) or that the capacity of any area to support numbers of human beings is finite. In more obvious senses, the increase of population involves a sort of equalization of "forces," both in the direct sense of birth and death rates and more indirectly as regards motives and conditions underlying these rates. But to admit that "there are limits" does not validate the treatment of population as "approaching a limit" in the sense that the condition of equilibrium may be stated in terms of other conditions taken as given. The essential fact for emphasis is the interconnectedness of all the growth elements involved in economic progress over against all those of the conditioning environment. Each changing economic element is a condition affecting the change of any other element or its ultimate stability of position, just as the features of the non-economic environment are conditions; but the former cannot be assumed "equal." It therefore appears to be misleading rather than helpful to describe the growth of population as a tendency toward any describable state of equilibrium. An equilibrium must relate to economic progress as a whole, to every factor treated as given in the static economy, not to any single element, just as in the static economy equilibrium must apply to all the variable elements simultaneously. (For brevity we pass over the physical composition of population, age, and sex distribution, etc., where the notion of equilibrium has a special but familiar application.)

Turning, secondly, to the psychological traits of peoples, we notice as the first growth-element the expansion of wants. The common assumption is that this is a cumulative rather than an equi-liberating tendency. The assumption need not be questioned as fact under modern conditions, though it is easy to see how a wave of any of several kinds of social-psychological contagion might nullify predictions based upon it. Any careful discussion of wants should also place in the foreground the fact that it is commonly the social implications of goods that are wanted rather than goods themselves, or their direct physical effects on the individual. Other psychic traits, such as knowledge, skill, personal energy, and morale, relate to man as producer rather than as consumer and in fact comprise the element of technology and business organization. Industry, or energy, and morale seem, like population, to be subject to an ultimate limit; they seem to approach a practical perfection (assuming that they do advance). Knowledge and skill present an interesting problem. There is surely a limit to what any individual can learn, or learn to do. A group, however, seems to remove the limit by specialization; but specialization calls for co-ordination, which is undoubtedly subject to increasing cost. In America the increasing proportion of the population which the census shows to be earning their living by telling others what to do is already a theme for viewers-with-alarm. In connection with the moral factor the bearing of knowledge may raise questions; business management may yet have to take seriously the poet's dictum that a little learning is a dangerous thing.

Looking at these psychological traits from a more strictly economic standpoint raises the question of cost. Even if it is maintained that progress in this field is "natural" (in accordance, for example, with the Darwinian principle of selection of favourable spontaneous variations), it can hardly be denied that most of the change which we see taking place is the effect of deliberate effort and expenditure, partly by society and partly by individuals, and in both cases largely under the influence of the expectation of an economic return. Again it is difficult to see how an equilibrium analysis can be realistically applied. The cost laws involved in this branch of "production," and the closeness of association between bearing the cost and receiving the return, present interesting problems too complicated to enter upon here. The production of changes in human nature is also affected by an especially high degree of uncertainty, the human attitude toward which is difficult to rationalize or to discover empirically.*

Coming now (3) to material productive resources (exclusive of man himself) economists have traditionally made a categorical distinction between the natural and the artificial, between land and capital goods. By definition, obviously, land would be fixed in supply for all time; in that direction there could be no growth; the land supply would be one of the permanently given conditions constituting the setting for progress, an extra-economic datum. However, the distinction between land and capital goods was never clear and has been

* Theorists generally assume that uncertainty is a psychological cost, but the evidence from gambling, gaming, and the like and that from "risky" types of business also, seems to the writer to run in the contrary direction, other things being equal. If it is attractive on the whole, in comparison with a fixed, known reward equal to the true actuarial value of the contingent one, then the average return to investment in advertising, for example, should be below the general average rate.

more and more called in question. It is difficult to define any actual category of natural agents the supply of which, known and available for use, has not been produced at a cost in work and waiting or will not similarly be increased in the future (though this may not hold for a particular politically bounded area). The surface of the earth is ultimately limited, but is not and is not likely to be in itself a factor limiting economic activity or growth. It appears to us, moreover, that on the one hand it is both impossible and futile to go back in time to the origin of resources, that is, to the advent of man on the earth, while on the other hand at any given time all resources are equally "ultimate," except on the other hand at any given time all resources are equally "ultimate" except in so far as they are known to be perishable and to require replacement.

To state our own position briefly, the facts seem to be that while most of the productive agencies in use at any time require maintenance and replacement, there are some which require only maintenance and a few perhaps which do not require even that. If the service of agencies which wear out are to be continuously available, a part of their earnings has to be set aside as a replacement fund. Under static conditions, as intimated above (footnote, p. 174), the matter would take care of itself. Every agency (i.e., its owner) would receive its current imputed product, out of which would be paid to "other agencies" whatever might be necessary (if anything) for permanent maintenance and replacement, only the residue being net income available for consumption. (Ultimately, the net residue is a payment for waiting, or more accurately for time itself.) The distinction between maintenance and replacement really has no particular significance, and would practically disappear in a static economy. In a progressive economy the supply of productive agencies is increased by saving and investment, in accordance with the principle that equal investments yield equal increments of perpetual net income (or actuarial probabilities of such, or more, or less, depending on one's theory of uncertainty). It is true that some productive agencies may be more freely multiplied than others, and there are various degrees of uncertainty and other differences. At the growing point or margin natural resources analyse into two elements, a cost of discovery, which is essentially the "production of knowledge," already discussed, and a cost of development, which is the same as any other investment of capital in the production of things under known conditions.*

This brings us to growth of capital as a general fund, embodied in particular goods, or ideas, but contrasting with any particular example of the latter. This is, of course, the problem of saving and investment, to which frequent reference has previously been found necessary. Avoiding the general problems of the theory of capital and interest, our question is whether accumulation is to be treated as an equilibrating process, and if so, what are the conditions of equilibrium. The neo-classical treatment of the interest rate typically proceeds from the proposition that it is a price and like other prices expresses equilibrium between supply and demand. This may have either of two meanings, referring to equilibrium under the given ("static") conditions, or implying that the process of economic growth really moves in time toward a condition in which the interest rate would be permanently stable. Not uncommonly the two views are confused in the same statement, especially in the sense that supply is assumed to be subject to growth, while the demand (general conditions, not absolute amount demanded) is assumed to be constant. An intersection of a demand curve with a curve of rate of increase in supply is of course meaningless.

Moreover, both the short-run and long-run equilibria, when clearly formulated, are in our opinion misleading and practically fallacious. This is so in the short-run because the supply of capital at any given time, like that of concrete factors, is virtually fixed (and variations to which it may be subject are dependent on other things than the interest rate), while the amount demanded depends upon the rate, and may vary substantially from zero to infinity if the rate is high or low enough. Hence the interest rate at a moment in a perfect capital market is a matter of the demand, the demand price for the given supply. The long-run case is more properly in question here, and

* This analysis of land into knowledge and capital goods may be contrasted with Schumpeter's analysis of capital goods into land and labour services, referred to above.

The only peculiar condition is that this particular field of knowledge seems to be in a somewhat special sense exhaustible, that there is a theoretical limit when the resources of the earth would be fully known, and in that sense this line of growth is equilibrating. (Nearly any scientific discovery is really and in economic significance an addition to the known resources of the earth as in another view it is an addition to technology, a human quality.)

more important. We may illustrate by Marshall's statement:"Thus then interest . . . tends toward an equilibrium level such that the aggregate demand for capital . . . is equal to the aggregate stock forthcoming . . . " (*Principles*, p. 534). His reasoning apparently is that saving is motivated by interest and that the accumulation of capital must bring down the interest rate (diminishing returns) and hence that the process will finally come to rest at a point at which the return is inadequate to induce further net saving. The essential fallacy we find in the argument is that other things which must be assumed equal not merely are not but cannot be, that accumulation itself has other effects than the equilibrating one, some of which work in the opposite direction. One such effect is that as new savings are invested the income derived from them reduces the difficulty of saving at the same time that incentive is reduced. It would seem to be impossible to say, *a priori*, which effect would predominate or to assert that if everything else remained unchanged saving would cease before capital became entirely a free good (which, as already observed, could not happen until all goods became free). In addition, we must note a further, less direct effect, that abundant capital and low interest rates stimulate invention, the general tendency of which is to elevate the demand-curve for capital. Moreover, the activities of invention and discovery themselves absorb capital (apart from that used in constructing and developing the results) and in this employment the law of decreasing returns seems to work in a slow and uncertain way.

In connection with these reverse influences must be noted the high rate of accumulation which we actually find in the contemporary world, with the absence of any clear tendency either for accumulation to slacken or the interest rate itself to fall. These facts alone would make the theory of a tendency toward equilibrium questionable, and prove that at least that condition is indefinitely remote in time, giving "other things" indefinite scope for action.

For methodology, the point is that the "other things" or "given conditions" assumed as the setting for any particular process form an interconnected system, while the process is also one of a number forming a similar system. For very small changes it is admissible to assume that while any element or condition changes, the others in the same group remain fixed. But in discussing trends over any consider-

able period of time this must not be done. The greatest caution needs
to be exercised in determining and specifying the systems of constants
or long-period processes, and of variables adjusting to them (and to
each other), if the notion of tendency toward equilibrium is to yield
sound results.

In regard (4) to the distribution of ownership of productive
capacity, specified as a constant in the static economy, the long-run
tendency would appear to be, as in the case of the expansion of wants,
definitely cumulative as opposed to equilibrating. Ordinary economic
forces tend toward a progressive concentration. Wealth does breed;
"to him that hath shall be given, and from him that hath not shall be
taken away." If such a trend is not empirically prominent, it is because
of various sorts of deliberate social interference, equally numerous
"accidents," and perhaps factors analogous to those which make any
large mass unstable. However, beyond a certain point again, other
things cannot be equal; the possessor of a vast fortune, especially if it
has been inherited, can hardly have the same motives and interests
as one just achieving business success.

Our general conclusion must be that in the field of economic
progress the notion of tendency toward equilibrium is definitely
inapplicable to particular elements of growth and with reference to
progress as a unitary process or system of interconnected changes
is of such limited and partial application as to be misleading rather than
useful. This view is emphasized by reference to the phenomena
covered by the loose term "institution." All speculative glimpses at
trends in connection with price theory relate to a "competitive" or
"capitalistic" economic system. But all the human interests and traits
involved in this type of economic life are subject to historical change.
Moreover, no society is or could be entirely and purely competitive.
The roles of the state, of law, and of moral constraint are always
important, and that of other forms of organization such as voluntary
cooperation may be so. Business life in the strictest sense never
conforms closely to the theoretical behaviour of an economic man.
Always history is being made; opinions, attitudes, and institutions
change, and there is evolution in the nature of capitalism. In fact
evolution toward other organization form, as the dominant type

begins before capitalism reaches its apogee. Such social evolution is rather beyond the province of the economic theorist, but it is pertinent to call attention to the utter inapplicability to such changes, i.e., to history in the large, of the notion of tendency toward a price equilibrium. Probably we must go further and reject entirely the use of the mechanical analogy, the categories of force, resistance, and movement, in discussing basic historical changes.

VII

COST OF PRODUCTION AND PRICE OVER
LONG AND SHORT PERIODS*

GREAT difficulties are met with in stating a clear and straightforward exposition of price theory because of the fact that the given conditions or data of the problem are so different according to the length of the time period which the explanation takes into account. The forces which immediately regulate prices are different from those which ultimately control, and there are degrees or stages in both immediateness and ultimateness. The average student of economics is likely to be quite baffled by these distinctions and to get no clear ideas at all; but he is still more baffled by differences in degree, where distinctions are not sharply drawn and statements are left in the form of "it depends." This paper looks rather to the problem of exposition from the standpoint of the student than to the correction of errors in accepted doctrine, but the course of the argument will have to note cases in which current phraseology is misleading to unwary readers if it does not represent fundamental misconceptions on the part of economists themselves.

I

The most familiar device for separating certain short-time and long-time aspects of economic problems is the fiction of the "static state," and our first critical duty is to raise serious question as to this conception in its current form. The writer doubts whether its popularization has represented an advance in clearness of ideas or a service to the science. Passing over the technical point that there is no discoverable analogy between the meaning of static and dynamic in economics and their established meaning in mechanics, our objections are more serious. All science is static in the sense that it describes the unchanging aspects of things. There is no sense in making statements that will not continue

* Reprinted by permission from *The Journal of Political Economy*, vol. xxix (1921), pp. 304-35.

to be true after they are made. The possibility of saying anything about a thing rests on the assumption that it preserves its identity, or continues to be the same thing in the respect described, that it will behave in future situations as it has in past. The essential fact in economics is that different changes take place at different rates, that for certain time periods certain aspects of the situation may be assumed to remain unchanged, while for longer periods some of these will undergo change. The data or given conditions are different when different periods of time are under consideration.

It may not, however, be true, and generally is not, that the different changes can be completely separated in this way. The effects of long-period changes are not generally in fact practically negligible over the shorter periods. But scientific treatment, in view of the mere limitations of the human mind and the necessity of considering one thing at a time, is forced to treat the separation as absolute. We must ascertain the separate effects of the different causes and combine them after we understand them. This would have to be done just the same if the causes did not generally operate in different periods of time, but the latter fact greatly simplifies our thinking. It is more realistic and intelligible to isolate a short-period effect, abstract entirely from perturbations due to the operation of more slowly working forces because for short periods the effects of the latter are in reality relatively less important. There are thus, in fact, as many "static states" as there are economic problems worth studying. All that is really involved in the static method is the use of analysis, the assumption in studying the effects of any one cause that the operation of other causes does not interfere.

Another serious confusion in connection with static hypotheses relates to the conception of equilibrium. It is true practically if not altogether without exception that the changes studied by any science tend to equilibrate or neutralize the forces which bring them about, and finally to come to rest. The simplest example perhaps is that "water seeks its level"; the movement is always the effect of a difference in level and its result is to obliterate that difference and come to a stop. In the same way the wind is caused by a difference in air pressure, the transfer of radiant energy is due to a difference in temperature, of electricity to a difference in electrical potential, and so forth, the change or movement in every case being of a character to equilibrate the forces which cause the movement.

In consequence of this fact it is a practical necessity to describe the action of any force by stating the *final* condition which it tends to bring about, the conditions under which it would cease to work. Any other description is partial and arbitrarily so. The only complete or logical procedure is to state the ultimate goal of the tendency in question. Such a statement or description does not imply at all that this final condition is likely to come about. When we say that the movement of water or air is of such a character as to obliterate the stresses which produce the movement we do not mean that these movements are likely soon to cease on the earth, just as we define north as toward the North Pole without implying that everything moving northward is bound for that goal. The final effect of even a short-period change may be an indefinite distance in the future, involving the practical certainty that in the meantime the original cause will change in character or cease to operate or be interfered with by innumerable other causes; it may be never so improbable that the final result will ever be reached, yet the proper and only proper way to describe the situation at the moment is to state a "tendency" toward this theoretical final result.

The static method therefore involves two fundamental but badly confused ideas. The first is simply that in describing any change it is assumed that "other things are equal." The second is that changes are described by stating the condition of affairs to which they would lead if they continued without interference until they equilibrated the forces at work and came to a natural end. These principles are the same in economics as in mechanics or any other science which attempts to predict effects from the knowledge of causes. Goods move in response to price differences from points of low to points of high price, the movement tending to obliterate the price difference and come to rest. Productive services are shifted from one field of use to another in response to differences in remuneration and the transfer tends to bring the remuneration to equality in all fields—to produce equilibrium.

After a considerable amount of experimentation the writer has tentatively settled, for instruction purposes, upon a division of the problem of explaining prices into four, or possibly five, stages, relative to the time length of the changes to be discussed.* In all these stages or "cases" the general principle is that price is adjusted to the point at which supply and demand are equal. They differ in that supply and demand have different meanings, especially the supply. The first stage in the explanation is to state the character and condition of equilibrium of the forces operative at a given instant of time. Here the motives of both sellers and buyers are based on speculative considerations, the former entirely and the latter almost so. Supply and demand are both functions of price, meaning that the amounts that sellers will offer and the amounts that buyers will take depend upon the price. In general, sellers will offer more and buyers take less, the higher the price. The reason is that the higher the price the less is the likelihood that it will go higher and the greater the likelihood that it will go lower in the immediate future. In the primary markets, where prices are determined, this is the only consideration in the mind of sellers, and the buying is also almost entirely speculative. For the moment the demand for goods for *immediate* consumption is practically negligible, and purchases are determined by opinions as to the probable course of prices in the near future.†

* This division differs from Marshall's four cases in important respects which will be developed at length. My five-fold division corresponds more closely to his four-fold one.

This article discusses the problem of the explanation of price. It is appropriate to say that I think we have talked rather too much about prices as such, and should strive to keep more in the foreground the forces which are measured by prices and the changes which they bring about. The real subject-matter of economics is the organization of production and consumption. The desideratum is to get students to see how in our social system, in so far as it is based upon private property and free contract, consumption is controlled by the prices of finished goods, how these prices are translated through entrepreneurs' calculations into price offers for productive services which control the utilization of the productive resources of society, and finally and most sadly neglected of all, the circular character of the whole process. The pecuniary demand for goods has little relation to their objective human significance. It depends on the existing distribution of ownership and opportunity and the facts as to consumers' tastes, both of which are largely moulded by the workings of the system itself.

† The situation in the market at a moment is represented by the familiar demand and supply curves. In the writer's view these gain enormously in reality and clearness by taking price as the base line, the independent variable, and interpreting the price point as the point where the amount offered is equal to the amount taken. (See Diagram I.) This is the procedure of the so-called mathematical economists. American textbooks generally plot quantity of goods horizontally and price vertically in order to make the demand curve identical with a curve of diminishing utility (utility as a

II

The second stage of the explanation deals with the production period for the good. From this point of view the supply is fixed and is on the market without reserve. The data are not sharply definable, but in general there is a fairly definite period within which supply is fixed. The situation is clear enough in the case of an agricultural product such as corn or wheat. Taking the season as a whole there is no possibility of a change in the supply between the time when final commitments are made for one season's crop and the time when the next crop becomes available. The growers may indeed market less of the crop, using more themselves, if the price is low, but if so* the fact is exactly like increased consumption by non-producers under the same circumstances. If the demand of the producers themselves is taken into account at all it should be regarded as demand and added in with the demand of non-producers, and not treated as a deduction from supply. In this case the suggestion made by Davenport† seems to be by far the most realistic manner of viewing the situation. The demand from the standpoint of the production period as a whole is the consumer's demand and is a decreasing function of price, represented by the same sort of curve as in the former case. The supply curve (again taking price as the independent variable) is a horizontal straight line. (See

function of supply). When it is remembered that utility in the sense in which it influences price is *relative* utility, measured in terms of money, the value of the utility analysis for explaining price becomes somewhat problematical, especially for purposes of elementary exposition. It is not clear that such utility curves add much to the mere statement that purchases are a function of price. Certainly they have to be translated into curves of purchases as a function of price before they are usable, for a utility curve can at most represent the facts for a single purchaser. There is no possibility of comparing or adding utilities for a group of individuals differing in taste and in income, and the only way of representing the *social* facts is to add the amounts of the good which different individuals are willing to purchase at the different prices.

In any case utility calculations are nearly negligible in relation to price at a given moment, since prices are fixed in primary markets where purchases are made far in advance of actual consumption. Purchases in advance of immediate needs by consumers, and still more by middlemen, and controlled by speculative motives, make up the effective momentary demand.

* Moreover the fact itself is improbable. If the wheat is the grower's main source of income it is at least as likely that he will consume more if the price is high, since the difference in his income due to the higher price of his produce is likely to be more important than the difference in the price as a deterrent to consumption.

† *Economics of Enterprise*, pp. 48–52.

Diagram II.) The theoretical price is the marginal demand price of the existing supply, the highest price at which it will all be consumed within the period before new supply becomes available.

Even in the case of wheat some qualification of this formulation is necessary. Some wheat is carried over from one production period to another and variations in this amount with anticipated changes in conditions in the next period may be appreciable. And the facts are somewhat complicated from the standpoint of any one country by

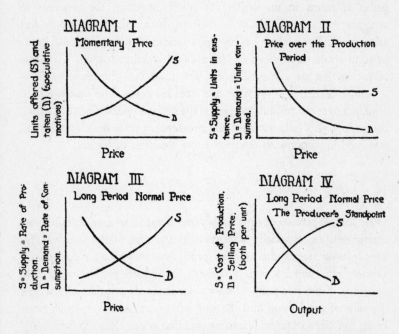

the fact that the market is international. But from the standpoint of the world-market as a whole the description is a fair approximation to the facts.

With respect to manufactured goods more serious reservations must be made. The production period is less definite and the amount of carrying over from one production period to another is much more important. For extreme price changes the supply, meaning the amount produced, is more flexible over short periods of time and anticipated changes in the conditions of production make themselves felt more quickly by affecting the rate at which existing stocks are thrown on the market. If prices promise to be higher, middlemen hold back supply, raising prices before the new conditions actually become effective, and if they promise to be lower, stocks are reduced below the normal levels, reducing prices.

These two cases, the situation at a moment and over that more or less definite production period within which supply is not subject to change, are thrown together in the conventional treatment of market price. It seems to the writer absolutely necessary for clearness to separate them. In neither, it is obvious, do conditions of production affect price. For a given supply once produced, the price which competition tends to establish is determined by demand alone. The costs of production are ancient history. The producer will get as much as he can, whether it is more or less than his costs. The *tendency* is to establish over the production period the highest uniform price at which the supply will be consumed and momentary price fluctuates around this level in response to the speculative estimates of traders.

III

Over longer periods of time supply and demand take on still different interpretations, especially important in the case of the supply. The supply now means the amount produced, viewed as a continuous average rate, and becomes a variable, controlled by producers' calculations. From this point of view price tends toward the point where the rate of production and the rate of consumption are equal, both being functions of price. It is axiomatic that goods cannot permanently be consumed more rapidly than they are produced and will not be produced more rapidly than they are consumed.* For short periods of time this quality does not necessarily hold, for the reason that accumulated stocks serve as a sort of buffer between production and consumption. Consumption may exceed production for a considerable

* The latter part of the statement does not fit certain types of "durable" goods such as gold, jewellery, works of art, ideas, etc., which are not strictly speaking consumed at all. The theory of normal price (price determined by cost of production) is wholly inapplicable to such things, in the form which is valid for ordinary consumption goods.

time, drawing down accumulations, and production may exceed consumption by building them up; but it is evident that neither difference can exist permanently or for very long.

The form of the functional relation between rate of production and price is the most complicated problem in price theory and to this problem the remainder of the discussion will be devoted. But one more distinction must be drawn by way of defining the data or given conditions of the problem. A change in the production of any given commodity may be associated with a change in the total productive power of the society as a whole or it may be related to a shift or transfer of productive power from one use to another. In general, again, it is a matter of the time interval taken into account. Over relatively short periods of a few years or a small multiple of the production period for the commodity, referred to under Case II, changes will generally represent transfers of productive resources and will be correlated with opposite changes in the production of some other good or goods. For such periods of a few years the total productive power of society does not greatly change. It is therefore as natural as it is necessary to separate the consideration of effects of changes in total productive power from those of transfers from one field to another.

The effects of these long-period changes in the total situation will not be taken up in the present discussion at all. We assume that the fundamental conditions of economic life in the aggregate, on both the supply and demand sides of the relation, remain unchanged. These fundamental conditions include (a) the total supplies of productive resources ("land, labour, and capital"); (b) the "state of the arts" or the knowledge of productive methods and processes; and (c) the "psychology," tastes and habits of the people. Significant changes in these things are generally progressive in character, in contrast to the readjustments to accidental fluctuations which make up the changes considered under the three cases already enumerated, and may be grouped under the heading of *Social Progress*. A social setting in which all such progressive changes are abstracted but in which unlimited time is assumed for all adjustments to the given conditions in these fundamental respects to work themselves out to their natural equilibrium results, is approximately what is meant by the "static state," or Marshall's conditions for the establishment of long-time normal price.*

We turn now to the crucial problem of the relation between the supply of a commodity and its price (meaning by supply the rate of production of the commodity), or in other words the problem of the form of the long-time supply curve. If supply is some function of price the meaning of the price point as the condition of equality between production and consumption is clear. Diagram III is drawn on the superficially natural assumption that an increase in price, other things being equal, will increase the production of the good, that supply is a direct function of price. Demand (rate of consumption) is, of course, an inverse function, as in the other cases.

The production of the commodity depends on the action of producers who are governed by profit-seeking motives and it is in this connection that cost of production exerts its effect on price. It goes without argument that cost affects price only as it affects supply, that any given supply put on the market will sell at a price determined by the demand, irrespective of its cost. The general character of the

---

* The expression "unprogressive society," though less compact, seems to the writer much better than the "static state" to designate this situation. The word "static" suggests the absence of *change*. The idea is not, however, to eliminate change, but only *certain* changes while discussing the natural readjustment of other things to the given condition of those assumed as unchanging for purposes of the argument. The term "dynamic" contrasted with "static" is still more objectionable and "progressive" has in this case the advantage of being more euphonious as well. The distinction between progressive change and fluctuations seems to be important enough to justify a generic division along this line. It is not always true that progressive changes become practically important only over periods of time long in comparison to those in which fluctuations work themselves out, but it is so generally true as to make the division all the more significant and to make it easier to visualize the separation.

The advisability of distinguishing between short-time and long-time normal price will be taken up immediately. If this is done we have five cases or sets of data for our analysis in place of Marshall's four (*Principles of Economics*, 6th ed., p. 379).

It is fundamental to price theory as a whole, in which no sharp separation is possible between the prices of consumption goods and the prices of productive services or distribution (since the costs of production are identical with the distributive shares), that the data for the long-time theory of the former are the same as the data for the short-time theory of distribution. Over the period under consideration (say a few years) the supply of any consumption good is variable, a function of price, while the supply of any fundamental productive factor is fixed. The theory of progress will treat of the remunerations of productive services under the influence of changes in supply, and of what Marshall calls "secular changes" in normal prices (of consumption goods).

reasoning is simple. If the price is above the cost of production (including a profit representing payment at the general market rate for the entrepreneur's own services), production will be stimulated and the increased supply will bring down the price. If price is below cost, production will be decreased and the price raised.

From this point of view it is obvious that the costs which influence supply and price are the money outlays necessary to production. Ultimately these are the payments for the use of productive resources. We shall neglect the effects of taxation. We have no concern with the pains or subjective sacrifices involved in production, since it is not at all in terms of such "costs" that the entrepreneur makes his calculations on the basis of which he decides whether to produce the good or on what scale. He takes account of sentimental costs only in so far as they influence the outlays he must make to secure the services necessary to production. That is, he is concerned only with the price measure of his costs. Their magnitude in some other aspect will not influence his decision. Pains and sentimental repugnances are undoubtedly an influence in limiting the supply of some sorts of services and raising their price, but in the aggregate they form a relatively unimportant element, and no one now contends that there is any tendency for the prices of productive services, still less of final goods, to bear any correspondence with these magnitudes. The relation between them is a separate inquiry, pertinent perhaps to an evaluation or criticism of the competitive economic order, hardly so to an explanation of its workings.

It would seem also to be almost too obvious for argument that in those costs which influence the entrepreneur's decisions and affect the supply and the price of a commodity, rent payments take their place among and in all respects on a parity with the outlays for other necessary productive services. They condition production. The entrepreneur must make these payments for the same reason that he must pay, say, wages; he must meet the offers of competing bidders for the use of the productive capacity represented. Even when all of these competing bidders are other producers of the same commodity, the service being useless in any other industry,* the payments are

* A condition doubtfully more often true of "land" than labour, bearing in mind that mineral resources are not economic land.

socially necessary as a means of effecting the distribution of the land among the different users and its rational combination with other agencies.*

Closely connected with the confusion involved in the interpretation of cost in subjective terms and the exclusion of rent is the notion of marginal cost, and the whole idea that one unit or portion of a supply costs or may cost more or less than another, under the conditions assumed for long-time normality. This point will be developed as we proceed,† but since other confusions are also involved in the error, it should be mentioned here.

For the present let us first be clear as to what the assumptions or given conditions of our problem are. Progressive changes are eliminated, but *unlimited* time is assumed for the making of productive adjustments. That is, we are describing the tendencies operative in the relation of production to demand in terms of their *final* results in the absence of interference, as insisted upon at the beginning of the paper. Later on will be taken up the question of the advisability of a separate formulation of their effects when they operate for more limited periods (Marshall's short-time normals).

Under these conditions the supply curve is identical with a cost of production curve. The supply is a function of price because the cost of production per unit is a function of the supply, the amount produced. It follows at once from the relation between cost of production and price (see above, p. 193) that the amount which will be produced at any selling price (per unit) is the amount which can be produced at that cost per unit. That is, the same curve which shows output as a function of price shows cost as a function of output. In order to discuss

* The separation of land from "artificial" productive goods is to the writer one of the hardest things to account for in the traditional economic speculation. It simply is not true that there is any productive power in land which has not been "produced" in the only sense in which men produce anything; its value is due to the form it is in, which represents previous investment, and the supply is determined by free investment in competition with other fields. The speculative element in such investment may be larger on the average but in the writer's opinion the reverse is more probably true.

These statements do not apply to mineral deposits and other *exhaustible* and *non-replaceable* natural wealth. There would be good ground for erecting these goods into a separate productive category; but this type of natural productive power is just what has been excluded from the category of land by the economists' definitions. But detailed discussion of the classification of productive resources is outside the field of this paper.   † See below, p. 199.

the relations from the producer's point of view it is therefore advisable to reverse the axes of the diagram, treating supply as the independent variable and cost and selling price as functions of supply. This gives the same curves as before, but as seen in a mirror or looking through the paper from the back. (It is also evident that the demand curve may be regarded indifferently as showing selling price as a function of supply or the amount saleable as a function of price, that these are two ways of looking at the same set of facts.) On the new diagram (IV), which represents a mirror image of Diagram III, the intersection of the curves shows in the more natural graphic way the equality between cost and selling price, which is the goal of producers' adjustments, though on either diagram, according to the direction in which it is read, it shows either equality of cost and selling price or equality of production and consumption.

Looking at the supply curve from this new point of view it is evident that decreasing costs would mean that at higher prices less of the commodity would be produced than at lower prices. This certainly seems paradoxical, and suggests that there is something wrong with the notion of costs decreasing as supply increases. The further course of the argument will show that decreasing cost as a long-run tendency is indeed impossible under a natural competitive adjustment of industry. Under the conditions assumed, an increase in the production of any commodity means a transfer of productive resources into the industry and a decrease in the production of some other commodity. But, other things being equal, this decrease in the production of other goods will raise their prices and increase the strength of the competing attraction which they exert on productive resources against the industry in question in which output is being increased. In simpler terms, an increase in the output of any industry involves increased demand for the productive goods used in it, which increased demand raises their prices, that is, raises the costs of production of the commodity turned out.

The implications of perfect competitive adjustment may now be briefly summarized and decreasing costs shown to be incompatible with the long-run tendencies of productive adjustments. In the first place a perfect market for productive services is implied, that is, uniform prices over the whole field. The costs cannot be different to different producers or for different parts of the supply of any one producer, on this account. In the long run the same productive goods will cost the same prices and all differences of every sort in productive situation will be evaluated at their true worth under the influence of competition and be converted into costs which function in the same way as all other costs in the producer's calculations. Most of the apparent differences in production costs are undoubtedly due to imperfect evaluation of cost goods, and the *tendency*, however slowly it may work itself out, is manifestly toward a correct, uniform evaluation. Every productive good tends toward that position in the total productive system in which it has the greatest possible value, and tends to be priced at the value which it has in that position.

In the second place, the conditions of perfect competition include the production of every commodity by an indefinitely large number of competing organizations, *each of the most efficient size*. The confusion between variation in the scale of operations of the single productive establishment with variation in the output in the industry as a whole is perhaps the most prolific source of error in this whole field of reasoning. Under perfect competition, neither increasing costs nor decreasing costs in the individual establishment affect output or price. All establishments will be forced to the most efficient size, and variation in the output in the industry means a change in the number of establishments, without change in their scale of operations individually. This does not mean that all must be of the *same* size, but that each, in the conditions in which it works, must be of the most efficient size and that the *efficiency* of all must be the same. This again is not the actual character of the competitive situation at any given time, but is its actual *tendency*, and it is the long-run tendencies which must first be grasped as a basis for discussion of conditions under which they are but partially realized.

The specification of a plurality of establishments each of the most efficient size eliminates at once both the possibility of decreasing costs due to increased efficiency under larger output and also the entire notion of marginal costs, referred to above (p. 196). If increased economies are available through larger-scale operations, then larger-scale operations will be introduced under competition, through an increase in the size of the establishment with a *reduction in the number* of establishments and *without an increase in the output of the industry as a whole*. The tendency to an increase in size and reduction in the number of establishments will go on, independently of change of output in the industry, until either all establishments reach a size of greatest and equal efficiency (not necessarily equal size) or else until there is only one establishment left in the industry. Competitive production is possible as a final adjustment only if the technological conditions and the demand for the product are such that a large number of organizations are left in the industry when all are at the size of greatest efficiency. Otherwise the tendency is toward the establishment of monopoly.

In the same way the notion of marginal cost is meaningless in relation to any final adjustment. Competitive price can never be determined in the long run by an equation of the cost of the final unit of the supply to the selling price, leaving a profit on earlier units. The final unit cannot be more costly than any other unit in the ultimate competitive situation; for (*a*) costs must in the long run be the same to all producers, as shown, and (*b*) there cannot be increasing costs in the individual establishment because that would mean that smaller establishments are more efficient than larger, and if so they will put the latter out of business or force their reduction to the most efficient size.

The same reasoning applies to different productive methods. In the long run all producers are forced to use the most efficient methods or give place to others who do. The long-run tendency is toward a price determined by the cost of production under the best possible conditions, not the worst, as so commonly stated, nor those of the average or representative establishment.

The final consideration and in some respects the most difficult of all is the relation between output and the capacity of fixed or specialized equipment in the industry. A considerable fraction of the productive equipment in an economic society can be transferred freely from one industry to another and another fraction can be transformed by being replaced by a different kind instead of the same kind when it wears out, but of another large part neither assertion is true.* From our

---

* The division lines cut across all the conventional productive factors. Some "land," some "labour," and some "capital" (capital goods) are transferable, some

long-run point of view the two former are equivalent; both amount to effective fluidity or mobility. But even ultimately it is not admissible to assume perfect mobility for all types of productive goods. Even if the tendency is finally toward some degree of mobility for productive goods generally, the time involved would be so very long that it is pertinent to grant the point and raise in the present connection the question as to the effect upon the cost function of assumed permanent specialization of cost goods.*

It is commonly and naturally assumed that if there is fixed equipment in an industry, not transferable to other uses, payment for its use represents a fixed cost and that a reduction in the output of the industry will be accompanied by an increase in the cost per unit. But if the entrepreneur's, i.e., the realistic, point of view is rigidly retained, it will be seen that this is not true. The entrepreneur's costs are the *payments for* the services of the cost goods and if the demand for a product decreases the rigidly specialized productive services used in making it will be *revalued* at lower levels and these costs also will decrease. In the long run, of course, such considerations as the fact that entrepreneurs may have contracted for these goods for a considerable period of time at fixed rates fall away.

What is true is rather that payments for permanently and rigidly specialized productive agencies do not exert a *causal* effect on the price of the good in whose creation they are employed. There is no exception to the principle that an increase in output represents an increase in cost per unit and conversely. Moreover, it is difficult to

transformable (over a longer or shorter period of time) and some rigidly specialized. Here as elsewhere the conventional division is irrelevant; the writer has yet to run across any real economic problem in relation to which it has practical significance.

* It should be noted that it is impossible to be sure that we are adhering rigorously to the assumption that progressive change in total productive capacity is absent. When productive goods are changed in form there is no clear and definite meaning in the assertion that they remain the same in amount. The equivalence can be approximately preserved, in so far as the new forms represent the same amount of some more fundamental productive resource (such as homogeneous labour) as the old, but some differences in the kind as well as amount of the ultimate investment are doubtless always connected with differences in the immediate form of the production good. The question really is, the extent to which production goods differing in form and specialized to certain uses do ultimately represent the investment of unspecialized resources. It is undoubtedly true that for the most part they do; but even then, some such investments never wear out and give back the unspecialized productive power which went into them for use in creating goods of some other specialized form.

give any definite practical meaning to questions of the causal relation between cost and price; such questions are metaphysical, having little bearing on problems of policy. The practically pertinent facts are summed up in the statement that under all conditions, (a) every productive resource *tends* to be employed in that way and place in which it will make the greatest possible contribution to the output of consumption goods as measured by pecuniary demand, and (b) that it (i.e., its "owner") *tends* to be paid for its use the value of the contribution which it makes. The statement that the cost of production and the price of any good are equal really signifies simply that productive resources are divided between the production of that good and the production of other goods for which they might be used in such a way that none of the resources can produce more value by being transferred either way. If cost is above price, some productive services are being used for the good in question which are worth more somewhere else, and if cost is below price, some productive services are being used for other goods which would be worth more to produce the good in question. To avoid false inferences commonly drawn, it should again be emphasized that there is no necessary connection between pecuniary demand and real worth, and hence this reasoning in no wise vindicates the competitive system, and would not do so even if its tendencies came to literal realization. Our present concern is merely the question of accuracy in describing its workings, in terms of their final, long-run tendencies, which should be done correctly before critical judgment is passed. Under the conditions necessary to competitive production, and looking to the final results of competitive tendencies, the cost of production is without exception a direct or increasing function of output.

A more or less important qualification relates to the *extent* to which cost necessarily increases with output. For commodities which do not represent an appreciable fraction of the demand for any productive resource which goes into them, the change in cost corresponding to probable changes in output may indeed be practically negligible. The function may represent virtually constant cost. For example, the case of steel rails may be contrasted with that of carpet tacks. A considerable change in the demand for steel rails means a considerable change in the demand for the ultimate resources used in producing them, and will make a marked difference in the prices of these resources, i.e., in the cost of production. No probable change in the demand for carpet tacks would make an appreciable change in the demand for any ultimate productive resource and hence within the limits of accuracy of economic measurement the long-run tendency is represented by constant cost. The supply curve of Diagram IV is for such goods a horizontal straight line, in Diagram III a vertical one. But constant cost is the "limiting case" which in strict accuracy is never met with. There is no place for a tendency to decreasing costs, when the conditions are correctly stated.

IV

All of this reasoning relates to the ultimate goal of the competitive tendencies, with unlimited time allowed for the adjustment of production to given conditions of demand (but with long-period progressive changes in the general conditions of both supply and demand eliminated). The next question is that of the relation between cost of production and price, the shape of the curve showing cost as a function of output and hence output as a function of price, over moderate periods of time. Two main sets of facts differentiate the short-period from the long-period tendencies. The first is the *physical immobility* of productive resources between different uses and the second is the comparative inflexibility of the *prices* of productive services, in terms of which the producer makes his calculations. When the price of a product changes, due to a change in demand, the entrepreneur cannot commonly change his price offers for productive goods immediately into correspondence with them. For many of these he is under contract over a longer or shorter period at specified rates. For others, notably labour services, psychological and social considerations prevent quick and accurate readjustments, not to mention that the entrepreneur himself does not come instantly and automatically into accurate knowledge of the facts. And when the price remunerations for "land, labour, and capital" do change relatively in different industries, transfers of these agencies from one industry to the other do not always follow quickly or freely. Even those agencies which are transferable without physical modification encounter a large amount of inertia and resistance. Others cannot be transferred without changes involving costs and still others are only indirectly movable; they must be allowed to wear out and be replaced with others of a different type. That is, the *ultimate* resources are largely mobile, but they are embodied in intermediate forms which are not; and finally, to some extent the ultimate resources are specialized and the only change to which they are subject is a revaluation.

In consequence of these facts of immobility the adjustment to changing conditions of demand is generally far from complete. And especially when it can be foreseen that the new condition of demand will probably be short-lived in comparison with the time required for perfect adjustment to it, the tendency to make these adjustments is enfeebled and for those adjustments which require an especially long time to carry out the tendency may be entirely abrogated.

To fit the theory more accurately to the facts of life the doctrine of short-time normal price has been formulated, notably by Marshall. The idea is that over short periods supply is a different function of price, cost a different function of output, from what is true of the ultimate adjustment. Marshall separates the two cases by saying that for short periods of a few months or a year supply means the amount which can be produced for the price in question with the existing stock of plant, personal and impersonal, in the given time, while for long periods, of several years, it means the amount which can be produced by plant which itself can be remuneratively produced and applied within the given time.*

* *Principles of Economics*, 6th ed., p. 379. It is to be observed that even Marshall's discussion of long-time normal price does not relate to the *ultimate* adjustment of production to fit given conditions of demand. This is in line with his general tendency to avoid clear-cut formulations and "soften" his principles to make them cover a broader range of facts. The present writer is inclined to a very different conception of scientific procedure, though not necessarily to the exclusion or displacement of "looser" forms of treatment. Another case in point is the concept of the "representative firm" already referred to. In our view general principles are to be stated with the most rigorous accuracy attainable and pure theory sharply separated from its application to reality. From this point of view the failure of a scientific principle to fit accurately any case whatever, much less any class of cases, may be a merit rather than a defect. It is not the purpose of such principles to describe facts in realistic detail, but to state with the greatest possible accuracy general relations which form a *common element* in large groups of real situations, even though they may not be the whole story, may not necessarily even give an approximately complete description, of any single case.

We question the validity of a separate formulation of short-period tendencies along the line adopted by Marshall or the recognition of a special "case" along any lines. It seems rather that the facts are sufficiently covered by recognizing that in a limited period only a corresponding part of the readjustment described as the final goal will be brought about. We argue that there is no division between short-period and long-period changes; that they are of the same character and differ only in the degree of completeness and that this variation in degree of completeness is smooth and gradual, without break or sudden change of character as the time interval considered is longer from zero up to indefinitely long periods.

Marshall's distinction between variation in output from the equipment, personal and impersonal, already in an industry and a variation due to a change in the amount of equipment itself, seems to involve confusion and difficulty if not definite error. It may be doubted whether a variation in the output from given equipment in response to variation in price is to be regarded as probable on a significant scale. To some extent the productive life of machinery in terms of total output may be greater at lower speeds (enough greater to offset the interest charge connected with stretching the yield out over a longer time) and if so machinery could be economically operated at higher speed as the price of the product increased. But it is improbable that this factor would be important, and the discussion quickly narrows down to the human element in the equipment. The argument assumes that at higher product prices, higher wages will be paid and that at higher wages, the same labour force will work the material equipment more intensively and turn out a greater output, through speeding up or overtime work.

Examination of this reasoning raises serious doubts. Everything depends on the assumptions as to the psychology of the workers. Suppose to begin with that the working day and speed are normal. It is pretty well demonstrated that what industry considers a normal* working day is too long and normal speed probably too high for maximum efficiency over even moderate periods of time. Labour cannot produce more than normal output except for a temporary spurt.

* Normal here means of course merely usual and has no connection with the use in "normal price" as the goal of tendencies at work.

Moreover, if the inducement is a simple increase in piece wages, it is at least as likely that workers will choose to work less hard as that they will choose to work harder, and if they behave like the rational economic man they will be more likely to choose the former. They will take *part* of their increased income in the form of leisure time, earning more money but doing less work as the rate of pay rises. We are therefore thrown back upon special forms of wage payment such as bonuses for extra production, higher rates for overtime, and the like. It is undeniable that such expedients may stimulate production to some extent for a short time, but accumulating observation, notably the experience of the recent war, shortens the time to very narrow limits, and emphasizes the stupendous cost of the temporary increase through reduced efficiency later on.

Moreover, it is quite clear that in fact the temporary increase in output going with high prices does not come altogether from the equipment, material and human, already in the industry. When prices rise the less specialized forms of labour and tools are taken on and when prices fall they are laid off; the longer the time available, and the greater the price change, the more highly specialized is the equipment, material and human, which will be involved in this change, varying continuously and smoothly in both directions and without limit.

When the fluctuation is below the normal (usual) working adjustment in the industry, the case is somewhat different. Here the dominating fact is that the entrepreneur usually bargains for his fixed equipment, or the capital which it represents, on long-term contracts and has to pay for its use whether it works or not. Under these conditions it is indeed true that the industry will be subject to decreasing costs. If the entrepreneur owns the equipment himself or hires it on terms of its momentary value to him, the long-run principle applies with the modification that *with reference to time periods for which* any particular equipment is specialized, its remuneration is not a price-determining factor, and this element in cost will be reduced by re-valuation of the service in question. In regard to labour, the more expert and specialized branches are in much the same position as fixed equipment. The entrepreneur cannot generally afford to lay off such men, and their wages are in large part a fixed cost with reference to short-period changes. With unskilled labour the tendency is to keep piece wages fairly constant for actual employment but reduce the number employed or the hours of work or both. It is by no means a negligible element in the actual calculation that both these facts mean increased labour efficiency at lower outputs, since in general the men laid off are the less capable, and the psychological influence of depression in the industry works in the same direction in other ways.

The facts as to the relation between output and price are represented

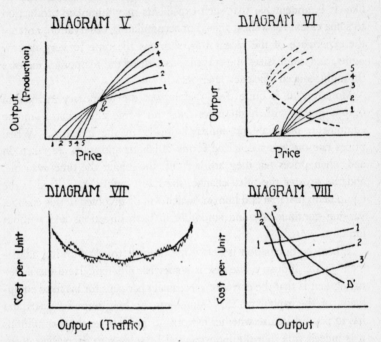

roughly in Diagram V. The point *b* corresponds to a normal adjustment in which price and cost are equal, which assumed as a starting-point. For increases in price the output may be assumed to increase in greater degree as the time for readjustment is longer, little or not at all for very short periods as shown by curve 1 and more steeply without limit as the time increases (curves 2, 3, 4, and 5).* For decreases

---

* A complete and accurate representation would require a three-dimension drawing, the curves being located at successive points along a time axis perpendicular to the paper and blending into a surface increasing in inclination to the price plane with increasing distance from the zero point of the axis of time-allowed-for-readjustment.

in demand the same curves would be continued to the left as shown, again becoming steeper with increase in the time interval taken into view. It may aid in visualizing the situation to imagine that the curves to the right of the intersection (*b*) represent output of some commodity, demand for which is greatly increased by the outbreak of a war, while the portion to the left of the intersection represents the facts for some luxury good, for which the demand is largely cut off; the different curves showing production according to different anticipated durations of the war. (It is to be assumed that the productive readjustments are effectuated by price motives alone.) With reference to a new commodity not previously produced the curves will start from a zero point on the price axis as shown in Diagram VI. The dotted curves in Diagram VI relate to the possibility of producing the commodity on an entirely different scale by an entirely different, more highly organized, and more efficient process; this possibility will be discussed presently .(p. 214). By this large-scale process small amounts of the good would not be produced or if they were the price would have to be very high; beyond a minimum point the rate of production will be an increasing function of both the price and the time allowed, as in the previous case.

V

The foregoing abstract formulation of principles may be brought down to earth, made concrete, and connected up with practical social policy by a brief discussion of what is in a sense the stock example of decreasing costs, the railway industry. The effects of so-called fixed charges or burden and the resulting decrease in cost per unit as output (traffic handled) increases are as conspicuous and as familiar here as in any field. The decrease in cost is a concomitant of *surplus capacity* in important elements of the equipment.* The crucial question is, *why*

* A well-known problem book in economics contains the question, if a railroad is already in existence between New York and Chicago and trains are running, what added cost will the railroad incur in hauling a five-pound box from Chicago to New York? Of course the Freshman is expected to answer that the cost would be slight, and to be duly impressed with the importance of fixed costs. No reference is made to the possibility that the trains already running may be full! The *added* cost of the particular small increment of traffic which compels the addition of even an extra car to a train will not be negligible. And locomotives also reach their capacity and new

do certain elements of the equipment contain surplus capacity? The answer, in the case of American railways, is obvious. The roads were built in the first place long in advance of the economic development justifying the investment, in order to pre-empt the locations and to speculate upon the unreflecting optimism of a frontier community, where every junction point habitually looks upon itself as a budding metropolis. And being built, they were (more or less wisely) laid out upon large lines, with a view to future expansion in the traffic. It requires no explanation that such an establishment, *while it is working up to the capacity for which it is designed*, will show large fixed charges and diminishing costs. It is just as obvious that this is a temporary condition.

The present confusion in the railway field in this country is in no small degree a product of the fact that for more than a generation the roads and the public were habituated to thinking of the industry as one of decreasing costs. The roads were encouraged by publicists and writers on railway affairs to make rates that would enable the traffic to move, oblivious even of the fact that the traffic increases were largely at the expense of other lines operating under the same conditions. The result is our impossible system of rate-basing and traffic classification. In the early years of the present century the country grew up to its railway system; since then the equipment has been behind rather than in advance of the needs, and railway finance has been floundering in bewilderment, trying to find itself in relation to a situation in which increased business is no longer an advantage.*

trains have to be added; and sometime, new tracks must be built if the traffic continues to grow, and ultimately it would be impracticable to increase the number of tracks. Perhaps about eight is a maximum before it would be cheaper to start an entire new system far enough removed from the first to avoid interference in switching and handling the shipments.

* In European countries generally the facts were different, the traffic demands being generally up to the capacity of the railways as they were built and expanded; the foreign literature on railways is relatively free from the heresy of decreasing costs and foreign railway policies from the disorganizing tendencies based upon the idea.

The doctrine that railway rates are determined according to the principle of joint cost seems to the writer especially hard to defend, since the operation of the equipment would be actually simplified if its capacity were all employed in handling a single class of traffic. The notion of joint cost adds nothing to the simple statement of diminishing cost unless different kinds of product result in *nearly fixed proportions* from the same productive operations, Compare Taussig, *Principles of Economics*,

The actual shape of the curve showing cost as a function of output (traffic) is intended to be suggested by Diagram VII.* Beginning at an exceedingly high cost for the first small increments of business—so high that a railway would not, of course, be built for them alone—the cost descends for a time, rapidly on the whole but very irregularly. There is an upward "kink" in it not only for every new car, train, track, etc., but for every freight-handler, freight shed, bookkeeper, etc., necessitated by the expanding traffic. For a time the drops in the curve are much larger than the rises and the trend is sharply downward. A ten-car train is more efficient than a one-car train, and a double-track road, than a single track. But soon this tendency slackens, and still later it is reversed. The writer is not a railway expert, but is told that beyond somewhere around three or four tracks the efficiency falls instead of rising, and surely it needs not to be argued that a road of twenty tracks would be quite unmanageable.

The foregoing assumes a *rapid* expansion. If the growth is slow and related to conditions accurately known far enough in advance, the curve will be smoothed out to the trend line, as shown. Cars can be built a little larger instead of adding standard cars one at a time. Even a man, the most indivisible productive unit, can generally be employed for part of his time only in any one occupation, or "smaller" men can be replaced by "larger" ones. Even the capacity of the given number of tracks can be increased by varying the amount of auxiliary equipment, and additional tracks may be added gradually, beginning with the busiest sectors.

Diminishing costs are generally real in the very early stages of the expansion of the demand. There are minimum limits to the divisibility

chap. lx, and a discussion of the subject by Taussig and Pigou in the *Quarterly Journal of Economics*, vol. xxvii.

The writer is inclined to believe that the "wise social policy" would be to require railways to make all charges on a ton-mile basis, over the best route, with allowance for special handling costs and any special service such as extra speed or the like. Of course this does not mean that they should be required to change quickly to such a basis from the present system, nor is the proposal expected to be taken seriously from the standpoint of that complex of auto-hallucination, humbug, and knavery which we call practical politics.

* The curve is of course a rough sketch and merely suggestive. Drawn accurately to scale it should never be steeper than a rectangular hyperbola through the point. A decrease in cost per unit at greater ratio than that of the increase in output would mean a smaller *total* cost for the larger output, which is absurd.

of important elements in cost. If a pipe is to be laid, a ditch must be dug wide enough for a man to work in, and the right-of-way for two railway tracks will not cost nearly twice as much as for one. Such gains, however, decrease very rapidly with expanding size, and though many of them will never fall to zero they are quickly offset by just as inevitable losses which increase from the first, the varied and multiplying costs of maintaining internal stability as size increases. No fallacy is more pernicious with reference to intelligent economic policy than the popular illusion that large-scale business is in general more economical than small-scale. If the scale of operations expands very far it will always run into increasing costs; and as the facts stand the gains are more conspicuous than the losses so that even careful study inevitably overestimates the advantages and underestimates the critical size at which increasing costs set in.

But it may naturally be objected that if decreasing costs are significant up to the capacity of two tracks and real, even if small, up to three or four, the operation of the greater part of the railway mileage of the United States would still in fact be subject to decreasing costs. This is doubtless true, in an accurate adjustment; and it may also be true to some extent that in a rapidly growing society it is wise at certain stages to overbuild the fixed equipment of public utilities in relation to current needs. It may even be true that a certain amount of price classification may be theoretically justifiable. But all consideration of the merits of the case serves to emphasize the very limited extent to which any of these conclusions hold and the importance of the practical considerations on the other side. The outstanding fact is that most if not nearly all the actual consequences of these policies are bad. Price differentiation either gets business at the expense of competing equipment operating under the same conditions or develops traffic which ought not to move, artificially distorting the natural lines of social growth, while the monopoly rate on the traffic which will "bear" it encourages socially unwise investment in the industry which makes the charge.

Getting business away from competing establishments similarly subject to decreasing costs raises again the question earlier discussed of the tendency of competition to force all the establishments to adopt the most efficient size. If a four-track railway is most economical, how can lines on a smaller scale continue to exist? The answer obviously is that only a part of the service rendered by a railway (the through traffic) is subject to competition, while a large part (local traffic) is a natural monopoly. The social problem as to how far the possibility of securing monopoly prices for local service ought to be allowed to influence railway building is a vast and intricate problem which cannot here be gone into in detail. While the effect of free competition in railway-building and rate-making would be to concentrate economic development to some extent along favoured transportation routes, the effect of forbidding new lines to compete with established ones at rates which would cut their traffic below the point of maximum efficiency would be to concentrate it much more. The policy of permitting free railway-building (and still more that of fostering competition), if consistently followed out, tends to diffuse population and industry over a wider area, reducing the natural advantage of proximity to superior transportation routes. As noted above, the writer would favour the policy of restraining competition. Then if "society" wants to encourage artificially the development of the newer regions or sub-sidize the movement of any particular class of freight* it should be done directly and consciously, out of taxation levied so far as possible according to the benefit conferred. But again, in practical politics, it is doubtless rash to suggest that society should do anything consciously and deliberately where it is possible to "muddle through."

VI

The foregoing discussion is all relative to an *expanding* demand. In our rapidly growing society contractions in demand are a relatively short-period phenomenon. When from any temporary cause an industry is working below the *correct* capacity of the fixed equipment, there is a tendency toward decreasing costs with their concomitant of cut-throat competition. Here the fixed costs represent either contractual remunerations not subject to quick readjustment or the

* It is by no means meant to imply that this should never be done. The writer would hold—in opposition for example to Taussig (*Principles of Economics*, chap. lx, sec. 1)—that in this field social interests very often outweigh economic advantage, as measured by pecuniary demand.

physical immobility of the intermediate forms in which ultimately mobile ultimate resources are temporarily embodied. The amount of such physical immobility depends upon the suddenness and extent of the change. At one extreme a large part of both the material and human productive resources of society would be included. At the other, practically nothing. It is the writer's belief that if we abstract from the disturbances due to progressive change in demand and in productive methods and from those affecting business as a whole (the "business cycle") the assumption of perfect mobility corresponds closely with the facts for all changes not so short in duration as to iron out through the mere tendency of business calculations to base themselves on average conditions.*

This high degree of mobility is to be sure largely the result of social growth or progress, making possible a shift in the relative investment in different industries through differential growth, without an actual transfer of equipment from one to another. Productive power, to repeat, is in its ultimate form either transferable from one use to another or else is not price-determining in its one special use; but at any particular time it is more or less largely committed to particular forms specialized to particular uses. It cannot be quickly recovered in its fluid form without loss, and for much of it the commitment is permanent or practically so. There is no contradiction between assuming a degree of mobility dependent in fact on the steady accumulation of capital and assuming at the same time the absence of disturbances due to progressive change. For, though accumulation is a phenomenon of progress, it is a type of progress which has no appreciable effect in upsetting business calculations or producing

---

* Professor Friday's interesting argument against the concept of "normal profit" (in *Profits, Wages, and Prices*, chap. iii) does not affect the proposition as stated above, if indeed it applies to any doctrine which economic theorists have traditionally advocated. He has not in any sense disproved a tendency of profit toward a normal level, nor even that this tendency is reasonably effective over a moderate period of time if the variables are accurately measured in price terms.

In this connection it may be suggested that the conclusion of Professor Friday that an excess-profits tax will not discourage production may be hastily drawn. In the first place, we may question whether the anticipation of unusual profits is not in itself a vital element in the incentive to business activity. In the second place, it is admitted that profits are closely connected with fluctuations in industry, and if the tax is levied annually a business which is actually losing money may pay a considerable amount of excess-profits taxes over a period of a few years.

fluctuations. In any case it is legitimate methodology to separate the effects of mobility from *other* effects of progress even if there is some connection between the two, if there is also a large degree of independence of one upon the other.

One of the most serious oversights in the discussion of decreasing cost is the neglect of the mixture of competition and monopoly which is a general characteristic of the type of business supposed to exhibit this type of cost function. Just as part of the traffic of a railroad is competitive and part monopolistic, nearly every manufacturing and mercantile business has a monopoly on *some feature* of its product; its good or service is differentiated from others in some manner and to some degree. To the extent that any business is monopolistic it may manifest decreasing costs due to the "economy of large-scale production." We have only argued that such a cost curve is incompatible with long-run competitive conditions.

The correct approach to the explanation of price in the case of partial monopoly would seem to be to apply the theory of monopoly, not that of competition. Instead of attempting to allow for a degree of monopoly in the supply, which there is no easy way of doing, it is vastly simpler to allow for partial competition as a phenomenon of *substitution*, on the demand side. No difficulty whatever is involved in assuming control of the supply (of the commodity defined in the narrowest sense) and allowing for competition by substitution of more or less similar goods in drawing the demand curve. And this is the more realistic view as it represents the way in which the producer would naturally envisage the situation.

In still another sense the presence of partial monopoly is a qualifying factor in determining short-run price. When an industry is in a depressed state, working below the capacity of equipment not transferable within the period in which reduced demand operates, a feeling of community of interest tends to prevent that reduction of prices to the level of prime costs which would follow from perfect competition. It is to be emphasized that a considerable degree of one or both sorts of monopoly exists over a large part of the field of manufacturing industry. The influence of both sorts of monopoly on price, i.e., of the striving after the greatest possible degree of real or fictitious uniqueness in product by different makers and the strengthening of a sort of "professional ethics" against price-cutting, has been emphasized by Professor Spurgeon Bell in his paper on this subject.*

One more phase of the problem of decreasing cost with decreasing output should be mentioned in conclusion. Without considering new inventions or the introduction of methods not previously familiar, there may be a possibility of using different systems of production in making a commodity, one method being more efficient for a smaller supply and another for a larger. This is under any probable conditions another phase of the variation in size of establishment, but in any case a confusion in the definition and plotting of the cost function should be pointed out. If it is true that a small output would naturally be produced by primitive methods while a larger one would justify a more elaborate organization with greater efficiency, it may well seem that the case is one of decreasing costs. There is a fallacy in overlooking the fact that any amount of the commodity *could* be made by any one of the methods available. A correct treatment of the cost in relation to output should plot a complete cost curve for each method separately, extending from zero output up to one of indefinite magnitude as shown in Diagram VIII. For the simplest method we shall have the curve of slightly increasing costs which represents the normal situation as shown early in the discussion (curve 1). For a more elaborate technology the smaller magnitudes of output will be much more costly, but as output increases up to the capacity of the equipment, costs rapidly decrease, to a level below that of the first method. Beyond this point the curve becomes parallel with the first (curve 2). And similarly for a still more capitalistic method, as shown in curve 3. The significant part of the figure presents therefore, not a curve of decreasing costs, but a series of curves of increasing costs at different levels. It is hardly supposable that there can be a plurality of equilibrium points in such a situation, at which production may go forward *under competitive conditions*. The substance of the matter is, as already brought out, that if more efficient methods, connected with larger-scale operations, are available, the number of organizations in the industry will be reduced until all are on the most efficient scale. Then if the demand is sufficient to maintain a plurality of organizations, each will be subject to increasing costs; if the demand is not large

* The *Quarterly Journal of Economics* for May, 1918.

enough for that, the industry will be a monopoly, in which case there is no tendency for cost and price to be equal (monopoly revenue not being counted as a part of cost).

VII

The main conclusion which we have attempted in this paper to establish is that decreasing cost with increasing output is a condition incompatible with stable competition in the industry. A significant degree of the phenomenon is probably rare outside of industries which are *both* naturally monopolistic *and* greatly overbuilt in speculative anticipation of future growth in demand. The significance of fluctuations also is sure to be greatly overestimated. The effective physical mobility of capital and labour, considered as physical productive power, is probably great enough in our society to make possible a very close adjustment of production to demand under ordinary conditions. The changes which upset business relations and throw costs and prices out of correspondence are *price phenomena*, and are due to miscalculated speculative contracts and to change in the value of the circulating medium. They affect business as a whole rather than the relations between different industries. Productive services as a class tend to be undervalued or overvalued relatively to finished goods. When the latter condition arises, industry has to stop and readjust itself, for under competition a business cannot operate unless it makes a pecuniary profit.

An error very different from that of treating price-determining cost as a decreasing function of output but not unconnected with it and very common, is the exaggeration of the economy of large-scale production and our highly organized industrial system as a whole. A spectacular saving is effected in certain operations, such as spinning and weaving; even when the labour which makes and maintains the equipment is considered, it is very large. But to make that saving possible large organizations must exist and the cost of internal cohesion in large groups of men is very high. Material must be collected and goods distributed over a wide area and the incredibly wasteful methods of purchase and sale are the best so far devised. There is much food for reflection in the smallness of the difference in cost between a tailor-made and a factory-made suit of clothes and the fact that the housewife who does her own sewing can often make higher wages than are paid to her sister for making the garments by "modern" methods.

VIII

FALLACIES IN THE INTERPRETATION
OF SOCIAL COST*

Arguments for social interference developed by Pigou and Graham illustrate common misinterpretations of the meaning of cost and its variation with output, 217.—I. The private owner of a natural opportunity secures maximum return from it by charging that rent which halts the application of investment at the point which is socially most advantageous, 221.—II. The notion of decreasing cost is a fallacy; competitive price fixation under decreasing cost or increasing returns an impossible situation, 222.—III. The law of comparative advantage in international trade is fundamentally sound, 230.—Importation a method of using resources to produce the imported good, and will be employed under competitive conditions only when more efficient than a direct method, 232.—The competitive system has important defects, but they lie outside the mechanical theory of exchange relations, 233.

In two recent articles† Professor F. D. Graham of Princeton University has developed an ingenious argument to prove that the classical theory of comparative cost as a demonstration of the economic advantage of trade between nations is "all wrong." He contends that a protective tariff may, after all, be a wise national policy in that it may enable the nation which adopts·it to secure a larger product from its resources than would be secured if free trade were permitted. It is the opinion of the present writer, and the contention of this paper, that it is Professor Graham's argument which is fallacious, though the way in which the classical theory has been formulated in many instances leaves much to be desired. The matter is of the greater importance because the most important argument, from the standpoint of general theory, in Professor A. C. Pigou's monumental work on *The Economics of Welfare‡* is, as I shall also try to show, marred by the same, or a very similar, fallacy.

* Reprinted by permission from *The Quarterly Journal of Economics*, vol. xxxviii (1924), pp. 582–606.

† *Quarterly Journal of Economics*, February 1923, November 1923.

‡ The Macmillan Co., 1918. This paper was written and submitted to the editor of the *Quarterly Journal* before the appearance of the March number of the *Economic*

If economic theory is interpreted as a critique of the competitive system of organization, its first and most general problem is that of determining whether the fundamental tendencies of free contractual relations under competitive control lead to the maximum production of value as measured in price terms. The problems of the validity of the price measure of "real value," and of the distribution of the value produced, are larger but subsequent problems, and belong to ethics as much as to economics; while the detailed comparison of the theoretical tendencies of perfect competition with the facts of any actual competitive society lie in the field of applied economics rather than that of theory. The theory of international or inter-regional trade is a special case under the more general problem, whether "society" can increase the production of exchange value by interfering with free bargaining relations: the case, namely, of bargains between its own members and members of some other society possessing a distinct body of productive resources. The peculiarity of international trade as compared with domestic lies in the immobility of population viewed as labour power. Natural resources are immobile even within a country, and capital goods enter into international commerce in the same way as goods ready for consumption.

Both Professor Graham and Professor Pigou reason to the conclusion that freedom of trade between regions may reduce the production of wealth in one or even both; and Professor Pigou extends essentially the same logic to cover the relations between different industries, irrespective of regional separation. The contention is that individual profit-seeking leads to an excessive investment of resources in industries of increasing cost (decreasing returns), part of which would yield more product if transferred by social action in some form to industries of constant or decreasing cost. The fallacy to be exposed is a misinterpretation of the relation between social cost and *entre-*

Journal. In that number Professor D. H. Robertson has an article covering some of the same ground and treating it with his usual analytic penetration and stylistic brilliancy. Moreover, in a rejoinder appended to that article, Professor Pigou admits the particular error in his analysis and states that it is to be eradicated in a forthcoming revised edition of his book. It seems inadvisable to recast and enlarge the present paper so as to include a discussion of Professor Robertson's argument, which is notably divergent from that presented herewith. I trust it will not be thought presumptuous to print without change the few pages which in some sense cover ground already covered by Professor Robertson.

preneur's cost. It will be convenient to take up first Professor Pigou's argument, which presents the more general problem.

I

In Professor Pigou's study the argument that free enterprise leads to excessive investment in industries having relatively upward-sloping cost curves is developed with the aid of a concrete example, the case of two roads.* Suppose that between two points there are two highways, one of which is broad enough to accommodate without crowding all the traffic which may care to use it, but is poorly graded and surfaced, while the other is a much better road but narrow and quite limited in capacity.† If a large number of trucks operate between the two termini and are free to choose either of the two routes, they will tend to distribute themselves between the roads in such proportions that the cost per unit of transportation, or effective result per unit of investment, will be the same for every truck on both routes. As more trucks use the narrower and better road, congestion develops, until at a certain point it becomes equally profitable to use the broader but poorer highway. The congestion and interference resulting from the addition of any particular truck to the stream of traffic on the narrow but good road affects in the same way the cost and output of all the trucks using that road. It is evident that if, after equilibrium is established, a few trucks should be arbitrarily transferred to the broad road, the reduction in cost, or increase in output, to those remaining on the narrow road would be a clear gain to the traffic as a whole. The trucks so transferred would incur no loss, for any one of them on the narrow road is a marginal truck, subject to the same relation between cost and output as any truck using the broad road. Yet whenever there is a difference in the cost, to an additional truck, of using the two roads,

* *Economics of Welfare*, p. 194.
† For simplicity, no account is taken of costs involved in *constructing* the two roads. The aim is to study the effects of the two types of "cost"—that which represents a consumption of productive power which might have been put to some other use, and pure rent or the payment for situation and opportunity. The assumption adopted is the simplest way of making the separation. The conclusion will not be changed if various types of cost are taken into account, so long as one of the roads has a definite situation advantage while the investment in the other can be repeated to any desirable extent with equivalent results in other locations.

the driver of any truck has an incentive to use the narrow road, but the advantage is reduced to zero for all the trucks. Thus, as the author contends, individual freedom results in a bad distribution of investment between industries of constant and industries of increasing cost.

In such a case social interference seems to be clearly justified. If the government should levy a small tax on each truck using the narrow road, the tax would be considered by the trucker as an element in his cost, and would cause the number of trucks on the narrow road to be reduced to the point where the *ordinary cost, plus the tax*, became equal to the cost on the broad road, assumed to be left tax free. The tax could be so adjusted that the number of trucks on the narrow road would be such as to secure the maximum efficiency in the use of the two roads taken together. The revenue obtained from such a tax would be a clear gain to the society, since no individual truck would incur higher costs than if no tax had been levied.

It is implied that the same argument holds good over the whole field of investment wherever investment is free to choose between uses subject to cost curves of different slope. Take, for example, two farms, one of superior quality, the other marginal or free land. Would not labour and capital go to the better farm, until the product per man became equal to the product to be obtained from the marginal land? If so, it is clear that the total product of all the labour and capital could be increased, as in the case of the roads, by transferring some of it from the superior to the inferior farm. This application of the reasoning will probably suggest the fallacy to anyone familiar with conventional economic theory. The statement does in fact indicate what would happen *if no one owned the superior farm*. But under private appropriation and self-seeking exploitation of the land the course of events is very different. It is in fact the social function of ownership to prevent this excessive investment in superior situations.

Professor Pigou's logic in regard to the roads is, as logic, quite unexceptionable. Its weakness is one frequently met with in economic theorizing, namely that the assumptions diverge in essential respects from the facts of real economic situations.* The most essential feature

* For the edification of the advocates of "inductive economics" it may be observed that the "facts" are not in dispute; that what is needed in the case is not more refined observation or the gathering of "statistics," but simply correct theorizing. There is, of course, also a large field in which the crucial facts are *not* obvious.

of competitive conditions is reversed, the feature, namely, of the private ownership of the factors practically significant for production. If the roads are assumed to be subject to private appropriation and exploitation, precisely the ideal situation which would be established by the imaginary tax will be brought about through the operation of ordinary economic motives. The owner of the broad road could not under effective competition charge anything for its use. If an agency of production is not subject to diminishing returns, and cannot be monopolized, there is, in fact, no incentive to its appropriation, and it will remain a free good. But the owner of the narrow road can charge for its use a toll representing its "superiority" over the free road, in accordance with the theory of rent, which is as old as Ricardian economics. An application of the familiar reasoning to this case will show that the toll will exactly equal the ideal tax above considered—though the application may need to be more careful and complete than that made by many of the expositors of the classical theory.

The owner of a superior opportunity for investment can set the charge for its use at any amount not greater than the excess of the product of the first unit of investment above what that unit could produce on the free opportunity. Under this charge investment will flow into the superior road up to the point where congestion and diminishing returns set in. (It is better in such a simple case to use the notion of diminishing returns than to use that of increasing costs, since in the large the practical objective is to maximize the product of given resources and not to minimize the expenditure of resources in producing a given product.) By reducing the charge, the owner will increase the amount of traffic using his road (or in general the amount of investment of labour and capital in any opportunity). But obviously the owner of the road will not set the charge so low that the last truck which uses the road secures a return in excess of the amount which it adds to the total product of the road (that is, of all the trucks which use it). This is clearer if we think of the owner of the road hiring the trucks instead of their hiring the use of the road. The effect is the same either way; it is still the same if some third party hires the use of both. The toll or rent will be so adjusted that *added* product of the last truck which uses the narrow road is just equal to what it could produce on the broad road. No truck will pay a higher charge, and it is not to the interest of the owner of the road to accept a lower fee. And this adjustment is exactly that which maximizes the total product of both roads.

The argument may be made clearer by the use of simple diagrams.* Chart A and B represents the case of constant cost or constant returns, the cost of successive units of output, or the return from successive units of investment on the broad road. In Chart C, the curve $DD'D_u$ is a *cost* curve for the narrow road, showing the cost of successive units of output. It starts at a lower level than the cost on the broad road, but at a certain point D', congestion sets in and increasing cost appears. Curve $DD'D_m$ is a curve of *marginal* costs on the narrow road, as Professor Pigou uses the term marginal cost; the marginal

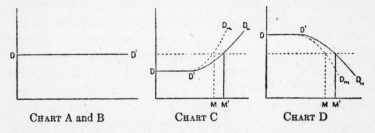

CHART A and B   CHART C   CHART D

cost of the nth unit of product is the difference between the total cost of producing n units and the total cost of producing $n + 1$ units. When costs begin to increase, the marginal cost will increase more rapidly than the cost of the added unit, since the production of each additional unit raises the cost of the earlier units to a level with that of the new unit. It must be observed that the cost of the additional unit is always the same as the cost per unit of the whole supply produced; much economic analysis is vitiated by a spurious separation of these two conceptions of cost.

Chart D represents the same facts as Chart C, but in terms of the product of successive units of investment instead of the cost of successive units of output, that is, as curves of "diminishing returns" instead of "increasing costs." The output begins at a higher level than on the broad road, but at the point D', which corresponds to the point of the same designation on Chart C, the return from investment begins to fall off. The curve $D'D_u$ shows the actual product of the added unit of invest-

* Cf. Pigou, op. cit., Appendix iii, pp. 931–8.

ment, and the curve $D'D_m$ its marginal product, its addition to the total. The latter decreases more rapidly, because the application of the additional unit reduces the yield of the earlier ones to equality with its own. The argument is the same, but stated in inverse or reciprocal form. As indicated, the viewpoint of Chart D is to be preferred, and it may be surmised that, if Professor Pigou had put his argument in this form, he would probably have avoided the error into which he was very likely misled by measuring efficiency in terms of cost of output instead of output of resources.*

The owner of the road will adjust his toll so that the traffic will take his road out to the point M in Chart C or D. It will *not*, under conditions of profit-seeking exploitation, be continued to M', as argued by Professor. Pigou. The actual output is the same as the "ideal" output, but it is the "ideal" output which is wrongly defined in Pigou's treatment (p. 937). Evidently, the adjustment is correct when the *marginal* product of the last unit of investment on the superior road is equal to the product of a similar unit on the free road. Confusion arises in translating this condition into terms of cost and selling price of product. Selling price will be determined by cost on the free road, or at least these two will be equal, however the causal relation is conceived. That is, the *money* cost of any unit of product is the value of the investment which is necessary to produce it on the free opportunity, where cost is constant, or, in general, at an opportunity margin where rent does not enter. Comparison of the two viewpoints shown by our Charts C and D above shows that under competitive conditions the application of investment to the superior opportunity will be stopped at the point where *marginal real cost* (cost in terms of the transferable investment) is equal to real cost on the free opportunity. When equal additions to investment make equal additions to output, equal units of output have the same cost. But the condition of equilibrium cannot be stated in terms of money cost and money selling price of product on the superior opportunity, *because*

---

* It may be noted that Robertson makes the opposite contention, that the concepts of increasing and decreasing costs are to be preferred to those of decreasing and increasing returns (loc. cit., p. 218). He gives no argument for this position. It seems to me that this is the entrepreneur's point of view, while that of either the investor or society is the inverse one advocated in the text above, and is distinctly to be preferred for general analysis.

these would be equal however the investment might be distributed, what
ever rent were charged, or whether the opportunity were appropriated
and exploited at all. The condition of equilibrium is that the rent on
the superior opportunity is maximized as an aggregate. The rent per
unit of output is a variable portion of a total unit cost which is fixed.

Extension of the foregoing argument to the general case of land
rent involves no difficulties and will not be carried out in detail. The
point is that any opportunity, whether or not it represents a previous
investment of any sort, is a productive factor if there is sufficient
demand for its use to carry into the stage of diminishing returns the
application to it of transferable investment. The charge made by a
private owner for the use of such an opportunity serves the socially
useful purpose of limiting the application of investment to the point
where *marginal* product instead of product per unit is equal to the
product of investment in free (rentless) opportunities; and under
competitive conditions this charge will be fixed at the level which
does make marginal products equal, and thus maximizes productivity on the whole.*

It is pertinent to add that in real life, the original "appropriation"
of such opportunities by private owners involves investment in
exploration, in detailed investigation and appraisal by trial and error
of the findings, in development work of many kinds necessary to
secure and market a product—besides the cost of buying off or killing

* It is a theoretically interesting fact that the rent on an opportunity which maximizes the return to its owner and brings about the socially correct investment in it is
its "marginal product," in the same sense as used to describe the competitive remuneration of other productive factors transferable from one use to another or ultimately
derived from labour and waiting. It is exactly the amount by which the product of
the whole competitive system would be reduced if the opportunity were held out
of use or destroyed, and the investment which would be combined with it were put
to the next best possible use. This point is brought out in Professor Young's chapter
on Rent in Ely's *Outlines of Economics* (pp. 409, 410 in the fourth edition). Professor
Young also pointed out the essential fallacy in Professor Pigou's argument, in a
review of the latter's earlier work on Wealth and Welfare (*Quarterly Journal of
Economics*, August 1913).

The relation between "investment" and "opportunity" is an interesting question,
by no means so simple as it is commonly assumed to be. In the writer's view there is
little basis for the common distinction in this regard between "natural resources"
and labour or capital. The qualities of real significance for economic theory are the
conditions of supply and the degree of fluidity or its opposite, specialization to a
particular use. In a critical examination neither attribute forms a basis for erecting
natural agents into a separate class.

or driving off previous claimants. Under competitive conditions, again, investment in such activities of "appropriation" would not yield a greater return than investment in any other field. These activities are indeed subject to a large "aleatory element"; they are much affected by luck. But there is no evidence proving either that the luck element is greater than in other activities relating to economic progress, or that in fact the average reward has been greater than that which might have been had from conservative investments.

II

While Professor Pigou constantly refers to industries of decreasing cost, or increasing returns, the principles at issue do not necessarily imply more than a *difference* in the way in which efficiency varies with size from one industry to another. Some of Professor Graham's reasoning in regard to international trade and international value depends upon decreasing cost as such. It seems advisable, before taking up his argument concretely, to devote a few paragraphs to this conception, which the writer believes to involve serious fallacies, and to the meaning of cost and its variation.

Valuation is an aspect of conscious choice. Apart from a necessity of choosing, values have no meaning or existence. Valuation *is* a comparison of values. A single value, existing in isolation, can no more be imagined than can a single force without some other force opposed to it as a "reaction" to its "action." Value is in fact the complete analogue of force in the interpretation of human activity, and in a behaviouristic formulation is identical with force—which is to say, it is an instrumental idea, metaphysically non-existent. Fundamentally, then, the cost of any value is simply the value that is given up when it is chosen; it is just the reaction or resistance to choice which makes it choice. Ordinarily we speak of cost as a consumption of "resources" of some kind, but everyone recognizes that resources have no value in themselves; that they simply represent the products which could have been had by their use in some other direction than the one chosen.

The notion of cost suffers greatly in logical clearness from confusion with the vague and ambiguous term "pain." In the broad true sense every cost is a pain, and the two are identical. Little or nothing can be made of the distinction between pain and the sacrifice of pleasure, or between pleasure and escape from pain. The subject cannot be gone into here from the point of view of psychology; it is enough to point out that the way in which a particular person regards a particular sacrifice depends mainly upon the direction of *change* in the affective tone of his consciousness or upon the established level of expectations. The essential thing is that the pleasure-pain character of a value is irrelevant, that the universal meaning of cost is the sacrifice of a value-alternative. This is just as true of the "irksomeness" of labour, as of a payment of money. The irksomeness of digging a ditch reflects the value of the loafing or playing which might be done instead. And there is no significant difference between this irksomeness or pain and that of using the proceeds of the sale of a bond to pay a doctor's bill when it might have been used to procure a fortnight's vacation.*

The natural and common rule in choice is necessarily that of increasing cost. In the exchange of one good for another at a fixed ratio, the further the exchange is carried, the more "utility" is given up and the less is secured. This is merely the law of diminishing utility. It is only when one commodity is given up in order that another may be produced by the use of the common and divertible productive energy that we ordinarily think of the variation of cost. If two commodities are produced by a single homogeneous productive factor, there is no variation of cost as successive portions of one are given up to procure more of the other by shifting that factor— except in the sense of increasing utility cost as met with in the case of exchange. Ordinarily, however, new considerations enter, as a matter of fact. If we wish to produce more wheat by producing less corn, we find that the further the shift of production is carried, the more *bushels* of corn (as well as corn value) have to be given up to produce a

* Besides confusion with the notion of pain, which has at last obtained in psychology a definite meaning independent of unpleasantness, the notion of cost encounters in economics another source of obscurity. This is in the relation between those values which do not pass through the market and receive prices and those which do. The "loafing" which underlies the irksomeness of labour is such a value, and there is a tendency to associate the notion of cost with these non-pecuniary values. In this connection it should be noted that not merely labour but all types of productive service are subject to the competition of uses which yield their satisfactions directly and not through the channel of a marketable product. Thus land is used for lawns as well as for fields, and examples could be multiplied at will.

bushel of wheat (and still more for a given amount of wheat value). This is the economic principle of increasing cost (decreasing returns) as generally understood reduced to its lowest terms and freed from ambiguity.

When costs are measured in value terms and product in physical units there are two sorts of reasons for increasing cost, one reflecting value changes and the other technological changes. The first would be operative if all productive resources were perfectly homogeneous and perfectly fluid. But this is not, in general, the case, and technological changes supervene which work in the same direction and add to the increase which would otherwise take place in the cost of a unit of the product which is being produced in larger volume. Principal among these technological changes is the fact that some of the resources used to produce the commodity being sacrificed are not useful in the production of that whose output is being increased, and in consequence the resources which are transferred are used in progressively larger proportions in the second industry and in smaller proportions in the first, in combination with certain other resources which are specialized to the two industries respectively. The consequent reduction in the physical productive effect of the transferred factors is what is meant by diminishing returns in one of the many narrower uses of that highly ambiguous expression. Another technological cause still further aggravating the tendency to increasing costs arises from the fact that productive factors are not really homogeneous or uniform in quality. As productive power is transferred from corn to wheat, it will be found that the concrete men, acres, and implements transferred are those progressively more suitable for corn-growing and less suitable for wheat. Thus each unit suffers a progressively greater reduction in its value in terms of units of either commodity, or it takes more units to represent in the wheat industry the value of a single unit in the corn industry, and the value costs of wheat mount still higher for this third reason.

All three changes so far noted clearly involve increasing cost in the real sense, the amount of value* outlay or sacrifice necessary to produce an additional physical unit of the commodity whose production is

---

* Value as used in this discussion means "real" value, relative significance or utility. No assertion as to exchange value or price is implied.

increased. In addition to these we have to consider two further possible sources of increased cost. The first is that, when an additional unit of, say, wheat is produced, and the factors transferable from other industries to wheat are raised in price, the quantities of these factors already used to produce wheat will rise in price along with those added to the industry. Should all this increase in cost be charged up to the production of the last unit of wheat produced, which causes it to appear? In a sense, this is in truth a social cost of this last unit. Yet the transfer of productive energy will not take place unless there has been a shift in the market estimate of wheat in comparison with competing commodities such as to justify it. That is, as the exchange system measures values, making all units of the same good equal in value, the increase in the total value of the wheat must be greater than the decrease in the value of the output of competing commodities. (A discrepancy— *in either direction*—may result from considering the potential significances of infra-marginal units commonly designated as consumers' surplus.) The second additional possible source of increased cost is the increased payments which will be made for the specialized factors used in producing wheat,* the cost elements which are of the nature of rent or surplus. These payments evidently do not represent social costs at all, but redistributions of product merely. Such redistributions may be "good," or "bad," depending on the moral position, according to some standard, of the owners of the two classes of factors respectively.

Decreasing cost (or increasing returns) is alleged to result in several ways, which can be dealt with but briefly. The most important is the echnological economy of large-scale production. When the output of a commodity is increased, the cost of the productive services used to produce it will be higher; but this increase in their cost per unit may, it is held, be more than offset by economies in utilization, made possible by larger-scale operations, which increase the amount of product obtained from given quantities of materials and resources consumed.† But technological economies arise from increasing the

---

* The fallacy of identifying specialized factors with natural agents and transferable factors with labour and capital has been referred to above. It will not be elaborated in this paper.

† Professor Graham says (p. 203, note) that decreasing cost is an "aspect of the law of proportionality." This is a form of statement frequently met with, but rests

size of the productive unit, not from increasing the total output of the industry as a whole. The possibility of realizing such economies— by the distribution of "overhead," or more elaborate division of labour or use of machinery—tends to bring about an increase in the *scale* of production, but this may happen independently of any change in the output of the industry. If competition is effective, the size of the productive unit will tend to grow until *either* no further economies are obtainable, *or* there is only one establishment left and the industry is a monopoly. When all establishments have been brought to the most efficient size, variation in total output is a matter of changing their *number*, in which no technical economies are involved.

The rejoinder to the above argument is the doctrine of "external economies," which surely rests upon a misconception. Economies may be "external" to a particular establishment or technical production unit, but they are not external to the industry if they affect its efficiency. The portion of the productive process carried on in a particular unit is an accidental consideration. External economies in one business unit are internal economies in some other, within the industry. Any branch or stage in the creation of a product which offers continuously a chance for technical economies with increase in the scale of operations must eventuate either in monopoly or in leaving the tendency behind and establishing the normal relation of increasing cost with increasing size. If the organization unit is not small in comparison with the industry as a whole, a totally different law must be applied to the relation between output, cost, and price.

Two other alleged sources of decreasing cost are the stimulation of demand and the stimulation of invention. Neither can properly be regarded as an effect of increasing output, other things being equal. Producing a commodity and distributing it at a loss might result in developing a taste for it, but would be no different in principle from any other method of spending money to produce this result. Inventions tend to enlarge the scale of production rather than large-scale production to cause inventions. It is true that an increase in demand from some outside cause may stimulate invention, but the action takes place

on a misconception sufficiently refuted in the text. It is true only accidentally, if it is true in any general sense at all, that a more elaborate technology is associated with a change in the proportions of the factors.

through first making the industry highly profitable. The result is not uniform or dependable, nor is it due to increased production as such.

These brief statements form a mere summary of the argument that, with reference to long-run tendencies under given general conditions, increasing the output of a commodity must increase its cost of production unless the industry is, or becomes, a monopoly. They also indicate the nature of the relation between social cost and entrepreneur's money cost. Under competition, transferable resources are distributed among alternative uses in such a way as to yield equal marginal* value product everywhere, which is the arrangement that maximizes production, as measured by value, on the whole. Nontransferable resources secure "rents" which equalize money costs to all producers and for all units of product under the foregoing condition; or, better, the rents bring about that allocation of resources which maximizes production, under the condition that money costs are equalized.

A further major fallacy in value theory which suffuses Professor Graham's argument will be pointed out in general terms before proceeding with detailed criticism. The reference is to the notorious "law of reciprocal demand." This so-called law, that the prices of commodities exchanged internationally are so adjusted that a country's exports pay for its imports, is at best a truism. To say that what one gives in exchange pays for what one gets is merely a statement of the fact that one is exchanged for the other. What calls for explanation in the case is the process which fixes *how much* of one thing will be parted with, and *how much* of· the other received in return.

III

We are now ready to take up concretely the proposed refutation of the law of comparative advantage. Professor Graham begins by assuming two countries, which he calls A and B, but which it appears simpler to designate as England and America respectively. Suppose then that in England

> 10 days' labour produces 40 units of wheat
> 10 days' labour produces 40 watches;

* "Differential" is the term in use in other sciences for the idea commonly referred to as a marginal unit in economics.

in America

> 10 days' labour produces 40 units of wheat
> 10 days' labour produces 30 watches.

America has a comparative advantage in wheat, England in watches.*
According to the accepted theory, trade at any ratio intermediate
between the two cost ratios will be of advantage to both countries.
Our author assumes it to begin at the ratio of 35 watches for 40 units
of wheat. Then, for each ten days' labour devoted to producing wheat
and exchanging for watches, America can get 35 watches instead of the
30 which could be produced by using the same labour in producing
the watches. England, for each ten days' labour devoted to producing
watches and exchanging for wheat can secure $\frac{40}{35} \times 40 \ (= 45\frac{5}{7})$ units
of wheat, instead of the 40 units which could be directly produced
with the same labour.

So far, well and good for the theory. But at this point Professor
Graham's blows begin to fall. Assuming that wheat-growing is an
industry of increasing and watch-making one of decreasing costs,
it will come to pass, as the two countries progressively specialize, that
the cost of both commodities is decreased for England and increased
for America. It clearly follows, first, that if the process goes on long
enough, America will begin to lose, and just as clearly, from the
assumptions of the article, that the process will go on for ever! For
the further it is carried, the greater becomes England's comparative
advantage in the production of watches and the greater becomes
America's comparative advantage in the production of wheat. Yet this
conclusion must arouse a suspicion that there is something wrong in
Denmark.

First, in accordance with the argument above, drop the assumption
of decreasing cost as a permanent condition in the watch-making
industry; then the two cost ratios in the two countries must come
together instead of separating as the specialization of productive
efforts progresses. Under any assumption whatever, *either* this must

---

* The use of labour as equivalent to productive power, or the treatment of labour
as the only factor which may be transferred from one industry to the other, is a
simplification likely to mislead the unwary, but it will not be criticized here. It is
of interest to note, however, that historically the whole doctrine of comparative cost
was a prop for a labour cost theory of value.

happen, *or else* one country must entirely cease to produce one of the commodities. In the first event, the exchange ratio will be the common cost ratio of the two countries (transportation costs being neglected, as usual in these discussions). If the second result ensues—that one country abandons one of the industries—*the exchange ratio will be the cost ratio in the country which still produces both commodities* (assuming, always, that monopoly is absent). Professor Graham "assumes" that the comparative advantage has become progressively greater as the result of specialization and then "assumes" (page 210) that, with the cost ratio in one country half what it is in the other, the market price may be established at any ratio between the two. In reality the only possible result under the cost conditions he states would be that America would stop producing watches at once and would exchange wheat for watches at the ratio of 40 for 40 (the cost ratio in England), thus making a *gain* of 20 watches on each ten days' labour so employed as compared with using it to produce the watches in America.

Next, the author proposes to consider the effect of interpreting his cost figures as representing marginal cost instead of cost per unit. He gets no further, however, than to average up the marginal with assumed infra-marginal costs, which amounts merely to a slight change in the numbers assumed for cost per unit. He nowhere gives an explicit statement of what he means by cost, and must be suspected of not having clearly faced the difficulties and ambiguities in the notion, as brought out in the argument of the first and second parts of this paper. Certainly it will not do to recognize a possible permanent difference under competition in the money cost of different units of a supply, or in their marginal real cost. The money costs which represent real costs differ in different situations, but the rent element always equalizes them, or produces *coincidence* between equality of money cost, which would result in any case, and equality of marginal real cost, which is the social desideratum. Value and cost are like action and reaction, axiomatically equal, and as in an exchange system the value of all similar units must be equal, so must their costs.

In the writer's opinion this also is socially and morally correct. We do not, and should not, value the first slice of bread more highly than the last, nor systematically value anything at more or less than its necessary cost. As between units of supply consumed by different persons, the case is different, because different persons do not come into the market with equal exchange power in the form of productive capacity. But the question is one of ethics, entirely outside the field of exchange as a mechanical problem. The famous surpluses have the same kind of significance as potential energy in physics. They relate to possible changes in fundamental conditions, but have nothing to do with the conditions of equilibrium in any particular situation. With reference to relations among actual magnitudes, cost curves and utility curves should always be interpreted to mean that, as supply varies, the cost, or utility, of every unit changes in the manner shown by the curve.

Marginal money cost, in the sense in which it is used by Professor Pigou, is meaningless with relation to competitive conditions. It is true that under monopoly the supply is so adjusted that the contribution of the last unit to total selling price (marginal demand price) is equal to the addition to total cost incurred in consequence of producing it (marginal supply price); but this is a mere equivalent of the statement that the difference between total cost and total selling price is made a maximum. Professor Graham seems to use the expression marginal cost to mean the particular money expense of producing the last unit of supply; but, as already stated, there cannot in the long run under competitive conditions be a difference between the cost of this unit and that of any other, or the cost per unit of producing the whole supply.

Professor Graham's article makes use at several points of the effects of different elasticities of demand for different goods, especially as between agricultural products and manufactures. He fails to recognize that, with reference to large and inclusive groups of commodities, demand, which is an exchange *ratio*, is merely a different view of a production ratio, and hence of a cost ratio. In discussing the sale of a single commodity in a complicated economic society and with reference to small changes, it is permissible to treat money as an absolute; but in reducing all exchange to barter between two classes of goods, this procedure is quite inadmissible.

Moreover, consideration of the actual course of events when trade is opened up will show that elasticity of demand has little to do with the special theory of international trade or international value. Each country continues to specialize in the commodities in which it has a comparative advantage, until there is no gain to be secured from further specialization; that is, until it will cost as much to secure the next unit of the imported good by exchange as it will to produce it within the country. Now at a certain point, a country will obtain as much of the imported good as it would have produced for itself under an equilibrium adjustment within itself if foreign trade had been prohibited; and in consequence of the saving of productive power effected by the trade, a part of the resources which in its absence would be used to produce that commodity will be left to be disposed of. *Beyond this point*, that is, in the disposition of the saved productive power, elasticities of demand come into operation. This fund of saved productive power will not all be used to produce either of the commodities concerned in the exchange with the foreign nation, but will be distributed over the whole field of production in accordance with the ordinary laws of supply and demand.

The foregoing paragraphs are believed to cover the main points in the writings criticized which involve fallacies in the interpretation of cost and so come under the title of this paper. The entire argument of Professor Graham's second article falls to the ground, as he has stated it, as soon as the principles of cost are applied to the determination of international values instead of "assuming" the latter. Many further points in his first article are especially inviting to criticism, but fall outside the scope of the present paper. It suffices for the solution of the essential problem of international trade to recognize that the production of one good to exchange for another is an *alternative method of producing* the second commodity. Under competitive conditions, productive resources will not be used in this indirect process of production unless the yield is greater than that obtained by the use of the direct method. The task of economic analysis is to show why the profit-seeking motive impels the private producer to put resources to the use which brings the largest yield. Now to the entrepreneur producers of wheat and watches, in a case like that used in the illustration, the choice is not a question of comparative advantage, but of absolute profit or loss. If ten days' labour will produce a quantity of wheat which can be exchanged for more than 40 watches, then that amount of labour will be *worth more* than 40 watches, and the business enterprise which uses it to produce the watches will simply lose money. It is an example of the common fallacy of thinking in terms of physical efficiency, whereas efficiency is in the nature of the case a relation between value magnitudes.

That free enterprise is not a perfectly ideal system of social organization is a proposition not to be gainsaid, and nothing is further from the aims of the present writer than to set up the contention that it is. But in his opinion the weaknesses and failures of the system lie outside the field of the mechanics of exchange under the theoretical conditions of perfect competition. It is probable that *all* efforts to prove a continued bias in the workings of competition as such, along the lines followed by Professors Pigou and Graham, are doomed to failure. Under certain theoretical conditions, more or less consciously and definitely assumed in general by economic theorists, the system would be ideal. The correct form of the problem of general criticism referred to at the outset of this paper is, therefore, that of bringing these lurking assumptions above the threshold into the realm of the explicit and of contrasting them with the facts of life—the conditions under which competitive dealings are actually carried on.*

When the problem is attacked from this point of view, the critic finds himself moving among considerations very different from the logical quantitative relations of such discussions as the foregoing. Human beings are not "individuals," to begin with; a large majority of them are not even legally competent to contract. The values of life are not, in the main, reducible to satisfactions obtained from the consumption of exchangeable goods and services. Such desires as people have for goods and services are not their own in any original sense, but are the product of social influence of innumerable kinds and of every moral grade, largely manufactured by the competitive system itself. The productive capacities in their own persons and in owned external things which form the ultimate stock-in-trade of the human being are derived from an uncertain mixture of conscientious effort, inheritance, pure luck, and outright force and fraud. He cannot be well or truly informed regarding the markets for the productive power he possesses, and the information which he gets has a way of coming to

* The great bulk of the critical material in Professor Pigou's *Wealth and Welfare* is of this character.

him after the time when it would be of use. The business organizations which are the directing divinities of the system are but groups of ignorant and frail beings like the individuals with whom they deal. (In the perfectly ideal order of theory the problem of management would be non-existent!) The system as a whole is dependent upon an outside organization, an authoritarian state, made up also of ignorant and frail human beings, to provide a setting in which it can operate at all. Besides watching over the dependent and non-contracting, the state must define and protect property rights, enforce contract and prevent non-contractual (compulsory) transactions, maintain a circulating medium, and most especially prevent that collusion and monopoly, the antithesis of competition, into which competitive relations constantly tend to gravitate. It is in the field indicated by this summary list of postulates, rather than in that of the mechanics of exchange relations, that we must work out the ultimate critique of free enterprise.

IX

VALUE AND PRICE*

MODERN economics is a study of the system of social-economic organization which functions through and in connection with the pricing process; price and pricing therefore constitute one of the central topics of economics. Three main sets of prices are generally distinguished: the prices of consumption goods and services; the prices of productive services, or of the uses of productive agencies; and the sale prices of productive agencies, or, in a non-slaveholding society, of property which, unlike human beings, can be bought and sold. Theoretically property prices are merely the capitalized prices of the uses which property yields, although the large speculative element in the knowledge of future services and their expected price makes the matter much more complicated in fact.

Since price is always the price of something and is a quantity or number, it is natural to think of it as the measure of some quality or attribute in the thing which bears a price. This quality or attribute measured by price is the simplest conception of value. Indeed it is this value concept which constitutes one of the two notions of value in a sense distinct from price in the *Wealth of Nations* as in most economic writing before and since. The second and very different value concept is related to social policy. The economic doctrine of Adam Smith and of the classical school as a whole is a mixture of a more or less scientific analysis of a price economy with what is really political propaganda for *laissez-faire*; and the advocacy of any specific policy implies some ideal of the end of social policy in general and a hierarchy of values based upon it. This broader concept of value is also involved in the thought of most economists of the other schools, for they too have combined scientific analysis with propaganda.

Modern systematic discussion of the phenomena of value (in the scientific sense) and price may be said to have begun with the classical school. It proceeded from two general theories which go back to the

* Reprinted from *The Encyclopaedia of the Social Sciences*, edited by E. R. A. Seligman. By permission of The Macmillan Company, Publishers.

earliest speculations on the subject among the Greeks—the theories which emphasize respectively "use value," or utility, and cost. The classical economists dismissed use value as a cause of price on the ground that there seemed to be no correspondence in fact between the two. Smith used the illustration of water and diamonds, which had appeared in the literature before, to show that the highest use value may go with the lowest price, and conversely. But in centring attention on cost as the determinant of price, Smith employed in different portions of his work two distinct conceptions of the nature of cost. In certain passages he obviously referred to absolute cost in labour, pain, or sacrifice, while in others he implied relative or alternative cost, a reflection of the competition of different uses for productive capacity. He never saw the relation between the two cost concepts and he gave the predominant place to a labour cost view. His first great successor, Ricardo, whose work gave the characteristic form to economic theory for the greater part of the nineteenth century, was concerned mainly with giving unity and consistency to Smith's system by developing the labour cost theory to the exclusion of the other conception. Even more exclusive emphasis was placed on labour cost as the basis of value by the post-Ricardian socialistic schools of thought.

Thus throughout most of the nineteenth century both orthodox and socialistic economics treated price as tending to measure or express value, more perfectly so as a longer run was taken into view, and found the essence of value in pain cost. It may well be suspected that the primitive idea of the curse of labour, as found in the Book of Genesis, had something to do with this attitude. At bottom the issue between the two cost conceptions reflects a confusion between ethics and science, between the defensible but not necessarily sound ethical principle that labour or sacrifice ought to be the basis of value, or at least of economic income, and the doctrine that in a competitive price economy price in fact is determined by, or tends to correspond with, sacrifice cost. The second position can be characterized only as an error, in view of the conditions of production which obtain generally in the modern world. A labour cost theory would have considerable validity if each commodity were produced by a different labourer or different kind of labour incapable of producing any other. But the truth is that in general each kind of labour competes for employment in connection with the production of a great many commodities, and that production generally involves agencies other than labour similarly transferable with more or less freedom from one use to another. In so far as productive resources are freely transferable but perform complementary functions in each use, the relative price of any two products depends upon the quantities of fluid resources used to produce a unit of each, and the relative price of any two transferable productive resources depends upon the quantities of products added to output by a unit of each productive resource. Non-transferable resources get a price-determined, differential or residual payment, a rent in the theoretical sense. If the essential resources are transferable to nearly every productive use all prices become interconnected into a system and any one price can be explained only in terms of economic equilibrium, which takes into account all the general conditions of economic life in the given system—the tastes of consumers, the supplies of the different kinds of resources and their distribution of ownership, and technology as known and applied. True, in such a system prices are affected by effort and intelligence, which may at least in part be considered as ethical factors, but they are also affected—and much more decisively—by considerations of economic power.

As the classical writers recognized, price may arise from any cause limiting supply. It is limitation and the resulting necessity of balancing one thing against another in choice which generate the idea of equivalence underlying the concept of price. The latter has no necessary connection with cost of production. It depends on relative attractiveness, which depends on relative supply. Where production is involved it affects prices through determination of relative supply, which in turn is conditioned by the allocation of productive resources among industries turning out different goods or services. This phenomenon is best studied at the point of equilibrium, where resources are allocated among the different uses in such a way as to equalize their productive values; it is this equivalence which is reflected in both prices and costs. Thus the cost of producing a unit of any commodity is the non-production of a determinate amount of other commodities. The pain or pleasure involved in production is operative only to the extent that it varies from one employment to another, and it has in fact little to do with prices. In so far as the owners of the resources have no preference as to their uses, it is irrelevant to the explanation of price whether the resources are property or free labourers and whether their functioning is painful or pleasant or unconscious.

Historically, breakdown of the pain cost theory of value and establishment of a more realistic doctrine was a by-product of the subjective value revolution. Although at first all cost theory was discarded in favour of the marginal utility explanation of value, gradually it came to be recognized that, while price immediately depends on marginal utility, under competitive conditions of production it is ultimately determined by cost in the sense just indicated. But the identification of value with marginal utility raised new problems in the handling of which social values and the propaganda interest played a part. A typical problem of this sort is the "rich-man-poor-man" difficulty, the fact that the price paid by the rich for food to waste is the same as that paid by the poor for food to sustain life.

As a scientific question the problem of economic utility is simply that of the comparative motivation of purchasers of a commodity. Since economic theory had grown up in the intellectual milieu of the hedonistic interpretation of human nature, the motivation stressed was the desire to increase pleasure and reduce pain. The pleasure theory, however, was always more or less ambiguous as between psychological and ethical hedonism; it did not make clear whether maximum pleasure to the individual is actually and necessarily the determining motive of every act or maximum pleasure in some of many possible and conflicting interpretations is the end toward which all conduct ought to be directed. Even ethical hedonism is ambiguous since it may refer to a moral duty of the individual or to an end at which social policy should be aimed.

For the purposes of explanatory analysis, however, ethical hedonism is obviously irrelevant. And the psychological hedonism, the theory of pleasure as the universal motive, is becoming increasingly untenable. Clearly, the motive underlying actual purchases must at least be modified from the pleasure which actually results to that which is anticipated, unless it can be assumed that the two always coincide, and they proverbially do not. From the question as to just what is anticipated, what later consequence of any behaviour constitutes its motive, one naturally proceeds to inquire just what part conscious anticipation in any form plays in the actual determination of conduct. This is the question of rationality. Critical students are more and more doubtful not only as to the degree to which people really foresee the consequences of their acts, but even as to the extent to which choices are consistently made with a view to any intended result, especially any result desired for its own sake. In modern psychology there is an increasing emphasis on unconscious motivation as well as on the "prejudice" and caprice in the conscious motives of men; again, it is recognized that the immediate, concrete aims of action are desired as symbols of social relations or social position. To the extent that rational action plays a part in economic life and social conduct at large its motives are increasingly regarded as analogous to the motives of a game in which the capture of opponents' pieces or the gain of points is not desired for itself but with a view to winning the game. This is far removed from such tangible and concrete results as are suggested by terms like utility or want satisfaction in the consumption of goods and services.

In any event, a growing recognition that many problems of economics are independent of any particular conception of the nature of motivation has resulted in an increasing tendency to treat motivation as a datum and to leave the discussion of its character to specialists in fields other than economics. The one fact which is essential to economics as a science is the law of the variation of relative intensity of the incentive or attraction to any particular line of activity as it is carried on in competition with other lines. Acceptance of this conclusion amounts to an interpretation of economic behaviour on the analogy of mechanics, with motive as the "force" which produces the act. It is doubtful, however, whether motive in this sense affords any place for the notion of value. Moreover, the concept of force in mechanics has itself been recognized as metaphysical rather than scientific in a strict sense. Again, the interpretation of motive as force is subject to serious objections. In mechanics forces are known and measured through their effects alone; consequently there is no ambiguity in the information about them, such as it is. In the field of human conduct motives are not inferred merely from the observation of behaviour; there seems to exist, on the contrary, a kind of direct knowledge of

motivation through the process of social intercommunication—and
the two sources of knowledge disagree. As a result of direct experience
it is known that behaviour does not correspond to intent as accurately
as the effect in mechanics is assumed to correspond to the forces
producing it; the relation between motive and act is vitally affected
by error absent from mechanical process.

For these reasons there has been a movement in economics to dis-
pense with motivation altogether. Although utility doctrine is still
ably defended in one of its early homes by Hans Mayer and his school
at Vienna, efforts have been made, notably by Gustav Cassel, to build
up a system of price theory without making use of utility or value
theory in any form.

In general, if explanation of economic behaviour in terms of motives
is to be abandoned, a number of alternative possibilities are open.
Perhaps the simplest is the one analogous to a trend in physics—to
do away with all "explanation" and merely to formulate empirical
laws; the result is statistical economic theory, having for its content
the objective phenomena of commodities and prices alone. A second
line of development away from the types of value theory represented
by classical or utility economics centres around the emphasis on the
social control of economic life with clearly implied advocacy of such
control. In the past generation this trend has been most marked in
Germany (socialism of the chair), in England (Fabianism and left
wing liberalism), and in the United States (as a phase of institutionalist
economics).

The third alternative to explanatory theory is that of treating
economic phenomena as essentially historical, which, of course, must
be done in any case if the concrete content of economic life at a particular time and place is to be explained. Historical economics again
subdivides into as many varieties as there are basic conceptions of
history and historical method. Two such varieties stand out. The first
treats history as far as possible in objective, empirical terms, and may
use statistics for the discovery and analysis of trends; logically this
procedure contrasts sharply with the search for repetitive laws,
analogous to those of natural science, which characterizes statistical
economic theory, but in practice the two conceptions run together
in the work of statistical economists. The second variety of historical

economics uses the more familiar humanistic conceptions of political and social history—individual ambitions, efforts, and failures in a given social-psychological setting. It represents essentially a revival or continuation of the historical schools of the nineteenth century, especially prominent in Germany. In so far as it arrives at generalizations, it may be described as institutional economics, a term which has come into use particularly in the United States. The related contemporary movement in the German literature is referred to as neo-historical or sociological economics, with Sombart and Max Weber as its most prominent leaders.

At the root of the differences and disputes between the old and the new economics as well as among the three new lines of theoretical development noted above are two problems: the relation between description and explanation and the relation between statement of fact and critical evaluation. The first, inescapable in any thinking about human conduct, is fundamentally the problem of the reality of choice, or "freedom of the will." It involves the essence of the value problem in the sense of individual values, and is at bottom the problem of the relation between individual man and nature. The second basic problem has to do with the relation between the individual man and society.

The crucial fact in connection with the first problem is that, if motive or end in any form is granted any real role in conduct, it cannot be that of a cause in the sense of causality in natural science. This is the supreme limitation alike of statistical and historical economics. For, if motive or end is used to explain behaviour, it must in turn be brought into the same relation with events and conditions antecedent to it, and then the motive becomes superfluous; the behaviour will be fully accounted for by these antecedents. Motive cannot be treated as a natural event. A fundamental contrast between cause and effect in nature and end and means in human behaviour is of the essence of the facts which set the problem of interpreting behaviour. There seems to be no possibility of making human problems real, without seeing in human activity an element of effort, contingency, and, most crucially, of error, which must for the same reasons be assumed to be absent from natural processes.

Thus motive or intent forces itself into any relevant discussion of human activity. But the subject of behaviour cannot be simplified even to the point of reducing it to a dualism. At least three basic principles must be introduced into its interpretation. The typical human action is explained in part by natural causality, in part by an intention or desire which is an absolute datum and is thus a "fact" although not a natural event or condition, and in part by an urge to realize "values" which cannot be reduced entirely to factual desires because this urge has no literally describable objects. Interpretation in terms of factual desires is the procedure of economics as represented by the bulk of the theoretical literature, in so far as it is objective in outlook. Yet this second principle of explanation is perhaps the most vulnerable of the three. It is doubtful whether any desire is really "absolute," whether there exists any desire that does not look to achievement of some change in a growing system of meanings and values; this is a different thing from changes in physical nature, even though rearrangements in physical nature are the only means by which values can be realized. Every act, in the economic sense, changes the configuration of matter in space. But this does not exclude the possibility of "acts" which change meanings and values without changing natural configuration, since reflection may yield new insight and effect a change of personal tastes. More fundamentally, it is doubtful whether one configuration is in itself preferable to another.

People report and feel two different types of motivation for their acts. There is the wish or preference which is treated by the actor and by outsiders as final, as a brute fact. On the other hand, people make value judgments of various sorts in explanation of their acts; and explanation runs into justification. In other words, no one can really treat motive objectively or describe a motive without implications of good and bad. Thus not only do men desire more or less distinctly from valuing, but they desire because they value and also value without desiring. Indeed, the bulk of human valuations, in connection with truth, beauty, and morals, are largely or altogether independent of desire for any concrete thing or result. That individual economic motivation itself typically involves some valuation and not merely desire is established by two other considerations: first, what is chosen in an economic transaction is generally wanted as a means to something else, which involves a judgment that it "really" is a means to the result in question; and, second, what is ultimately wanted for its own sake can rarely, if ever, finally be described in terms of physical configuration, but must be defined in relation to a universe of meanings and values. Thus there is an element of valuation in the notion of efficiency in the realization of a given end; and, in addition, the real end contains as an element a value concept.

The dual conception found in motivation is reflected also in the more narrowly economic concept of value. The latter contains definitely more than the notion of a quality measured by price; it is always imperfectly measured under actual conditions. Price "tends" to coincide with value, but the notion of value also involves a norm to which price would conform under some ideal conditions. This norm includes two ideas: that of a goal aimed at but only more or less approximately realized because of errors of various kinds (which tend to be corrected); and that of a "correct" goal of action in contrast with incorrect goals as well as the actual goal. In a society based upon competition as an accepted principle, the competitive price, or price equal to necessary costs of production, is the true value in both senses; aberrations are to be attributed to two sets of causes—accidental miscalculations, and wrong objectives of action. This statement overlooks, of course, the existence of different technical conceptions of competitive price relative to the short run or local conditions; and a deeper ethical criticism may condemn given conditions other than the tastes of consumers which fix competitive price, especially the distribution of income and economic power.

To make the main point clear it is necessary to notice the difference in the conception of ideal conditions in economics and in mechanics. In the latter field the most notable of the ideal conditions is the absence of friction; an apparently similar conception of ideal conditions is one of the familiar features, almost a cliché, in economic theory. As generalized description the conception of perfect competition, reached by abstraction from the features of the economic situation which make competition imperfect, is like the conceptions of frictionless mechanics and is similarly justified. But to assume that the specific thing abstracted from in the theory of perfect competition bears the same relation to behaviour as does friction to mechanical process would be utterly misleading. Friction in mechanics involves a transformation of energy from one form to another, according to a law just as rigid and a conservation principle just as definite as the law and conservation principle which hold good for mechanical changes where no energy disappears. There is nothing corresponding to any of this in the economic process. What is abstracted in equilibrium price theory is the fact of error in economic behaviour. Perfect competition is, among other things irrelevant here, errorless competition; fundamentally it is not comparable to a frictionless machine. The familiar "tendency" of competition to conform to the theoretical ideal is no mere possibility of experimental approximation, but a real tendency in so far as men are supposed to endeavour with some success to learn to behave intelligently. It cannot be treated as a tendency toward an objective result, but only as a tendency to conformity with the intent of behaviour, which intent cannot be measured or identified or defined in terms of any experimental data. The ideal conditions of economics involve perfect valuation in a limited sense, perfect economic behaviour which assumes the end or intention as given. The correctness of the intention is an ethical question, from which the economist abstracts just as he abstracts from error which causes the behaviour to end otherwise than according to the intent.

Thus far two levels of interpretation of economic behaviour have been discussed. The first is that at which behaviour is reduced as far as possible to principles of regularity by statistical procedure; it may or may not be thought convenient to impute behaviour to some "force," but if it is so adjudged, the force must be assumed to correspond with the behaviour observed. The second is the interpretation of behaviour in terms of motivation, which must centre on the difference between motive and act and on the fact of error. It is at the third level of interpretation that the international end of action itself is submitted to valuation or criticism from some point of view. Here the relation between individual and society, the second main problem suggested above, and the concept of value as related to social policy become central topics of discussion.

In fact even at the second level two forms of social reference must be recognized: the individual ends as they are given are chiefly social in origin and content; and in societies in which economic thinking has any relevance there is a large social-ethical acceptance and approval of individual motivation in the abstract. Modern society, for instance, has accepted the right and even the duty of the individual to pursue his own ends within wide limits; in other words, individual liberty itself is a social value and not merely a fact. Thus the second level of interpretation tends to break down. If the notion of economic behaviour is effectively separated from mechanical process, if the ends are regarded as ends and not merely as physical effects, the discussion is already in large part at the third level. Factual ends as desired cannot be maintained unless they are given a large element of valuation in addition to desire. The "desires" for economic goods and services cannot be held to be final or to have a self-contained, independent reality. The least scrutiny shows that they are very largely rather accidental manifestations of desire for something of the nature of liberty or power. But such objects of desire are forms of social relationship and not things, and the notion of economic efficiency has only a limited applicability to their pursuit and attainment. Treatment of such activities, if it is to have any general, serious appeal, must be a discussion of social policy relative to social ends or norms and social procedure in realizing them.

The serious difficulty in economic theory in this connection has been the tendency to confuse advocacy of a policy of political non-interference (or the opposite) with description of a social organization based on free contract. Even when the authors have not deliberately intended to preach as well as to analyse, the difficulties of keeping the two types of discussion separate have been too great, especially in view of the requirements of an exposition which would be intelligible, not to say appealing, to any considerable reading public. In this field the interest in values, and especially in social policy, is in fact predominant. Thus economic theory, growing up in an atmosphere of reaction against control, clearly over-emphasized this side of the case and neglected the other. It is now just as obvious that there are equally sweeping and complex limitations to the principle of liberty in the economic sense, that is, to the organization of economic life exclusively through free contract among individuals using given resources to achieve given individual ends. Society cannot accept individual ends and individual means as data or as the main objectives of its own policy. In the first place, they simply are not data, but are historically created in the social process itself and are inevitably affected by social policy. Secondly, society cannot be even relatively indifferent to the workings of the process. To do so would be ultimately destructive of society and individual alike. This conclusion is strongly reinforced by the fact that the immediate interest of the individual is largely competitive, centred in his own social advancement relative to other individuals. In such a contest it is the function of the public authority to enforce the rules impartially, and still more to make such rules as would tend to keep the "game" on the highest possible level. To this end it must maintain a standpoint distinctly different from the interest in which the individual, always more conscious of conflicts of interests than of community of interest with the social body as a whole, tends to be absorbed.

These reflections point to a logical error underlying the value theory typical of the classical economists. It was not ostensibly their contention that liberty as such is a good. Notoriously, they were hedonists; their argument for liberty made it instrumental to pleasure, on the ground that the individual is a better judge than government officials of the means to his happiness. It is not denying weight to this argument to point out that liberty itself is unquestionably a good to the individual, and in addition an ethical good more or less apart from the degree to which the individual actually prizes it. Certainly an individual may desire liberty and claim a right to it without contending that he will uniformly make decisions more wisely than they would be made for him, from the standpoint of his own material comfort and security. And just as certainly it can be maintained that the individual should within limits make his own decisions and abide by their consequences even if he may not choose to do so. In other words, the classical economists did not realize, and the "scientific" spirit of the age has made economists generally reluctant to admit that liberty is essentially a social value, at least when it is advocated or opposed, as is any other social system or social relation.

The actual interests or desires expressed in economic behaviour are to an overwhelming extent social in genesis and in content; consequently they cannot be described apart from a system of social relations which itself cannot be treated in purely objective, factual terms. To a limited extent they can be conceived by an individual in such terms;

they may even be described by one individual to another as matter of fact. But the parties to such a communication place themselves in the role of spectators rather than members of society or participants in the phenomena. Thus any published discussion, presupposing a general appeal to readers as members and participants, necessarily takes the form of stating a case for a policy, possibly with more or less equal attention to both sides. In this conflict between the spectator's interest in seeing and understanding and the participant's interest in action and change, the philosopher or methodologist cannot possibly take sides. The question whether economics as such should be one or the other is to be answered only by recognition that it must be both, with more or less emphasis one way or the other according to the aims of a particular treatment; but always by implication it must be both, however one-sided the emphasis, since each interest presupposes and is relative to the other, and every writer and reader as a human being is motivated by both interests. What is desirable is that in any statement the relation between the two sets of interests should be clear. But what tends to happen is the reverse: he whose interest is primarily in truth tends to reinforce his statements by identifying truth and value, and he whose interest is in values tends to strengthen his statements by giving them the quality of truth.

While in the period of development of the classical economics the practical social interest centred almost exclusively on liberation from an antiquated system of control, at present the pendulum has swung definitely the other way. The new problem raised by the confusion of scientific and evaluative interests is enormously more difficult than the old. Society is positively seeking a basis of unity and order instead of negatively attempting to abandon an unsatisfactory basis. Moreover, the current standards of thinking have come under extreme domination of the scientific ideal, which has little if any applicability to the problem. The ultimate foundation of group unity must be of the nature of morale and sentiment rather than knowledge. There is no intellectual solution of conflicts of interest. Only values can be discussed, but the discussion does not necessarily lead to agreement; and disagreement on principles seems morally to call for an appeal to force. It is also of interest to note that the tendency to "rationalization" causes conflict of interest and disagreement regarding principles each to take on the quality of its opposite, and that in practice they are inseparably mingled.

The extremist wings in the advocacy of change recognize the inapplicability of purely intellectual knowledge. Both "fascist" and "communist" schools incline to treat the truth or falsity of propositions in economics as a matter of indifference or even as illusory, judging the doctrines only by their conduciveness toward the establishment of the desired type of social order. This view is, of course, "untrue" from a narrower "scientific" point of view; in any social order the results of certain choices affecting production and consumption, by whomever made, come under certain abstract, essentially mathematical principles which express the difference between economy and waste. At the other extreme—at the first and second levels of interpretation indicated above—there is an equally energetic movement in the interest of a rigorously "scientific" treatment of economics. Analysis at the first level, disregarding motivation and considering only the results of action in the form of commodity statistics, leaves no real place for any concept of economy. Moreover, it cannot be carried out even literally, for commodities must be named and classified and the treatment must take account of similarities and differences in use as well as physical characteristics. And economics at the second level, treating desires as facts, is subject to very narrow limitations. Desires really have no very definite content, and of what they have the student can have no definite knowledge. The conception can be made the basis of a purely abstract theory, but it has little application to reality. To give the data any content, the desires must be identified with the goods and services in which they find expression, and the second method then is reduced to identity with the first. Moreover, the only desires which can be treated as at all akin to scientific data are purely individual, and any discussion of social policy must draw on values or ideals entirely outside of such a system.

X

INTEREST*

HISTORY OF DOCTRINE

INTEREST in its primary meaning is the payment for the use of money; more broadly, it may mean the return on investment in any form. In theoretical analysis it is generally taken to mean a "pure" remuneration for the use of money, or yield on money capital; pure interest is deduced from nominal interest by elimination of all elements imputable to cost or effort of administration, to insecurity of payment of interest or principal, to prospective changes in the purchasing power of money and to amortization necessary to maintain the principal intact. The word interest came into use in the late Middle Ages, replacing the term usury. The Greeks called the interest payment *tokos*, meaning offspring, whence Aristotle's statement that "money does not breed." The modern term comes from the Roman law expression for an indemnification for damage due to the delay in the interval (*interesse*) before repayment, one of the chief forms under which payment for loans came to be tolerated by canonical and civil courts. Interest in the modern sense was in the Middle Ages merely an important type of usury; since then the term usury has become specialized to mean interest at exorbitant or illegal rates.

In tribal and economically undeveloped societies there is a strong sentiment against lending money at interest, which is usually prohibited as between members of the social group. The repugnance to interest has been ascribed to the danger of weakening the group in a military sense, since citizens capable of equipping themselves for war might be reduced to penury or slavery through debt. In Greece and Rome, where the ownership of landed estates was the gentlemanly source of income, the opposition to money lending was ostensibly grounded in ideas of social respectability; the opposition tended to disappear when money lending was regularly conducted on a scale which permitted the capitalist to live according to the genteel standards

* Reprinted from *The Encyclopaedia of the Social Sciences*, edited by E. R. A. Seligman. By permission of The Macmillan Company, Publishers.

of the old aristocracy, and in the period of high civilization the law permitted interest at restricted rates. In the Middle Ages the prohibition was premised on religious and ethical principles. A loan was usually made under stress of special need for consumption purposes, and it was considered that to exact interest under such circumstances was to take advantage of a brother's need. Indeed it was admittedly a compromise with strict Christian tenets to require repayment of the principal. The doctrinal basis of the opposition to interest was found in the concept of objective value, any departure from which was looked upon as unjust. It was argued that no value could attach to the use of a consumptible good separate from the good itself, and money was regarded as consumptible because it could be used only by parting with it. Another argument was directed against the payment for time, over which no man could claim ownership. Church apologists therefore contend that medieval practice never seriously interfered with loans made in the course of business, where the use of funds had a money value to borrower and lender, provided only that the charge was "just." Moreover, the payment of rent for the use of land or durable goods was never condemned by the churchmen or the canon law.

As trade and industry developed and a general loan market came into being, lending ceased to be treated as different from other market transactions. The role played by the Reformation in this connection has been disputed. Some attribute to Protestantism an important part in the disintegration of the medieval effort to apply ethical ideals to business relations, while others contend that it was rather a reaction, centring in relatively backward Germany, against the advanced humanistic tendencies of the Renaissance. In any case the prohibition of usury became increasingly difficult to enforce. Legal devices and forms which to the modern student seem merely disguises for loans at interest came into general use; these forms were troublesome and their interpretation by the courts was uncertain. During the sixteenth century there developed a movement to abolish the prohibition; its literary champions were the Protestant leader Calvin and the French jurist Dumoulin. The first legal action was in England, where at the close of the reign of Henry VIII the prohibition of usury was replaced by a legal maximum [37 Henry VIII, c. 9 (1545)]; after a reaction this legislation was restored under Elizabeth [13 Eliz., c. 8 (1571)]. Other countries soon followed.

In the two following centuries the justice of charging interest was still the subject of controversy in voluminous theological and political writings but no attempt was made to discuss interest as an economic problem. The attack ran in the old moral and religious terms; and the defence was based on the supposedly evident fact that the use of money is a source of gain, is therefore of value to both the debtor and the creditor and hence should be treated by law like other articles of commerce. In the latter half of this period the demand for regulation was based more on mercantilist grounds: English writers, for example, argued that low interest cost was necessary to help English business to compete with foreigners in the export trade.

The next stage in the historical development of interest theory, comprising the work of the classical school of economists, extends for more than a century after 1776, the date of publication of Adam Smith's *Wealth of Nations*. Writers of this school contributed a little toward the formulation of an integrated distribution theory, in which interest theory falls. They regarded the problem of distribution not as one of pricing services furnished to production but as one of dividing the total income of society into the shares of the three economic classes which they recognized. The landlord's share, rent, was explained as a "surplus," on the ground that it did not enter into the price of the final product stated in terms of pain cost. Wages were explained by the simple observation that the labourer must live. Thus the way was opened for treating the share of the capitalist, which was called profit, as a residue after the other shares were paid. J. S. Mill, for instance, regarded it as a settled doctrine that profit arises because labour produces more than is required to sustain the labourer; in other words, because industry produces more than the labourers get. Yet the explanations of wages given when the topic of wages and not that of profit is explicitly under discussion run in very different terms; the most famous of these explanations, the wages fund theory, even assumes profit as previously determined (or negligible) and makes the wage share either the total capital or the portion actually used to employ labour. The classical school never faced the problem of the nature of capital as a quantity and hence could not have said anything very illuminating about the rate of interest. Their general conception of capital was that, like products generally, it is produced by labour and hence is really the embodiment either of a certain quantity of labour or of the subsistence goods on which the labourer lives while performing that labour.

In contrast to their vagueness regarding fundamentals, classical writers showed profound insight in many partial analyses and especially in practical conclusions. N. W. Senior in particular, following up hints in Ricardo, developed brilliant ideas in connection with capital and its return; and his lesser known contemporaries, Rae and Long-field, came near to explaining interest on the ground of capital productivity. Senior made the general character of capital and its function in production one of the four fundamental propositions from which he wished to develop the whole science of political economy. In his effort to bolster up the pain cost theory of price at one of the weak points recognized by Ricardo, Senior argued that the essence of capital as an element in cost is the pain of abstinence. Yet it is indefensible to attribute to him, as Böhm-Bawerk does, an abstinence theory of interest. Besides his clear and repeated explanations of the productivity of capital Senior stated expressly that abstinence has nothing to do with the return after capital has changed hands through gift or inheritance. In his discussion of profit he assumes that the sacrifice of abstinence would prevent the return from ever falling to zero but explains the actual level first as a residual and finally, after a very tortuous argument, by the proportion between capital and labour in existence; this is true but incomplete.

Economists of the classical school achieved progress also in their discussion of the various elements into which the gross return on capital must theoretically be analysed. Adam Smith himself made it clear that in typical cases part of the return must be treated as essentially a wage—later called wage of management—and another part as compensation for risk, true interest being different from both. J. S. Mill even had fairly clear notions of a further differentiation between payment for risk in the sense of an insurance premium against a recognized hazard and mere accidental deviations from a normal return because of miscalculation or unforeseen changes. These beginnings developed into the tendency to treat profit not as the gross income including interest, which was the usage of the classical writers, but as the final residual income of the entrepreneur after a deduction of both interest and wages of management.

The confusion in the classical reasoning between the causality problem of the market value of services of various kinds and the ethical question of remuneration for sacrifice explains in part the contemporaneous development of another system of economic thought which treated all property income as exploitation of labour. The socialistic and anarchistic schools, from Godwin and Thompson to Louis Blanc, Rodbertus, and Karl Marx, have held that the modern economic order based on "economic freedom" has merely substituted the economic power of property ownership for the physical and military power of slave owner and feudal lord as a means of enabling the upper class to live by the sweat of the masses. Practically every detail of socialistic theory can be taken almost verbally out of the classical treatises, which habitually referred to labour as the producer of all wealth. Abstinence as a justification for interest was particularly vulnerable to ethical attack, since most of the abstaining seems to be done by persons who have first consumed all they can or at least more than they need. This point was used with telling effect by Lassalle in Germany. Whether they do or do not explain how property income is possible, exploitation theories do not offer a cause and effect analysis of the proportions obtaining between property and labour incomes. As to the ethical challenge which they present, it goes without saying that in competitive society every income is based on economic power. Whether or when or how far property income is defensible on grounds of abstract right or of social expediency is a question to be answered by the ethical or political philosopher rather than by the economist. Interest is merely a form of payment for the use of real wealth transferred from one person to another. Hence no special objection can be directed against it ; its merits and demerits are those of private property and of a social order based on ownership. Moreover, it is questionable, at least in theory, whether a clear-cut distinction can be drawn between property and labour incomes. As was emphasized by Smith and Senior among the classical economists, a large part of the earning power of individuals paid for as labour is really the fruit of an investment no different in principle from any other; and another large part is the result of inheritance or chance.

Discussion of interest theory during the generation preceding the World War centred around the work of Böhm-Bawerk. Before him the English economist Jevons had given a mathematical version of a type of productivity theory along with a very penetrating discussion of the relative valuation of present and future goods. But Jevons's work received only limited recognition until similar views were presented in more popular non-mathematical form by the Austrian school, which for interest theory practically means Böhm-Bawerk, although Wieser's variant of the productivity theory is more in harmony with accepted doctrine of to-day. While it appears to rest on the preference for present as against future goods Böhm-Bawerk's view of interest is really a productivity theory, since the possibility of productive investment is the most important, at least from a short time point of view, of the three "reasons" advanced by him for such a preference. Jevons, Böhm-Bawerk, and the writers who have followed their line of approach interpret capital as meaning essentially the substitution of more indirect or "roundabout" for more direct methods in production, as an increase in the time length of the production process with a resulting increase in efficiency of the use of primary factors. This is similar to the classical conception of capital, except that the earlier writers lacked the notion of correlated variation in elements of complex situations; they tended to think of capital as conditioning in an absolute sense rather than of the amount of product as subject to increase by increasing proportions of capital. Böhm-Bawerk also laboured to establish a distinction between the psychological preference of present to future and the notion of abstinence. He had a great influence, especially in the United States, where particularly Fetter and Fisher took his work as a point of departure in constructing time preference or eclectic theories.

In recent years attention has been centred on Schumpeter's theoretical construction which regards interest as belonging essentially to a dynamic economy. The innovators among the entrepreneurs who bring forward new and more efficient methods of production and business management obtain a surplus over cost, a part of which is returned in the form of interest to banks and other suppliers of capital funds without which the new projects could not be executed. In the absence of new inventions and other advances there is according to Schumpeter no room for interest. In application to statics Schumpeter's theory is similar to Marshall's in that it deals with the long run equilibrium rate; while for Marshall this rate is determined by the inter-relation of "waiting" and productivity, Schumpeter assumes that the rate is zero. It is difficult to see the reasons for this assumption: there is no limit to the use of capital even in the absence of new inventions, although the rate of return would of course fall indefinitely low as investment proceeded. Intellectually Schumpeter's dynamic interest is related to subsequent attempts to explain interest on loan funds in terms of banking cost.

GENERAL THEORY

The theory of interest begins properly with two facts. The first is the existence of various kinds of goods, the use of which has economic value as distinct from the objects themselves; it is actually bought and sold, and the payment, based on the length of use, is called a rent. The value derived from possession of an item of wealth for an interval of time may be of three main kinds: immediate satisfaction, as in the case of durable consumption goods; assistance in producing other goods, as in the case of producers' goods; increase in sale value of the item itself through time, whether through natural increase in its quantity, improvement in its quality, or change in the conditions of supply and demand. An effective increase in value must of course exceed any direct cost incurred in connection with it. The second fact is that many kinds of rentable goods can be produced under conditions and at a cost more or less accurately known. Both of these facts are of a technical sort; that is, they are data for the interest theorist, although they may be problems for the business manager.

The peculiar feature of interest which makes it a special problem for economics is that it is not a rent paid directly for the use of property in the concrete sense but is a repayment for the use of money (and as such takes the form of an abstract number, a ratio, or percentage). Yet while the borrower obtains and repays a money loan, it is the use of goods which the borrower wants and gets by means of the loan. If loans for consumption are left out of account, as they may well be since under modern conditions their terms depend upon those of loans for productive purposes, the rental or yield of goods the use of which is obtained by means of the loan provides under normal conditions the income paid out in the form of interest. Competition tends to bring about equality of return from equal investments; the ratio of this equalized return to investment is the rate of interest. Since the income from property is a given fact, the problem of the rate of interest is that of explaining how the amount of the investment, the capital, is determined in monetary terms; in other words, it is the problem of the evaluation of productive property.

The psychological or time preference or agio theorists solve the problem of capital according to the immediate facts of demand and supply, buyers' and sellers' offers, viewed psychologically. There is in the market, they argue, a certain aggregate of such goods, on which the owners set a certain estimate and which prospective purchasers likewise value according to individual tastes and means. The value set on an item of wealth is, of course, the value of the stream of income which it is expected to yield in the future in comparison with similar units of service or satisfaction at the moment. The competition of buyers and sellers will set on income yielding wealth a price which makes the amount demanded equal to the amount offered at that price. This price involves a uniform market rate of discounting future values. Thus if at the equilibrium point it takes $1 in hand to buy $1.05 payable one year from date, it will also take $20 to buy a piece of property yielding a perpetual income of $1 per year; all other income bearers will be valued on the basis on the same arithmetical proportion and the rate of interest will be 5 per cent. Taking into consideration the ordinary form of loan, involving repayment of principal, and ordinary investment and accounting policy, which reckons return only after full provision for maintaining the investment in perpetuity, the correct standard for comparison is that of a perpetual income of given size with the value of the wealth yielding such an income. As regards any particular item of wealth the process of evaluation takes the form of capitalizing its income, with allowance for its expected duration, at the general market rate.

The productivity theorists approach the problem of capital valuation from a different angle. They do not question the validity of the time preference reasoning but find that it lacks finality as an explanation under actual conditions. They observe that as regards unique and non-reproducible durable goods there is no objection to the capitalization theory of evaluation, as a first approach at least; and if all durable wealth were of this character, in other words, if there were no possibility of producing it, there would be no objection to the theory as a final explanation. But the possibility of more or less closely reduplicating existing types of wealth or of producing new types of wealth yielding future satisfactions places the matter in an entirely different light. If the capitalized value of any income bearer is more than the known cost of producing items yielding an equivalent income stream, people will instead of purchasing the existing items set about producing new income-yielding goods and these will sell not at their capitalized value but at the lower level set by cost of production. Conversely, no new wealth will be produced for the future unless the capitalized value of the expected income is greater than the cost of production. Hence if new wealth of more or less durable form is actually being produced, all such wealth must sell under competitive conditions for precisely the cost of producing items of any physical type yielding the same income (after all deductions necessary for perpetual maintenance).

If goods are valued for the sake of their future yield, then their physical character is a matter of indifference; all such goods viewed economically form a perfectly homogeneous class, and the value of any item depends only on the amount of the future income maintained in perpetuity. It is characteristic of the psychological theory itself that only the future income as such is valued. Hence if it is possible to produce any goods yielding future income, the cost of production of these must determine the value of all goods of the class. Under equilibrium this value will be equal to the value as determined by capitalization, but that is because the supply of any good yielding more than interest on its cost will be increased as long as this relation holds. For non-reproducible goods or goods yielding less than interest on reproduction cost capitalized value with rate determined at the investment margin and cost of production of equivalent goods are in fact different ways of saying the same thing—as long as any kind of durable wealth is actually being produced. In a society or a world in which there is actual growth the rate of interest is determined by or simply is the ratio between perpetual annual income and the cost of income yielding goods at the margin of growth. New investments will not be made unless they offer more than the purchase of old ones, which forces the writing down of the old ones to the level of the new.

That interest is the ratio between perpetual income and cost at margin is true only under "perfect competition." In actual markets economic adjustments work themselves out more or less slowly and imperfectly. Perhaps the most typical result in real life is to "overdo the thing" in expanding or contracting investment and thus to set up oscillations in the rate of return. Since neither the yield nor the cost of new wealth items can be exactly foreknown at the time when productive commitments are made, any piece of new property may from the start yield more or less than the interest on its cost and the longer the item lasts the more uncertain becomes the relation between return and cost. When an unforeseen change in conditions occurs, the owner of wealth affected by it receives a speculative profit or suffers a speculative loss through appreciation or depreciation of his investment. The capital value of an investment is measured directly in the case of new, free capital just flowing into concrete forms of wealth and is arrived at by the capitalization process in case of all concrete items of wealth in existence.

Another variant of the productivity theory is that advanced by Jevons and Böhm-Bawerk, which states the basic facts in terms of the length of time elapsing between the application of labour (and any other primary factors) and the enjoyment of the fruits and in terms of the efficiency in the use of these factors as a function of the time length of the production process. There is obviously a rough correspondence between this notion and the one expounded above which relates the cost of income-yielding goods to the net return obtained from their utilization. While Böhm-Bawerk's view may be more appropriate for some theoretical analyses, it is fatally handicapped by the lack of a general and accurate conception of the length of the production process. In a certain loose historical sense capital goods may be resolvable into labour and time or into labour, "nature," and time; but no particular item can be so treated for the simple reason that in the production of any capital good the use of pre-existing capital good is always involved. There is no working distinction between capital and other factors. Without the presence of the element of uncertainty all natural resource values at once become capital; from the standpoint of the market itself they are capital in any case. Much the same must be said of a large element in labour power, which is a produced good; it is social institutions which justify any separation of labour from capital, as the case of the slave suffices to prove. Nor is there a computable time length of the production process in any particular case; still less is there an average length in a literal sense. Much capital is completely permanent unless made obsolete by unpredicted changes and a series containing infinite items cannot be averaged. An average can be found only theoretically by dividing the annual maintenance and replacement into total capital value, a calculation which presupposes that all the data of the capital and interest relation are previously known. In fact it is always intermediate products, not the application of labour over more time in a literal sense, which produce the increase in output. Interest must be treated as the productive yield of capital, defined and measured by its cost or the cost of equally productive items, in terms of sacrificed immediate goods.

Eclectic theories generally make use of the demand and supply scheme of analysis to combine the psychological and the productivity explanations of interest. To complete the exposition it is necessary therefore to consider the problem in terms of demand and supply. In this connection it is not clear what is supply and what is demand, what is being priced and what is the price, since both the commodity and its price are stated in money terms. One may regard interest as the price of the commodity, use-of-capital, or savings as the price of future income. The former is the more familiar view: the supply of the commodity, use-of-capital, comes from saving, while the demand for it comes from the people controlling opportunities for investment.

In this view the supply is the total amount of productive wealth in society, and the savings made in any short interval constitute merely a small addition to it. The rate of saving, which is only the rate of increase in the supply of capital, may or may not depend on the interest rate; but in any case the supply as such keeps on increasing always, at all rates. The supply is thus highly inelastic: strictly speaking, it is absolutely inelastic at any instant of time. Demand, on the other hand, is highly elastic, since it is indisputable that the opportunities for investment would absorb large amounts of capital with only a gradual lowering of the rate of return. Hence demand determines the price, supply being a "datum," a given condition but not a cause.

The other view of the interest transaction as a purchase of future income for present wealth in hand corresponds to the statement of the problem as essentially that of the valuation of productive wealth. Now, if the commodity is future income, supplied through the production of income-yielding goods, and the demand comes from savings, then the supply is indefinitely elastic and the demand inelastic. The virtually unlimited possibility of using more capital in production means that future incomes can be provided in correspondingly large volume at a slowly increasing cost. Other things being equal, it is true that a given investment—that is, cost incurred—does tend to yield income at a decreasing rate as the amount of investment increases, since capital as a factor in production is subject to diminishing returns; but this decrease is very slow in comparison with the total magnitudes involved. It appears, for example, that in the United States the elasticity of demand for capital is around unity; that is, the total supply of capital, which includes the entire national wealth, would have to be doubled before the interest rate would be reduced to half its value at the beginning of the test. This would call for saving for a full generation at a high rate, so that it is correct to consider the supply of future income at a given time as practically unlimited, indefinitely elastic. The demand for future income, represented by the amount of savings available for investment, is at a given moment narrowly and almost absolutely limited. In the theoretically perfect adjustment it would at any instant be zero in absolute amount, a mere rate of flow, disappearing in investment as it appeared in saving. In this situation, as in the case of any commodity produced under nearly constant cost, demand conditions—the psychological comparison between present and future—can operate only to effect the volume of savings without an appreciable influence on the price at which they are invested. Men with different estimates of future in terms of present satisfactions will save different amounts (or conceivably consume varying amounts of capital already in hand); but the effect on the interest rate of the resulting changes in total supply of capital will in any short short interval, even a year, remain negligible.

In the long run the yield on new investment depends in part on the amount of capital previously invested (in all past time) and thus reflects variations in the amount of savings in the past, which may be said to depend on comparisons made in the past between present and future. This does not affect the conclusion that at any given time the supply of capital is a datum and that the current psychological estimates have no effect on the rate. Moreover serious objections arise with regard to the historical view itself. At the rates of pure interest which have obtained in modern times it would require a generation for a saver to get in income a total sum equal to that given up in making his investment. In reality the net accumulation of capital depends on the fact that savers maintain their capital and leave it behind when they die. At most they consume the income; and the classes which make substantial savings even reinvest a part of income through life. It does not seem very realistic to call the decision to save and invest, looking beyond one's own life, a choice of future rather than present satisfaction. It may, of course, be put in that form in order to construct a rationale of economic choice. But there is no reason to believe in the reality of "impatience" or of preference of present to future as a general principle of conduct, if conditions are correctly stated to isolate this comparison from other factors, particularly if interest itself is eliminated as a factor. A realistic discussion of the motives involved in decisions as to saving would run rather in terms of interest in security and power, of living standards, of forms of social emulation, and of similar facts of social psychology and culture history.

Nor is it legitimate from a long time point of view to assume that other things remain equal in connection with the law of diminishing returns on investment. As new investment tends to lower the point of equilibrium on a descending demand curve for capital, other social changes are always and inevitably acting to change the position of the curve itself. In fact these two sets of changes have roughly offset each other through history, so that there has been no clear trend of the interest rate upward or downward, especially in the modern industrial era. The relative constancy of the interest rate has aroused the curiosity of many economists and provoked much speculation.

An older view, held by Henry George and Alexander Del Mar, found a physical basis for interest in the average rate of growth of animals and plants, while Cassel has made the ingenious suggestion that it may be connected with the length of human life. A sufficient explanation is found in the tendency of practically every form of social progress both to make saving easier and to increase the demand for capital, raising the curve vertically if drawn with quantity on the base line. Even if invention and all forms of social progress ceased and saving went on at an indefinitely high rate, the interest rate would never fall to zero; for there is no limit to the possibility of using capital to increase the supply of innumerable commodities which could never become free goods. There is no empirical evidence or abstract reason even for the belief that under such conditions the point of long run equilibrium—a naturally stationary supply of capital—would be reached. It appears therefore that Marshall's long run equilibrium theory is just as untenable as the short or long run psychological theories.

The long run may be discussed only in the manner of the philosophy or theory of history. The interest rate tends to fall or rise as the effect of accumulation runs ahead of or behind the effects of other types of social change, notably increase of population, development of natural resources, invention of new technical processes, and opening up of new fields of demand. Accumulation itself likewise depends on the general movement of taste and the people's outlook on life. Here analysis of the type of price theory in terms of tendency toward equilibrium under given conditions has no applicability whatever. The problems and theories are necessarily sociological or institutional, and comparatively little help may be expected from any sort of deductive theorizing yet devised.

From the standpoint of computation there are two ways of looking at the interest relation. One is the everyday view of the interest loan or other investment in which the investment itself is maintained permanently. From the gross yield of the property is deducted, first, all operating expense; second, direct upkeep cost; and, finally, a sum which accumulated to the point of retirement from service will replace the original investment. The remainder is a perpetual net income; when divided by the cost of the property it shows the rate of interest.

It is evident that both the cost of a capital good and the annual contribution to a sinking fund for replacing it involve the interest rate itself.
Another method of formulation is more suited to the bond market
and amortized loans. In a continuous market under stationary conditions any investment can theoretically be made, continued, or
realized at will; hence the accumulated cost (less return if any) up to
any point in time must equal the discounted net return looking forward
from the same point. Both of these facts may be stated as equations
with the interest rate as the unknown; a few algebraic operations would
simplify the two equations into the same form. It is most realistic to
take as the equating point the moment when construction is complete
equating past cost with future return. If S dollars per year are saved
and invested for C years and the resulting property yields a net rental
of R dollars per year for a service life of L years (with no scrap value),
then $SA^L(A^C - 1) = R(A^L - 1)$, where interest is compounded
annually and for simplicity A is written for $(1 + i)$, unity plus the
interest rate. The first view more clearly corresponds to the realities
of the situation than does the view of discounting. The essence
of the matter is that artificial capital goods yield during life a
total net rental greater than their cost; the difference is, roughly
speaking, interest on the cost for the period, which must be distributed
equally through time. To do this exactly calls for compounding
continuously instead of annually by the use of the same type of
formula as that given above.

HISTORICAL, DYNAMIC, AND SOCIOLOGICAL ASPECTS

A survey of the general theory of interest serves to emphasize the
vast territory which would still have to be covered in order to give
much concrete information about the factors determining the rate on
a loan under varying historical and social conditions or even on loans
of a different character in the same country and year. In the first place,
the general theory itself is abstract in a sense beyond that implied in
generality: it explains in terms of given conditions which are taken
for granted in every aspect except the quantitative. Back of the motives
affecting choice immediately, at the time and place in which the
decision is made, is an infinite complex of why's and how's, ultimately
including most of human history. A final explanation of any economic

choice would have to include these factors in their concrete character, giving a sociological or institutional treatment instead of one based on the analogy of mechanical forces. In the second place, there are considerations which affect the terms of loans and investments in greater or less degree in different classes of cases, large or small, running into unique circumstances of the individual case. Some of these considerations are of such a character as to supplement the general theory, some rather of the nature of interfering forces which prevent competitive tendencies from finding effective expression.

Even in the most highly developed loan market hardly two loans are alike within significant limits, and many divergent types must be recognized. Superficially viewed, this is something of a paradox, since the commodity dealt in is the use of wealth in its most abstract form; yet loans are in fact much less amenable to standardization than many concrete commodities, such as wheat. But in addition to the unlimited diversity of circumstances among different loans and capital commitments at any given moment there is the supreme fact that they all look to the future for their value. And with reference to the future both in intrinsic uncertainty as to facts and an even wider divergence of human opinions and attitudes defy specification.

Even in the most advanced countries there is no one general interest rate and no one general money market, although there is a perfect market for certain securities dealt in by name and an approximation to a general market for loans of very short duration and unquestionable security. In practice in virtually every case the making of a loan is a matter of negotiation, and negotiation is the antithesis of what happens in the perfect market of economic theory. A few governments and large corporations are in a position to issue securities within limits and to offer them to the public through an impersonal marketing organization, but even with them a new loan of considerable size will be floated by negotiation. Even within the field where standardization of loans is carried farthest, it is normal for the bank rate to be about double the rate on the best bonds, while call money may go at a fraction or at a multiple of the latter. Farm mortgages plod along very steadily at an intermediate level, while the others fluctuate in their respective ranges, largely independent of one another. Outside the field covered by organized markets the loan rate may be almost rigidly uniform through widely varying conditions—an instance of the "customary price" in connection with loans—or may fluctuate within the widest limits from case to case; the latter is of course the more usual situation. Generally the rate is much higher than in organized markets. Thus in the south in the United States Negroes are said to borrow $5 at the beginning of the week and repay $7 at the end of it, an interest rate of 40 per cent per week. Loans made to the very poor on furniture and similar articles are said to range from 100 per cent up. In instalment selling, a method by which a large fraction of the automobiles and a smaller fraction of many other goods are regularly marketed in the United States, the terms involve a rate of interest from 11 to 40 per cent; it is to be noted that these rates are charged to persons of good credit standing and on quite sizeable sums. The Uniform Small Loans Act, designed to curb the exactions of loan sharks and adopted by over twenty states, prohibits interest above the monthly rate of $3\frac{1}{2}$ per cent.

Because of the overwhelming difficulty of the task no study of the general interest rate through history has as yet been undertaken; even the investigations of limited periods in the history of single countries are not detailed enough to permit confident generalization. Until the nineteenth century the available information relates to specific cases which may or may not be typical; yet even when allowance is made for their uncertain representative value, the data are sufficient to illustrate the extreme divergence of nominal interest rates in different epochs. This, however, should not be taken to imply qualification of the statement that the rate of pure interest has been surprisingly constant through history.

Thus W. H. Dubberstein's study of numerous clay tablet records extending over many centuries found that in later Babylonia the rate of 20 per cent recurred with monotonous regularity; the rate was twice as high in the neo-Babylonian and Persian periods (650–325 B.C.). In Ptolemaic Egypt the regular rate was 2 per cent per month (Westermann, W. L., *Upon Slavery in Ptolemaic Egypt*, New York 1929, p. 32). In Greece the rate at the time of Solon was about 16 per cent; at Corcyra in the second and third centuries B.C. loans on good security commanded 24 per cent, while the common rate at Athens in the time of the orators was from 12 to 18 per cent (*Palgrave's Diction-*

ary of Political Economy, vol. ii, new ed., London 1923, p. 429).
Mommsen states that in Rome the rate in the time of the monarchy
was probably about 10 per cent per annum (*The History of Rome*,
tr. by P. W. Dickson, vol. i, new rev. ed., New York 1905, p. 195).
Under the late republic interest was usually stable and low, normally
ranging from 4 to 6 per cent. In Asia, where invasions, inefficient
government, and indirect business methods made for insecure posses-
sions, 12 per cent was a low rate even in times of peace (Frank, T.,
An Economic History of Rome, 2nd ed., Baltimore 1927, p. 294). The
Byzantine law of Justinian limited the rate of interest to 12 per cent
for loans on cargoes, 8 per cent on loans for business purposes, and
6 and 4 per cent in other cases (Ashley, W. J., *An Introduction to
English Economic History and Theory*, vol. i, 4th ed., London 1909,
p. 210). In the early Middle Ages Byzantine commerce could raise
money at the moderate rate of 8 to 12 per cent; the rate was lower
still in the tenth century, which was quite unusual for the rest of
Europe (Boissonade, P., *Life and Work in Medieval Europe*, tr. by
E. Power, New York 1927, p. 51).

For western Europe in the Middle Ages it is difficult to make
definite assertions regarding the interest rate, because the fact of
interest was concealed or disguised in consequence of the usury laws.
Interest was certainly high for most loans. Ashley states that the rate
which the Jews were permitted to charge in England in the thirteenth
century was two pence per week on the pound, or approximately 43
per cent per annum (p. 203). According to Sombart the rate permitted
to the Jews by a regulation of 1243 in Provence was 300 per cent,
while that specified by the emperor Frederick II the next year was
173 per cent (*Der moderne Kapitalismus*, 2nd ed., Munich 1916, vol. i,
p. 626). In contrast Boissonade states that during the Hundred Years'
War commerce in Italy and Germany obtained credit at the rate of
4 to 10 per cent (p. 288), and M. M. Knight asserts that commercial
interest rates in southern Europe became standardized from the
thirteenth century at 10 to 17 per cent (*Economic History of Europe
to the End of the Middle Ages*, Boston 1926, p. 116).

For the Renaissance and the following period data have been made
available by Ehrenberg (*Capital and Finance in the Age of the Renaissance*, abr. and tr. by H. M. Lucas, London 1928) from the Fugger

records and other sources. Ferdinand and Isabella sold annuities bearing 10 per cent (p. 24). In the sixteenth century the rate on commercial loans on the Antwerp bourse, an effectively organized market, was from 2 to 3 per cent per fair, i.e., 8 to 12 per cent per annum (p. 247). In a list of thirteen short-period loans made to various governments between 1519 and 1521 the rate varies from 7 to 27½ per cent besides "considerable" brokerage charges (pp. 259–60). In the decade 1532–41, it is asserted, there was a slow reduction in the rate of interest, which varied from 13 to 20 per cent in 1535–6 (p. 265). For the years 1546–7 there is available a list of loans in which the Fuggers were borrowers, chiefly from other south German banking families, and another list of loans by the Fuggers to various courts and governments; in the former the rate varies from 8 to 10 per cent, in the latter from 11 to 13½ per cent (p. 269).

The first modern bank, the Bank of England, was founded at the end of the seventeenth century in connection with the first funded state debt. From that date one may speak of a general rate of interest in a sense not previously possible, especially as London has since been the central capital market of the world. The transactions of such a bank and dealings in such funds involve a publicly known rate, and publication is the main consideration in standardization. The initial loan to the state, which was a new dynasty of questioned status engaged in a major war, was at 8 per cent; but the rate fell rapidly and after the conversion of 1750 the English government was borrowing from the bank at 3 per cent. In 1751 the government issued 3 per cent consolidated annuities; but later the consols fell far below par, fluctuating with the wars and the progress of the industrial revolution. In Holland in the second half of the eighteenth century, as Adam Smith observes, the government was borrowing at 2 per cent and private persons at 3 per cent (*Wealth of Nations*, bk. i, ch. ix.).

Modern conditions may be said to begin after the post-Napoleonic settlement and the final establishment of English coinage on a gold basis. Since the first quarter of the nineteenth century information on interest rates becomes increasingly abundant both for the London money market and for other markets. An analysis of such data reveals the existence of permanent differences between rates on the same type of loan in different markets as well as between rates on different types of loans in the same market. Only when allowance is made for the fact that each type of rate in each money market seems to have its own zone of variation do the fluctuations of the rates appear more or less correlated. If the level of the interest rate after 1825 is to be judged by the yield of British government consols, which by many authorities is taken as the nearest available approximation to pure interest, it will be found to have fluctuated between 3 and 3½ per cent until the 1880's; the trend after that was downward until the turn of the century, when the rate began to rise, reaching its customary level by 1910. Similar data for the United States are available only from the last quarter of the nineteenth century. Thus F. R. Macaulay's index of bond yields, based on the quotation for the "best" railroad bond—that is, the one with the lowest interest rate—indicates that the interest rate was approximately 5½ per cent in 1875; it fell fairly steadily to about 3¼ per cent in 1900, rose to about 4 per cent by 1914, reached its post-war peak at 5 per cent in 1921, and has fluctuated since in the neighbourhood of 4½ per cent.

There is no great difficulty in indicating the general lines along which changes in the general interest rate and divergences between various types of nominal interest rates are to be explained. The most important immediate causes producing changes in the interest rates in modern times (acting apart from or through the intermediary of real investment opportunity and real savings) have been the fluctuation of business conditions in the now unpleasantly familiar cycle, war and the opening up or saturation of new fields of investment, of which the railways are the stock example. The main causes of divergence in the rate from one type of loan to another at a given time are included in the categories recognized by Adam Smith and his followers; namely, trouble or expense in connection with the loan and uncertainty of payment of interest or principal. To these should be added the case of monopoly: special conditions may cut a borrower off from the general market and give a lender power approaching that of exclusive control over a necessity of life.

Administrative expense clearly accounts for the excess of the bank rate over that on good bonds. Indeed some economists have held that the interest rate under modern conditions is determined by the operating expenses of banks, a statement to be interpreted in connection with the entire theory of the relation between currency and interest. Again, a pawnbroker may lend at a rate per month equal to that yielded in a year by good securities and still make no more than the same net rate of interest, if account is taken of the expenses incident in the conduct of a pawnshop and the competitive wages to which the pawnbroker may lay claim.

Uncertainty, which is a better general term than risk, affects more or less every loan or investment, depending especially upon how far into the future the commitment looks. The measurable element of uncertainty, risk in the proper sense, can be eliminated by applying the insurance principle in some form. But the subjective and individual element of uncertainty is not susceptible to standardization; it is a matter of how much confidence one feels in his opinions about the future course of events and of how much courage he has in acting upon his convictions. Uncertainty, more or less connected with expense, explains the major differentiations in interest rates between different sections of the money market. Rates are high in new countries and frontier areas, partly because experience offers no basis for accurate prediction of the future or objective estimation of risk and partly because the lenders typically live far away in the older centres and have to depend on sources of information in which they place limited confidence. There is also the cost of obtaining, transferring, and validating such information as is available as well as special mechanical costs of administration at a distance. Such considerations also apply as between loans separated by other than geographical distinctions, particularly between older and newer types. In addition most capitalists are more informed or feel more confidence in their information about certain types of investment than about others. The fact probably does not produce important permanent differences, but it certainly retards the flow of capital from one field to another in response to rapid changes in real investment prospects.

One phase of the factor of uncertainty has to do with changes in the general price level, to which Irving Fisher has given special attention. Apart from any connection with general business conditions changes in prices should obviously affect the interest rate, if they are generally foreseen. If the value of money is expected to fall between the contraction and the maturity of a loan, the borrower should be correspondingly more disposed to borrow and the lender less disposed to lend until the rate goes high enough to compensate for the change. Perfect foresight would clearly mean foreknowledge of conditions during the period of the loan and not an adjustment of the rate on the assumption that the rate of change at the time the contract was made would hold good for ever, as Fisher assumes; but the latter interpretation of foresight may more nearly describe the way men think and act. People do not have the necessary foreknowledge, in the full sense of the term, and even in the face of actual changes they inveterately tend to consider the value of money as absolute unless it is visualized in some concrete speculative price, such as the quotation of one currency in terms of another. As a matter of fact, to the extent that the effects of anticipated changes in the value of money do appear in the history of interest rates and prices they are largely due to an indirect influence; namely, the relation between price changes and business conditions. Rising prices mean large profits, because wages and other basic costs tend to lag, and hence an increased demand for loans. Also capital owners may be more disposed to go into business for themselves rather than to lend their funds at a time when things are "booming," which would mean a reduction of apparent supply as well as increase in demand.

However the matter is viewed, the problems of interest, of the price level and of the business cycle overlap. Certain economists, notably Fisher, consider the business cycle essentially a phenomenon of price level changes, a "dance of the dollar"; while others would regard price changes as effect rather than cause, some of them suggesting even that the primary phenomenon is precisely the artificial stimulation of the creation of capital through credit expansion. The obvious relationship between the interest rate and cyclical price movements arises from the fact that in the modern business world the great bulk of the medium of exchange consists not of money in the primary sense of a money commodity, such as gold, but mainly of bank credit and to a lesser degree of government credit. Bank credit, whether in the form of deposits or of banknotes, represents a right to obtain gold on demand and under a gold standard depends for its validity on the power of the banking system to make this right good. But only a fraction of the normal total volume of bank deposit and note obligations is represented by gold stored up anywhere to meet the demand; the primary backing of such credit consists of the presumably liquid assets of borrowers from banks. Deposits and notes for the system as a whole are created through loans by banks to their customers. Since the banks lend money chiefly for productive purposes, taken in the broad sense to include merchandising, there exists a close and inseparable connection between the phenomena of money and circulating credit on the one hand and those of capital and interest on the other; a new bank loan is an addition at once to the supply of effective currency and to that of effective capital, for the proceeds are used by the borrower in the same way as is a loan based on real saving.

If "other things remained equal" it would be fair to argue that the creation of capital by bank loans represented a tax on the owners of money through a reduction in the purchasing power of each unit. For the writing of slips of paper and the making of book entries by bank clerks do not directly create any more goods or productive capacity, and the new purchasing power placed in the hands of borrowers must be subtracted from that of the effective money previously in circulation; the dilution of the circulating medium must manifest itself in a rising price level. It is arguable, however, that new purchasing power may serve to bring into use existing wealth or productive power previously idle and so to increase the total output and circulation of goods instead of raising prices. Then in effect the new real capital created through the loan will represent no real cost to society as a whole other than what may be involved in putting idle capacity to work, and this may even be a gain.

Apparently both of these effects are represented in some degree in what actually happens. An expansion in the volume of bank loans is associated with both an increase in the total volume of production and a rise in the price level; the latter is higher than it would have been in the absence of credit creation, even though it may not rise absolutely. In the past business expansion financed by created media of exchange has turned out to be a process which ultimately reversed itself, giving rise to cycles. Precise proof of what is causal in the process depends on a very accurately measured statistical knowledge of the sequence and timing of changes or upon the successful control of the phenomena by actual manipulation of some element in the situation.

Until such proof is available it is not possible to say positively even that the process is necessarily self-limiting and reversing or that this feature is necessarily connected with the use of credit currency and with expansion and contraction in its volume.

For the student of interest the important fact is that all these phenomena exert a large and at times overpowering influence on the loan market, acting on both the supply and demand sides. One effect is a fairly sharp separation between short term and long term loans, the latter being relatively much less affected. In the market for short term loans the fundamental investment conditions, with which the general theory of interest is concerned, may be eclipsed at crucial points in the cycle by the special situation generated by the cyclical movement. The demand for loans may be dominated at the moment by the state and prospects of business from a cyclical standpoint and by the necessity for business men to meet outstanding obligations and keep solvent. The supply of loanable funds may be just as completely dominated by the state of bank reserves and the general banking position and by the vicissitudes to which money incomes in general are subject because of monetary changes.

The effects of the cycle exercised through phenomena associated with long term capital are more varied. The fluctuations of profit connected with cyclical movements of business affect the magnitude of corporate savings which have become an important source of supply of new capital. Although corporations invest reserves to some extent in public securities or in those of other industries, the bulk of their savings represents plant extensions and improvements; the increase in corporate savings based on rising profits is thus a factor contributing to the overdevelopment of industries momentarily prosperous, which tends to unbalance development and to aggravate the cycle. The fact that interest on long term loans is a fixed charge which does not rise with the general upswing is one of the factors responsible for the lag of costs during prosperity and contributes to unsound expansion. On the downswing the bond or mortgage interest becomes a heavy charge on industry; and the long term creditor oftens becomes complete owner of the business, entirely wiping out the equity of the active direct owners.

Interest as a form of property income which does not involve its recipients in direct participation in active processes of business and production is bound up in a capitalist society with group antagonisms. There is a tendency to regard as parasitic people who live from a fixed and assured income completely divorced from effort or concern with the work and life of the masses. The antagonism between the active business group and its silent partner, the outside investor of long term capital, creates the opportunity for abuses such as insiders' profits or the shift of losses to investors; while the presence of such a party as the innocent investor, whose property must not be affected, makes regulation by public authority difficult and sometimes unfair, since most of its burden is apt to fall on the owners of the equity. At the same time the shrinking in the value of fixed incomes during prosperity and the passing of productive enterprises during depression into the hands of people who neither want nor are fit to assume the responsibility of management create social problems of far-reaching significance. These social antagonisms and problems tend to become increasingly vital as industrial civilization makes more use of accumulated wealth both in providing for the satisfaction of consumers' wants and in playing the game of power in the national and international arenas.

Capital and interest are commonly regarded as peculiarly characteristic of the capitalist order. Thus while the regulation of wages by public authority and the limitation of profits by taxation were accepted as interesting experiments not vitally affecting the foundations of the capitalist system, the emergency decree of December 8, 1931, reducing interest on private loans in Germany was interpreted by many as evidence of the passing of capitalism. Yet there is no abstract reason or experimental evidence, in so far as any is available, to justify a belief that interest will disappear in a socialist or communist society. The use of the pecuniary calculus to maintain the existing stock of capital and to increase it by accumulation as well as to distribute it among the various branches of production must lead to the employment of an interest charge for the use of capital. As long as capital is merely maintained, the interest charge may be nothing more than an accounting device and the interest income received by the national authority may be returned to the producers either as a uniform reduction in the prices of all goods below cost or in some other form. But if new capital is accumulated, the presence of interest as an element of cost would mean that only a part of the total output is distributed to the population in the form of consumers' goods. In a socialist economy, however, the class living on interest income would disappear and with it also the social problems and antagonisms to which rentier incomes in a capitalist society give rise.

XI

ECONOMIC THEORY AND NATIONALISM*

In this essay I propose to consider briefly three systems of economic institutions. These are economic individualism, economic democracy or socialism, and fascist-nationalism. The world of what we call European civilization appears to be in a state of transition from the first to the third; the second is not really an intermediate stage, but rather an alternative goal which the historical movement, as might figuratively be said, once tentatively chose, but after a little progress in that direction, changed its mind.

PART ONE

ECONOMIC INDIVIDUALISM: ECONOMIC THEORY AND REALITY

I. NEGATIVE CONSIDERATIONS

§1. Economic theory is not a descriptive, or an explanatory, science of reality. Within wide limits, it can be said that historical changes do not affect economic theory at all. It deals with ideal concepts which are probably as universal for rational thought as those of ordinary geometry. Our first main step must be to clarify the relation of such theory to economic reality; and the first subdivision —and perhaps the one most needing emphasis—will deal with negatives, with what the relation is not.

Economic theory, in the meaning which the expression has actually come to have, includes two branches, or, in a sense, stages. The one deals with a type of individual behaviour, the other with a type of social organization. To both, the adjective "economic," or perhaps even better, "economistic," may be applied, in harmony with established usage. At the same time, both, like all human behaviour, real

---

* A preliminary draft of this essay was presented to a meeting of the American Economic Association at Chicago, December 28, 1934. Not previously published.

or idealized in any relevant and useful way, are social, which is to say, institutional.

A. INDIVIDUAL ECONOMIC BEHAVIOUR

§2. Economic theory treats of economic behaviour in much the same way, up to a certain point, that medical science treats of hygienic and therapeutic behaviour. It is no part of its task to describe actual behaviour, the activities of "consumers" or "producers," any more than it is the task of medical science to describe medical practice. It is only necessary to mention the contrast between the content of a description of, say, classical Greek or Chinese medical practice and that of a treatise on medicine. Actual medical practice is also a legitimate and interesting subject for study, but its study falls under other disciplines than medical science, such as history, and perhaps sociology. Similarly for economic behaviour and economic science.

(1) No generalizing science, even a natural science, is concerned with describing events in time and space. The statements that arsenic is poisonous and that salt is soluble in water are scientifically true, whether or not anyone is ever poisoned by arsenic or any salt is ever dissolved. And it might or might not be necessary to have one or more instances from experience to suggest such a proposition or to establish its truth.

(2) Moreover, not only may the practical significance or relevance of such propositions be independent of the occurrence of instances, but the practical significance of the propositions typically is that knowledge of them prevents instances from occurring. This is true to the degree that possible events which we desire to prevent outnumber those we desire to bring about, which is a very high ratio indeed. "Arsenic is poisonous" is again an illustration (as regards its effect on human beings).

(3) A "science" of human behaviour, to be relevant or practically significant, *must* describe *ideal* and not actual behaviour, if it is addressed to free human beings expected to change their own behaviour voluntarily as a result of the knowledge imparted. Reference to medicine as an illustrative case should make this clear without further argument (the doctor being the person whose behaviour is

to be changed—the relation of the patient to medical knowledge is somewhat different).

(4) Since economic theory, like medical science, does not deal with actual behaviour, it is no more explanatory than descriptive.*

(5) There is a sense in which a science of ideal behavior is incidentally "explanatory"; the *desire* and *effort* to preserve or restore health may serve to explain actual behaviour, and may do so whether or not the act is effective in realizing the end pursued. The meaning of explanation where an act is explained by an end of action is *teleological*, as contrasted with the positivistic meaning, and with what is meant by "scientific" in the literature advocating scientific procedure in the social disciplines. The fact that description of ideal behaviour in part explains actual behaviour operates as a source of confusion; the notion that economics is a science explanatory of actual behaviour is the most important single confusion in the methodology of the science.†

(6) Economic behaviour is ideal rather than actual in two sharply distinct senses (both distinct from theoretically ideal conditions in physics). It is ideal in the sense of being an objective which the individual does in fact strive to realize, and also in the further sense of a "value," an end which the individual recognizes that he, and others, "ought" to pursue.‡

* In the positivistic conception of scientific method, explanation is, of course, a kind of description, namely generalized description in terms of relations of coexistence and sequence, with especial emphasis on uniformities of sequence in time.

† The notion of "perfectly" economic behaviour and of explaining actual behaviour by a tendency to approximate this ideal is only figuratively and in a misleading sense analogous to the methodological device of the frictionless machine in mechanics. Mechanical friction is definable in terms of objectively measurable dimensions, none of which, except the time dimension, applies, or has a literal analogue, in economic analysis. In many connections, the reduction or elimination of friction is a practical as well as a theoretical ideal, but it is such, of course, from the standpoint of the human student-manipulator of an apparatus, not that of the apparatus itself.

The second phase of economic theory, dealing with social organization, is concerned with a "perfect market," which is ideal in a somewhat different sense from that of perfect economic behaviour of an individual; but it is largely or wholly derivable from the latter, and is equally divergent from the type of "ideal" represented by the frictionless machine.

‡ It should be pointed out that the evaluative or imperative quality attached to behaving economically—the feeling that there is something "wrong" or defective about not doing so—is entirely apart from the concrete end of the action. With this end, or

(7) The conception of behaviour as *amenable* to *complete* explanation, or to description in terms which would apply to future as well as past behaviour (i.e., complete prediction), would exclude all relevant or practically significant discussion of it, all possibility of formulating ideals which might operate to change the actual by appealing to the behaving persons as free agents. Discussion would be limited to historical description or to formulae for manipulation from without, implying that the subjects whose behaviour is to be affected do not so much as know what is going on.

(8) Moreover, the *view* of human behaviour as a mechanical sequence or as completely describable or explicable in natural-science terms, is *impossible* to human beings. For the description itself, the act of describing, would be behaviour, and any activity in which subject and object are identical is a contradiction in thought. The principle can be illustrated at the physical level. It is impossible to draw a picture which includes the drawer in the act of drawing; such an act would obviously involve an "infinite regress." The statement that "man is a machine" involves saying either that "I am not a man" or that "I am not saying anything," i.e., "I say that I am not saying anything," and the contradiction is unescapable.

(9) In several respects, economic theory is much more remote from reality than medical science.

(a) Health is a *more or less* objective idea; how far and in what sense objective is not clear, but the point need not be discussed; in any case the doctor can empirically study examples of the condition he seeks to bring about whether thought of as a healthy body or

the question whether it is good or bad, or its pursuit wise or foolish, the notion of economy has nothing to do. It refers to a mode or quality in action directed to any end; the end may be good, bad, or indifferent without affecting the degree to which the action is economic.

No two of the three conceptions of behaviour can be coincident, neither actual behaviour with what is actually aimed at, nor what is actually aimed at with the normative ideal. Ethical ideals have meaning only if what ought to be desired is more or less different from the actual desire; and an actual goal or intention has meaning only if it is imperfectly realized. In particular, the concept of "economy" has no meaning in connection with a mechanical process. Thus we face the paradox that perfectly economic behaviour, which would reduce to mechanical response to conditions, is not economic at all. And still less is it ideal in the other, or ethical, sense; the unethical character of an individual who should practice perfectly rational self-seeking needs no elaboration. But there is a kind of formal analogy among all meanings of the word "ideal"—otherwise it would not be used as it is.

hygienic living. The economic quality of behaving is purely subjective; no outside observer has any way of knowing the degree in which activity is "economical," and even the individual subject cannot know at all accurately, even afterwards, and is in still deeper ignorance beforehand.

(*b*) Pure theory, in economics as in any field, is abstract; it deals with forms only, in complete abstraction from content. On the individual side, under consideration at the moment, economic theory takes men with (*a*) any wants whatever, (*b*) any resources whatever, and (*c*) any system of technology whatever, and develops principles of economic behaviour. The validity of its "laws" does not depend on the actual conditions or data, with respect to any of these three elementary phases of economic action.

(*c*) As a matter of fact, men obviously do not want their wants satisfied either completely or without difficulty and effort. We *want* not only wants but also resistance to be overcome in satisfying them. Ultimately, the real ends of action are not mainly of the concrete quantitative sort represented by utility functions, but consist rather in such abstract motives as interesting activity, satisfying achievement, self-approval, fellowship, and social position and power. There is no end completely "given" in terms of sense data. Every end is more or less redefined in the process of achieving it, and this redefinition is one reason for desiring the activity.

(*d*) It is worth repeating that the notion of perfectly economic behaviour involves contradiction or antinomy. It is essentially a concept of "limits" in something like the mathematical sense, but at the limit the behaviour would cease altogether to be economic and would become decidedly the reverse; it is not "economical" (nor moral) to attempt to behave "economically"!

(*e*) Economic analysis must run in terms of variables treated as quantities. But they are not really quantities, since no subjective state is measurable. (One vessel of water is hotter than another by a certain multiple in a physical interpretation, but not to the sense of temperature.) To some extent, the notion of an "index function' with the property of varying in the same direction as the non-measurable economic magnitude meets this difficulty, but it cannot do so in any fully satisfactory way. For economic variation must be discussed in terms which imply curvature as well as slope, and probably higher derivatives of the functions as well.*

B. The Unreality of Economic Theory in its Social Aspect

§3. In its second aspect or stage, economic theory deals with social, in the sense of inter-individual, relations. But the "economic man" is not a "social animal," and economic individualism excludes society in the proper human sense. Economic relations are *impersonal*. The social organization dealt with in economic theory is best pictured as a number of Crusoes interacting through the markets exclusively. To the economic individual, exchange is a detail in production, a mode of using private resources to realize private ends. The "second party" has a shadowy existence, as a detail in the individual's use of his own resources to satisfy his own wants. It is the market, the exchange opportunity, which is functionally real, not the other human beings; these are not even means to action. The relation is neither one of cooperation nor one of mutual exploitation, but is completely non-moral, non-human. It particularly needs emphasis that economic competition implies no feeling of rivalry or emulation. The economic man feels no such emotions, and does not "compete," in the ordinary sense of the word, at all. This is one of the main differences between the economic man and the real human being. In a perfect market there is no higgling or bargaining and no effort to manipulate other human beings in any way. The relation is theoretically like the "silent trade" of some barbarian peoples. Economic theory takes all economic

* Although this essay cannot be in any sense a treatise on economic theory, it seems needful for clearness to supplement this negative view of economic behaviour with a brief positive description. In general economic behaviour is defined by the notion of economy or efficiency, which carries with it that of a *maximum* realization of ends with given means, or "perfect" economy. Difficulty is more likely to arise in connection with two more or less conflicting sets of ends normally pursued by the individual and pursued by use of the same general stock of means. These are the ends respectively of satisfying one's current wants and of improving one's position, especially by sacrificing current want-satisfaction in achieving a fuller satisfaction of wants in the future. The notion of maximizing *either* current satisfaction *or* increase in means—with the present means devoted to the one or the other purpose—is fairly simple; but the notion of a maximum attainment of the two results combined involves a comparison not so easy to view in rational terms. In the real world this comparison finds quantitative expression in the rate of interest. The first of these two phases of economic behaviour, individual or social, is referred to under some such term as "stationary conditions"; the second is economic growth or progress.

individuals in an organization as *data*, not subject to "influence," and assumes that they view each other in the same way.*

II. Positive Relations to Reality

A. In a "Scientific" View

(AA) Individual Economic Behaviour

§4. (1) The economic quality of behaviour is *real*; it is not only real as a moral ideal, that waste is "wrong," and as an actual goal which men do strive to realize, but actual behaviour is *more or less* economical.† In that sense the conceptions of economic theory are "descriptive" in a formal sense, though an infinite variety of behaviour will fit the principles.

(2) All theorizing which aims at relevance takes for granted if it does not specify some of the more general conditions of actual behaviour, conditions under which economy is to be achieved. That is, the theory places some restriction of a factual sort on the nature of the "wants, resources and technology," making them relevant to the world in general and to certain regions in space and time. In particular, it recognizes the general character of the social situation in which the individual lives.

* See P. J. H. Grierson, *The Silent Trade.*

Economic theory assumes an organization of "economic men," each made up of the three elements or sets of elements: (*a*) "wants" expressible as a utility function or surface; (*b*) productive capacity, in various forms and amounts—all assumed to be measurable, at least to the individual himself in the sense of quantitative comparability which is necessary to intelligent choice as regards their use; (*c*) a stock of technological "knowledge."

All this, it should be noted, applies strictly in the "stationary economy." Economic theory also takes account of phenomena of growth which affect all three sets of elements, as listed, but only in so far as the change can be brought under the form of accumulation of means in the measured sense of "capital," and in so far as in this respect the individual can be assumed to act "intelligently." In acts looking to the future, intelligent action requires perfect foreknowledge. Particularly as regards activities which change the conditions of action for other individuals, there seem to be insuperable difficulties in the way of formulating perfectly satisfactory theoretical postulates; and this is more or less true of all acts which have a real time aspect, i.e., which change the conditions of future action even for the acting individual. Rigorously speaking, the theory is restricted to stating conditions of equilibrium; it could never determine the path of movement toward that state from any other.

† This is probably true universally of all conscious behaviour, play as well as work, and even the play of children and animals. Even in walking for exercise, we prefer to go somewhere and typically take the most direct route.

(BB) Social Organization

§5. Here much greater concessions have to be made to reality. Any attempt to say definitely what is meant by an abstractly ideal "economic" organization raises at once a number of possibilities too complicated to treat impartially and exhaustively, and among which choice must be made on grounds of practical relevance. Undoubtedly the notion of individual behaviour which has the character of "economic" in a maximum degree implies social organization through voluntary exchange, i.e., a market organization of some sort. But there are theoretical difficulties in the notions of a perfect market, and perfect competition, and serious ambiguity in the notion of a system of market or competitive organization of an economic society.

With respect to content on the side of social organization, economic theory has actually developed and flourished only in societies where the form of organization is more or less typically that of "enterprise economy." In this type of organization, individuals get a living in two stages; first they sell productive services, of "person" and "property," for money, to enterprises, which carry on actual production; second, with this money income, they buy, from enterprises, the products which they consume. In addition, these societies have undergone a transition from individual to corporate enterprise during the historical period in which enterprise was becoming established, and evidently as a phase of the process of its establishment. Enterprise is especially to be contrasted with "exchange economy," in which individuals (families) produce and exchange products. In an exchange economy, the phenomena most important from a theoretical and practical standpoint in economic theory as now studied would not be met with at all. There would be no pecuniary distribution; the phenomena of wages, rent, interest, and profit would not exist.*

---

* Economic science based on reality in this way is still "theory," in so far as the empirical data used are a matter of completely general knowledge and are not in dispute. Such data may be treated as "axiomatic"; it is, of course, possible to maintain that this is the only meaning of axiomatic principles in any connection.

The process of transforming an existing society into a new type gives rise to problems calling for factual study of the existing type as well as theoretical analysis of the type proposed. Recurring to our former imperfect analogy, the doctor must study both the healthy body and the diseased. But while his study of both may be empirical, the economist must construct imaginatively his ideal society, but he studies by observation the existing one.

B. Positive Relations to Reality from a Practical Point of View

§6. (1) First, a brief note is called for on the relation between knowledge and social ideals and social activity.* We have taken the view that the justification for theory in human affairs is practical significance. The function of theory is to formulate and clarify some conceptual pattern of action to the end that men may better conform to it if it is already accepted, either as desired or as (normatively) desirable, or so that its appeal may be better judged if it is in question— or even so that it may be more surely avoided if already recognized as bad. These principles give rise to serious intellectual difficulties even at the level of discussion dealing with individual behaviour patterns, but the difficulties are still greater at the social level. Yet if the formulation and clarification of social patterns or systems of organization are to be fruitful in the same way, we must be able to assume that society also is in some sense, as a unit, a free agent in moulding itself.†

(2) The development of modern economic theory has undoubtedly been due in the main to the practical drive of concern for social policy as expressed in political (legal and administrative) action. It became a pure science, to the extent that it become such, by way of an interesting development from directly hortatory or propagandist political discussion. Smith's *Wealth of Nations*, from which modern economic

---

* This subject is discussed at greater length in the concluding section of the essay.

† It is necessary to distinguish this view from *two* very different lines of intellectual attack on economic phenomena, one of which excludes practical relevance while the other makes room for it in a vitally different sense. Both of these other views, separately, or in various mixtures, have achieved considerable attention under the name of "Institutional Economics." The former, which best fits the name, is essentially a continuation or revival of the historical standpoint. But if human and social phenomena can be completely explained in terms of their own history, the result is the same as that of a complete mechanical explanation; there is no such thing as purposive activity or as practical relevance. (The same explanation would account for the explainer and his behaviour in explaining, which reduces it to absurdity.) The other view is that economics should provide techniques for the "control" of economic process, in the manner in which natural science provides techniques for the control of nature. Under this view the principles would have practical significance indeed—to the *controller*, who is implied if the notion of scientific control is to have meaning, but not for the society subject to control. The view here adopted, abstracting from both of the above, treats social institutions as a product of social choice based on social knowledge of patterns between which choice is made, and has meaning only in so far as such social choice may be real.

theory may be dated, has with much justification been called a political pamphlet. A relatively small fraction of the work requires inter- pretation in terms of an interest in pure-science, and its main signi- ficance is that of propaganda or preaching of policy. Yet it is also the first important general work in scientific economic theory. It becomes scientific without ceasing to be chiefly concerned with advocating a policy. The preaching of a policy naturally takes on the character of a science, when the policy preached is negative, when it is the policy of allowing events to take their natural course. For then the content of the discussion consists chiefly of description or analysis of a "natural" course of events, in the absence of con- scious human interference, and this is obviously the character of a science.*

(3) The argument just given will show why in discussing the practical significance of economic theory there is no call for distin- guishing between individual and social viewpoints as was done under previous headings. The political ideal of the age was negative, indi- vidualistic. Its ideal was individual liberty; i.e., there should be no ideal of individual life enforced by society. It looked toward making society a mutual aid organization of a mechanical sort, by which each individual would achieve maximum efficiency in using his own means to his own ends. In the main, this ideal still stands, though it is visibly crumbling, in America and other countries which have not yet repudiated democracy outright for a dictatorial regime. There is a "burden of proof" against any proposal of a sweeping change away from free labour, private property, and a free market.†

* *The Wealth of Nations* is the first "scientific" work on economics in that it first gave a fairly clear and coherent picture of the nature and workings of a social economic organization on the pattern of free enterprise, with a reasonable minimum of political interference or control. In the course of time, England and the United States, and some other countries to a lesser degree, largely adopted this system of organization. Then the character of the practical problem changed. It became a question rather of examining the defects in the system and comparing its results with those to be obtained through some form of political control or by outright substitution of a "political" system of organization (for there is no other general alternative; after the question is raised a voluntary return to a traditional system is impossible).

† In the literature of economic theory, the concept of the "economic man" has indeed been attacked and generally rejected, verbally. This was intellectually a step backward, since the notion is essential to scientific analysis, and the only hope was to use it while making its limitations clear. In essentials it has been revived in the concept of the indifference function of the mathematical economists. But while certain so-called

(4) A little examination will show, however, that the ultimate moral and social ideal of the Liberalistic period (we may say, for short, the nineteenth century) was not that expressed in the conception of economic efficiency. The economic man, and his concomitant in society, the dual order of negativistic political democracy and economic *laissez-faire*, represent a rationalization carried to extremes, of a direction in which people wanted to go from a preceding state embodying the opposite extreme. On its face, the system treats liberty for the individual and mutuality in the relations between individuals as instrumental, i.e., as conditions for maximizing individual want satisfaction, and treats the individual as an absolute datum in his three aspects of wants, ultimate resources or productive capacity, and knowledge of processes.*

But in a reasonably generous interpretation of the accepted values of nineteenth-century civilization, neither liberty nor mutuality are properly instrumental to maximum individual economic utility. Rather, they are themselves ends. And they are ends in the two senses already distinguished. Not merely are individuals assumed to want liberty and mutuality, even at some sacrifice of objective material well-being, but these are moral ideals, which the individual "ought" to want even if he does not. It was definitely a principle of social policy that the individual should not merely be free to make his own mistakes but should be expected and required to assume his own responsibilities. This was conceived as a part of the dignity of man, which it is the obligation as well as the privilege of the individual to assume. Thus personal liberty is made, in more or less set

economists, notably the "historical schools" of Germany and England, were repudiating the idea without understanding it, much of its content in the bad, absolutistic sense was being preached with even less understanding by social philosophers and politicians. Among the former were especially Spencer; under the latter head come the Manchester Liberals. The British classical economists are comparatively guiltless, but less can be said for the French. Meanwhile, many of the vicious aspects of *laissez-faire* were put into effect in the legal system of the common law as interpreted by Blackstone, and in the United States through judicial review, under the Bill of Rights and especially the fourteenth amendment of the Constitution.

* It is hard to imagine this view being taken seriously, if it is understood; for it is obtrusively evident that society as politically organized for purposes of policy cannot possibly treat the individual as a datum in any of these aspects, or if it does so, that it places absolute reliance on non-political agencies functioning in a political capacity. The individual as a contracting unit obviously becomes what he is in all these respects under the influence of social conditions.

terms, an "inalienable right," in the constitution of every liberal state.*

As to mutuality, too, there can be no fair doubt either of the general acceptance in the modern commercial era of the principle of "a man's a man for a' that," or of the fact that the so-called "commercial spirit," more accurately the "spirit of enterprise," as it actually worked out in the era beginning with the Industrial Revolution, was a spirit of individual achievement. It worked for tolerance and for the rating of all men in accord with moral and personal qualities to a degree incomparably beyond anything seen in any previous civilization.

III. The Dualistic Institutional System of Liberalism; Reasons for its Decline

A. The Historical Setting

§7. The practical problem of economic organization is a political problem. The words politics and government refer to and mean the mechanism by which any social group acts as a unit, by which it formulates and carries out group policies, whether positive or negative. In the main, the political changes involved in the historical movement toward realization of the economic ideal of individual liberty, with the "automatic" forces of market competition as the mechanism for securing ordered cooperation, were negative changes. They consisted in reducing the functions of government; but by no means altogether to zero. An economic system of "free" market relations, even in its maximum development, must operate in a framework of political order, to protect property and enforce the rules of the market.

The new political order corresponding to the greatly reduced and chiefly negative or "preventive" functions of government was· *Democracy*, in the modern sense of representative government, both political, in the narrower meaning, and legal. It seemed to the statesmen of the revolutionary age of the later eighteenth century that the problem was to prevent government from usurping improper functions, and

* Paradoxically, it is out of this inalienable right that the special handicaps of the propertyless individual arise; because he cannot sell or mortgage his personal capacities, and must satisfy fundamental needs continuously, he finds himself in a weak bargaining position.

interfering with the liberties of the people, and that the solution was to place government as directly as possible under the control of "the people."* In practice, the system of economic individualism and political *laissez-faire* or negativism began to disintegrate before it was far advanced toward complete establishment. Its history almost from the start was a race between growth and decline.†

An attempt to give "reasons" for the decline, which in our own day threatens to become a debacle, must begin by inquiring as to how it was able to arise. Relatively little examination seems necessary to show that this nineteenth-century system could not permanently survive, and could only seem to approach realization in a highly unique material setting. Two points call for emphasis. The first is that the setting for individual liberty was a complex of physical conditions created for modern European civilization by the geographical and scientific discoveries extending from the later Middle Ages to the nineteenth century. The second is the fact that these conditions were inherently temporary and that liberalism in any form dependent upon them could only be correspondingly evanescent.‡

* The struggle out of which modern democracy really grew was more the fight for religious than for economic liberty, though we now tend to take the former for granted as an incident of political and economic freedom. The statement of the text ought to have considerable elaboration and qualification, if space permitted. The course of history was different in different countries, especially as regards the actual establishment of universal suffrage, which has been achieved for the feminine half of the adult population only in our own day.

For fairly obvious reasons, it was in the United States, of all the great nations, that the constitutional forms and accepted ideals came to represent the most thoroughgoing embodiment of the liberal principles, especially the negative ideal of government as a system designed to preserve "law and order," but so compounded of "checks and balances" that it would be prevented from undertaking positive functions which would interfere with individual liberty. Here was a new nation starting relatively free from older traditions, populated predominantly from the European country most advanced in the liberal direction (and indeed with people selected in large measure for an attitude of dissent), and also immediately dominated by frontier conditions. To our founding fathers, this connection between democracy and economic *laissez-faire*, meaning political negativism, was so obvious that they were hardly conscious of it. And in western Europe, the political evolution of the nineteenth century was toward democracy in the American sense.

† The economic system of "natural liberty" certainly did not reach its maximum growth in England until well along in the second half of the nineteenth century, but the first "factory act" was passed in 1802.

‡ In this analysis we must keep in mind the conceptual and methodological assumptions already emphasized. If historical changes can be accounted for in terms of historical

The effect of the new physical situation was manifested in somewhat different ways in Europe itself, in the regions of old civilization brought under European domination, and in the relatively unoccupied barbarian lands opened up to colonization; but it may all be summarized by the single expression, "an open frontier." The geographical discoveries and technological advance referred to virtually removed the confining boundaries of action for the European man and opened up an almost unlimited field, in which anyone with energy and ambition found before him more than he could appropriate; there was no occasion for serious overlapping or clashing with the interests of others. A large part of the opportunities thus created called for little in the way of either organized activity or previous training or accumulated "capital," but chiefly qualities of physical stamina, courage and ingenuity in the man himself. Particularly in the wilderness, but to a considerable degree in Europe itself, social organization on the large political scale became relatively unimportant—after the political sovereignty over the new regions was settled by war.

For reasons which are as obvious as they were overwhelming, such a situation could not last. The main interest which moved men to go to the geographical frontier for settlement depended on a prospect of developing later a very different kind of life, if not for the first pioneer himself, at least for his heirs. With the filling up of this wide-open world, conditions were bound to change fundamentally. Getting ahead in the world would come again to mean, as it had before, a

causality, then all economic theory, as a discussion of social ideas for the guidance of a free society, is words without sense. But this is not to deny that historical causes play some role, along with the free choice between ideals. This would be absurd in general, and in the present instance some causal analysis will contribute greatly to the understanding of our problem, as the changes now going on certainly are not due entirely to new intellectual light on the meaning of ideals.

The general problem of historical explanation or interpretation cannot, of course, be gone into here. Besides the view that material conditions in some sense and in some way "control" the process as a whole, there are two other main views. The first of these holds that "culture" is an entity or group of entities having a fairly independent existence and its own (or their own) "laws" of growth and change. The second, that change comes about through the creative activity of exceptional individuals—the "great man" theory. All three views contain a large element of truth, and all must be taken into account if we are to have a defensible view of history. In a revolutionary age such as the present, the third view tends to be over-emphasized. It seems self-evident that no one individual is likely to have much influence on the course of history, and also that the nature of the influence which the exceptional historical personality does or will have is highly problematical and is not generally in close accord with his own ideas or wishes.

more direct struggle with other people rather than with nature, and a struggle for power over other people, which is overwhelmingly the human meaning, immediate or ultimate, of power over nature itself. The pioneers looked forward to life under these changed conditions.* In different words, the economic aspects of life largely reflect interests which are ultimately political, in so far as the motive which drives men is the urge to get ahead in the world. The economic interest ending in material things could take precedence only temporarily in the open spaces, technical and geographical, and as these regions filled up, the political phases of the struggle were bound to gain the ascendancy. For the nineteenth century social philosophy of liberty accepted, and even emphasized, the driving motive of the desire to "get ahead in the world."

B. Disillusionment with Economic Individualism

§8. Under this dominant motive, and historically normal conditions of life, economic liberalism in the negative sense of extreme individual *laissez-faire* is impossible, for two fundamental reasons which were generally overlooked in the accepted theory. The first reason is the fact that wealth can be used to get more wealth; for, the more of it anyone has, the more advantage he has in the struggle to get still more. Consequently, under individualistic freedom, and under the condition that men want more wealth, for whatever reason, it will be used to get more, giving rise to a cumulative growth of inequality. Two further consequences naturally follow in turn: (a) With "gross" inequality in the distribution of wealth among individuals, all ethical defences of freedom lose their validity; and (b) the automatic system of control (market competition) breaks down, for competition requires a large number of units, every one of negligible size.

Moreover, elimination of competition may result from the organization of individuals in large units as well as inequality in individual wealth. The fact that monopoly is usually more remunerative than competitive production furnishes a powerful incentive to form such organizations, and free competition naturally tends to become a

* To be sure, there was in the drive to settlement a certain element of pure romanticism, and of the negative urge of escape, but the "beautiful savage" mentality is neither very deep nor very widespread nor, especially, very enduring under contact with the realities of primitive conditions.

contest in the establishment of monopoly. In an individualistic-utilitarian view of life, freedom means freedom to use power, and economic freedom means freedom to use economic power, without political interference or restraint. Such freedom may in effect become slavery for the person who has little power at his disposal, since life itself requires practically continuous control of a certain minimum of economic power.

The second oversight was the failure to see that skill in verbal utterance, or capacity in any form to "influence" other persons, is a form of economic power. Men have lived by their wits from time immemorial; it was no doubt one of the earliest uses of language. Persuasive power is, in the first place, a form of "productive capacity" in that skilful "puffing" makes a product more desirable to a pur-purchaser and consumer, who in an individualistic system is the final judge of the merits of products. But even more important in economic relations is the same sort of power used in selling "indirect goods," including productive wealth and economic opportunities and organization devices of all forms, and functioning "executive ability" in general. Adam Smith and the classical writers, in advocating freedom of access to the market, do not seem to have thought about the possibilities of personal influence as a serious factor in economic relations; advertising and selling technique assumed importance after Smith's day. But in "business" itself (as to politics, see below) there is hardly a limit to the distortion it may produce, if allowed to work cumulatively. Nor did they appreciate the importance of the fact that freedom to compete means freedom to organize to eliminate competition. As will be emphasized presently, personality power, ability to persuade and to organize, is both one of the forms of power most unequally distributed by nature and in addition is one capable of most rapid development through its own exercise, which naturally leads to the cumulative inequality already referred to.

It is surely evident that, if social life is to be a contest, and a contest for anything limited in supply and which itself is or confers power in the contest, it can only lead to such a concentration of control over the object of struggle as will put an end to such a social form. This tendency is enormously intensified by the fact that in the underlying motivation in what is called economic activity, it is in large measure power for its own sake which is the real object of striving, rather than any material use or fruit of power. Such a contest cannot go on very long without systematic provision for a "new deal"— meaning a new deal, and not merely a questionable change in the rules, which the phrase has come to signify in current political slogan-mongering. Through the inevitable response of human nature to such a situation, any "game" of this sort will tend to degenerate into appeal forms of power more elemental than mere skill or capacity in play. The game is, or soon becomes, so "unfair" that the losers can hardly be morally condemned if they refuse to abide by its rules and results. Something of this sort has been taking place in the economic life of the western world. The further steps in the argument will show that the same principles naturally are and have been operative in other departments of culture, and especially in politics, with the same consequences, which are more, and not less, disastrous in these other fields.

PART TWO

POLITICAL INDIVIDUALISM OR DEMOCRATIC SOCIALISM

I. FROM BUSINESS TO POLITICS

§9. When the "economic game" of free enterprise becomes intolerable through the growth of individual inequality and of monopoly, the next recourse of the masses who get the worst of it—or of their more or less self-appointed saviours from the ranks of the labour movement and the social-reform minded intelligentsia—is to politics. This has meant, in the first instance, to *democratic* politics. It was natural to assume that with a distribution of power in the equal basis of one-man-one-vote, the economic reorganization of society in favour of the "toiling masses" as against the privileged or parasitic few, would follow automatically, or as soon as the mass could be made to see the issue and to realize its own power.

It is especially interesting that in England, the original home of modern industrial enterprise, we begin to hear of a "New Liberalism" at just about the date which historians set for the "passing of the frontier" in the New World. The New Liberalism represented an inversion of the old as to basic political principles; it rested on the conception of the state in positive terms as the main instrument of economic cooperation, rather than in negative terms, as an umpire or order-maintaining agency in an automatic process of interaction between individuals. In England, the new liberalism grew into the Labour Party movement, while the Social Democratic Party in Germany embodied the same social philosophy, as did also, in a mild form, the "Progressive" movement and then the "New Deal" in the United States.

This movement, which came to be referred to as "Socialism," proposed, in brief, to use the political machinery of the democratic state to effect the organization of economic life, in place of the system of private property and competitive free enterprise. As to what concretely might be involved in this, the propagandists for the change were comfortably vague. A few remarks on this subject will be offered below in another section; in the present connection the point of interest is that the movement—in different degrees in different countries—lost popular support, and even the adhesion of its former leaders, before reaching political power and the test of application. It gave place to a theory and a propaganda which not only renounced but violently denounced democracy as a political form, and all its works. Herein it followed, with more or less lag, the evolution of Marxian thought.* The new movement, still proclaiming the ideal of economic equality, or economic "justice," as against "exploitation," calls itself Communism. It has, of course, achieved power only in Russia, and there through a course of events in sharp contrast with the historical predictions of its earlier theorists.

In the meantime, partly under the threat of political party Com-

---

* It is unnecessary for our purposes to comment in detail on the political movements in various countries. But some mention should be made of the role, and especially the evolution, of "Marxism." In his earlier phase, Marx accepted the position indicated, that economic equality would follow automatically with the achievement of political equality. But he was soon disillusioned by the course of events in America, where a generation of manhood suffrage had led to no such result, and by the episode of the Paris Commune. Official Marxism then evolved toward an entirely different political theory, called the "dictatorship of the proletariat," meaning the dictatorship *over* the proletariat, and annihilation by proletarization of other classes, by a closely organized minority party, posing as the custodians of Communism, now set up as a remote ideal. But the radical liberal parties which commanded real strength in the western nations adhered until recently to democratic principles, even if they used Marxist phraseology.

munism, and partly as a direct reaction to the recognized shortcomings of the liberal system of free enterprise and negativistic democracy, there has arisen another type of movement toward minority party dictatorship. It is generally referred to somewhat loosely as "Fascism," from the name of the first party of the type to seize power, in Italy. With the accession to power of a somewhat similar regime in Germany, and smaller countries, and the rise of strong movements in the same general direction in still other lands, it becomes a question of by no means merely academic interest to inquire into the strength and weakness of "free" institutions in the political as well as the economic realm.

The significance of the actual development to date of dictatorships will be variously estimated, especially because the revolutions, and more outstanding developments in the direction of revolution, have taken place in countries where democratic forms were relatively new and not deeply rooted. Our concern here is rather with the theoretical analysis of free institutions as such, and especially with respect to basic theoretical weaknesses overlooked by the exponents of liberalism in its day of ascendancy, which may help to explain the trend toward new forms. In the foregoing section, we glanced at the economic side of the dual system; in this, we are concerned especially with the political side.

What seems to be the fundamental weakness of democracy is briefly to be told, after the foregoing analysis of economic individualism. In principle, democracy is political individualism. The pure or direct democracy of the town meeting or small city-state, governed by an assembly of its entire citizenship, is the nearest approach to pure political individualism short of anarchy, and democracy in the sense of representative institutions is an adaptation necessary for larger communities. The essential point is that, as it has worked out in practice in the modern world, *democracy is competitive politics*, somewhat as free enterprise is competitive economics (though inherently a competition for a monopolistic position), and shows the same weaknesses as the latter. In ideal theory, neither is competitive in the psychological sense.

Political democracy, with representative institutions and majority rule, cannot be individualistic in quite the sense of enterprise economy

—at least not if the government undertakes positive functions beyond its merely preventive role of enforcing the rules of a free market and maintaining its freedom. For it is the nature of political decisions to be binding upon all. But ideally, even under representative institutions, the decisions of a democracy should be based on universal free discussion, with equal participation by all full citizens.*

As no one needs to be told, the realities in both business and politics have been very different from these ideals. The reality in the two realms has this in common, that one of the main interests providing the drive for action is the competitive interest in the psychological sense of emulation or rivalry. And the main weakness is the same in both cases, as compared with an ideal system in which "each should count for one and none for more than one"; it lies in the natural, cumulative tendency toward inequality in status, through the use of power to get more power. The main error on the political side, in the theory of liberalism as expounded by its advocates, is that competitive politics is not better than economics in this regard, but definitely worse.

The error is a natural one, resulting from a superficial view of the facts. In economic relations, there is the visible fact of property, an objective and durable medium for accumulation lacking in politics; and in economic affairs men nominally exercise influence in proportion to income, while democratic politics rests on the principle of one-man-one-vote. But a little critical examination will undermine the contrast. On the side of business, as we have seen, the most important substantial constituent of power is not the ownership of material things, which is so prominent to a superficial view, but personal power in widely various forms.

In the political system of democracy, what was in economics an especially important factor in individual power becomes virtually the whole. Democratic politics works out in practice as campaigning, electioneering, and "organization," featuring the type of human capacity suggested by such terms as "spell-binder," "boss," and "machine." Such abilities are more unequally distributed among men

---

* The principle of majority rule must be taken ethically as a means of ascertaining a real "general will," not as a mechanism by which one set of interests is made subservient to another set. Political discussion must be assumed to represent a quest for an objectively ideal or "best" policy, not a contest between interests.

by nature than is economic ability or power of any other kind, and also tend more strongly to cumulative increase through their own exercise. This growth through exercise does not come about solely or even chiefly because a technique improves with practice. A far more important reason is that the largest element in the ability to influence people is prestige, reputation, or prominence. Only persons of some degree of prominence find it easy to get a hearing at all, and one who is prominent enough, for whatever reason, is readily accepted as an authority and guide on almost any subject—regardless, in both cases, of real knowledge or competence, or even moral trustworthiness.

Thus liberal economics and liberal politics are at bottom the same kind of "game." The fundamental fact in both is the moral fact of rivalry, competitiveness, and the interest in power. Democratic politics in the nineteenth century was a power system, a phenomenon of the use of power, and especially of its use to get more power. Given the moral condition of an interest in power, whether for the sake of some result or fruit for which it is to be used, or for the sake of power itself as an end, the forms of organization are of secondary importance. Yet both theory and experience go to show that the cumulative tendency to inequality and to consequent disruption of the system is likely to be actually stronger in the political field, where the power is purely moral and psychological, than in the economic field, where such power is supplemented by, or competes with, control over material agents. (This control or ownership to be real must be accepted by others, for psychological or moral reasons, or it must rest upon political power.) In view of the way in which psychological principles work in politics, equal suffrage (even *if* it is respected in practice) provides little or no guarantee of equality in that field. The overwhelming majorities rolled up in plebiscites (more or less fairly conducted) on the question of dictatorship show where the realities lie.

Of course, any black-and-white separation and contrast would be misleading. Wealth power is used in economics and in politics to acquire and enhance persuasion and prestige power, and reciprocally; and the direct power of political and military coercion stands in the same reciprocal relation to both. But these facts do not affect the principal argument. This argument is three-fold: (*a*) that *any* form of power may be used to get more power in the same or other forms, (*b*) that in a culture in which men's chief interests and psychological drives centre in power, it will be so used, and (*c*) that the consequent, inevitable concentration of power will destroy freedom, or reduce it to an empty form. A game in which winning increases power to play cannot go on for long without a real "new deal"—to be distinguished from problematical changes in the rules referred to by that term in current American political slogan-mongering. This argument should make it clear that the appeal from competitive economics to democracy, under such moral conditions that the latter means competitive politics, is no cure for the self-defeating tendencies of economic competition, but is rather a jump "from the frying pan into the fire." It is not due to accident or mere human perversity that "Socialism" never made sufficient headway to come to a test as a system.*

There are other important reasons why the self-defeating tendency is likely to be stronger in the political than in the economic struggle. Business, including industry, does have a foundation in substantial reality and material needs; it does provide "goods" and services which are of importance in themselves for life, comfort, and aesthetic

---

* The situation as regards the self-defeating tendencies of any system of individual liberty is of course aggravated, to the extent that men seek power for "political" reasons (the desire for power over others for its own sake) rather than for "economic" reasons (the desire for the fruits of power). One of the more serious fallacies of liberal theory was the assumption that in "economic" life the motive is really "economic," with the related assumptions that market competition is impersonal and that conflicts of material interest form the principal basis of the problem of social order and harmony. The same man who will say "you first" to another, in a natural catastrophe where the saving of life itself is at stake, may fight *à outrance*, and resort to treachery as well, over a social humiliation. Even in what we call economic consumption, i.e., the personal use of material goods and services, the motive is largely competitive, "keeping up with the Joneses"— and getting ahead of them. This of course is true in a progressively greater degree as we move upward in the income scale, but even what are called economic necessities are in very large measure a matter of conformity to social standards. (Poverty is of course a no less terrible thing because it is largely a matter of social degradation or because the physical suffering and menace to health, and even to life, which is real, is so largely the result of sacrificing physical needs to the necessity of keeping up a "front.")

The doctrine taught in economic classes, that money is a means to goods and services as an end, is false in both its aspects; money is an end as well as a means, and goods and services are a means—to social conformity and distinction. In the reading prescribed for all students of economics a special place should be given to a few realistic behaviour studies such as the story of the conversation in Plutarch's *Life of Pyrrhus*, between the King and his counsellor Cineas, or Mark Twain's story of how Tom Sawyer got his fence whitewashed.

satisfaction, and not merely as instruments of prominence and power, while the latter make up practically the sole objective in politics. Again, business leaders, more or less in spite of themselves, must appeal to men as individuals and in terms of individual interests; there are limits to their opportunities to create the conditions for crowd psychology and to exploit it. But in politics the appeal is almost exclusively to the crowd.* It is worth emphasizing, too, that prominence and power are subject to the principle of scarcity to an indefinitely greater degree than any economic commodity having substantial utility. It is a simple matter of arithmetic that in a "public" of any considerable size only a small fraction of the individuals can be the object of attention or obedience by any satisfying fraction of the whole, either directly or through their written words, for any satisfying fraction of the time. Finally, it seems that power and prominence belong in that class of satisfactions, along with certain drugs, which, over time, obey a principle of "increasing utility;"† in consequence, the struggle for power and prominence does not tend toward saturation and a position of stability; in the nature of social power, it is impossible for any individual to get *all* power, while excessive concentration tends to strengthen opposition and to generate weakness in the power-holding group. The result to be expected is (as Plato and Aristotle saw) a cyclical oscillation, from freedom to autocracy and back to freedom by way of revolution.

* The founding fathers of democracy, notably in America, were by no means undisturbed by the possible role of persuasive power in politics, as Adam Smith and the other founders of *laissez-faire* were oblivious of it in economics. On the contrary, our Constitution makers strove to erect effective safeguards against appeal to the passions of the masses. But no special analysis is needed to show why such safeguards were bound to go by the board in the exigencies of practical politics. Any party or group which by extending the suffrage confers political power on a new sector of the population naturally attaches to itself the allegiance and voting strength of the new electors for a long time in the future. The staunch Republicanism of the ex-slaves of the American South is, for special reasons, an extreme example, but illustrates a general principle. In England, the details were different, the Conservative Party often astutely taking the lead in suffrage extension and other reform measures, as a backfire against more radical changes. But the result was the same. In England, this "Tory-Socialism" was contemporary with the "New Liberalism," and differed little from the latter in its historical political significance.

† Such a principle is not, of course, on the same level as the law of diminishing utility operative at a given moment, and does not contradict the latter; increasing utility with the passing of time is a matter of the shift in position of a diminishing utility curve, not a movement along it.

Historically, the development of democratic political forms was an accompaniment of the growth of the automatic market organization in the economic realm. As already suggested, the founders of democracy themselves took it for granted that democracy was an inseparable aspect of the dual system based on the principle of *laissez-faire*, leaving to government few serious positive functions in time of peace. Both abstract reasoning and the historical course of events following the attempt to convert liberalism into a "new liberalism," seem to show that they were right. The free political institutions of the nineteenth century were dependent upon a delegation of the problems of economic relations to non-political automatic devices. (And, as we have seen, the working of the automatic economic system was dependent upon anomalous and inherently temporary material conditions.) In the centuries following the Middle Ages, government had come to be regarded as chiefly economic in meaning and function; and when it was relieved of its economic functions it sank into a position of relative unimportance. In the nineteenth century men commonly treated politics as a kind of sport. The interest in it was chiefly dramatic. Neither the specially informed nor the bulk of the population thought that it really made any vital difference who was selected. When democracy did confront a serious issue, such as slavery in the United States, the issue was settled by fighting to the exhaustion of the weaker party. And it is a commonplace that in the face of a serious war—the original and always the primary function of government—democracy "folded up," with no serious protest from any quarter.

The ultimate reasons for the inability of democratic machinery to meet serious issues raise the problem of the political intelligence and the moral qualities of human beings. It would be easy to make out a strong case for the view that the requisite qualities do not exist in human nature at all, that people generally neither have them nor want them, and do not admire them in others when they are occasionally manifested. Observation of social and political phenomena, from the primitive peoples down, and of the behaviour of very young children and of animals, tends to suggest that "human nature" craves a human contest and loves victory and power first of all, and admires them in others when it cannot get them for its individual self. Worse still for the prospects of democracy, it does not seem to have educated in this direction, but rather the contrary.* For this realistic study of human nature, it would appear that we should give at least equal consideration to the spontaneous activities of recreation, as compared with those of work. When we are freest to do what we want to do, the first thing we generally do is to start a competition of some sort, either to engage in directly, or as a spectacle which we enjoy by vicarious participation; and the interest of the direct participants is largely dependent on the size and character of a spectator group. And, as already observed more than once, the activity which we call economic, whether of production or of consumption or the two together, is also, if we look below the surface, to be interpreted largely by the motives of the competitive contest or game, rather than those of mechanical utility functions to be maximized.

The methodological implications of this fact of competitiveness cannot be developed here. It should be sufficient to remark that the interest in a game is only within the narrowest limits, if strictly speaking at all, to be promoted by the discovery and application of correct procedures in the manner of science and technology. "Science" plays a part, if at all, only in connection with the interest of the individual in *winning* the game; it plays none in having the game go on, still less in "improving" it. Even in winning, it is certainly a small

---

* Mention of education calls to mind the familiar proposal, from various quarters, to "change human nature." This notion cannot be discussed here as it deserves, but I must say that I find the argument puzzling, not to say depressing, in several regards. In the first place, as to the logic used by the proponents. Within a year, I have clipped from several supposedly high sources of intellectual enlightenment the argument that human nature has changed and that this proves that it "can be" changed. If this is not a perfect *non sequitur*, I should like to see a better example. Even the premise that human nature has changed is nonsensical rather than true or false, or even debatable; it is true, and false, and debatable, each in as many senses as anyone cares to take the trouble to distinguish. The conclusion merely states that the premise means something which it does not mean; to say that human nature has changed, may argue that it *may* change again, but it does not argue that anybody can change it. If anyone really possessed the power to remould human nature at will, he would certainly have to exercise it in effective secrecy or "human nature" would promptly kill him, and it would be right in doing so. Proposals to change human nature, or radically to reform society in any way, or to "plan" its activities, or to exercise "control," typically emanate from some pretended impersonal "we." To ask about the antecedent of the pronoun ought to be as superfluous as the original statement is nonsensical. The question whether "we" either ought to or are going to change, plan, or control ourselves, is one very difficult to talk about in a way that makes even grammatical sense. Later sections will inquire into the possible meaning of social self-change.

part, and relative to the opponent's "science." Doubtfully and to a slight degree at most is the "science" of fencing or poker or any other game science at all; it is beyond even the skill and judgment, which are things not communicable by verbal propositions or other symbols. Effectiveness at a game depends upon outguessing and outwitting, "out-deceiving," an opponent.

But the important fact is that interest in winning and the interest in the game tend to run into conflict; too much interest in winning first spoils a game and then breaks it up altogether, converting it into a quarrel, or beyond this into a fight. Unless people are more interested in having the game go on than they are in winning it, no game is possible. And the social interest, which is the concern of the social scientist, is precisely the interest in keeping up the game, preventing it from deteriorating, and beyond that in making it a still better game. From the social point of view, the question of who is to win does not and cannot arise—except of course in the sense that the "best man" should win, which is just one aspect of the statement that it should be a good game.

The "natural" tendency is for a game to deteriorate, if the participants follow their primitive impulses without conscious exercise of moral restraint. No game is possible unless the players have the attitudes and interests to which the term "sportsmanship" is understood to refer. This is the organization of people pursuing individual interests; and the problem of morale is probably harder in an individualistic organization than in a group united under some mystical common purpose. In general, the group as a unit must also exert some pressure on its members.*

The minimum political problem in society is that of preventing (too much!) "cheating" and unsportsmanly practice. The operation

---

* The game presents an ideal example on a small scale of the whole problem of government. Belief in anarchism consists essentially in the faith that the informal pressure of "public opinion" will be sufficient. In connection with the larger socio-politico-economic game, relatively few persons hold this faith—and it may even be questioned whether the pressure of public opinion, in any form in which it might conceivably be effective ("Mrs. Grundy"), would be morally preferable to frank compulsion, in the best achievable form of the latter. It is equally unreal to conceive of society without a moral attitude, which means a religion of some kind, enforced by approval and disapproval, and without an organized mechanism of sanctions. The two (or three) must work together effectively to keep infractions of rules at a low level.

of the tendency to cheat is insidious; if one player cheats "a little," or even creates a suspicion that he is cheating, the thing tends to become contagious and progressive. If in any game there is a considerable amount of cheating going on, the individual who wants to maintain the game in its integrity confronts two alternatives: he may either organize group pressure to correct the evil, or withdraw from the game. But in the larger, political game, peaceful withdrawal is impossible, and those persons who care for ordered society must face the problem of organized compulsion, i.e., of law. The alternative is that the game itself descends to progressively lower levels of strategy, then to worse and worse disorder, and finally to civil war or the *bellum omnium contra omnes*.

Enforcement of rules and prevention of cheating is, however, but the minimum function of the political system. In any state of affairs yet seen in the world, men of good will must aspire to have it do much more; the game of social living has never approached satisfactory ideals in the fairness of its rules, to say nothing of the inherent quality and dignity of its objectives and the type of play employed in reaching them. This is the real social problem, the problem of progress, and it is obviously one of enormously greater difficulty than merely keeping things going at a given level. Yet it may not "really" be harder, for it seems likely that a society cannot merely keep going at a given level without progressing, but must change in one direction or the other, either upward or downward. This seems almost certainly true in a culture in which the individual is dominated by the motive of improving his own condition, for his struggle in this direction must force social progress or social disruption. In any case, it is in connection with change and progress that serious issues arise in society.*

* Of course the problem of economic organization is further complicated by the fact that economic activity does and must supply vital material and cultural needs of man. We have no thought of belittling this aspect, or the evils of stunted lives on one hand and excess on the other. But the physical considerations are inseparable from the social-competitive and would largely take care of themselves if the "game" were made and kept "fair." The main problems would be: to prevent continued concentration of power in the hands of individuals or organizations; to assure to all a really equal start, or at least one as fair as possible, through an "equitable" sharing of the material and cultural inheritance; to arrange such "handicaps" as would give everyone a "chance"; and to provide the best distribution of prizes for making the contest interesting to participants and spectators. In this view of social life as a contest, enforced

The settlement of issues by free general discussion is at best a costly process in time and mental effort and patience, even when the group is very small—even at the ultimate minimum of two persons. It is much simpler to have someone in charge. Reflection on what actually happens in the simplest cases—say the discussion of presumably scientific problems by two social scientists—is hardly conducive to faith in the possibilities when larger groups and more tangible differences are involved. It is surely self-evident that organized social action on any large scale, unless conditions are purely traditional and stationary (except for such unconscious "drift" as characterizes linguistic change), must depend on *leadership* and the general willingness to accept and follow leadership.

But there is and can be no mechanics of intelligent and moral leadership. A little reflection about the simplest type of problem in the field of leadership, say, that of the relation between a technical counsellor and his client, or more specifically, a physician and his patient, will show four things: First, it is impossible for a leader to be selected intelligently, in the scientific sense. In order to select his doctor scientifically, the patient would have to know all the medical science known by all the candidates under consideration, and in addition know how much of this knowledge was possessed by each separate candidate. Secondly, the relation between leader and follower must be a moral relation, one of confidence and trust on the part of the client and of moral integrity and of candour tempered by judgment on the part of the counsellor. Thirdly, where the leader is chosen by the follower or client on the basis of active competition for the position, the follower becomes the real leader; for the methods of competition by those seeking appointment will run largely to competition in promising to do what the client wants done, and by debating technical details will make him the judge of these, and in promising results of whose probability of realization the counsel-seeker must judge. And all this is the more certainly true where the follower is a group, amenable to manipulation through crowd psychology. Fourthly, active competition for positions of leadership, especially leadership

equalization would be absurd; a game is not bad or unfair because some win and others lose, but on the contrary its interest and value depend in part on the fact. (That, however, says little in defence of the inequality which we actually have.)

of groups of considerable size, means the progressive degradation
of the entire system through the use of salesmanship or "influence,"
—flattery, cajolery, outright deception, and sheer pressure of suggestion and assertion. This means appeal from intelligence to the most
irrational emotions. The methods of competition adopted by aspirants
to positions of leadership must be those which "work"; candidates
in any way restrained by "principles" will simply be eliminated.
And it goes without saying that competence to persuade is only
accidentally and improbably associated with competence to counsel
and to lead.*

Specific illustration of the working of these principles in nineteenth-
century democratic politics is sadly superfluous. Enough has been
said above in general terms about campaigning and party machines.
The public reaction to the testimony at a recent political trial of a
mayor of New York City made it clear that men need not lose popular
admiration even by downright graft on the most colossal scale as
long as they "get away with it"—without running into the clutches
of the law in the hands of someone who is not for sale or whose
price cannot be met. The growth of advertising relative to productive
activity in business has the same implications for the principles of
leadership as campaigning, though less serious consequences. The
workings of competition for leadership in the "higher" fields of
science and religion will call for notice later.†

* Of course some will work on the basis of building and maintaining a reputation
—others on the principles of "getting away with the goods" and that of "one is born
every minute."

† We may remark here that perhaps the profoundest ground for doubt regarding
the possibilities of a workable and ethically tolerable democracy lies in the failure of
the intellectual leadership of the nineteenth century. Under the special conditions of
the time, men were for a few generations placed in a position to indulge rather largely
in the luxury of pursuing and proclaiming the truth. Relative freedom from economic
and social pressure, and the general freedom of opportunity going with open frontiers
in several dimensions, placed those with genuine intellectual interests in a position to
be impartial—if not absolutely, at least in a degree far beyond what can be expected
under historically more typical conditions. But the best social thought of the time, in
societies most completely dominated by liberal sentiments, did not grasp the difficulties
of a free social order, or see that the freedom which existed was dependent upon a
remarkable and temporary concourse of circumstances; and of course it did not attack
the problem of what is necessary to preserve liberty in the long run. The contemporary
discussion of fundamental social problems—or at least that which got a substantial
hearing—ran in terms either of apologetic or of criticism of such quality that the two
now seem to vie with each other in irrelevance.

II. Economic Theory and Socialism

§10. Socialists, perhaps wisely from the standpoint of their propaganda purposes, have been chary of details as to how their system would be organized or would function in practice. Space limits exclude any thorough discussion of the problem here, but a few notes seem necessary by way of support for the essential observation that the differences between democratic socialism and free enterprise are certain to be greatly exaggerated by anyone who judges superficially or without serious study of the problem.

For our purposes, we assume, in accord with the liberal ideals actually cherished by socialists, and to promote which they advocate the system: First, that the governmental system will remain democratic, in the meaning of control by majority vote, with campaigning and balloting "free," i.e., free from outright coercion and the cruder forms of fraud. Second, that such a government will try to follow individualistic ideals (a) in leaving each person free to choose his own ends and values in connection with consumption and with his contribution to production, and (b) in using available productive capacity in such a way as to secure maximum results under the criterion of such free choices. The workings of the system are to be interpreted on the further assumption that "human nature is unchanged," i.e., that men show the same major interests and drives as in nineteenth-century economic and political life, and that political activity conforms to the best norms of intelligence and public spirit reasonably to be expected in view of modern experience. Under these conditions, we have to inquire into the theoretical differences between a democratic-political system and one of private property and competition such as was found, for example, in the United States in the generation before the World War. Since most of the argument will apply to any system of political control, whether democratic or not, in so far as it follows the ideal of maximum individual material well-being, as judged by the individuals affected, it may be in order occasionally to note comparisons with the Russian system.

(1) The only possible general policy for approximating the ideals indicated would be to retain a money economy, the individual (or family) receiving his share in the distribution of the product in some

form of fluid purchasing power or money, with freedom of expenditure for products at known prices. For the purposes of economical management, the productive contributions of individuals would have to be measured by the saleable value of the product, and the remuneration for the service would have to vary with this value. It would not have to be equal to it, but the simplest way to effect any other scale of remuneration would be to compute the pay according to product value and modify the result by taxation or subsidy out of taxation.*

(2) Traditional demand-and-supply analysis (in its abstract-descriptive and its normative sense) will fit such a system with practically no change. The principles governing the organization would be identical with those of enterprise economy, however different the concrete material data. The familiar "economic laws" of diminishing utility and diminishing returns and the process of imputation on the basis of small increments would be valid without modification. In so far as the system worked "economically," productive resources would be apportioned among uses on the principle of equalizing the increment of product value from an increment of resources—with some modification, but in the main not much, by sentimental preferences among occupations. Entrepreneurs *and property owners*—the idleness of the idle rich is much exaggerated—would be replaced by administrative officials, who, like their prototypes, would theoretically have no discretionary power over production, the details of organization being determined, just as under the theory of enterprise, by consumers' choices.

(3) The chief differences would affect resource ownership, with wants in a second place, due to differences in social norms (education and sales promotion), but differences in wants are highly problematical; there is no ground for assuming any important difference with respect to technology—at least if inventors were rewarded in some correspondence with the value of their performance, and even that reservation is questionable. Superficially, there seems to be a fundamental difference in the fact that power of control is distributed on the basis of one human adult one vote under socialism, one dollar one vote

* Taxation in such a system may look like giving with one hand and taking away with the other, but it is what the Russians have found expedient; in fact, they also employ as a part of their financial system the still more anomalous device of selling interest-bearing securities to wage earners.

under free enterprise. In the United States, for example, individual incomes (in the statistical, accounting sense) have run as high as a hundred thousand times the model for all incomes. That is, ignoring negative incomes, the distribution curve is skewed (as measured by range from the mode) in the ratio of a foot to fifteen or twenty miles. Yet the more one goes behind such superficial facts, the more it becomes doubtful whether real distribution would be less unequal under socialism than under free enterprise. It is in this connection that major fallacies in socialistic theory call for correction.

As we have shown at sufficient length, equal suffrage does not mean equality in control of voting power, but may mean almost its ultimate antithesis when voters come under the influence of effective propaganda and "machine" organization. (Recall, again, the overwhelming majorities by plebiscite in favour of dictators.) Even less, if possible, does equal voting right imply equality in the distribution of the favours in the power of voters to grant. For the practical effects on the side of consumption, we have our own political system as an indicator. The executive household of our Federal government certainly costs more money than is spent for consumption by any private person.* It must especially be kept in mind that only a fraction of the large nominal incomes of most persons of great wealth is used for personal consumption even in the most inclusive sense; for the very largest incomes, it may be a fraction of one per cent. The great bulk of such income is reinvested, and the recipient cannot generally do otherwise than reinvest if he wishes the income to continue. Allowance must also be made for taxes, gifts to causes of all sorts, and the value of unpaid public services rendered by persons of means.

After all, as we have sufficiently emphasized, the significance of consumption itself is largely symbolic; the inequality which really

---

* This of course is but one case, and space limits exclude full discussion. This would raise complicated questions as to what is meant by consumption, especially the line between personal consumption and expenditure in the line of duty, both in the public service and in business. In the expenditure for display rather than utility, in the working quarters, only the banks, of all private enterprises, could compete at all with our capitols, court houses, etc. At best, inequality in consumption is greatly exaggerated by the money figures; the part which pays for natural scarcity would largely cancel out through price adjustment if incomes were equalized. No distribution of money income will make it possible for everyone to enjoy the "choice cuts," of meat, dwelling location, artistic products, or fruits and wine. (And the same is true of choice among "jobs.")

"hurts" is the unequal distribution of dignity, prestige, and power. Neither abstract reasoning nor the evidence of experience affords ground for belief that, given the moral drive toward such values as the dominant motive in society, democratic political process could fail to distribute them even more unequally still than does competitive business.*

(4) The practical problem in relation to inequality, whether in consumption or in social dignity and power, is that of its natural tendency to cumulative increase. Again, we have sufficiently stressed the point that the use of power to get more power is a tendency naturally more extreme in an organization based on vote getting than in one based on dollar getting. But there is one serious question raised by this argument, one which is especially pointed in relation to the current trend toward dictatorships. It comes up when we look beyond the individual life into the matter of inheritance of place and power. On one hand, the legal systems of the western world have taken inheritance in the natural family, more or less modified by testamentary freedom, as an inseparable feature of property as an institution. On the other, the minority party dictatorships are being set up in accord with the opposite principle. In abstract theory, there is no necessity in either arrangement, or in one more than the other; we can think of the other perquisites of ownership without that of inheritance and bequest, and the regular inheritance of political authority and social rank is the familiar arrangement in history. From a practical point of view, the contrast is more important. Society can indeed easily abolish the right of inheritance, but to allow effective ownership of property, with

* Mention of this issue raises problems of infinite complexity and difficulty. In the first place, almost nothing can be said in general terms of the reasons which make people envious or condescending, or especially as to why dignity and indignity are attached to particular functions in society. Furthermore, it is arbitrary to assert that equality is "better" than inequality. The fact seems to be that people do not actually want equality, that the next best thing to being a hero is to have a hero to look up to. Under certain conditions, there is no question that men literally love punishment, even physical torture; they also rather characteristically love a grievance; they love compulsory conformity to arbitrary patterns, and at the same time love to break rules for the sake of breaking them, and to act irrationally because it is irrational. And so on without end; these are merely a few suggestive hints. Economic rationality is not relatively a very important principle in the interpretation of life. Man is a romanticist. Truth and right themselves are, in themselves, dull, prosaic, commonplace; they are interesting only if they are novel, or in dispute, or the violation shocking, or, especially, if they are a means to distinction and power.

freedom of management, and yet prevent owners from making dispositions looking beyond their own lifetime, if they want to do so, would be difficult. But on the other hand, in a propertyless system, if the family and the sentiments which make it significant are to persist, it will also be difficult to prevent the holders of privileged positions from using them to secure special advantages for their children.* Even in American politics, a tendency toward the formation of dynasties has been noted.

(5) These suggestions again force into view a major aspect of the economic problem which we have mentioned before. Economic life at a "stationary" level is one thing, but under "progressive" conditions the social-political problems presented are very different. Growth, or any tendency toward cumulative change, is a fundamentally disruptive force, and a conscious effort toward progress further intensifies the problems of order and efficiency almost beyond comparison. One of the main advantages of the enterprise system has been its promotion of progress, to a degree undreamed of in any other region of history.† But it broke down precisely in failing to solve the problems which have arisen naturally out of progress, especially the cumulative tendency to

* This applies also to other favoured individuals. Even if the family were abolished and society organized on a Spartan-Platonic plan, it is difficult to see how any political machinery could prevent the formation of other primary groups. All this, again, involves assumptions as to what people want to do, as to what is "human nature." It is especially interesting to note that while it is difficult or impossible for the western man to imagine a society in which people do not have "friends" and "enemies" in various degrees, and make important differences between people at different points on the scale, yet the religious-ethical, the political, and the economic systems of the western world are all based on theories of the impersonality of organized social relations. The Christian, the ideal public servant, and the economic man, divergent as they are as types, are alike in having no preferences or prejudices as between persons.

† It is no wonder that primitive peoples have a deeply ingrained antipathy to change, for an unprogressive society requires little conscious direction and raises few practical problems of organization. But any conscious effort at improvement is an effort toward progress in some sense, and in the very nature of discussion of policy it must deal with the problems at the more difficult level of progressive conditions, if it is to be realistic.

In the literature of economic theory, the treatment of growth and historical change is one of the most unsatisfactory divisions—partly because activities looking to the future are affected with uncertainty to such an extent, both as a fact and as a source of interest, that the concept of rational anticipation has very limited validity. The conflict between the two interests, maximum satisfaction and improving one's condition, has already been mentioned. The relation between individual and social interests in connection with progress has been discussed in economic literature chiefly in the fields of population, of saving and, less extensively, of invention.

inequality. In connection with a socialistic organization, it is a vital question whether it might not solve the problem of progress, if it solved it at all, by preventing progress and so defeating its fundamental purpose—unless stopping progress is itself a desirable mode of progress. It is one of the perennial subjects of debate in connection with socialism, whether a bureaucracy would be irresponsibly experimental or "woodenly" conservative. It might be either, or even both; but the second alternative seems more probable as a type.

(6) The question of progressiveness, or at least that of meeting changes impinging upon the system from the outside, is virtually identical with the problem of *efficiency* in a social organization. For under stationary conditions social problems tend to disappear. But the concept of efficiency in this connection can hardly be given any definite meaning, and it is certainly not susceptible to measurement. The question whether any type of political machinery will work "better" or "worse" than another is consequently a matter of opinion. It should be understood that our property system is really an essential part if not the major part of the modern political constitution, in its aspect of economic control. It is one method of selecting, motivating, and remunerating the functionaries who actually direct a social-economic organization, and is to be compared with other types of machinery for effecting the same result. All other possible types are "political" in a narrower sense and come under the head of *bureaucracy*, a word which has a certain connotation in consequence of which it is usually avoided by propagandists for such a change.*

(7) On the question of efficiency and of motivation, it must be noted that socialists have not usually proposed to get away from the stimulus of emulation. Yet, with little indication of the precise mode of the appeal to emulation, they assume that socialism would avoid what are clearly the effects and accompaniments of the principle as such regardless of circumstances. In fact, they do not even propose to abandon the graduation of "material" rewards in accord with the "material "value of services performed, and there is no way in which

* In the same way, and for similar reasons, the advocates of "planning," and "control," avoid clear reference to the fact that these conceptions mean planning for and control over the masses of the people by human beings chosen by some political process and given the necessary powers—unless they assume that the economic life of, say, the United States could be managed by a "town meeting" of the whole population.

it could be dispensed with while keeping production directed toward economy in the creation of such values.

Our special concern at this point is with the phenomena of salesmanship and demand creation, manipulation, or "education," already mentioned as a field in which a socialistic system "might" present appreciable differences from competitive free enterprise. But in fact the differences to be expected are entirely problematic. The slogan, "production for use and not for profit," may state an appealing ideal—to people who do not ask what it means*—but it answers no practical question in any other way than by begging it. Under socialism as under any other system, in a society where the competitive spirit prevails, retail organizations, and sales people individually, as well as productive units, would compete with each other; and any mechanism which "introduces" products and potential consumers to each other at all effectively must "push" sales. It is only a question of the manner and degree. That under socialism it would be done purely in the consumer's interest is merely an assertion and an improbable one; even assuming it true, it cannot be assumed that a social system will function better if individuals strive to promote each other's interests than if each strives to pursue his own. The question is only in part the effectiveness of the urge toward efficiency in creating values as measured by consumers' individualistic choices. In so far as maximum consumption is taken as the ideal, the consumer must choose between looking after his own interests and being taken care of by a paternalistic state. His choice is a hard one, for the first he cannot do; but the details of the manner in which a paternalistic state will take care of its citizens need hardly be discussed here, for the essential fact is that it cannot take care of them and leave them free, and our concern is with free society.

(8) We are now confronted with another fundamental question, namely the scope of activity to be included in the socialistic system of control. The very meaning of socialism and of economics is involved

* Is "profit" taken in the accurate sense of an excess of value return over outlay? If so, there probably is none on the whole, under free enterprise, but more likely a loss. Or does it mean a more or less contingent return, and if so is it contingent upon (a) effort, (b) foresight, (c) results? And is the uncertainty of estimates and acts separated from that of unpredictable changes? Or does profit mean simply gain or advantage of any and every kind? and if so, why are people supposed to engage in production and to accept division of labour? Or, finally, is the slogan a mere question-begging condemnation of return from capital or property?

in this question. The proposal is for the "government" to own and administer the more important "productive resources." But even as regards the external, non-human instrumentalities of production, the problem is necessarily one of degree. In an analytical classification, even clothing and personal effects are agencies of production, or "capital;" the real product or final consumption good is the *services* which they render. Clothing indeed is sometimes leased by its owner to others as a source of money income, and this pecuniary in contrast with direct utilization is very important in connection with living quarters.

But the major difficulty lies beyond all this, in the field of the most important "productive resources," the economic capacities of the people themselves. Under present conditions, not only do these make up from three-fifths to three-fourths of the total productive capacity in the United States, but income from such sources is *very* unequally distributed, doubtfully less so than income from "property," if we take income as personal consumption, instead of book income. Nor will it do to think of large personal-service income as indirectly derived from property—like that of business executives, corporation lawyers, or purveyors of "fancy" services to the rich. We have already mentioned the consumption of public servants in our own democracy; and the earnings of such persons as movie actors and pugilists, not to mention political bosses, contain further pregnant suggestions as to what might be expected if all economic life were "democratized."

The plain truth, which "reformers" consciously or unconsciously ignore, is two-fold; first, no great change could be brought about by "socializing" (meaning politicizing) the more important forms of material wealth; and second, no defensible clear distinction can be drawn from the point of view of either ideal ethics or practical politics between external wealth and personal powers as a source of income. As to the magnitudes involved, the confiscation of all consumed property income, in the narrow sense, would not, in the United States, as much as double the amount which our governmental agencies already spend in normal times; if it were doubled, the fraction would only be increased from eight or ten to fifteen or twenty per cent of the total national income.

The second fact mentioned, itself a two-fold one, needs much more discussion than is possible here. First as to ideal ethics. In genesis, the two forms of earning capacity called labour power and property are derived from the same three or four sources, namely, inheritance, the more or less intelligent and conscientious use of productive capacity previously possessed in one or the other form, the general working of social processes, largely independent of individual choice, and miscellaneous factors which must be grouped under the concept of "luck." Personal capacity, like "property" (more accurately, *other* property) is either inherited, or it is produced by deliberate action which is essentially investment. In either case, the one form has no more ethical claim to special compensation than the other; and moreover, the government would find it difficult or impracticable to carry out any such distinction. If individuals were prevented from accumulating, and bequeathing, in the form of external property, they could find ways in plenty, both to accumulate and to bequeath, by investing in themselves or their children or others in the form of personal training and situation advantage.

(9) The argument carries us back to the ultimate problems of democracy, already discussed in the preceding section. The special issue here is whether the problems of the dualistic organization, i.e., of the free market and representative political institutions, would be more or less satisfactorily solved or advanced toward solution by greatly reducing private property and enterprise and making the state the chief property owner and the chief entrepreneur. We encounter the interesting argument that the weaknesses of democratic institutions are due to its contamination by relations with business enterprise.* On this particular point, we must first refer again to the general misconception regarding economic motives already stressed in several connections. Rigorously speaking, there is no such thing as an economic interest, or a material interest. That is, the economic interest is never final; it is an interest in the efficacy of activity, and of the use of means, in promoting real or final interests of any sort. And these final interests do not inhere in particular physical things or physical changes, but are all, at bottom, social interests. Even the food interest, the "most" material of all, is in concrete content overwhelmingly a matter of

* This argument was eloquently stated in a paper read before the American Economic Association at its 1931 meeting by Professor Rexford G. Tugwell, now a prominent member of the "New Deal" administration. See *American Economic Review*, Supplement, March 1932.

social standards. In general, it seems impossible to find any concrete end of action which is not a means to some continuing interest which is essentially social and "spiritual" (*geistlich*), and it is an equally plain fact that human activity is governed by preferences *and value judgments* among means as well as ends. It is true that men's opinions are influenced by their interests, but just as true that their opinions *are* interests, over which they are just as ready to fight as over any others. And on the other hand the most spiritual interests are promoted by the use of material means, as no one is so unfamiliar with religion and education as not to realize.

Again, if we simply look at the facts, we find "politics," in the connotation which the word has in everyday usage, about as conspicuous in organizations having as little connection as it is possible to have with business, or "pelf," as where the so-called material interests are the primary concern. One would like to know, for instance, whether the academic advocates of the position under examination have found college class politics, fraternity politics, and faculty politics essentially different from "political politics." Even in religious organizations, dedicated to the "saving of souls," as well as in learned societies, dedicated to the pursuit of truth, we find the same motives manifested in action in much the same way. The social problem is at bottom a moral problem, and not one of substituting one type of organization machinery for another.

To be sure, "material" considerations, in a broad sense, are rarely or never entirely absent. There are few forms of "competition"—which is the chief moral issue—in which "material" power does not play some role, both as end and means. Men "have to live," and usually have decided preferences as to their mode of life, of a sort which quite directly involve material means. This is chiefly to say that the "material" circumstance of life constitute the most fundamental and universal field of competition among men. In consequence, they do not generally "serve God for naught," even in intellectual and artistic creation or soul saving; and what reason is there to think that politicians would do so in a socialistic state? There are of course limits to the possibility; but if men generally strove to approach these limits, either for idealistic reasons or because that were the objective in social competition, the social problem would have to be discussed in utterly different terms, and the form of organization is relatively a secondary matter. It should hardly be necessary to point out that in a society dominated by the same moral drives as ours, the politics of a socialistic control organization would be as closely involved with material emoluments, along with such interests as "service" and "honour," and power, and victory, as is true of either politics or business under the dualistic system.

(10) At the other pole from the glowing claims on behalf of socialism on the score of efficiency and devotion to the public weal, we have to face the question whether it is reasonably possible for a democratic government to exercise control over the details of economic life at all. That is, might it not simply collapse under the burden, or yield results so bad as to lead to revolt and revolution? This would mean the establishment of a dictatorship in some form—presumably, under present conditions in the European world, some variety of either fascism or communism. A few observations on the way in which, in the liberal era, governments used their admitted powers and carried out their undisputed functions in the field of economics will make a favourable answer seem doubtful.

The crisis conditions, which have led to most of the recent talk about the "breakdown of capitalism," have undoubtedly been due in large part to the lack of a scientific monetary system with adequate governmental control. But there was never any question, among the most extreme advocates of *laissez-faire*, that effective control of the circulating medium is an essential power, and duty, of the government. In the United States, the Constitution was framed with this as one of the main objects in view. A secondary cause of the crisis and threatened breakdown has been the growth of monopoly; but again, the most extreme advocates of individual economic freedom never defended monopoly. The evil of inequality in wealth and income suggests as its most direct and natural remedy a wise use of the taxing power; but no limit in principle has ever been set to the power or the right of the government to tax, and it is an established doctrine in American constitutional law that it includes the power to destroy. It is problematical whether there would be any really serious resistance to the most drastic taxation, if men generally believed that the taxes would be equitably assessed, honestly collected and spent, and effectively used

for purposes indubitably promoting the public weal. The fact is that
on the grounds of experience men generally do not believe this, but
believe the opposite. The relief of destitution has also been an unquestioned duty of the state since the latter superseded the church in
this field at the close of the Middle Ages. But the history of poor relief
is a tale of horror, and not primarily because there was not enough
money collected and spent.* There is probably no point to arguing as
to just what these facts prove. All I am interested in showing is that it is
difficult to discuss the main issue in terms of fact and logic,† and that
extreme opposites of the claims for socialism are as reasonable as the
claims themselves.

(11) We should not leave the discussion of democracy without
emphasizing again that political behaviour is the most speculative of all
real or practical problems. There is no *necessary* reason why individuals
as voting members of a group should act on the same principles that
they follow when making purely personal choices as consumers or
producers. Thus it would be perfectly intelligible that an individual
who could not resist the temptation to buy alcoholic liquor on seeing it
offered for sale, might be the first to vote for prohibition. It is arguable
in the abstract that a group, making decisions through discussion,
might be vastly *more* intelligent and moral than its component individuals would be in choosing among alternatives as presented. If
individuals exercise much intelligent or moral restraint in choice, it is
undoubtedly because they have really made the choice in advance, by
reflection and "self-legislation" in the famous "calm, cool hour."
Freedom itself can have little meaning apart from such a process of
self-legislation, and the necessity of reaching a consensus in a group

* In one middle-western American state there are, or recently were, counties which
were spending more for the upkeep of their poor than it would have cost to maintain
them all in the most expensive hotel in the state.

† What seemed to me one of the strongest "proofs" of the proposition that a
socialistic state would not remain democratic (contrary to the assumption granted at
the beginning of the section) came from reading Emma Goldman's denunciation of the
"betrayal of the revolution" in ruthless suppression and tyranny by the Russian
Bolsheviki. Two things seemed evident from her account, read openmindedly. First,
that no government responsible for feeding a modern nation could possibly brook
opposition or real threat of opposition, or indulge in the luxury of general discussion
of its policies, however much its personnel might individually wish to do so. Second,
that no government would be likely to get such responsibility unless made up of men
who believed in and enjoyed the use of force. Certainly the Russian Bolshevik revolu-
tionaries as individuals were no exception to this latter statement.

might seem to make such reflective decisions far more probable. And *sometimes* all this is true.

But unfortunately, the group may also be much less intelligent than the individual. Just as the individual may and often does act from impulse, prejudice, or passion, the same motives are often still more dominant in group decisions. Unfortunately, experience seems to indicate that the truly deliberate process of seeking truth and right through co-operative discussion is met with chiefly in small intimate groups, and is rare enough even there. "Politics," on any large scale, seems pretty definitely to run to "politics." Enough has been said above regarding competitive campaigning and political organization. They necessarily follow the methods actually most effective, as far and as fast as experience shows what these are, and it is pointless to criticize the "politician" for accepting the conditions of being in politics which are made what they are by his constituents. The only hope for democracy is in the intelligence and public spirit of the citizenship as a whole, for in the nature of democracy, whatever teachers and leaders it pays heed to must be chosen by itself.

PART THREE

FASCIST-NATIONALISM

I. Possible Alternatives to Liberalism

§11. When the system of government by discussion, organized and administered through agency relations,* breaks down, the first aspect of the practical situation resulting is the impossibility of going back to any unconscious or traditional process. There is no way in which a thinking process, once set going, can "turn itself off." It may happen, but in the nature of the case it is not a policy which can be put into

---

* Whatever proportion of the actual organization of life is left to individualistic market dealings, it is the political framework which is "fundamental," since the latter must make and enforce the rules according to which a market economy operates. Consequently, the market economy, in whatever form and degree it exists, must be regarded as the creature of the sovereign state, and an expression of its policy. This is no less true if the state acts permissively rather than positively. This reasoning also holds for all voluntary associations, the plural-sovereignty theorists notwithstanding, and in full view of the fact that associations possess and exercise political power.

effect voluntarily, and is not an alternative of action for the purpose of discussion.*

The possibilities which suggest themselves are three: An ecclesiastical or theocratic system of some sort, "Communism," and "Facist-Nationalism." These are in reality not at all mutually exclusive, and the three names in no sense represent a scientific analysis or distinction between principles. But such an analysis cannot be entered upon here, and the designations must stand with whatever meaning they have. The first must be dismissed with the mere statement of opinion that it is not really "in the cards" as far as western nations are concerned. And as to communism, much the same must be said. Even the Russian system is not communistic and is not likely to become so, but on the other hand is increasingly nationalistic; and looking to the future, the difference between communism and facist-nationalism is probably much exaggerated, and will tend to disappear. But communism, even in the Russian sense, does not seem to be a possibility in the other nations of European civilization, with the possible exception of Spain.†

Fascist-nationalism, then, seems to be clearly indicated as the next stage in the political evolution of the liberal democracies, including the United States. There will, of course, be very great differences between different countries or "nations." But even the possibilities of prediction in this field cannot be discussed here. Nationalism itself confronts enormous difficulties, in view of the existent world map of peoples in relation to basic resources; but it is hard not to believe that

* We are not unconscious of the argument which can be presented against any social change whatever being "really" the result of a voluntary social choice, or of the intellectual cogency of such argument. We merely note that discussion of policy must assume the reality of choice based on discussion in a sense which contrasts with meaningful communication from various causal and explanatory points of view. Like all simple generalizations in this field, however, this needs qualification; the individual may in a sense voluntarily stop thinking about general problems by putting himself in the hands of a hypnotist or psychiatrist, or even by driving himself to think about something else. The second alternative does not seem to be open to a society, but something akin to the first may be, for a society may voluntarily establish a dictatorship with the expectation that the dictator will "educate" along appropriate lines. Indeed, this seems to be the essence of the policy of establishing a dictatorship, in so far as it is done through conscious policy of a society as such. (What the dictator will actually do, after receiving full power, must of course be taken on faith.)

† With reference to the communists' own theory of history, it is interesting that events seem to prove their system to be possible only in a region which has not experienced a natural development of industrialism. But in a real sense no development after the first one could be "natural."

the greater nations in something like their present form are with us for the visible future. Indeed, liberalism itself evolved out of a kind of nationalism, and throughout its history never ceased to be nationalistic, in varying degrees and in changing meanings of the word.*

The argument of the preceding sections has indicated that in the absence of some revolutionary change in the moral and intellectual world-view of western civilization, democratic institutions probably must give place to an authoritarian system of some kind. For, on the one hand, democratic government cannot organize and control modern economic life and remain democratic (the inversion of liberalism into "neo-liberalism" is impossible), and on the other hand, social order cannot be maintained, especially on the scale demanded by modern technology, in the absence of a *social* religion, in contrast with one of individual "freedom" and "self-expression." Even the existing nationalities, anomalous as they are, and different as they are from the primitive tribe or any primary group, yet seem able somehow to afford a setting for an essentially tribal psychology. This psychology it seems defensible to regard as a fundamentally "natural" human attitude. Men show a tendency to gravitate into groups in which one of the main effective bases of internal unity is a sentiment of opposition to or competition with other groups—rather than either economic efficiency or a pure fellowship interest; the latter seems to be effective only in groups quite small in size, approximating the "primary group" of sociological jargon. The crucial matter is that of a sentiment able to establish unity for internal organization, which seems to presuppose unification "exteriorly;" a feeling of unity seems to imply a feeling of difference. For this purpose, the sentiment of patriotism apparently has no serious competitor in our actual world.†

* It is true that, going further back, the "nationalism" of the post-Renascence centuries evolved out of a kind of theocracy; but it seems impossible to take seriously the notion of a reversion to that stage, even though it is advocated in high quarters.

It is worth noting that if this reasoning is sound, the conceivable alternatives to economic organization through market forces have all been tried, though under "conditions" very different from those of the present. All except anarchist communism have been fairly recent stages in the history of liberal civilization itself, and in modern times we have had examples of communistic experiments in great variety.

† The so-called cosmopolitanism of Medieval western Europe had many of the same features. The regions loyal to the Roman Church were never very extensive in comparison with the world, and the attitude of the Church toward "schismatics" and "infidels" is not hard to classify as between tribalism and universal brotherhood. Of

II. Toward the Understanding of Nationalism

§12. As a political order, the liberal system is in the way of proving to be self-defeating, for reasons which have already been indicated. When the frontier world filled up, and the spirit of "getting ahead" came into serious conflict with the requirements of a human social life, the moral ideals of sportsmanship and humanitarianism were not strong enough to stand the strain. The natural tendencies (a) of power-seeking toward concentration of power and (b) of any contest to degenerate into a quarrel and then an appeal to force, came to the fore.

From such a set-up, based on such ideas, reaction was inevitable, and the type of revolutionary change represented by nationalism is one which it seems natural to expect. Furthermore, speaking as one perhaps second to none in hatred of nationalistic dictatorship, I must still confess to seeing in the nationalistic philosophy a central core of profound truth. Social-moral motivation must rest on more than pure, abstract ethical idealism. It has a quality properly called religious. As there is really no human life apart from group life, so there is probably no group life without real "devotion," in a religious sense, of the members to the group as a more or less "mystical" entity, and beyond it to some set of values for which the group is supposed in an especial way to stand. I offer this as a simple fact, a fact of "observation" in the only sense in which really human data ever are observed. The degree to which this element in motivation is present is of course variable. Some individuals, such as great world conquerors and great "crooks," may be nearly free from it, looking upon society not in terms of participation, but as something entirely outside themselves, to be treated as a toy or an instrument for purely private ends. But such cases are hardly pure types and are exceptional.

Complete indifference to the interests of one's group is hardly conceivable. The concept of devotion as a motive applies conspicuously to men at both ends of the scale of thoughtfulness. For those who are distinctly thoughtful, and attempt to rationalize their existence as

course the whole question of group sentiment is very complicated; it is easy to find an indefinite multiplicity of "tribes" in any extensive region at any time, and the notion of tribe is like that of social "class," in the impossibility of giving it definite meaning.

individuals, the craving for such a super-individual end or object of devotion is an outstanding fact, and if it is not more or less satisfactorily gratified, symptoms of morbidity are likely to appear. On the other hand, it is apparent that the great mass of men have always lived in some society characterized by a religion which each accepts and organizes into his own system of values. They seem to require for normal living the feeling of a "destiny" and mission pertaining to a group to whose life they contribute. This motif is conspicuous in Medieval ideals; the individual lived to save his own soul, but salvation consisted in "belonging" to the Blessed Community, the City of God.

So it seems to me natural that we react from individualistic instrumentalism to an opposite extreme. We pass by way of a crushing competitivism to a worship of emotional unity, and by way of intolerable insecurity to morbid craving for security. And this is what nationalism seems to mean. The individual gives up the effort to treat the world, material or human, as his oyster, and tries to put himself in mystical unity with his group, meaning the more or less racial, cultural "nation" which is already the object of his strongest political allegiance. Along with this growth in a kind of sentimental gregariousness, he swings from an active to a passive attitude toward society, and from a reflective to an emotional, impulsive attitude toward the world at large. He swings from "rationalism" to "romanticism."* In particular, the individual reacts from the notion of reaching validity by general discussion—which he has seen degenerate into a contest in "selling"—to a faith in "strong" individual *leadership*, which also represents a reaction from moral and intellectual equalitarianism to hero worship. The movement also involves a shift from the actor interest to the spectator interest in society, and in part to a merging of the two in an experience of mystical participation. Men want action, but by the group, i.e., the government or its outstanding personalities. They do not want to act. It is as if the peoples of the western world were turning from a "sadistic" to a "masochistic" attitude toward society and government.

---

* Such a statement must be coupled with the recognition that romanticism may be rational in its own way, and that rationalism was in its own way romantic; yet in general being "reasonable" does not appear to be very satisfying to the normal human craving for romance. Rationalism is of course used in the sense of planned activity, only remotely related to the epistemological rationalism.

The relation between the nationality and its "Leader" is an interesting one. He is its symbol, its hero; yet he does not do much real leading; he leads chiefly by following. His chief attribute is an absolute and fervid faith in his own "call" to the position of representing and speaking and acting for the group, and a belief that all opposition reflects immoral motives, or hopeless stupidity. His own conviction on this point is contagious by its intensity. At bottom this is because he is peculiarly endowed with the sense of unity which others crave, and with an especial sensitiveness to popular ideas and sentiments. The situation represents essentially the phenomenon of the mob and its leader, on a greatly enlarged scale. There is little truth in the idea so popular among liberals that nationalism is manufactured and "put over" on the general population by a few astute and unscrupulous individuals. This is never true of any social movement, not even a fashion in dress. Great events happen "in the fullness of time." The real social leader always leads by following; and theory and observation concur in showing that "dictatorship" will come and will operate by "democratic" process, if any action of a social group is ever democratic.

It will perhaps be most democratic in its policy of forcibly suppressing freedom of discussion. In fact, "discussion" needs little formal suppression. There is little evidence that any large mass of people ever wanted to discuss or attend to discussion, of serious issues, involving real intellectual effort. Real discussion is rare even among professional intellectuals, and their "argumentation" commonly illustrates the tendency of a contest to deteriorate. Debate, and the preaching of unorthodox views, which are very different from discussion, may or may not be popular, depending on the aesthetic character of the performance. The successful dictator will have to provide suitable entertainment along these lines without permitting anything really dangerous. It is, of course, a delicate problem to stage verbal gladiatorial combats and supply the craving to be shocked without running some risk of arousing loyalties competing menacingly with loyalty to a particular leader or party, and we do not know how long on the average any regime is likely to be successful in keeping competing loyalties from growing too strong. The mixture and interaction of different main forms of power—persuasion, "bribery," and outright violence, and the relation of all of them to the basic urges of the crowd mind, which in turn reflect mysterious historical tendencies, are questions of detail which can only be mentioned.

What all this means in connection with "economic" life is fairly obvious and cannot receive detailed development here. Ostensibly, it means a turning away from economics and all its works, and a devotion to "higher" and more "spiritual" objectives. It is of course in the mental, moral, and social—or in general the "spiritual" (*geistlich*)—realm, that the revolution which is in progress is deepest and most positive in character. The instrumentalistic conception of nature does not seem to be on the way to reversal, though probably to a considerable loss of interest and importance, through suppression of free initiative in applying science to industry. But its application to war will assure generous financial support and a fair amount of scientific progress, as in the early modern period. In politics, however, the relation between individual and society is being definitely reversed. The state under liberalism existed for the individual. It was in theory an association of individuals formed for the narrow purpose of keeping order in a more positive organization through market dealings for the quest of economic well-being by the exploitation of nature. Under nationalism it will be more and more a super-individual, "mystical" entity, in and for which the individual "lives and moves and has his being." It may even be that in sacrificing himself to it he will more and more find his highest fulfilment.

All this is "in theory," and in profession. Actualities are generally, to objective analysis, more or less divergent from pretensions. In the liberal era itself, the real end of individual striving was progressively less economic well-being and progressively more the purely sentimental values of social position and power. Under nationalism, the attention paid to individual economic well-being must be very considerable. This has always been the case with civilizations professing ascetic or sacrificial ideals. The rulers in such a society do not work for ascetic rewards, and there is always a more or less general competitive struggle to achieve a place in the ruling group. For its own purposes, then, including both what may reasonably be called group ends and the personal uses of its officials as individuals, the nationalistic state will require resources and will have to practice economy.

In addition, a minimal attention to the material well-being of the masses is obviously necessary from the standpoint of the rulers, in order to prevent discontent and insurrection in time of peace, and in order to provide in war and preparation for war the needed quantity and quality of cannon fodder. There is little doubt that the nationalistic state will be more solicitous for the well-being of the poorest people than either the state or business has been under the liberal system, and the standard of living of an undetermined fraction at the bottom of the economic scale—and especially its security against downright want—may well be higher. But under nationalistic tutelage, the conception of material well-being held by the mass itself will naturally be different. It will be a new age of bread and circuses; and since the requirements for physical comfort of human beings are comparatively limited, there will undoubtedly be less emphasis on "bread" and more on "circuses."

In so far as any regime practices economy, in so far as it administers its resources economically, it will act in accord with the general principles of theoretical economics, specifically those of "marginalism," irrespective of the concrete ends pursued or the resources used and technological system followed. But the extent to which it will actually behave economically is another question, and the language it will use in talking about its policies is still another. Discussion of unescapable economic problems will naturally take the form of a new "Cameralistics." The amount of such discussion, its character, and the amount of circulation given to it, outside the bureaucracy itself, and inside it, are all questions of policy for the leaders to decide.

Coolly considered, the life ideal of bread and circuses would hardly be considered "lower" than that suggested by the "economic man." Yet I must enroll myself among those who do not like the change from liberalism to nationalism, and who look with regret upon the passing of freedom, as an ideal to be striven for, and to an important degree an actuality.* There seems to be no room for doubt that commercialism, while it lasted, made for tolerance and humanity, and to a significant extent practised as well as preached the doctrine of "live and let live."

* The question of how much freedom there really was under liberalism at any time and place could of course be argued endlessly. Freedom of expression perhaps tended to outlast economic freedom; but the two affected different groups and strata, and economic liberty also remained up to the actual revolution in any country, for those possessing a sufficient share of power.

It encouraged friendliness and good humour, and the sense of a basic human equality, among men of divergent rank and station. This was surely true to a degree far beyond anything ever seen in any other type of culture. And this was in addition to its incomparable multiplication of the means necessary to a decent existence and the even more remarkable diffusion of these means among the masses.

It is true that in beauty and pure "refinement," the age of liberalism had its shortcomings, though an effort to get the consensus of critics as to just what they were would encounter difficulties. But in discussing other civilizations, we are inclined to romantic exaggeration about these things, and inclined to judge other times by a peak of achievement reached only by an infinitesimal fraction of the population, standing in a parasitic relation to a general mass which lived in squalor. It is doubtful whether anyone can be impartial in a comparison of his own culture with another, or find fair standards of judgment. General theories and forms of bias, for the familiar or the unfamiliar, for the new or for the old, are perhaps more serious obstacles to objectivity than the more familiar forms of prejudice. Similar difficulties must be faced in passing any judgment in advance upon culture under a dictatorship, which will also have its distinctive values. We cannot tell how the comparison will look to people who have lived under the system for a few generations. Perhaps they will like it, extol its moral superiority to other systems, and view its displacement of liberal ideals and forms as a great step in progress. In that case, the designation of "free" can be withheld only by giving to freedom a highly transcendental meaning. But it will be a society based on lying and deceiving. Are men free when they act under such influences? And do they care? In any case, if we are to view the social problem in terms of intelligent choice, we must try as far as we can to analyse the alternatives.

PART FOUR
SOCIAL SCIENCE AND SOCIAL ACTION

I. Conceptions of Social Phenomena and of Social Science

§13. Apart from what we might call the standpoint of "humane naïve realism," it would be abstractly possible to discuss human phenomena in terms of at least a half-dozen main categories or viewpoints.* Every one of these contains a large element of truth, which is to say that no one can be accepted as true in a sense which binds one to view the others, or any other, as false. All these are really inseparable aspects of a unitary reality, yet any one of them may be, and every one often is, arbitrarily adopted and used within wide limits to explain, arrange, or interpret the subject matter. Without attempting any exhaustive classification or comprehensive treatment of the question raised, we may list for brief notice the following six "approaches," which, as will be observed, present in part a series of "levels" of interpretation: (1) the positive-physical-scientific, (2) the biological or vitalistic, (3) the concrete-motivational or economistic, (4) the abstract-motivational, which includes a number of sub-species, (5) the institutional or historical, and (6) a viewpoint or collection of viewpoints, which for want of any better name we may designate as "groupism" or "societalism," the term socialism being excluded by political connotation.

These abstact conceptions need at least a few words of explanatory comment, and may be taken up in order. Human phenomena centre in human beings, which, to begin with, are unquestionably physical objects, which again may either be viewed as units or analysed into elaborate complexes of physico-electro-chemical mechanisms. In the second place, the human being is a biological organism and can be discussed in the terms pertaining to that field of knowledge, such as adaptive response, competitive struggle to exist and to multiply according to type, natural selection, long-run morphological adaptation, etc. Both these viewpoints fall within the domain of what is called natural science. The subdivision could be carried much further, as there are obviously various "levels" within the phenomena called physico-chemical (impact mechanics, electro-magnetism, chemism,

---

* By "humane" naïve realism we mean especially to distinguish the position from any scientific realism. It is the standpoint exemplified in the writing of history and biography when it is not done with some special theory in mind. It is highly pluralistic, presenting under analysis a combination of logically incompatible postulates, including most or all of those to be specified below, and no doubt others. To begin with, it is *dualistic*; it assumes human beings as conscious, thinking, deliberating beings, who make "free" choices and initiate changes in the course of events in an environment characterized by the opposite of all the above-named traits. More accurately, it is not dualistic but "triplistic," for it also recognizes that "man is a social animal."

radioactivity, etc.) and also in those called biological (from the "lowest" to the "highest" forms of plant and animal life).*

This approach to social phenomena excludes any possibility of practical significance of the study, *unless* it assumes the point of view of a student and manipulator of the material studied who is outside of and apart from the material itself, and is active toward it while it is completely passive and inert towards him. Also, if knowledge becomes the basis of action, it is purely in the interest of the knower, as the material viewed in objective terms has no interests. No (human) interest or problem is recognized in such a study except the "idle curiosity" of the student and of other students, if the results are communicated to others. A science on these lines has practical relevance on either of two conditions; (*a*) in the manner of astronomy and meteorology, that it does not lead to any change in the phenomena studied but enables the student to predict their course and so to live more intelligently in relation to them; (*b*) that it confers on the student

---

* The general problem is obviously that of a hierarchical arrangement of sciences in accord with the decreasing generality of qualities to be found in the subject matter, made famous by Comte and elaborated in various ways by other writers. It is evident that there is a certain claim to exhaustiveness in the different systems of categories, particularly at the lower levels. The laws of mechanics seem to claim to explain everything, leaving nothing to be said from other standpoints. What we—the scientifically sophisticated modern Western mind—tend to call explanation consists largely in "reducing" higher phenomena to terms of lower—the evaluative life to biology, biology to physics and chemistry, etc., ending in the pure mechanics of mass, momentum and impact. These concepts have a peculiar finality of intellectual satisfying power, but are untenable from this point of view even in physics (as Mach showed long before the "modern" developments in that science). As a matter of fact, many of the ultimate philosophical issues in the interpretation of human life are hardly escapable in any thoroughgoing examination of the most elementary physical process, the communication of motion by impact. At this lowest level, we confront as a condition of intelligibility the notions of force and a stable equilibrium of forces, and force is not a physical concept. (Comte insisted on a hierarchy in subject matter, but only one methodology, without interpretative concepts of any sort!)

In this brief sketch, many problems have to be solved arbitrarily without discussion. We simply pass over a possible "psychological" level in the sense of "scientific" introspective-analytical psychology, in which the phenomena of consciousness are examined for uniformities in themselves and in relation to conditions in the physical world. Consciousness is here considered only when it is assumed to make a difference in organic behaviour, i.e. in the role of motivation of some sort. It is to be noted too that by the biological view of human behaviour we refer only to individual human beings as organisms, not to the figurative conception of society itself as an organism. Such a view of society comes into our scheme, if at all, only in the sense of the sixth heading, "societalism." We also omit all "metaphysical" views (using the term in the Comtian sense) of interpretations of behaviour in terms of "drives" or "wishes," other than conscious or "subconscious"—potentially conscious—motives.

"power" to "control" the phenomena through disruption of their natural sequences by interference from without. In social science it could make possible either prediction or control only if not communicated to the human beings composing the society studied, and it is relevant to control only if the scientist is in the position of a dictator or adviser to a dictator.

Above these levels is the conception of motivated behaviour, which must be further subdivided into two categories, according as it does or does not assume given, physically concrete ends. Under the first assumption, we have the "economic" or "economistic" view already discussed in the first sections of this essay, the standpoint of the traditional or "classical" economic theory. If, on the other hand, concrete ends are not taken as data, with efficiency in achieving them as the only "problem" (see below) in the behaviour, a number of attributes of motivation, neglected in economics, must be taken into account. In an inclusively and critically realistic view of human behaviour, the motives are not in general concrete ends or goals of action. As already observed, concrete ends, though taken as final in economics, are in fact rather instrumental. The ultimate motives or interests must be referred to by such terms as exploration, problem-solving, fellowship, power, beauty, rightness, etc., which are not descriptive in an objective sense.

. Leaving biology aside as an ambiguous case (unconscious teleology) the first, third, and fourth conceptions of behaviour form a natural series, with respect to the notion of problem-solving. In the first view (mechanism), behaviour involves no problem to the behaving material or entity, but may present to an outside observer a "scientific" problem or other intellectual problems. In the third (economism), the procedure for realizing ends is problematic to the subject, while the ends are not, being *data* in the behaviour problem. In the fourth, the view of behaviour as explorative, problem-solving or value seeking, the ends themselves are recognized as problematic. In fact, the discovery or precise formulation of the end is usually an essential element in the motivation.

Two opposed types are included under this fourth head. The extreme example of one type is purely explorative activity. The relation to economic motivation is illustrated by the difference between looking for a particular object and looking simply out of curiosity to see what one will find, with no special interest in what its character will be. In the other direction, the end is normative. The best example is moral conduct, taken in the extreme sense of *fiat justitia ruat coelum*. Behaviour affected by aesthetic norms, and all value-realizing or problem-solving activity is also in point. Obviously, when one is trying to solve a problem, one is looking for a particular "correct" solution, or the best possible solution, but it is of the essence of one's interest that the solution is not concretely known in advance. It is probably true that all motivated behaviour presents some mixture of the three principles, the pursuit of a given end, effort to find the correct or best end, and pure exploration. The end of action seems rarely if ever to be given in advance in such precise form that it is not more or less redefined or further defined in the process of realization. In the economistic view, action is also affected by norms, being right or wrong in relation to "given" ends.

The fifth general viewpoint, the institutional, is characterized by taking its subject matter as strictly social, not individual, and not in the form of "behaviour" in a literal sense, at all. It deals with social forms, products, or manifestations of activity, such as language, law, etc., as species of social process "as such," as a unique order of existence. It employs "positivistic" assumptions in the sense in which these are applicable to the data. There is a difference between "observation" involving intercommunication with the object, as truly social phenomena are exclusively known, and the observation of physical phenomena by means of the senses. But the notion of "laws of history," or uniformities of co-existence and sequence in cultural manifestations, has meaning, and most types of social phenomena, including those called economic,* may be studied from this point of view. Like that of

* Whether a theory stated in non-economic terms, of the section of behaviour referred to in general usage as economic, is to be called economic theory is debatable. But it ought not to be so called; for any such theory would at the same time fit into other recognized branches of inquiry, such as sociology, cultural anthropology, and the science or theory of history, and there is an "economic" view of behaviour which has undeniable reality and distinctiveness. The practical question raised is one of the advantageous division of intellectual labour. One must be especially impressed by the opinion held by nearly every specialist in any branch of the social studies that his particular speciality is the one correct vantage point from which to essay both a general interpretation of society and its problems and the charting of the course which the future "ought" to follow.

mechanism, it implies a denial that voluntary or conscious *control* of social phenomena by human beings is possible or has meaning. Historical explanation also rests on the assumption that phenomena behave in accord with an unchanging set of characteristics, the "nature of things," the discovery and formulation of which is the purpose of science and all that it can possibly do. It differs from mechanics in conceiving its subject matter as social, which is to say ideal, instead of physical by nature. With respect to content, it is the science of traditions. The group, whether considered as a collection of individuals or as an "organic" unit of some sort (see following paragraphs), might be conscious of its traditions or not conscious, or conscious in any form, cognitive or emotional, as long as the fact "makes no difference" in the laws governing them, and these laws are to be discovered inductively by "observing" the phenomena. In social as in physical phenomena, the laws may describe either cumulative change or recurrence.

History as usually written embodies a varying mixture of modes of interpretation. The notion of pure history, as a methodological concept, or what we here call the institutionalistic treatment of social phenomena, is most easily defined by using as an illustration the study of language, which is in a sense the most fundamental social institution. Such an institution is studied as a phenomenon bearing to the society in which it exists, or goes on, much the relation which a plant bears to the soil in which it grows. It is described in terms of itself, and regarded as having its own laws of growth and change. A plant "is," in a sense, soil (and air), and an institution "is" social and ultimately individual behaviour (and this in a strict natural-scientific view is ultimately physical process); but relatively little, and most of that negative in import, is to be learned about plants by studying soil; and similarly, one would not learn much about the nature of language by observing the physical behaviour of individuals or examining their physical structure and physiological processes.

But the term "institution" is *doubly* ambiguous. In the first place, it refers either to a social activity or to a social organization-form connected with the activity—on one hand a law, on the other a legislature or law school. In the second place, the organization and the activity may embody and represent either the semi-conscious, non-deliberative, traditional type of social usage exemplified by language or the contrasting sort established and maintained deliberately, by a social choice. The best example of the latter is perhaps a written political constitution. We must distinguish sharply between institutions which "just grow," and those which are "made on purpose," i.e., created by a community for community ends.* The institutional view of social phenomena refers of course to the former class. Most "institutions" represent some mixture of the two types, or aspects. Language is a nearly pure type at one extreme, while social usages, laws, and political constitutions, written as well as unwritten, undoubtedly contain a large mixture of this element; how large, is an extremely controversial point, as no objective discrimination is possible. Moreover, a change in the character of law from traditional growth in the manner of language to deliberate legislation—by a law-giver or by group discussion, or by agents or "representatives" of the group—is one of the main threads of "progress" in human history. (There is, of course, no implication that progress, or any historical change, has been continuous or homogeneous in character over the world.)

The sixth general standpoint, here called groupism or societalism, takes social phenomena as expressing a *motivated social choice*. There are various ways in which we may think of the choice as being made, and the general viewpoint might be divided up and treated as a group under different captions. The minimal conceptualization of social choice, involving the least departure from the institutionalism just referred to, and different only in a nominal or metaphysical sense, would simply postulate a "group mind" of some sort as a metaphysical interpretive concept, instead of taking persistence, and change in accord with law, in institutions as a matter of empirically discoverable fact.†

* We should also mention the fact that an individual may be said to start or found an institution. But it is the social process of acceptance which makes it an institution in our sense.

† The problems raised by the concept of a social mind cannot be argued out here. Since our remarks, being written in the English language, are addressed primarily to a public steeped in the over-simplification of naïve economistic-individualistic voluntarism (along with the contradictory one of naïve physical-positivistic realism) we must emphasize the fact that social phenomena cannot be completely accounted for in terms of interaction between individual minds taken as *data*.

The objections to the "atomistic" theory that society is merely an aggregate of individuals in certain "relations" more or less closely parallel those applicable to the interpretation of animal or plant life in terms of the behaviour of atoms. The irreducibly social residuum, which is an "observed fact" in the sense relevant to social phenomena,

At the next level in the conception of social decision, the folk-mind has an individual spokesman and interpreter, a shaman-king or whatever he may be called, from whom group decisions immediately emanate. The function is almost inevitably developed and organized and spread over a more or less definite inner group or caste. No historical or anthropological precision is in question in this schematic analysis, and the widest overlapping of fundamental principles would always be met with in fact. But if we may think of the evolution of the social constitution in the terms of the famous formula suggested by Sir Henry Maine, and designate the stage of traditionalism by the term *status*, it seems to be true in a general way that a stage of autocracy or oligarchy generally intervenes between this and the "higher" stage of *contract*. The position of rulers, priests, or other leaders under primitive conditions is itself overwhelmingly traditional, but with varying mixtures of "force," and also of a kind of rational acceptance.*

must be recognized as having the same general properties, powers, or "faculties" as an individual mind, especially emotion, cognition, and will. The substance of the concept (as of all concepts) inheres in the fact that it is recognized by individual minds. In this case, it takes the form of the individual's awareness of a difference, running into actual or potential conflict, between his own opinions, interests, and intentions, and those of the group to which he belongs. Again, we are undoubtedly dealing with a fairly definite moral hierarchy and evolutionary order. The greater prevalence and greater intensity of this felt opposition between self and group go with a more "advanced" social life. The "lowest" level of the phenomenon might be pictured as a kind of idyllic primitive anarchy or communism, in which the individual is completely merged in the group. At the lower levels, too, the unity of individual and group as present to consciousness will be predominantly of a spontaneous-emotional rather than a deliberative and cognitive sort, the kind of thing represented by the *mob*.

The validity of communication and of knowledge of mental content is presupposed in the notion of objective knowledge of physical facts. No laboratory or other scientific observation is taken as real unless it is confirmed or "verified" by a plurality of observers, who must be assumed to know somehow that they do see the same thing.

* A modern individualistic student tends to view the relation in terms of individual power, i.e., some mixture of persuasive power and what is more commonly called force; he will argue that the individual has by hook or crook worked himself into the position of leadership (or some small group or coterie has done so) and then proceeds to "put it over" on the other individuals making up the group as a whole. The group decision would be regarded in this interpretation as based upon some "special interest" of the individual or clique or the achievement of leadership would reflect the interest in power as such, and the general perquisites which naturally go with political power. This interpretation is really much more applicable to fascist-nationalism (page 318), where a more advanced society has retrograded into tyranny. In this case, the social-psychology of the situation is doubtless much more emotional than in primitive society, where it is more largely spontaneous and unconscious; but it also has more of the cognitive-deliberative element characteristic of the higher level, though the acceptance reflects in part a choice between evils rather than ideals.

The third level or species of social decision would seem to be the notion of democracy. It should be considered first in the ideal sense of "social contract," where decisions would represent a consensus or near-consensus reached through deliberation and discussion in intellectual and moral terms among the individual members of a group. The process, of course, implies the reality of individual deliberation and free choice, and requires in addition a social process of discussion leading to agreement, which is perhaps even more mysterious and scientifically repugnant. It seems impossible to visualize it as real without postulating a "value cosmos," a world of objective, super-individual norms, to be thought of as discovered, or progressively approached—though undoubtedly at the same time partly created—in the discussion process.*

The close relationship thus established between social choice and the effort to realize norms or values—our fourth level—will be apparent. (They are not identical, as there is a sphere of private ethics.) Democracy, which has been defined as "government by discussion" must rest on an accepted common system of ethical principles, and the connection between agreement and objectivity need not be elaborated here. However individualistic a society may be, this is still true. Individualism itself is an ethical principle, and it must be defined and interpreted in an elaborate code covering economic, political, social, and religious relations. The rational social acceptance of ethical principles is to be distinguished from traditionalism, unconscious or dogmatic-emotional. In a true democracy individual relations rest

* The maximum simplification of this system of ethical norms—short of the anarchistic postulate of spontaneous and complete but conscious agreement on all questions affecting group action among all members—is no doubt that of modern liberal democratic social philosophy. Here all other ethical principles and values are subsumed under two, the economic-ethical principle of the right of the individual to do as he will with his own (including the use of it to get "more") and the political-ethical principle of majority rule. Unfortunately, as sufficiently emphasized in the earlier sections of this essay, both principles are subject to serious limitations, and the two may come into conflict to any degree, so that neither one nor the other, nor both together, afford workable answers to many questions for which a social group is compelled under modern conditions to find practical solutions.

The description above applies to pure or direct democracy, which of course is impossible of literal realization, and the more so as the group in question increases in size. Actual democracy must also have its leadership. But in ideal theory the leaders secure their position through an active intelligent and moral selection within the group, not merely the passive "consent" of the governed. Some of the difficulties of the conception of such selection of leaders have already been suggested.

on a system of acknowledged and felt obligations on one hand and conscious "legitimate" expectations on the other.

The type of groupism presented by the social philosophy of fascist-nationalism is best viewed as authoritarian leadership under conditions of reversion or degradation from a previously more advanced, more ideally democratic level, as already suggested. Decisions emanate from an individual "Leader" (surrounded by a special coterie calling them-selves a "party") as spokesman for the group, but ostensibly come ultimately from the group itself considered as possessing a group spirit or folk mind. The position of the leader rests in part on deliberate acceptance by the group, based on failure to secure adequate unity by democratic methods, in part on "force," and in part on an artificial manipulation of group or "crowd" emotion, really a disguised method of applying force. Of course, the notion that decisions reflect any "special interest" opposed to other special interests within the group—whether on the part of the political leaders as individuals or some "class" with which they are identified, or the interest in power and its perquisites—would be indignantly denied. Characteristically, too, the group interest as formulated may take a direction to which any pro-portion of the individual members feel themselves opposed. The leader and his clique are assumed to know and express the "true" group mind, and those who diverge to be ignorant or corrupt. Essentially the same philosophy applies to communism as to fascism. Actual leadership is in the hands of a party composed of a small minority, and having an individual head. The party is supposed to consist of the "advanced" and "class conscious" members of the "proletariat," including the great mass of the people and destined to destroy other strata or to absorb them in an ultimate classless commonwealth.*

For the practical purposes of methodology in social science, i.e., of achieving clarity as to the terms in which it is possible to discuss social phenomena in verbal propositions which may be defended as

---

* The opinion in the mind of an individual that he is especially competent to voice the true interests and opinion of a social group, in opposition to the indifference or contrary views of other members, naturally invites interpretation from various stand-points.

In addition to these three conceptions of the process of social decision, it could also be divided, as in the case of individual decisions, into two problem stages, the selection of ends and the selection of means to realize ends.

"true" and "relevant," the issues must lie, to begin with, in the field of the last four standpoints enumerated. Whatever anyone's general dogmatic pretensions may be, there is no serious danger that an effort to account for social phenomena by the principles of physics, chemistry, and biology will be made, or if made will do any great amount of damage.* Details and individual occurrences may be intelligently treated, within limits, at lower levels, but these cannot give any view of social process in the large or as as really social. Social problems begin where those of the natural sciences leave off. We take it for granted that social behaviour will be in accord with the laws of physics and biology; our questions regarding it relate to matters on which such data shed no light—a statement which might serve as a definition of the social as a category.†

Positivistic history should also be impossible as a complete account of phenomena to anyone who really thinks about what he is doing; the historian will hardly care to deny either that his writing of history

* Our special concern is with economics, and no one has seriously proposed to construct a science of economic phenomena as a branch of either physical mechanics, chemistry, or biology. When the concepts of these sciences are employed, they are taken in an analogical, even rather figurative, sense. It *has* been, and is, seriously proposed to make of it a natural, positive science along lines roughly corresponding to the conception of "behaviouristic psychology," meaning behaviourism as a substitute for psychology (but distinguished from neurological and bio-chemical interpretations). Such a view takes the individual human being, the organism, as a unit, and attempts to discover "uniformities of co-existence and sequence" in the "raw" phenomena in the field called economic. Behaviouristic economics commonly considers the phenomena as collected in relation to some recognized human aggregate or "group," or even the human world. The content is statistics dealing with physical magnitudes, chiefly "commodities," including certain physical activities of human beings themselves ("labour"). Such a treatment is descriptive, not interpretive, and explanatory only in the positivistic sense of generalized-description. Its most distinctive characteristic is the elimination of everything naturally or properly called "human" or relative to any human interest.

The essential mystery of the procedure is the reason for selecting any particular phenomena as "economic" or the meaning which that term may have in relation to a sequence of phenomena viewed as a matter of cause and effect, viewed in turn as bare phenomenal invariability under given antecedent conditions. "Commodity" is obviously another concept which can be given no definition in physical terms without depriving it of the meaning it actually bears in usage, and "demand" is still another. (The case of "supply" is somewhat different.)

† It is possible, of course, to abstract from the mental-communicative aspect of society, and it seems to be possible even to deny its reality (though it involves denying the possibility of denying!). But if this is done, there is no special subject matter for discussion, beyond the mechanics of organic response. In a physical view, "other" organisms are, for any particular organism, simply details in the physical environment and the relation between them is one of physical interaction.

is conduct and is part of the social process, or that it is motivated and more or less intelligent. In any case, as already sufficiently emphasized, the postulates of the historical or institutional approach exclude the possibility of viewing society, the subject matter of the discourse, as an entity facing and solving problems of its own.*

The third or "economistic" viewpoint is as easily and briefly eliminated as a possibility for the study of phenomena in a truly social aspect. By the nature of its fundamental conceptions, theoretical economics is an *individualistic* science. As explained at length in an earlier part of this essay, the "economic man" is not a social man, and the ideal market dealings of theory are not social relations. The science takes its economic individual as a datum, in his three aspects of wants, resources, and technical knowledge, ignoring all question of his origin; and it abstracts from all his relations with other human beings, except those of the perfect market, which are really relations to commodities as such.† A social science is concerned with "economic" data in the aspects excluded from economics as an analytical science, the historical and genetic explanation of the individual himself, the phases of market dealings which do not fit the pure theory of exchange, and especially the moral and legal framework in which economic life is lived, the field in which practical social problems take their rise.

We have left as viewpoints from which to discuss problems of social decision of action, the fourth and sixth of our list. These regard behaviour respectively as problem-solving or value realizing, for the behaving individual, and as involving social decision. But for practical

---

* There are partial exceptions to such a statement. We shall refer later to the "learning curve" as a scientific result. But obviously, a society which is warned by a historian that in accord with the "laws of history" it is heading for disaster, and which in consequence changes its course of action, "breaks" the "laws in question in doing so."

† The rational self-interest which is abstracted from other aspects of human nature as the basis of economic theory plays a large role in a realistic explanation of the events described in written history. It operates in two ways: First, the tendency to equilibrium in the system of economic relations of a human group acting under given conditions, or specifically in response to changes in given conditions. In the second place, the changes in given conditions themselves result in part from action more or less in accord with principles of economic motivation. The concept of economic motivation, it must be remembered, involves two elements more or less in conflict; resources may be "rationally" used either to yield current satisfaction or to create an increase in the total means of satisfaction (including technical knowledge and skill) available in the future. (They may also be used by an individual owner to change the wants and attitudes of other individuals, which action may be to some extent in accord with economic principles.)

purposes, these two views are largely (though by no means entirely) identical, as already indicated. We may now leave the discussion of the problem of viewpoints or approaches, and turn to that of social decision itself, and the meaning and role of intelligence in the solution of social problems.*

II. Social Action as an Intellectual Problem

§14. Our next and final task is an attempt to indicate the meaning of an "intelligent" solution of a social problem, with especial reference to the contemporary crisis in the modern venture of democracy, or social self-direction. For this purpose, as should already be clear, the

* In this sketch it has been necessary to pass over philosophical issues, and also inumerable questions which lie on the surface of the argument. The six-point classification itself is not to be viewed as presumptively final, not necessarily so even in general outline. The purpose has been to emphasize the fact that there are different ways of looking at human-social phenomena, that they, so to speak, take place in a number of different universes of discourse and can be, and in any full account must be, discussed in terms of different sets of categories. To reconcile these, or make them fit together in an intelligible general synthesis, seems to the writer the supreme problem of philosophy. The ever-present and obtrusive mind-body problem is one phase of this pluralism, but we think the argument shows that it is only a beginning of the complexities that must be faced.

Such a "linear" classification has an especial weakness in obscuring the different kinds of bases of distinction involved between the different approaches. This raises a large problem, which can only be suggested here, not taken up for discussion. Perhaps the main distinctions are somewhat as follows: First, one of subject matter, material *versus* ideal; second, one of methodology, positivistic *versus* what for want of a better term we may call participative—a difference which goes with a contrast between non-telic and telic subject matter; third, there is a somewhat inscrutable but profound difference between individual and social teleology. Out of these distinctions can be built up the five (or four) cases (keeping in mind that individual value judgments are in large part social decisions), and excluding the biological, which presents the particularly recalcitrant problem of unconscious teleology.

The most controversial of the conceptions is likely to be the last, the notion of social teleology, involving the "group mind." In connection with it, the writer would like to suggest that the present essay itself is a social phenomenon, and to state that it is presented as *discussion*, which has no meaning unless there is or may be such a mind, in the formation of which an author can participate without manipulating other individual minds, either for their good or his own. The writer assumes also that interchange of meaningful discourse is something more than a detail in an absolute cosmic process, whether clash of atoms or dialectical dance of categories. (All discourse, including social science, is a social phenomenon and any *general* explanation of social process would have to be applicable to the explanation itself and to the explainer in all his behaviour.)

The great philosophical problem, unsolved and probably unsolvable to minds with the modern critical conception of the meaning of a problem and a solution, is twofold; first the ancient metaphysical enigma of freedom for the individual, and over and above this the meaning of free choice for a group of free individuals acting as a unit.

main point for emphasis is a multiple negation. The beginning of talking sense about social phenomena from the standpoint of relevance to the intellectual direction of social process by a society and in its own interest, is the recognition that the general concepts of such a discussion are *not* those of natural science. In this statement, the notion of natural science covers all knowledge of invariants in phenomena, including persistence without change, change in the sense of recurrence under given conditions, and cumulative change (history in one aspect); and it applies regardless of whether the phenomena are natural or human, physical or ideal, and of whether or not the knowledge affords any formula for interference in and control over the phenomena by the knower as a planning and choosing agent external to the phenomena, or for guidance of his activity in relation to them as "absolutely" given.*

The study of human society by methods more or less akin to those of natural science is possible in a few fields, such as mob psychology and language, *because* these are *not* treated as rationally purposive behaviour, and in general because the results established are not to be communicated to the groups (or individuals) whose "social behaviour" forms the subject matter; they are not communicated to most of the population in question at all, and are not communicated to any one with a view to getting him to change his behaviour as described and explained.† Theoretically, social phenomena may be described and analysed "scientifically" in a physical or a biological

* It would certainly conduce to clarity in thought and expression if all use of the term science were restricted in its reference to the intellectual methodology for the study by an *active* student, of a *passive* subject matter, a subject matter observed and/or manipulated without recognition of any interest or "point of view" of its own, and which consequently is not consulted either about the study itself or about the meaning or use of its results. The scientist does not study a phenomenon by discussing the motives of its behaviour with the subject matter itself, and does not predict or control a subject matter or develop methods for its prediction and control, by arguing with it as to how it ought to behave. He does not get his data by conference with the phenomenon or communicate his results to the phenomenon after they are obtained.

† All such generalizations admit of partial exceptions. Linguistic and other studies of social phenomena may prompt or psychologically stimulate efforts to change the phenomena, and may become data in the discussion of change. But if the efforts face any possibility of success, the case is highly and necessarily exceptional, and is narrowly limited by the fact that there can be but one controller of the same subject matter at a given time. But most important of all it *must* represent either one-sided control from without or self-control based on agreement between knower and known which violates and changes the formula or law describing the previous course of events.

view,* or as historical culture products; i.e., in accord with either the first, second, or fifth of the six approaches distinguished in the previous section. But in so far as man, individual or social, is viewed as a problem-solver, in either of the two possible senses (ends only or both ends and means problematic), his behaviour cannot be an object of positive, predictive knowledge. To predict problem-solving behaviour would mean prediction of the problems which the behaving subjects will confront, in the forms in which they will be apprehended, and also predicting the solutions, right or wrong, which will be reached.†

It is true that there is some limited possibility of predicting human problems and their solution, even when the solution will be "wrong," and also that it is possible, within some limits, for *some* human beings to exercise control over *other* human beings, individually or in groups, by manipulating the conditions of the problems which they will meet and anticipating the mode in which the problems will be solved, "rightly" or "wrongly," in action. But three facts are to be emphasized. The first is that the human relation involved, whether in private or public life, is virtually what we define as immoral. In politics the name for it is tyranny. In any connection it is the antithesis of the basic ethical principle that humanity, whether in one's own person or that of another, is always to be treated as an end, never as a means.‡

The second point is closely related to the first, and reinforces it.

* Biology is really positivistic only in so far as its phenomena are reducible to physical process. We should somewhere remark that no one, however emphatic his assertion of "mechanism" as against "vitalism," actually studies biological phenomena from physico-chemical data or can give an intelligible definition in mechanistic terms of the distinctive biological concepts listed above. Whether a person who knew "everything" about physics and chemistry as studied from their distinctive point (or points) of view would ever suspect the possibility of the existence of any living being if he had not directly observed such things is a question hardly worth raising.

† Again, partial exceptions can be thought of. It is possible, within limits, to predict learning curves on the basis of previous observation of other individuals, whether rats or men, given similar organisms set to work on the same or a similar "problem." But this is limited to repetitive situations and at best is possible where the problem of the learner is not a problem for the observer. Usage would even allow us to speak of a plant or a botanical species as solving problems, and correspondingly of its "economy."

‡ Control of others for their own good, in so far as it is real, is a partial exception raising ethical problems which lie beyond the scope of the present discussion. It will be noted that such control involves treating the controlled individual as something less than a complete adult person. It is to be distinguished from the educative or consultant relation intelligently chosen by the passive party, already referred to in various connections. The latter does not involve "control."

This is that the procedure or technique employed in the prediction and control of the behaviour of human beings is utterly different from that used in the prediction and control of natural phenomena. The procedure takes such forms as threatening, "coaxing," emotional appeal, exhortation, suggestion, etc. These are familiarly summed up in legal terms under the heads of "force" (or "duress") and "fraud." The crucial element in all of them is deception. Even in the crudest forms of "force," the basis is secret preparation and surprise.* But the special point here is that not one of the crucial terms or concepts involved in the exercise of control over persons has the least meaning in connection with our relations to natural objects; these we neither abjure, conjure, entreat, or constrain. The "logic" of the insistence on treating human beings in scientific terms implying a technique of control, which has been and in the main still is characteristic of modern social science, would seem to be that the best minds of the race, having finally learned, after millennia of struggle and groping, that natural objects are *unlike* human beings, that an "animistic" inter-pretation of their behaviour is false, that they are "inexorable," have drawn the conclusion that human beings must be *like* natural objects in that respect.

But the fact that prediction and control of human behaviour rest almost entirely on the prediction and control of the interests and opinions of the behaving subject is perhaps the smaller half of the story. To an at least equal degree it is the opinions and sentiments of others which men are directly interested in knowing and manipu-lating, rather than the associated behaviour. Commonly it is the two together. We want to know how others will act, and to know why; and we want them to act in a way satisfactory to ourselves and to do it for the right reasons. This relationship is particularly important for ethics. The ethical quality of the motive is more important than *that of the behaviour itself. And as regards control, viewed as unethical,

* It is unfortunate that the term "force" is ever used when "compulsion" is what is meant. Use of literal force on human beings is restricted to such procedures as "knock down and carry out," and in the concrete even these generally rest on "strategy." This necessity of secrecy in itself means that the possibilities of prediction and control are in general very narrowly limited. (Some qualification as to the requirement of secrecy is necessary in connection with political life, where men may be born into superior or inferior status, and where control over one part of a population may be made instru-mental to control over the rest.)

the wielder of power is often more interested in the deference, adulation, or fear which motivates those in his power and by which he dominates them than he is in what he makes them do. But of course if he is indifferent to what they think or feel, the relation of domination is still unethical.

The third fact is that phenomena involving relations of control by human beings over other human beings are not social phenomena in the proper sense of the word. Social relations between human beings differ as much from the "prediction and control" relation, where it obtains between one or more human beings and another or others, as this differs from "scientific" prediction and control in the proper meaning of the term, in connection with relations between human beings and natural objects. Prediction and control cannot be mutual. Two beings cannot so much as act intelligently in relations such that each takes the other's behaviour as a datum in planning his own. And it is, if possible, even more of a contradiction for each to control the other's action; this could be true only in the sense of mechanical interaction, which eliminates all planning and choosing and all problem-solving character from the behaviour. Moreover, no *common* factual knowledge can be the basis either of unilateral control, or of individual planning.* If any behaviour involving two or more subjects who form part of each other's behaviour situations is to be planned, the plan itself must be common and preconcerted (including the case of leadership freely and intelligently chosen), or one party must control the others, and the process of any true control must be secret. Social behaviour *means* behaviour jointly planned, and the social problem *is* the problem of joint planning, of establishing agreement or consensus on a common plan. In group life, and in an organization, it becomes under realistic conditions chiefly the problem of agreeing upon a process and a mechanism for securing agreement on particular issues, i.e., on a "constitution." It is the problem of social self-constitution; it is analogous to the moral problem of personality formation through self-legislation in the individual life, but vastly more subtle and complex.

* A simple illustration is the case of two friends who get separated, say, in a department store, and want to find each other. No conflict of interests is present, and yet no science or knowledge of fact or principle is of practical value apart from a preconcerted plan.

This fact determines the nature of any social "science" which has for its objective the solution of *social* problems. The only possible starting point is the "humane naïve realism," referred to at the beginning of the preceding section, taking individual and group and the problems of conflicting individual and group interests, which make up the social problem, as they "are"—i.e., seem to be, to competent and unbiased persons—at any given time and place. The social problem is, in the main, the current political problem, or group of problems, the problem of changes in laws and political constitution; for these are the institutions by which a human group acts consciously and deliberately as a unit, by virtue of which it is a group in a human, i.e., intellectual and moral, sense. It is, again, a social problem, only in so far as it is present to the social consciousness as a problem for conscious and intelligent solution. Any social science relevant to social problems is therefore restricted, as already observed, to the sixth of the list of our possible approaches. It must take as its subject matter a society that is capable of making and actually makes choices. The other approaches merely provide data and set limits to the alternatives of social choice.*

In so far as men live in a political organization, it must be the *same* organization; it is not a thing which each can have according to his individual taste—whether mere individual preference or imperative ideal of value. The limits of agreement are the limits of political organization, and these are the limits of agreement. The question is, first, how far and on what scale life is to be politically organized, and second, what is to be the nature of the process of agreement. For a

---

* The "machinery" for making decisions is not strictly limited to formal political and judicial process. Political action again is largely indirect—the making of rules for making rules and selection of persons to administer and to make rules. Actual administration and execution of decisions may well be in the hands of "experts" of innumerable sorts, appointed by the political functionaries, whose delegated authority includes especially this right to re-delegate details. Armies and other organizations generally have three types of leadership consisting of, or corresponding to, line and staff officers and technicians.

The first and overwhelmingly most important task of government is the two-fold one, (*a*) of fixing the "sphere of government," i.e. of deciding upon a general division between the sphere of activity which is to be jointly planned and executed and that which is to be left to individual planning, and (*b*) of maintaining its own monopoly of governmental functions by preventing any individual or group in society, other than the duly constituted authorities, acting in their legally defined sphere, from exercising any "control."

group made up of individuals who think politically at all, there are in the abstract the two possibilities (always combined in reality)— voluntary and intelligent consensus, and domination of the citizenship as a whole by some group within which there is a consensus of some sort. (A truly individual dictatorship would be possible only to one who could make his subjects believe him to be God.)

Domination will rest upon some mixture of "force," in the narrow sense of a threat of violence, with "psychological technique," "propaganda," or, in plainer language, deception, fraud, "humbug." In this connection, the modern developments of technology in the field of social communication and of the "science" (a quasi-natural science) of psychology, have together created a new basis for tyranny on the part of a group which once gets in a position to monopolize and control the press, radio, etc. Under these conditions a consensus may be consciously voluntary and yet forced or manipulated; assent may be enthusiastic and yet not intelligent and hence not really free; men may be "made" to act in a prescribed way and also "made" to like it. The concepts of tyranny, despotism, and exploitation have received an entirely new content, and the notion of liberty, at best more or less an intellectual "surd," has become enormously more difficult still to define. It seems not unlikely that a future historian of the period we call modern may find this the really important consequence of the scientific movement. From this standpoint, the carrying over of the utilitarian-instrumentalistic or "pragmatic" categories of natural science into the field of social relations in the attempt to build a social science on natural-science principles, without recognition of the intellectual and moral limitations of the project, would appear as the outstanding intellectual event of the age, the supreme catastrophe in the history of freedom, the suicide, or attempt at suicide of intelligence itself.

Any conscious effort of any group of persons to exercise choice on the basis of a genuine consensus is an intellectual project in that it represents an effort to reach *correct* solutions for problems, to discover and clarify *valid norms*. The effort to agree on the solution of any common problem means an effort to find the "right" or "best" solution.* Thus a political problem is an intellectual problem, but in

* This does not imply that the "principle" underlying every social rule must be formulated before the rule itself is stated, or even that it must necessarily be formulated

a sense very different from that of the problems of natural science. It involves cognition and understanding, but its character is as remote as possible from that of discovering "invariants" in the environment, whether the natural environment of the race or the human environment of an individual or limited group, the parties to the "scientific" interchange.* In this field the things to be discovered are values, ends of action, in contrast with the instrumental character which all natural existent things have for knowledge. The process of discovery, moreover, is *purely* intellectual, involving no manipulation of material by the body-machine of the investigator. It is like scientific work in being a concurrent co-operative activity of the minds concerned ("verification"), though in a much higher degree, and even in being normative (there can be no science of physics if physicists have no moral integrity!), but in the quest of values minds work internally to an ideal world as subject matter. Such activity must be distinguished equally from that of investigation in objective science and from the creative play of individual fancy.

The philosophical problem of the nature of validity in connection with values and its relation to that of the truths of science and mathematics or logic cannot here be further pursued, but one point does call for emphasis. It is that in the field of political ethics as in the domains more usually recognized as affected by truth, the recognition of validity in any conclusion excludes the role of *force*, and equally of *persuasion*, in any form, in securing agreement. Acceptance must rest on *discussion* of the objective merits of the question itself.†

at all. In political ethics, as in natural science, there is an interaction between the two processes of knowledge, from general to particular and from particular to general.

There are, of course, cases in which only the fact of agreement is important, the choice between the alternatives a matter of indifference. Here the issue may be settled by drawing lots, or otherwise left to "chance." Examples are choice between turning to right or left upon meeting, and the definition of words. Where agreement is vital and an objective basis difficult to find, a working adjustment will naturally be reached through *compromise*.

* Or, more accurately, these plus a bureaucracy of "controllers" for whom the scientists would certainly work and by whom they would be controlled, and *not* conversely, as they often seem to assume.

† A few brief statements may be added, in the hope that they will be taken in the spirit of suggestion or challenge, not that of dogma.

1. In both science and political ethics, the establishment of objectivity, but not the objectivity itself, depends upon the acceptance of the conclusion by a "competent and impartial" group (which presupposes valid intercommunication). Agreement is the *test* of validity, but the concept itself rests on the assumption, or faith, that validity is more

All thinking about policy or about action of any sort means thinking about *changes* in some given situation. Consequently, the starting point is knowledge, in some descriptive sense, or senses, of the existing situation at the point where action is to begin. But again, the "existing" situation may be in process of change from causes other than conscious interference and control, and these "natural" changes must also be a matter of descriptive knowledge before intelligent interference is possible. All such data are to be learned about through the study of the past, of history in the inclusive sense, remote and recent.

Thus, on the face of it, there is in intelligent social change an element of positive science, in the sense in which social data are scientifically knowable. But in general the situation cannot be inter-

than the fact of agreement. In neither field can validity be "proved." There is no answer to the sceptic who does not see, or who denies that he "really" sees what he seems to see, without giving reasons which outweigh the fact of seeming. On the other hand, there is no argument against the validity of the "best" conclusion in morals or aesthetics, which does not also apply in the field of science. The only general difference is that the range of disagreement is actually narrower in science, due especially to the availability of accepted techniques of measurement. It is undeniable that the moral judgments accepted in any society are more or less relative to its culture, and to that extent may be regarded as "historical accidents"; but the same is true in greater or less degree of scientific truths.

2. Ultimately, science and the criticism of norms rest on common principles. Truth is a value! But functionally the two are complementary. Scientific knowledge is relevant to action because of two sets of facts. First, human beings as minds, have a *limited* "power" through the "voluntary" muscles and related mechanism of nerves and bones to break into and redirect the "invariant" physical sequences, beginning with their own bodies (and sometimes ending with them). Second—or more properly first—human beings have ends differing more or less from the course of events as it "would be" in the absence of interference.

3. These ends may be either purely individual references or "objective values"—a distinction which every person constantly makes in thought and in practice. Where action is to realize ends for more than one person, they may of course happen to agree in their preferences. But to the extent that they do not—which in fact is large—the matter becomes a subject for *discussion*, or for one-sided control (or for conflict, ending in the destruction of one of the parties, or of both). It is "self-evident" that expression of personal preferences is not discussion and indeed leads definitely toward conflict, that rational agreement involves recognition by all parties of super-individual norms.

4. Since control of the material environment is effected *exclusively* through moving objects or portions of matter in space by means of "voluntary" movements of our bodily members, our thinking in this realm naturally takes on a geometrical pattern in space-time, with force and resistance as an additional (fifth) dimension. The tendency to use spatial-mechanical concepts such as position, direction, movement, velocity, inertia, friction, etc., is one of the most baffling sources of confusion in the use of language in thinking about social problems.

5. In view of the virtual deification of science, in modern thought, as the only mode of valid intellectual activity, the point needing emphasis is the large number of kinds

preted at this simple level. For any discussion of change will bring into the critical consciousness facts of a situation, including persistence and change, which were only in part present to consciousness before. This will generally reveal habits and subconscious motives in the process, which will not continue to function in the same way when brought above the threshold of consciousness. Quite typically, the raising of a problem makes it necessary to work out some deliberate, more or less rational solution. After we have once become critically aware of a situation which previously took care of itself without thinking, it will no longer do so. And in general it is impossible to "set the clock back" and return to the previous no-problem condition. Thus the shift from unconscious or habitual to deliberate action is only part of the story. As soon as men turn to look critically at their previous course of behaviour, they find that it rested on "principles" of various sorts, and it is especially these traditions, faiths, and more or less rational but not fully conscious beliefs which actually come under critical examination.*

This brings us to the observation that in determining one's general

of mental activity which have to be regarded as intellectual and affected with validity. The black-and-white dualism of the modern empirical-utilitarian world view—the notion that every statement relates either to a physical world in which truth is absolute or to "subjective" preferences, any ascription of validity to which is either illusion or arrogant presumption—is a major heresy of our civilization. The truth is rather that opinions in both fields have greater or lesser degrees of validity. Truth is an ideal in which we must believe to give meaning to thought and to life; but there is no way of knowing that any particular belief is true, and every belief must be held subject to revision—except the belief that there are better and worse reasons for believing.

6. To say that there is an intellectual element in the solution of the social-political problem is to say that some modes of associated activity, some "games," are "really better" than others. The superiority may lie in the objective or in the rules of play. The figure is rightly drawn from "play" rather than "work," because the ostensible, conscious objective cannot be in itself good. What activity directly does is to change some physical configuration, which commonly includes altering the character of a continuing natural process. But in itself one physical configuration is no better than another. The value must be in the process of play and the conscious experience involved or in some effect on the players as human beings, or through them on other human beings. (Reference has already been made to the variety of roles played by intelligence in the game situation.)

* These facts no doubt form the basis of the idea of a "fall" into responsibility and effort from a previous state of passive insouciance. The contrast between the ideal life as active, responsible decision, self-determination, and achievement, and as "peace and quiet," undoubtedly represents the greatest of all moral dilemmas. One of the extremes is represented by the Faust spirit of eternally insatiable striving, the other by the doctrine of Nirvana, which is perhaps the religious spirit per se.

attitude toward social problems, there are very weighty presumptions in favour of a generally "conservative" position. One of the evils which has resulted from carrying the natural science conceptions over into the field of social discussion is the common delusion that by the happy discovery of some formula, it may be possible to change the character and constitution of society in a way comparable to the modern development of technology through science. The two problems are utterly different, and the natural consequence of any such a belief is to create a danger of social disintegration and the destruction of culture and of life.

All reflection on the problem of a society changing itself tends to emphasize the necessity of "gradualness." The use of intelligence, even in the scientific sense, and in fields where conditions are most favourable, involves a tremendous "overhead cost," especially in the form of time. It is feasible only in connection with the establishment of data or data-elements which will be applicable to large classes of recurrent problem situations. For different reasons, which are obvious enough, the making of political decisions, where group consensus in a value judgment is required, is even more costly and time consuming. Moreover, even after the decision to change has been made, it is literally, and in fact obviously, *impossible* for society to transform itself fundamentally or rapidly without disorganization. Political society is a game which must go on under rules, or very quickly collapse into a war of each against all. It cannot be suspended while changes in the rules are under deliberation or in process. Even transition from one set of rules to another already agreed upon is, if the difference is at all considerable, and if the group is of considerable size, extremely difficult without more or less disorder. Moreover, it is equally evident that men do not want to spend a large fraction of their time and effort in making and changing rules of action. For the most part, the object is the game, the rules being instrumental and changes in the rules a necessary evil—or an evil necessity.*

Even more serious is the question of the adequacy of human intelligence, as revealed to itself by any candid and competent criticism, in its capacity to determine what political decision is wise. Serious

* But rule making and changing may also be, within limits, a game on its own account.

scrutiny of the problems which must be solved as a prerequisite to an intelligent social decision in any matter of consequence raises questions of principle on which the best minds have been at work at least as far back as records go, and on which they are still far from agreement. Such general principles as either philosophers or men generally will accept have extremely little content or specific value for guidance. They tend to be of the sort expressed by saying that it is better to do right than wrong or that circumstances must be taken into account. They are truisms; they are not for that reason non-sensical or unimportant, but their function is rather moral than intellectual.

The notion of the "experimental" determination of political issues, again, is an especially vicious analogy from natural science. Experimentation by society upon itself is both limited and terribly dangerous, especially since what it really involves is mainly the experimentation upon society as a whole as a sort of "guinea-pig" by some political official or group. It would be a very good law, if it could be enforced, to compel all discussion of action by "society," or "the whole people," to substitute for such terms the phrase "a government made up of politicians." The problem of social action is almost wholly a problem of leadership.*

The attitude of caution is reinforced by observation of the intellectual and moral qualities of men in general as manifested in everyday life. These qualities are not seriously inadequate for the maintenance of social life under stable conditions; with relatively few exceptions, men have good intentions and the ability to learn a routine of action, are amenable to discipline, and under discipline have courage. Moreover, the majority of men have a fair amount of ingenuity in meeting exceptional predicaments, *as individuals*; in the physical environment; and, in addition, the race seems to produce an adequate supply of individuals especially endowed with capacity for scientific investigation and analysis. (Only a limited number of these can be given employment, and only a limited amount of the fruits can be digested.)

A large proportion of men also have abundant ingenuity in meeting

* Politicians are, it will be kept in mind, of two sorts, either democratic or autocratic; i.e., they hold their positions by competitive persuasion or by monopoly based on outright force. In concrete reality, power always rests on a complex mixture of principles.

social and political predicaments, *as individuals*. But, unfortunately, the exercise of this form of ability is a force making for the *disruption* of order, and is in fact one of the chief roots of the social problem. But the proportion of human beings who could invent a game, which anyone would care to play, even a game for two contestants, or a very small group, is a question on which the range of disagreement will not be important for the present argument; *the proportion is small.* The notion that the general mass of mankind, taken on the scale of a modern national state, can quickly and reliably think out and apply important constitutional changes, is tragic nonsense. The conditions under which human nature evolved, through the millennia from the animal to the human level, and the further millennia of pre-history and of history—in comparison with which the era of attempted political self-determination is almost negligible—were not such as to develop the intellectual and moral capacities required for combining effective mass action on a large scale with individual freedom of self-expression, to say nothing of political competence. And such qualities did not develop.

Moreover, the "common man" must be given credit for sense enough to know that he and his fellows do not possess such qualities. When ordinary people think of large-scale mass action, they do not think of individual liberty and intellectual deliberation and public discussion. The simplest activity involving concerted action, even when rules for every contingency are given and accepted in advance, as in organized sports or the group rendition of a piece of music, is hardly thought of without a leader having practically absolute authority in the premises. On the political arena also the masses instinctively and unequivocally turn toward strong leadership in a time of crisis or serious tension. And the authority of a leader must rest on a moral-religious basis, which must be emotional, non-rational, in rough proportion to the amount of leading he is to do, i.e., to the amount of action, change, and meeting of situations which are called for.*

We are thrown back upon the problem of leadership, which is to

---

* In political society, it is impossible to have even fairly specific rules along with much change, and in fact practically the whole of the problem consists in interpreting, "enforcing," and changing the accepted rules.

say "politics," where the oustanding facts are no more reassuring·
It is fairly evident that the individuals conspicuously active in urging
extensive social changes are not generally those who are even relatively most competent in their judgment of social facts and values
and the consequences of possible measures. Humility and modesty
go with deep insight, and those who see farthest into the problems
see their difficulty and are reticent about writing prescriptions even for
admitted evils. (This is commonly interpreted as favouring the evils.)

And still less can the advocates of extensive reforms be regarded
as disinterested. Almost in the nature of the case, they would be the
agents to carry out the changes proposed, and to administer the new
system if adopted; and their interest can hardly be unaffected by the
realization of this fact. In short, advocacy of extensive reform is
practically the solicitation of the position of king on the part of the
reformer. And under competitive conditions the solicitation tends
to take a form in which it will be effective in gaining power for the
agitators, which does not mean clearness, and inclusive accuracy,
regarding the changes to be brought about. The reformer typically
has in fact little in the way of a definite programme, but preaches vague
ideals in terms admitting of little dispute. In an age of experimental
science, he also rather typically advocates experimental procedure—
with himself as experimenter and society as experimented upon.*
When a "leader" of a revolutionary movement acquires any considerable following, it is usually obvious to anyone but himself, if not even
to him, that it is based on mob-mindedness, on the romantic craving
of the crowd for a hero, and for easy and pleasant cures for serious

* This country and every democratic country has been flooded, especially during
the depression period, with propaganda of innumerable kinds as contradictory among
themselves as most of them are foolish from any sound critical standpoint. (Among the
worst in America is that put out over the signature of Professor John Dewey, America's
most widely followed and quoted philosopher.)

The *supreme* stupidity and crime to be laid at the door of reformers is of course the
doctrine of the class war. The intellectual absurdity of the notion that any developed
society is divisible into tolerably homogeneous economic classes in any limited number
(a war nearly has to be between *two* parties) is surpassed if possible by the intellectual
and moral monstrosity of the doctrine of moral reformism based on the philosophy
of materialism—forcibly construed to mean that the only way to promote reform is
to secure and employ superior force. But the dominant school of reformers, the Marxists,
have carried this position to the point of making their completely visionary and justify
any means and of denying that there is any truth or right except being on the "right
side," meaning their side in a struggle for power.

maladies, and on general emotional and intellectual befuddlement. A large mass of people simply does not form a cohesive group and act as a unit (in situations calling for rapid or effective action) on an intellectually critical basis; and intelligence must recognize this fact as a datum in all its deliberations about social problems. Leadership on a religious-emotional basis is an indefinitely more natural, an easier, and less costly system of order than any other.* The weakness of such a system is its excessive strength, its tendency toward rigidity. If freedom is to be maintained, the rate of change must be limited— with perhaps some provision for *temporary* recourse to authoritarian rule in times of crisis.†

The ideal of free society is that social problems should be settled in their large outlines by discussion in which all normal adults participate equally, and in further detail by leadership intelligently chosen by all through public discussion and leading with the intelligent and moral consent and co-operation of the masses. The first question raised, and a terribly serious one, is that of how far any moral basis of unity can survive open discussion. The very attitude of critical intellectual examination seems to be intrinsically individualistic, both as regards the intellectual process itself, and—even more seriously for the social problem—as regards an inherent tendency toward the individualization of ends. It certainly is inherently disruptive of the traditional and emotional-religious attitude, and that of passive acceptance in general, whether of tradition or of leadership, traditional or self-imposed, which together have formed the basis of social unity throughout history.

Discussion itself, moreover, is a social activity in the true sense, a "game" which has to be carried on in accord with rules, and these rules must be respected for "absolutistic" or "spiritual" reasons and not from individual utilitarian motives. The player must be more

* It is too easy for the idealist to fall into a contemptuous attitude toward order. Of course, we can have too much of it, but without a fair degree of order social achievement is impossible, society itself non-existent, and the life of man "nasty, brutish, and short."

† Under frontier conditions, even though growth and change are fairly rapid, not much unity in action is necessary, and a high degree of individual liberty is possible. Under modern conditions of social and economic pressure and of social, economic, and technological complexity, the maintenance of order requires an enormous amount of restraint. Intellectual *and moral* progress, as well as technical, are a source of tremendous strain on the mechanism of order.

concerned to maintain the game and have it a good game than he is to win. But discussion seems to manifest in an especial degree the tendency of games to deteriorate, through "cheating," first into ill-will, and ultimately into disruption or even violence. From this point of view, the history of intellectual activity, in science, criticism, and philosophy, is surely far from encouraging. The specialized, professional intellectuals have shown little enough capacity to maintain the spirit of discussion, even in small groups and under what should be extremely favourable conditions; and of their ability to settle issues and solve serious problems by discussion among themselves, it is more pleasant not to speak. In the natural sciences, the issues finally get settled by unmistakable objective tests, the results of which are plain even to the non-specialist. In the field of morals and politics —to say nothing of religion—it is questionable whether the net result has been progress toward consensus or the multiplication of controversy.

To recapitulate: The central theme in a sound treatment of the nature, functions, and problems of social science should be emphasis of the "paradox" that a non-practical, "pure science" of society— in the interpretive and normative-critical sense in which truth and knowledge have meaning in this field—is a practical necessity. In this connection, the parallelism and the contrast between social and natural "science" are equally important. It is a pet observation of the writer that we should probably not have had the modern development of electric lighting, power transmission, and communication if Franklin, Volta, Faraday, and the other founders of electrical science had been set to work on the problems of lighting, power transmission, and communication. There seems to be a general principle of indirection permeating human conduct; we do otherwise than we intend, and by aiming at one goal reach another, which may be better or worse. But while in dealing with social problems, we require objectivity just as much as in the thinking by which we understand and use the natural environment, the problem of objectivity is almost infinitely more subtle and difficult in the field of norms and values than in the instrumental realm of physical invariance. The fact that we feel so vague and timorous about it is sufficient evidence of the difficulties.

To begin with, in thinking about ideals and rules of action, even from an individual standpoint, we are thinking, in a much more direct sense than is true in science, about ourselves and our thinking, and this involves something akin to lifting oneself by one's own bootstraps. We unquestionably do it, more or less; we make judgments about ideas and ideals which are better or worse, and which may be made better by effort and pains. But we cannot expect to understand fully the process itself. When social phenomena, ideas and rules of associative life, are in question, the issues are further vexed by the moral factor already repeatedly emphasized; there is a universal "temptation to attempt to secure the agreement of others which confirms an opinion as true (or at least meritorious) and which is absolutely necessary to any expression of political thinking in action, by an appeal from "reason" to "force"—meaning any procedure except reliance on the inherent power of truth itself.

The moral issues involved in the notion of truth affecting moral issues must be understood and faced. Every honest worker for truth must recognize the moral limitations of human nature in himself as well as in others, along with the intellectual limitations, and the theoretical difficulties which arise from the combination. No one is free from pride of opinion or from a pathetic liability to error in forming judgments. Everyone is too ready to reach "conclusions" and then to make of any position a personal interest and proceed to "fight" for it. The notion that men naturally and spontaneously think correctly or alike, or would do so if they were only free from the influence of tradition and authority, is the great romantic heresy of the modern age. The fallacy is well illustrated by the tendency to indefinite multiplication of sects which followed upon the breakdown of the traditional-authoritarian religious unity of western Europe by the "Reformation." The "natural" thing is rather to follow some "line" of what seems to be reasoning to some result which looks big and interesting and important and then to assume that it is "sound" and that disagreement and opposition are due to selfish motives or to incompetence. It requires an astonishing amount of painful effort in the original construction and in the pondering of criticism to reach any justified assurance that an opinion has merit, in a field where terms cannot be objectively defined and results objectively tested.

Once a man's mind is liberated and set thinking, he becomes an inveterate "theorizer" and is as partial to his own ideas as he is to his own children, or to any individual interest whatever. Even sound logic is of little help in this situation, for the issues lie predominantly in the meaning of propositions, and not in their formal manipulation. When an idea gains acceptance, other data are easily harmonized with it and made to confirm it. This quality of human nature is abundantly manifest in the history of natural science itself prior to the age of experiment.

At the same time, we must recognize that there is in our field no objective test for separating either truth from opinion or the urge to promote an opinion "believed" to be true from the craving for personal aggrandizement.* No intelligently candid person will claim the right to be a judge of his own cause, or pretend that a difference of opinion does not set up a conflict of interests. Thus the belief that one has the truth on any new or controverted point can never be impartial, and ethically speaking must be held tentatively. But to hold a belief is to believe it better than conflicting opinions, and love of truth is humanly inseparable from the wish to spread the belief in what one believes to be true.

The fundamental moral issue faced by any individual is set by two opposed conceptions of the way in which truth is to be promoted. At one extreme is the view that truth will win in a contest with error, i.e., that in a contest between human proponents of conflicting positions, God or the universe will give victory to the right. According to this view, one ought to fight unhesitatingly and unreservedly for one's opinions. It does not really matter whether the position one fights for is right or wrong, but only that all possible positions be represented and energetically advocated. The intellectual theory of modern democracy has gone far in this direction. (Cf. especially the nature of a legal trial.) At the other extreme is the doctrine that truth will win out over error by its own inherent power if stated objectively and dispassionately—"lifted up." In this view, any personal contest

* There are many other loves which conflict with the love of truth and interfere with its quest and promotion. But in our contemporary liberal culture, the love of personal aggrandizement is the worst, or includes most of the others. And the very fact that in "science," knowledge has become a means to distinction and power, has created a "respect" for it which aggravates the difficulties.

is a mere test of relative power and has nothing whatever to do with truth or right.

All aggressiveness, all spirit of assertion against opposition, all personal identification with a position or wish to change the position of others, is vain, arrogant, and evil. (Modern civilization characteristically professes this view following chiefly the other.)

No doubt both of these extreme positions are wrong, and it is also right for different persons to compromise at widely different points along the scale between them. But it seems clear to the writer that, relatively speaking, with reference to our modern western culture, strong emphasis needs to be placed on the second alternative —our preaching in contrast with our practice. We need much more "intellectual pacifism," more consecration, and less controversy, than we get or are likely to get. Our civilization is excessively romantic; it needs more discipline and faith in discipline—and more patience, and in the field of morals and politics vastly more real intellectual work. Men on the average need to be *much* surer that they are "right" before they "go ahead" to convince their neighbours and convert the world. And while the contest motive cannot be repudiated altogether, it seems even clearer that when men do enter the lists for a position they should be much more restrained and "conscientious" in their methods of striving for victory. The belief in competition as a principle seems to carry with it recognition of the necessity of having and obeying rules. Otherwise, every difference of opinion would be the occasion for a fight—to the death and without rules.*

On the other hand, there can hardly be any danger of going too far in the direction suggested. Under a free system of government, all political issues which really are issues must be settled formally by an open contest between advocates, presumably in accord with rules, but with the inevitable tendency to "stretch" the rules and employ methods which lead to victory. The apparently universal

---

* I do not see how one can be an "absolute" pacifist or an absolute anything. (The word should be "pacificist," as Norman Angell says.) No doubt, we must admit that the end always justifies the means to some extent; and *perhaps* there may be cases in which it does so absolutely, where it comes to be simply "thy life or mine" between men, parties, states, or civilizations. But there must surely be the strongest possible presumption in favour of minimizing the test-of-strength element in favour of genuine discussion as a method of settling differences; and the very concept of discussion excludes all use of force, including persuasion, in any form.

human desire for victory itself must work with the interest in the issue to this effect. There will always be a need for moral pressure in the other direction all along the scale, for moralizing the contest and for minimizing the contest spirit in favour of true deliberation and discussion.

With reference to social science in particular, in a world where freedom in practical affairs means personal competition, something like the extreme position of absolutely eschewing contention in favour of dispassionate objectivity would seem to be the correct position. In the first place, it seems to be a reasonable creed for those who believe at all in the validity of principles other than force and "strategy" to trust in the potency of truth and in co-operation in the quest of truth. The alternative, which is to promote truth by setting its devotees to competing with each other, along with charlatans and demagogues, with the inexpert and romantically disposed public to pick the winner, does not seem promising. And again, it may on the one hand be doubted whether social science can maintain any distinctive existence on any other basis, and on the other it is fairly clear that the modern social situation has need for just this type of leadership.

First, as to possibilities. Effective maintenance of the "pacifistic" ideal of an absolute faith in truth, presents itself as the only escape from the progressive deterioration already referred to, with ultimate mergence in the pragmatic, time-serving of power politics—which in turn could only go on to the establishment of tyranny. What naturally happens when social scientists lose interest in a cloistered role and go out into the arena in the endeavour to influence the course of contemporary events is that the specialists abandon the effort to discuss issues among themselves and engage in a competitive solicitation of the "ignorant masses" for support against each other. The entire intellectual quality of the procedure accordingly gravitates toward the level of a demagogic appeal for a personal following, and/or for exlistment under slogans (the two are always combined in practice and are only in part analytically separable). The process is going on visibly and has already reached a point where the economists and sociologists known to the public as such are chiefly popular lecturers and journalists. Again the thought recurs that the future historian may record as the crucial result of the modern intellectual movement, "bigger and better mobs." Such a contest must surely result in suicide for social science.

In society as a whole, the direct leadership in a free system must be political, i.e., by "politicians." Here the natural tendency of a competitive game to deteriorate is accentuated by the influence of the material interests at stake. Both abstract considerations and the study of history suggest that the only way to maintain "moral" standards, even tolerably free from force and chicane, is to have a special class so constituted as to be somewhat protected from the natural tendencies of competition. But for this task, a religious priesthood in the old sense, as the only indirect, consultative leadership, auxiliary to the political, proves inadequate. Religion is too exclusively a conservative force for modern conditions, though it served the purpose tolerably well when the social problem was simply that of preventing individuals from departing too far from the beaten paths of tradition. The ideal of freedom creates its own problems and dangers. Modern conditions require a more complicated division of labour among types of leadership. Religion must be supplemented by an intellectual, critical, and constructive "learned" class, which of course corresponds with what has happened in the modern period. The difficulty is that under the influence of natural science, which has objective standards, this class in becoming separated from the priesthood, as was necessary and proper, has tended to lose the status and attitudes of a priesthood, which it needs to retain.

It seems reasonable to believe that if it were possible to maintain professional groups in the fields of special knowledge and research covered by the social sciences, including ethics, and religion as a social phenomenon, and if the workers took a "consecrated" attitude toward their common work, "devoting" themselves to a truly co-operative quest of the right or "best" solutions for problems, absolutely renouncing interest in individual prominence and power, and going to the public only with dispassionate statements of fairly established results, the politicians might find it good politics both to allow them to live and to take their work seriously. Members of such groups would of course have on the one hand to be protected in the use of appropriate designations and on the other (equally important) allowed to use them only on condition of abstaining from irresponsible utterances outside their spheres of special competence.

This of course is only the beginning of the necessary division of labour in the whole field of guidance. Between the professions definitely consecrated to truth, and politics in the ordinary sense, there would be a relatively free field for interpreters and popularizers. Below the "political" organs of policy determination—the media of popular responsibility—would be the whole system of administration, in the hands of a wide variety of specialists in such lines as law, engineering, social work, finance, medicine, etc. It is not our task here to go into such details, but merely to indicate the nature and functions of social science. It seems to be that of providing a necessary element of intellectual-moral leadership alongside the moral-religious. And both these auxiliaries to political leadership must be kept completely out of politics, and as free as possible from the spirit of competitive individual advancement in any form.

INDEX

GEORGE ALLEN & UNWIN LTD
LONDON: 40 MUSEUM STREET, W.C.1
CAPE TOWN: 58–60 LONG STREET
TORONTO: 91 WELLINGTON STREET WEST
BOMBAY: 15 GRAHAM ROAD, BALLARD ESTATE
CALCUTTA: 17 CENTRAL AVENUE, P.O. DHARAMTALA,
WELLINGTON, N.Z.: 8 KINGS CRESCENT, LOWER HUTT
SYDNEY, N.S.W.: BRADBURY HOUSE, 55 YORK STREET

Planning and the Price Mechanism

by James Edward Meade *Cr. 8vo. 8s. 6d. net Second Impression*

To plan or not to plan? This book outlines a solution of our present economic problems which makes the fullest use of the price mechanism and of free initiative and competition, but which involves the socialisation of certain monopolistic concerns and the State control of the price mechanism in such a way as to maintain full employment, to achieve an equitable distribution of income and property and to restore equilibrium to our international balance of payments. It is an outline of that "middle way" which the author calls the Liberal-Socialist solution.

The author is at present Professor of Commerce dealing with international economic problems at the University of London. He taught economics at Oxford from 1931 to 1937, and wrote the League of Nations' World Economic Surveys in Geneva from 1937 to 1940. During the war he was a member of the Economic Section of the Cabinet Secretariat and was Director of that Section for the first two years of post-war reconstruction, being a member of the United Kingdom delegations to various international conferences. In this book he has drawn on his wide domestic and international experience to apply his principals of Liberal Socialism to a great range of current economic problems.

"Altogether this is a valuable little book which should make not only the rationale of enlightened Socialism and the mechanics of planning but the nature of Britain's present economic dilemma a good deal clearer to its readers."—*Spectator.*

The Economic Basis of a Durable Peace

by J. E. Meade. *2nd Printing. Cr. 8vo. 6s. net*

"The conclusion which he reaches is important. To all who seek ways of establishing peace and international justice this book may be commended as a very gallant attempt to aid their endeavours."—

Lionel Robbins in *The Spectator.*

"Salutary in its insistence on certain plain economic truths."—

G. D. H. Cole in *The New Statesman.*

Secrets of Industry

by Lewis C. Orde. Introduction by Sir George Usher.
Demy 8vo. 9s. 6d. Fourth Impression

How efficient is British Industry? Who would run it? What should be done to make it serve the nation better? Mr. Ord offers new and revealing facts on these topical subjects which become increasingly urgent.

"Interesting and suggestive especially so in his study of the growth of mass production and the effect of standardisation."—*Daily Telegraph*

Careful research into industry, with measurements on the job made by the author and others, give new approach and new values for industrial efficiency. Comparisons are made of various industries and in various countries. The information is of interest to industrialists. It is expressed simply and affords the non-technical reader a revealing and understandable appreciation of industry and some of its secrets. Incidents drawn from real life aid explanations. The book is a contribution to the study of the industrial problem from the point of view of the national need.

Industrial Peace in our Time

by Hubert Somervell.   *Demy 8vo.   15s. net*

Throughout industry to-day there is a movement to destroy the psychological and social barriers that have stood for so long between management and men. Evidence of this may be seen, for instance, in the increased use of joint consultation.

But the movement is thwarted throughout by a failure to reorganize the economic structure which dates from the earliest days of capitalism and which embodies the conception of labour as a commodity. If the worker is to be treated as a sharer of industrial wealth rather than as a cost in its production, the wage-rate and profit system must be replaced by a new economic formula.

Basing his argument largely upon certain American experiments, the author of this book suggests how our present system might be developed to express the new relationship of management and labour to each other and to the industrial unit in which they work.

The author was for some years a joint manager and director of a well-known and progressive manufacturing concern. He was engaged for the most part on the reorganisation of its production necessitated by the enormous change in conditions following the first world war. During this period the Company doubled its output. Mr. Somervell can also claim to be one of the small band of industrialists who were trained for managerial responsibilities in America, and he has kept in touch with American ideas through the connections he made at that time. Latterly he has beome increasingly attracted to economic research and, after retiring from his firm, is at present on the research staff of the National Institute of Industrial Psychology.

Mr. Somervell, therefore, brings to this study exactly the peculiar practical and theoretical knowledge it requires. The result is an obviously valuable and original contribution to a discussion whose vital importance has only recently been acknowledged, but to which Government and both sides of industry are now devoting attention.

Freedom under Planning

by Barbara Wootton.   *2nd Printing.   Cr. 8vo.   6s. net*

Barbara Wootton deals with the effect of economic planning upon such freedoms as the right to choose our jobs and to spend our incomes as we please, the right of Trade Unions to bargain about wages, and the citizen's freedom to form or to join the political party of his choice, and to bring about changes of government by democratic election and not by force. Her aim is to look at what are real and topical, if often neglected, problems, and to search for constructive solutions. Hence this is anybody's—and everybody's—book, and not one particularly for economic specialists.

"Mrs. Wootton, with the skill and precision of a first-class surgeon, has here performed an important service . . . an admirable and timely book because it is in method as honest as in clarity it is remarkable."—*Manchester Guardian.*

"A valuable and timely book : lucid, never pontifical, and not too long."—*The Observer.*

GEORGE   ALLEN   &   UNWIN   LTD